Parables in Midrash

PARABLES IN MIDRASH

Narrative and Exegesis in Rabbinic Literature

David Stern

HARVARD UNIVERSITY PRESS
Cambridge, Massachusetts
London, England
1991

Publication of this book was assisted by a grant from the Lucius N. Littauer
Foundation

This book is printed on acid-free paper, and its binding materials have
been chosen for strength and durability.

Library of Congress Cataloging-in-Publication Data

Stern, David, 1949–
    Parables in Midrash : narrative and exegesis in rabbinic
literature / David Stern.
        p.   cm.
    Includes bibliographical references and index.
    ISBN 0-674-65447-1
    1. Parables in rabbinical literature. 2. Narration in rabbinical
literature. 3. Midrash—History and criticism. I. Title.
BM518.P3S74   1991
296.1′42066—dc20   91-2809
                        CIP

In memory of my mother, Florence Sherman Stern, *zikhronah livrakhah*, and for my father, Kurt Stern, *yibadeil lehayim arukim*

Acknowledgments

An ancient tale tells of a young man who as a youth began to write a short book on the parable. But as the young man grew older, the book grew longer; and as the book grew still lengthier, the young man grew still older. Until, finally, the youth was very old, and the book was very lengthy. But all the time the parable remained exactly the same.

This book, too, has been a long time in the making. On the path to its completion, I have acquired many debts of gratitude. The first of these is to the Society of Fellows at Harvard University, which afforded me the time, freedom, and comfort to shift my field of specialization from classics to Hebrew literature. My earliest work on the midrashic parable was done in the form of my doctoral dissertation, completed under the direction of Professors Isadore Twersky and Morton Bloomfield. An American Council of Learned Societies Fellowship under a program funded by the National Endowment for the Humanities, as well as a research grant from the Memorial Foundation for Jewish Culture and the Sir Simon Marks Fellowship from the Los Angeles Jewish Community Council, allowed me to spend the year 1983–84 in Israel, where I began to turn the dissertation into a book. As a guest of the Hebrew Literature Department at Hebrew University, I was able to avail myself of the resources of the Israel National Library and the Institute of Microfilmed Hebrew Manuscripts in preparing the critical texts in Appendix B. I offer my thanks to both institutions and their staffs. A summer research fellowship from the University of Pennsylvania Research Foundation supported further work on the project, and a generous subvention from the Research Foundation helped to allay publication costs.

Earlier versions of sections of Chapters 1, 2, and 6 have appeared in *Prooftexts* 1 (1981); *Jerusalem Studies in Hebrew Literature* 7 (1985); and *Parable and Story in Judaism and Christianity,* ed. Clemens Thoma and Michael Wyschogrod (New York and Mahwah, N. J.: Paulist Press, 1989). I wish to thank the editors of all these publications and Paulist Press for permission to use this material.

In the course of writing this book, I have been the beneficiary of the intellectual and personal generosity of many colleagues. Gregory Nagy first helped me unlock the secret of the mashal's traditional composition. James Kugel, Gerald Prince, Raymond Scheindlin, and Elliot Wolfson offered helpful suggestions for improvement of the manuscript and valuable criticisms that saved me from mistakes. Michael Fishbane graciously helped me to reconceive the book's structure. Judah Goldin, whose sensitivity to midrash is unequaled in our time, read the completed manuscript with his special eye for the telling detail. Elaine and Arthur A. Cohen gave much appreciated encouragement early on, as did Jacob Elbaum, Michael Meyer, and Edward Said. Josef Stern was the first to instruct me in the self-reflexive relationship of the mashal to its nimshal, and vice versa. Margaretta Fulton and Camille Smith of Harvard University Press have been the kind of editors that writers dream of. For all the time I have worked on this book, and for longer than he probably wishes to remember, Alan Mintz has been a steadfast friend, a generous critic, and a tireless listener.

My wife, Kathryn Hellerstein, has nurtured this book and its author throughout, giving unstintingly of her literary and critical gifts. And my children, Rebecca and Jonah, have been constant reminders for me of the difference between parable and reality.

The dedication of this book is only a token of the gratitude and love I feel toward my parents: my mother, Florence Sherman Stern, of blessed memory, who never stopped telling me, "Just sit down and finish the damned thing!" and my father, Dr. Kurt Stern, whose life has taught me the meaning of intellectual integrity.

Contents

Abbreviations

ARN A and B: *Abot d'R. Natan*, with two versions, A and B, ed. S. Schechter (repr. New York, 1967)

Arukh: Nathan b. Yehiel, *Aruch Completum*, ed. A. Kohut (1890; repr. Jerusalem, 1970)

B.: *Talmud Bavli* (Vilna, 1886; repr. frequently)

Bam. R.: *Midrash Bamidbar Rabbah*, as printed in MR

Ber. R.: *Midrash Bereshit Rabba*, ed. J. Theodor and Ch. Albeck (1912–1936; repr. Jerusalem, 1965), 3 vols.

BH: *Bet ha-Midrash*, ed. A. Jellinek (Leipzig, 1853–1873; repr. Jerusalem, 1967)

Dev. R.: *Midrash Devarim Rabbah*, as printed in MR

Dev. R. (Lieberman): *Midrash Debarim Rabbah*, ed. Saul Lieberman (Jerusalem, 1974)

Eikh. R.: *Midrasch Echa Rabbati*, ed. S. Buber (Vilna, 1899)

Eikh. Zuta: Eikhah Zuta, in *Midrash Zuta*, ed. S. Buber (Berlin, 1894)

EJ: *Encyclopaedia Judaica* (Jerusalem, 1972)

Esther R.: *Midrash Esther Rabbah*, as printed in MR

Even-Shoshan: A. Even-Shoshan, *Hamillon HeHadash* (Jerusalem, 1981), 3 vols.

HTR: Harvard Theological Review

HUCA: Hebrew Union College Annual

J.: *Talmud Yerushalmi* (Krotozhin, n.d.; repr. Jerusalem, n.d.); cited by chapter and halakhah

JAAR: Journal of the American Academy of Religion

Jastrow: M. Jastrow, *Dictionary of the Targumim, the Talmud Babli and Yerushalmi, and the Midrashic Literature* (New York, 1886–1903; repr. frequently)

JBL: Journal of Biblical Literature

JJS: Journal of Jewish Studies

JQR: Jewish Quarterly Review

JSJ: Journal for the Study of Judaism

JSOT: Journal for the Study of the Old Testament

JTS: Journal of Theological Studies

Koh. R.: *Midrash Koheleth Rabbah,* as printed in MR

Lekah Tov: *Pesikta Zutarta (Midrash Lekah Tob),* ed. S. Buber (Vilna, 1884)

M.: *Shishah Sidrei Mishnah,* ed. H. Albeck (Jerusalem, 1957)

MaHaRSHA: Commentary of Samuel Edels (1555–1631) on B., printed at back of many Vilna editions

MaHaRZU: Commentary of Wolf Einhorn on MR, completed in 1856, printed in MR

Mekhilta: *Mekilta de-Rabbi Ishmael,* ed. J. Lauterbach (Philadelphia, 1933–1935; repr. 1949)

Mekhilta de-RSHBY: *Mekhilta d'Rabbi Sim'on b. Jochai,* ed. J. N. Epstein and E. Z. Melamed (Jerusalem, 1955)

MGWJ: Monatschrift für Geschichte und Wissenschaft des Judentums

Mid. Hagadol: *Midrash Hagadol,* ed. M. Margulies (Jerusalem, 1947–1956)

Mid. Tann.: *Midrash Tannaim,* ed. D. Hoffmann (Berlin, 1908–1909)

Mid. Teh.: *Midrash Tehilim,* ed. S. Buber (repr. New York, 1947)

MK: Matanot Kehuna, commentary of Issachar Baer b. Naftali Katz Cohen (Cracow, 1587); abr. version printed in MR

MR: *Midrash Rabbah* (Vilna, 1878; repr. frequently); also ed. M. Mirkin (Tel Aviv, 1959)

NTS: New Testament Studies

PAAJR: Proceedings of the American Academy for Jewish Research

PR: *Midrash Pesikta Rabbati,* ed. M. Friedmann (Vienna, 1880)

PRE: *Pirkei Rabbi Eliezer* (repr. New York, 1946)

PRK: *Pesikta de-Rab Kahana,* ed. B. Mandelbaum (New York, 1962)

RaDaK: Commentary of David Kimhi (1160–1235) on the Hebrew Bible

RaDaL: Commentary of R. David Luria (1798–1855), printed in MR

RaSHaSH: Novellae of R. Shmuel Straschun (first pub. 1843–1845), printed in MR

Ruth R.: *Midrash Ruth Rabbah,* as printed in MR

Semahot deR. Hiyya: *Masekhet Semahot deR. Hiyya,* in *Masekhet Semahot,* ed. Michael Higger (New York, 1931)

SH: Scripta Hierosolymitana

Shir R.: *Midrash Rabbah Shir Hashirim,* ed. S. Dunski (Jerusalem, 1980)

Sh. R.: Chaps. 1–14 in *Midrash Shemot Rabbah,* ed. A. Shinan (Tel Aviv, 1984); all other chapters as printed in MR

Sifra: *Sifra De-Bei Rab, Torat Kohanim,* ed. I. H. Weiss (Vienna, 1862; repr. Jerusalem, n.d.)

Sifra (Finkelstein): *Sifra on Leviticus,* ed. L. Finkelstein (New York, 1983), vols. 2–3

Sifre Deut.: *Siphre ad Deuteronomium,* ed. L. Finkelstein (Breslau and Berlin, 1935–1939; repr. New York, 1969)

Sifre Num.: *Sifre ad Numeros,* ed. H. Horovitz (Leipzig, 1917; repr. Jerusalem, 1966)

T.: *Tosephta,* ed. M. S. Zuckermandel (repr. Jerusalem, 1936)

Tan.: *Midrash Tanhuma* (Warsaw, 1879)

Tan. B.: *Midrash Tanhuma Hakadum,* ed. S. Buber (Vilna, 1885)

TAPA: Transactions of the American Philological Association

TDE: *Seder Eliyahu Rabbah and Seder Eliyahu Zuta (Tanna de-Bei Eliyahu),* ed. M. Friedmann (repr. Jerusalem, 1960)

Vay. R.: *Midrash Wayyikra Rabbah,* ed. M. Margulies (1953–1960; repr. Jerusalem, 1972)

VT: Vetus Testamentum

YA: Yefei 'Anaf, commentary of R. Samuel Yaffe Ashkenazi (Venice, 1597); printed in MR

Yalkut: *Yalkut Shime'oni* (Venice, 1566; repr. frequently)

Zohar: *Sefer Hazohar,* ed. R. Margaliot (Jerusalem, 1978)

Parables in Midrash

Note on Translations and Transliterations

All translations of parables and other Rabbinic sources are my own unless otherwise noted. For translations of verses from the Hebrew Bible, I have generally used *TANAKH: A New Translation of The Holy Scriptures* (Philadelphia, 1985); from the New Testament, *The New Oxford Annotated Bible with the Apocrypha* (Revised Standard Version), ed. H. G. May and B. M. Metzger (New York, 1973).

Transliterations of Hebrew and Aramaic words are provided solely for purposes of identification. In order to simplify the transliterations, I have omitted all diacritical marks as well as super- and subscripts; for example, the letter *het* appears as a plain *h*, as does the letter *he*. The letter *aleph* has been left unmarked, but I have marked the letter *ayin* with an apostrophe.

Introduction

This book is about the intersection of two orders of discourse: narrative and exegesis. The particular form of narrative is the parable. The specific type of exegesis is midrash, the study and interpretation of Scripture practiced by the Rabbis in Late Antiquity.

In the last decade, midrash has won a recognition that no one could have predicted. Although midrash has long been known to many scholars, it has usually been treated as a marginal subject, as an exegetical curiosity, or as a source to be mined for information about the history of ancient Palestinian Judaism or early Christianity. Even in Jewish tradition, midrash has tended to be neglected in favor of Talmud, which has been viewed as the more serious and weighty branch of Rabbinic literature; and when midrash has been studied, it has been almost solely for its philological or theological interest. In the past ten years, all this has changed. Partly as the result of a fresh curiosity about midrash in post-structuralist literary circles, and partly out of more internal developments within the discipline of Hebrew literary studies, midrash has come to be seen as a literature in its own right. As exegesis has been recognized as a primary bearer of meaning in Jewish tradition, midrash has reassumed its place as the exemplary mode of Jewish commentary, and its history has become the focus of much new and exciting research.

Even so, virtually all this attention has been devoted to midrash as a hermeneutic, as an exegetical act. Little interest has been shown in midrashic discourse itself—in midrash's own literary language, the rhetorical and poetic forms and modalities in which midrash as exegesis, as a hermeneutical act, is preserved in the texts of Rabbinic literature. While this book stands at the juncture between several intellectual disciplines—Rabbinics, the theory of narrative and general literary criticism, scholarship about parables, those in the New Testament in particular—it is especially about one subject: midrash as discourse.

The specific mode of discourse treated in this book is the midrashic parable, or *mashal*, particularly in its conventional form as the *mashal lemelekh,* or king-parable, in which the narrative's protagonist is a king symbolizing God. The king-mashal is the preeminent form of narrative in Rabbinic literature. Nut-like, sweet and hard simultaneously, it epitomizes all the imagination and cleverness that the Rabbis brought to the study of the Bible. As examples of narrative art, the parables' aesthetic achievement alone makes them worthy of critical literary attention. In addition, however, the study of the king-mashal raises a whole number of separate issues: the relationship of Rabbinic literature to the New Testament and that of Rabbinic Judaism to early Christianity, the Rabbinic conception of God, Hellenization and ancient techniques of representation, the approach to midrash as literature, the place of midrash in Hebrew literature, problems in narratology and genre theory in general. In short, the mashal provides a point of entry into nearly every aspect of Rabbinic literature and its interpretation.

Yet despite all its points of interest, the Rabbinic mashal, like most midrashic forms, has hardly been investigated or discussed in past scholarship. And where it has been, it has nearly always been looked at for an extrinsic reason—as background, say, to the New Testament parables, or as a putative source for Roman history. The few attempts to describe the mashal on its own terms have been very fragmentary and limited in scope. This book differs radically from these earlier works by offering a full description of the mashal: of its compositional and exegetical techniques, of its rhetoric, poetics, and thematics, of its role in midrashic discourse and, finally, of its place in the history of Hebrew literature, from the Bible to the modern period.

To describe all these features of the mashal, I have drawn upon a range of examples of the literary form from different Rabbinic and classical Jewish texts, offering them in translations that will, I hope, convey the flavor of the originals. The parables that are the real foci of attention in this book are, however, a group of twenty-four meshalim which are discussed and analyzed in detail. These meshalim are all drawn from a single collection, Eikhah Rabbah, the classical midrash on the Book of Lamentations. Because the Rabbis used the study of Lamentations as the medium through which they expressed their own theological and ideological responses to the historical catastrophe of the destruction of the Second Temple (in 70 c.e.), perhaps the formative event in the history of Rabbinic Judaism, this midrash and its contents are more focused than other collections, and in its various interpretations the Rabbis seem to have invested special imaginative efforts. Whatever the reason, the meshalim in Eikhah Rabbah are among the most extraordinary in all Rabbinic literature. They therefore offer a particularly auspicious and opportune group for study. Unfortunately, there exists as yet no satisfactory critical edition of this midrash, and as a result I had to prepare critical texts of the meshalim before analyzing them. These Hebrew texts are printed in Appendix B.

Rabbinic literature is notorious for forbidding easy access to those not initiated into its literary secrets. But the Rabbinic parable, as I argue here, is not an esoteric literary form but a decidedly exoteric one, and I have tried to follow in its path by writing this book for readers who are nonspecialists as well as for specialists in Rabbinics. I have consequently tried to keep my discussions as untechnical and unesoteric as possible; wherever possible, philological and textual matters have been relegated to notes or appendixes.

1

Composition and Exegesis

The Rabbinic Parable

> Simeon, the son of Rabbi [Judah], prepared a [wedding] banquet for his son. He went and invited all the sages, but he forgot to invite Bar Kappara, who thereupon went and wrote on the door of R. Simeon's house: After rejoicing is death. So what value is there to rejoicing?
>
> Who did this to me? R. Simeon asked. Is there anyone we did not invite?
>
> One of his men told him: Bar Kappara. You forgot to invite Bar Kappara.
>
> R. Simeon said: To invite him now would be unseemly. So he went and made a second banquet, and he invited all the sages, and he invited Bar Kappara as well. But at every course that was brought before the guests Bar Kappara recited three hundred fox-fables, and the guests didn't even taste the dishes before they grew cold. The dishes were removed from the tables just as they had been brought in.
>
> R. Simeon asked his servant: Why are the dishes all coming back untouched?
>
> The servant replied: There is an old man sitting there. At every course he tells fables until the dishes grow cold, and no one eats.
>
> R. Simeon went up to Bar Kappara: What did I do to make you ruin my banquet?
>
> Bar Kappara answered: What do I need your banquet for? Didn't Solomon say, "What real value is there for a man in all the gains he makes beneath the sun?" (Eccles. 1:3)? And what is written after that verse? "One generation goes, another comes, but the earth remains the same forever" (1:4).   (Vay. R. 28.2)[1]

Unhappily, this passage tells us nothing about the three hundred fox-fables that Bar Kappara recited over every course at

R. Simeon's banquet; indeed, it does not bother to record even a single example, possibly because the fables, entertaining as they must have been, were not considered sufficiently "serious" compositions to be preserved in writing. Even so, the anecdote is a valuable one, and not only for what it tells us about social mores and table manners among the Rabbis in Palestine in the third century. Even more revealing is what the anecdote suggests about the fable and its function. In this case, the very act of reciting a fable served an ulterior purpose: it offered Bar Kappara a clever if nasty weapon for revenge.

The generic name in Rabbinic literature for fables like Bar Kappara's and for parabolic narratives in general is *mashal* (pl. *meshalim*). And though revenge is admittedly an unusual purpose for the mashal to serve, both parables and fables operate surreptitiously as literary forms, expressing allusive messages through indirect means. A fable utilizes anthropomorphic animals or plants to portray the particularly theriomorphic or phytomorphic features of human behavior.[2] A parable suggests a set of parallels between an imagined fictional event and an immediate, "real" situation confronting the parable's author and his audience. In both parables and fables, though, the literary form tends to imply the parallel rather than explicate it. The task of understanding the parallel and its implications, or levels of implication, is left largely to the audience. Neither a simple tale with a transparent moral nor an entirely opaque story with a secret or esoteric meaning, the mashal is a narrative that actively elicits from its audience the solution of its meaning, or what we could call its interpretation.

Parables and fables are hardly the property of Rabbinic literature alone. They can be found in the literatures of virtually every culture throughout the world. The Rabbinic mashal's own tradition can be traced back to the ancient Near East. It is represented in the Hebrew Bible as well as in the New Testament, specifically in the three synoptic gospels, in the parables attributed to Jesus, which happen to be our earliest datable testimony to the literary form that is more comprehensively preserved in later Rabbinic literature. And after the Rabbinic period, parables continued to be composed throughout the Middle Ages, in ethical, mystical, and philosophical Jewish texts, right down to the contemporary period when early modernist Hebrew writers like Agnon self-consciously imitated the Rabbinic mashal in its classical form. But by this time the mashal had become an acknowledged archaism, a late vestige of tradition itself.

Native homes for parables and fables tend to be traditional cultures that still possess oral literary traditions.[3] Of these perhaps the foremost example is ancient Greek epic, which possesses a literary genre, the *ainos,* that is directly analogous to the mashal. "An allusive narrative told for an ulterior purpose," as one scholar has defined it, the *ainos* as a genre includes the fables of Archilochus and Aesop as well as such tales as the one Odysseus tells Eumaios in the *Odyssey* (14.462–505) when he tries to persuade the shepherd to lend him a cloak for the night.[4]

This definition of the *ainos* as "an allusive narrative told for an ulterior purpose" aptly characterizes the mashal as well. Consider the following celebrated fable. According to this account of an otherwise unknown, possibly legendary event,[5] R. Joshua b. Hananiah (90–130 C.E.) is said to have recited the fable in order to dissuade his fellow Jews from rebelling against their Roman rulers:

> In the days of R. Joshua b. Hananiah, the evil kingdom [i.e. Rome] decreed that the Temple could be rebuilt. Pappus and Lullianus set up tables of provisions from Acco to Antiochia and they supplied the pilgrims with all they needed.
>
> The Cuthites [i.e. the Samaritans] went and said to [the Romans]: "Let it be known to the king that the Jews who came up from you to us have reached Jerusalem and are rebuilding that rebellious and wicked city; they are completing the walls and repairing the foundation. Now let it be known to the king that if this city is rebuilt and the walls completed, they will not pay tribute, poll tax, or land tax, and in the end it will harm the kingdom" (Ezra 4:12–13). [In this verse, the word] "tribute" means the land tax; "poll tax," the head tax; "land tax," forced labor.
>
> [The Roman emperor] said to them: What shall we do? We have already issued the decree!
>
> [The Cuthites] answered: Send the following [message] to the Jews and tell them: You must move the Temple from its place, or you must either add five cubits to its measurements or subtract five cubits. And they will then withdraw their request of their own accord.
>
> The community of Jews gathered in the Valley of Bet-Rimon, and once the letters [with the emperor's orders] arrived, the Jews began to cry, desiring to rebel against the empire.

Some people said: Let one wise man go up and calm the mobs. They said: Let R. Joshua b. Hananiah go up, because he is a scholar of Torah.

R. Joshua arose and preached: There was a lion that was eating its prey when a bone got caught in its throat. The lion said: Whoever will come and extract the bone will receive a reward. An Egyptian heron with a long beak came. It put its beak inside the lion's mouth, and removed the bone. Then it said to the lion: Give me my reward. Answered the lion: Go and boast saying that you entered a lion's mouth intact (literally: in peace) and that you came out of it intact.

So, too, it is sufficient for us that we entered with this nation intact, and that we came out of it intact.   (Ber. R. 64.10)

This mashal's resemblance to certain Aesopic fables has drawn the attention of folklorists who have suggested that its narrative may represent a universal tale-type found throughout the world.[6] Within this passage, though, the fable's meaning is almost entirely context-specific: "You are fools to wish to rebel against Rome!" R. Joshua tells his audience of contentious Jews. "Do not stick your heads into Rome's mouth a second time! You were lucky to have survived with your lives—'intact'—the first time!" This message of warning is the mashal's "ulterior purpose."

This text is a good illustration of the literary form as it may have been used in a real-life situation. One can easily imagine how R. Joshua's audience would have deduced his message from the parable; to do so, they would not have needed to draw a parallel between every detail in the mashal's narrative and their own situation; the immediate context would have given them all the information they needed, as the frame narrative suggests.

Most meshalim in Rabbinic literature, however, are preserved not in narrative contexts but in exegetical ones, as part of midrash, the study and interpretation of Scripture. There is no important formal or functional difference between meshalim recorded as parts of narratives and those presented as exegeses or midrashim of verses. In both, the Rabbis used the mashal as a rhetorical device. But it was primarily in the literature of midrash, in the anthologies in which the Rabbis' biblical interpretations were eventually collected, probably after being transmitted orally from teacher to disciple, that the mashal assumed its normative, standard form. The following mashal, Eikh. R. 4.11, is attributed to

R. Eleazar b. Pedat, an early-fourth-century Palestinian sage. The mashal is doubly exegetical: it begins as a comment upon Ps. 79:1 and concludes with an interpretation of Lam. 4:11:

> It is written, "A song of Asaph. O God, heathens have entered Your domain" (Ps. 79:1). A song! It should have said, "A weeping"!
>
> R. Eleazar said:
>
> It is like a king who made a bridal-chamber for his son. He cemented, plastered, and decorated it. One time his son angered him, and the king destroyed the bridal-chamber. The pedagogue sat down and began to sing. [People] said to him: The king has destroyed his son's bridal-chamber, and you sit and sing! He said to them: For this reason I sing: For I said: Better that he poured out his anger upon his son's bridal-chamber, and not upon his son.
>
> Similarly, people said to Asaph: The Holy One, blessed be He, has destroyed His temple, and you sit and sing! He said to them: For this reason I sing: For I said: Better that the Holy One, blessed be He, poured out His anger upon wood, stones, and dirt and not upon Israel. That is what is written. "And He has kindled a fire in Zion, which has devoured the foundations thereof" (Lam. 4:11).

Like nearly all Rabbinic meshalim, this text has two parts: a fictional narrative about a king, the *mashal-proper;* and the narrative's application, the *nimshal.* Both the mashal-proper and the nimshal begin with formulaic phrases: "it is like" (*mashal le* or a variant) and "similarly" *(kakh).* In addition, the nimshal usually concludes by citing a verse, the mashal's prooftext. That verse offers the mashal its exegetical occasion, and the exegesis serves as the mashal's literal climax. In this mashal, it is a radically literalist reading of the verse: "God's fire has devoured *only* the foundations of the Temple." This interpretation reiterates the same allusive message implied by the narrative. That message is a response to the destruction of the Second Temple in 70 C.E. that, somewhat paradoxically, praises God for having destroyed the Temple because by doing so He spared the people of Israel.

In rhetorical terms, R. Eleazar's mashal can be described as an apologetic parable: its aim is theodicy, and perhaps, too, rationalization of the Destruction. Like the warning in R. Joshua's fable, its implied apologetic message is the mashal's "ulterior purpose."

Yet while the message is inscribed—enacted, as it were—in both the narrative and the accompanying exegesis, it is never stated explicitly; indeed, the mashal's effectiveness in persuading its audience of the truth of its message lies in its refusing to state that message explicitly, thereby making the audience deduce it for themselves from its two enactments. By reproducing the message in duplicate, the structure of the mashal provides a framework for the interpretive act that its audience must perform. The duplication serves both as a hermeneutical safeguard—since the audience can "check" their interpretation of the narrative against their understanding of the exegesis, and vice versa—and as an opening for additional subtleties of meaning, since by inserting discrepancies into the space between the mashal-proper and the nimshal, by introducing differences into the larger pattern of resemblance, the mashal's author can deliberately complicate his audience's act of interpretation as well as the mashal's own message. As we shall see, the play of doubleness against duplicity is a critical factor in the mashal's narrative poetics.

The bipartite structure of R. Eleazar's mashal is the normative structure for the midrashic mashal. I will call this structure the mashal's regularized form, and the process through which it assumes this form, regularization. This process is the key to understanding the mashal's compositional techniques. As we will see, the regularized form can already be identified in many of the meshalim preserved in the Tannaitic collections. It becomes most easily identifiable, however, in meshalim recorded in texts attributed to Amoraim. By the Amoraic period, it appears, the Rabbinic mashal had reached its full maturity.

Mashal, Parable, and Allegory

The word mashal is derived from a root that, according to many philologists, is related to the ideas of likeness and similarity—a not unlikely beginning for a word that later comes to designate stories that draw lines of resemblance.[7] As the word appears in the Bible, however, the noun mashal seems to refer to any kind of language used in a special way: to figures of speech, like metaphors or similes, to proverbs, and to allegories—though never, curiously enough, to the specific narrative forms that we call parables or fables.[8] Only in Rabbinic literature does the word mashal become a formal generic title for parables and fables, though it continues even then to bear all its earlier meanings of allegory, metaphor, proverb, and so on.[9]

The conventional translation of mashal as "parable" ultimately derives, it seems, from the Septuagint, which first renders mashal as *parabolē;* somewhat later, the synoptic gospels also designate Jesus' mashal-like narratives as *parabolai.*[10] The Greek word *parabolē,* however, has its own history. Literally "something set aside," it is a term used by ancient rhetoricians like Aristotle to describe the brief comparisons, usually fictitious, that orators invent (as opposed to borrowing them from history) to serve as proofs or demonstrations in their speeches.[11] In Aristotle, these "parables" are in fact closer to similes than to genuine stories; for the latter type, Aristotle in fact employs a separate rhetorical term, *logoi,* a word usually translated as "fables." Among other ancient rhetoricians, however, the word *parabolē* comes to assume the sense of "an illustrative parallel," and eventually it includes narratives that serve as illustrations. Hence its application by scholars to Jesus' parables, which were understood to be essentially illustrative and pedagogical in purpose.[12]

Although the term *parabolē* or an equivalent never appears in Rabbinic literature, the midrashic mashal has also been understood by most scholars as a parable in the Greek rhetorical sense, if only because mashal scholarship has always been strongly influenced by Christian scholarship about the New Testament parables. Since Adolph Jülicher's seminal work on Jesus' parables, it has therefore been a commonplace to speak of both Jesus' parables and the Rabbinic meshalim as "illustrative parallels"—that is, didactic tales whose meanings were absolutely clear to their original audiences.[13] And in more recent scholarship, this sense of parable as illustration has been extended still further. While Jülicher conceived of the parable in Aristotelian terms as akin to simile, contemporary scholars have argued for a connection between parable and metaphor, proposing to read Jesus' narratives as "extended metaphors" that "concretely" realize their meanings in their narratives.[14] In this view, the parable is not a mere text. It is closer to what linguists call a "speech act" or a "language event," which by its very utterance creates a new reality (not entirely unlike the way the Bible describes God as creating the universe). As one adherent of this view writes about the "parabolic experience," it is "a way of believing and living that initially seems ordinary, yet is so dislocated and rent from its usual context that, if the parable 'works,' the spectators have become participants, not because they want to necessarily or simply have 'gotten the point' but because they have, for the moment, 'lost control' or as the new hermeneuts say 'been interpreted.'"[15]

The very hyperbole of this statement only emphasizes its view of Jesus' parables as being virtual revelations of the Divine Word. This is not, to be sure, a surprising testimony to be found in the writings of devout Christians, for whom Jesus' parables *are* revealed truth. But it is also a view implicit in much contemporary critical scholarship about the parables, and one not always fully acknowledged although it has been highly influential nonetheless. Of all its influences, the most important has been a nearly unanimous consensus among scholars that parabolic discourse excludes all traces of allegory—indeed, that the parable as a literary form is the opposite of allegory.[16] First predicated by Jülicher, partly out of the conventional nineteenth-century view of allegory as an artificial, intrinsically inauthentic mode of language, and hence as a particularly unsuitable medium for Jesus' divine speech, this belief has had a powerful impact upon all subsequent research on parables. Features in individual parables exhibiting "allegorical" characteristics, sometimes parables in their entirety, have been labeled as additions made by later editors or redactors to the authentic "original" gospel text. In Rabbinic scholarship, in turn, the mashal's allegorical features, particularly during the Amoraic period, have been interpreted by some scholars as evidence of the literary form's degeneration, its fall from "parabolic purity."[17]

My purpose in mentioning this scholarly consensus is not solely to dispute its exclusion of allegory from the literary form of the parable. Rather, I wish to suggest that the terms allegory and parable, as they have figured in past scholarship, are simply not helpful in understanding the mashal. Granted, if the term allegory is taken in its largest sense, to describe all discourse that is referential, then the mashal possesses allegorical features: the characters portrayed in its narratives, the deeds those characters perform, the situations they find themselves in—these all routinely refer in meshalim to something beyond themselves. But even if the mashal overlaps with allegory in this respect, it is not itself a mode of literary discourse as allegory is, a type of speech that says one thing and means another.[18] Rather, the mashal is a literary-rhetorical form, a genre of narrative that employs certain poetic and rhetorical techniques to persuade its audience of the truth of a specific message relating to an ad hoc situation. Even if a mashal's narrative personifies abstract concepts, entities, and relationships—God, the Community of Israel, the covenant—those features of the mashal, be they called allegorical or symbolic or referential, exist only for the sake of enabling its audience to grasp for themselves the ulterior message that the mashal bears.

To read the mashal as narrative—as narration of human deeds or actions—rather than as allegory, or not-allegory, also means, in effect, to abandon a certain theological investment in the parable's status as a type of privileged language. In the view that parable is not-allegory, or that parable is metaphor, it is possible to detect a nostalgic yearning for language as a virtually unmediated presence, for an almost revelatory experience of divine fullness. The term allegory itself in this view seems to be less a literary category than an emblem for interpretation, for the inevitable necessity of interpretation. As its very name suggests, interpretation is always, inescapably "a presence between," a mediation. The proponents of the claim that parable is not-allegory are really expressing a desire for a word, perhaps The Word, that will somehow exist in a realm beyond the interventions of interpretation, within a magic circle impervious to the intrusions and interferences of an interpreter. Conversely, the notion of parable as metaphor stands for a totalizing identification of literature *and* life, for speech as epiphany, for the parable as Logos.

If such a yearning for Absolute Presence stands behind the parable-as-metaphor position, then we might say that the real opposite of metaphor is not allegory but metonymy. For where metaphor reveals similarity among things that are different by asserting their complete identity, metonymy draws equivalences between separate, unrelated entities by association and contiguity: between part and whole, cause and effect, object and attribute. These equivalences are by definition partial, always somewhat accidental and random; insofar as they are not absolute or conditioned by necessity, they necessarily partake of temporality and its contingencies. They are, in short, closer to the stuff of prose and of narrative than to poetry and metaphor.[19]

Because the word parable carries with it all the theological and scholarly baggage I have just described, I have preferred in general to use the Hebrew *mashal,* which is in any case the term the Rabbis use to designate parabolic narratives. The reader should note, however, that where the word parable appears in this book, it does not mean anything different from mashal. For the same reason, I have used the Hebrew *nimshal* to refer to the so-called explanation or application accompanying the narrative, or mashal-proper; here, though, the reader should know that the word nimshal does not appear in this usage before the Middle Ages.

Mashal and Ma'aseh

When the mashal is not misidentified with allegory, it is often confused with the *ma'aseh.* Literally a "happening" or an "occurrence," the ma'aseh most resembles what Aristotle called a *paradeigma,* an example, or exemplum: an anecdote told to exemplify or illustrate a lesson, moral or otherwise.[20]

Like the mashal, the ma'aseh is a brief narrative form whose function is openly didactic. But where the mashal's narrative is fictional, the ma'aseh purports to tell a story that actually took place. To be sure, this claim is primarily rhetorical; it has no bearing on the separate question of whether the incident in the ma'aseh actually did occur as narrated.

Yet as a rhetorical claim, the assertion of historical veracity is a valuable key to the ma'aseh's basic narrative strategies. The ma'aseh marshals historicity as proof of its truth, the rationale for this being close to what Aristotle had in mind when he remarked, in describing the similar feature in the *paradeigma,* that "the future as a rule resembles the past."[21] Since what happened once is likely to reoccur in the future, the fact that a particular form of behavior once won reward or punishment is a revealing index to its virtuous or wicked character. Moreover, since whatever the ma'aseh narrates did actually happen (at least according to its own claims), the audience of the tale are assured that the ma'aseh's implied or explicit promises of reward and punishment are not based on its author's private fantasies. Indeed, one of the more striking characteristics of the ma'aseh is that the more improbable and fantastic its narratives, the stronger are its claims to historicity, and the more effective its exemplariness.

Consider the following ma'aseh, which appears in the Babylonian Talmud (Berakhot 53b) in the course of a controversy between the two early Rabbinic schools, the Houses of Hillel and Shammai, over the following legal question: If a person forgets to recite grace-after-meals, and only remembers later, after he has left the place where he ate, must he return in order to recite the obligatory blessings, or can he say grace wherever he happens to be? According to the ruling of the House of Shammai, the person must return to the original site. According to the House of Hillel, he need not—provided that he truly forgot; if he neglected to say grace and later regretted it, even the House of Hillel concedes that he must return. After some discussion, the Talmud records the following ma'aseh:

> Once there were two students.
> One forgot [to say grace] and acted in accordance with the House of Shammai, [and when he went back to the original site,] he found a purse of gold.
> The other disciple willfully [neglected to say grace], acted in accordance with the House of Hillel [and did not return,] and a lion ate him.

The opposite fates of the two disciples point to a common lesson: the great importance of observing the commandment of saying grace in the place where one has eaten. Whatever the precise status of the controversy between the two Rabbinic houses on this question—in the second story, even the House of Hillel would have agreed that the disciple should have returned to the original spot because he willfully neglected to say grace—the exemplary, didactic force of the narrative as a whole rests upon both its unspoken humor and its intentional exaggeration or hyperbole. One must believe that the two students actually met their fates as narrated in order to be persuaded at all of the ma'aseh's lesson. The fact that both reward and punishment are way out of proportion to deed or misdeed is precisely the point.

Hyperbole is one strategy the exemplum uses. Another is repetition. In the ma'aseh just discussed, the separate stories of the two disciples are clearly the products of a single rationale; they coincide, not by repeating the same story but by reenacting the identical logic, and thus making that logic explicit *through* its repetition. In this way, as Susan Rubin Suleiman has remarked, exemplary narratives expressly "entail" their meaning, virtually speaking for themselves.[22] The simplest technique for achieving this, the same kind of explicit moralizing, is through the epimythium, the moral saying appended to the exemplum, usually at its conclusion. In either case, the effect is what Suleiman calls "redundancy," or what Roland Barthes has referred to as "the excessive naming of meaning."[23] In the exemplum, excess or redundancy serves as a guarantee that the narrative's meaning will be understood without any ambiguity. By reducing all openings for doubt or question in a narrative, redundant features simultaneously eliminate the possibility of plural readings, and reiterate a single meaning through multiple narrative options.

The mashal, in contrast, operates through a technique that is the opposite of redundancy: it deliberately gives the impression of naming its meaning *insufficiently*. It uses ambiguity intentionally. Yet the mashal achieves this appearance—the appearance of ambiguity—not by being authentically ambiguous but by shrewdly incorporating suggestive openings for the questioning of meaning; in this way it artfully manipulates its audience to fill those openings so as to arrive at the mashal's correct conclusion. To be sure, in the exemplum the excessive naming of meaning can also be rhetorically manipulated; redundancy is not synonymous with repetitiousness, or with semantic tedium. But what one most obviously witnesses in the exemplum is the ambition "to make everything absolutely clear." The exemplum, one might say, epitomizes Abby Warburg's famous saying that God resides in the detail. In contrast, the mashal has God, or meaning, residing *between* its details, in the shifting sands that lie between the narrative and the nimshal, where story does not exemplify truth but simply alludes to it. The consequence of this difference is that one literary form, the ma'aseh, lends itself to closure; the other, the mashal, does not. A mashal's message can rarely be paraphrased in a single statement like an epimythium.[24]

The exemplary narrative about the two students is, in fact, only one of several types of ma'asim found in Rabbinic literature. Yet all its types serve openly didactic ends, although they use somewhat different rhetorical and poetic strategies to achieve this purpose. Because these forms of narrative, which are ubiquitous in Rabbinic literature, are often confused with the mashal, I have provided a brief taxonomy for the different varieties of the ma'aseh, as well as for the other main genres of narrative in Rabbinic literature, in Appendix A. This taxonomy will, I hope, help situate the mashal among the orders of Rabbinic narrative, and further clarify its singularity.

The Origins of the Nimshal

If the mashal does not expressly entail its meaning, as I have just argued, then what is the nimshal? What purpose is served by the so-called explanation or application of the mashal's narrative? The answer to this question—the purpose of the nimshal—is in a way the linchpin of the conception of the mashal that underlies this book. It therefore requires an especially careful exposition.

Now in most scholarship on the parable and mashal, the nimshal is indeed treated as a secondary feature of the literary form: as a kind of epimythium indicating belated allegorization.[25] For if the meaning of a parable was absolutely clear to its original audiences, as has been assumed, then an explanation for the meaning is unnecessary. Unless, of course, the explanation is intended to provide a new, revised meaning for the parable—either because its original one was unacceptable, or because it has been forgotten.

This argument from allegory against the authenticity of the nimshal is unsatisfactory because, as I have already argued, the mashal *is* to some extent allegorical. But the mashal is allegorical—or as I would prefer to call it, referential—only to the extent that it must allude to the ad hoc situation that gives it a concrete meaning. For a mashal preserved within a narrative context, that narrative supplies the information that makes it possible to understand the mashal's allusive meaning. In the absence of a narrative context, as in most midrashic literature, the normative presence of the nimshal as part of the mashal is to be understood as a device of compensation for the missing narrative: instead of a narrative frame, there is now an exegetical context, which is provided through the invention of the nimshal.[26]

It will be easiest to understand the nature of this invention if we imagine three different settings or situations in which a mashal can be delivered and interpreted:

1. *Real-life settings.* To what degree the meshalim recorded in the documents of Rabbinic literature derive from compositions

once recited before live audiences is a question whose answer we will probably never know. But if and when a particular mashal is recited before an audience, we can assume that the audience will be familiar with the ad hoc situation to which the mashal's allusive narrative is directed. We can also suppose that, on the basis of their first-hand knowledge, the audience will be able to figure out for themselves the mashal's message.

2. *Narrative settings.* This is a literary setting that attempts to reproduce a real-life setting so as to provide its audience—readers or auditors—with all the information that would be available to someone in a real-life setting. The most obvious illustration for such a setting would be that of a mashal originating in a real-life context that was later transmitted orally or committed to writing; in the later setting, the mashal's new audience, no longer intimately familiar with the context in which the mashal was first given its meaning, will have to be supplied with enough information about the mashal's origins and its setting to understand its allusive message. The easiest way to do this is with a narrative about the original setting.

Even so, that narrative will offer at best a second-hand account of what the reality was, and since that is all the new audience will have, their understanding of the mashal will not be the same as that of the mashal's earliest audience. This acknowledgment does not diminish the value of the "second-hand" audience's understanding of the mashal; it simply explains how and why the mashal's meaning will inevitably undergo alteration in moving from an oral to a literary setting even when the latter is a narrative.

3. *Exegetical settings.* This is the case relevant to most Rabbinic meshalim, which are preserved within exegetical—that is, midrashic—contexts; indeed, these contexts, as preserved in the literary anthologies of midrash, may in fact be *the* original contexts. These settings are doubly removed from a real-life setting: they are literary, and they do not provide a narrative about a real-life setting. Instead, their occasions tend to be exegetical—the study and interpretation of a verse—but these occasions are not in themselves the full setting for the mashal's meaning. In these exegetical contexts, the nimshal gives the audience all the information they need to understand the mashal.

As Barbara Kirshenblatt-Gimblett has noted, the meaning of a parable lies not only within its narrative but also "in the particular and variable meanings which the participants give it in specific social contexts."[27] As the context changes, a parable's meaning will also change; and it will change even more when the mashal shifts mediums, ceasing to be an oral composition delivered in a real-life context and becoming instead a text preserved in a literary document. Such changes are, in other words, inevitable; the nimshal is merely a device for facilitating understanding, not necessarily an attempt to conserve the original or true meaning.

To be sure, once the nimshal had become a normative part of the mashal, its presence could be exploited. One of the most common techniques the Rabbis use to complicate the interpretation of a mashal is to plant inequalities and inconsistencies between the mashal's narrative and its nimshal. Yet even in these cases the nimshal's function does not significantly differ from that of a narrative context. The "fit" between a good parable's application and its setting is never perfect; when it is, the mashal is either predictable or tendentious. Even a typical nimshal usually tells us less than we need in order to know the mashal's full explanation; rather, it tends to supply only enough information to enable the audience to apply the mashal's rhetorical message to the exegetical context. In fact, it is not uncommon for the nimshal to consist solely of a prooftext—if that happens to be all the context needed to grasp the mashal's meaning.

The rationale for the nimshal's presence in the mashal as a device of compensation rather than as an "allegorical" explanation is consistent with the ubiquitous tendency of midrash to subordinate every context—narrative, historical, sociological—to the all-encompassing context of Torah: to make the words of Torah literally embrace every detail in the universe. "Turn it and turn it over," the sage Ben Bag Bag counseled the student of Torah. "For everything is in it" (M. Avot 5.25)—provided you know how to read Torah: that is, to study midrashically. Viewed from the perspective of midrash at large, the normative presence of the nimshal in the mashal's overall form is simply a token of the mashal's own midrashic context—of the "midrashizing" of the mashal, its adaptation to the requirements of Rabbinic exegesis.

The invention of the nimshal is the first and most important feature of the process of regularization the mashal has undergone in midrashic literature. Aside from the nimshal, two other features of that process need to be described. Both concern the mashal's narrative.

The King-Mashal

The first of these features pertains to the narrative's characters. As the mashal became regularized, it was assimilated to the literary form of the king-mashal. The protagonist of the narrative conventionally became a king, and its other personae, members of the royal court—the king's advisers, counselors, generals, the soldiers in his army, the subjects of his provinces, and so on.

This aspect of regularization is partly a stylistic phenomenon. Many king-meshalim have nothing intrinsically royal about them, and in some, the character of the king could easily be replaced by an anonymous man, an *adam* or *ehad,* without changing the mashal's plot or meaning. A father who gets angry at his son might be anyone, a king or a commoner, as might a man hopelessly in love with his wife.

But the use of the king as conventional protagonist is not solely a matter of style. Typically, the character of the king symbolizes God. This symbolization derives from ancient Near Eastern traditions, and is already close to a cliché in the Bible.[28] It also pervades Rabbinic literature outside the mashal, particularly the standard liturgy in which God is normatively addressed as king of the universe; indeed, according to some Rabbis, a blessing that does not designate God as king of the universe is not a valid blessing.[29]

Yet the king portrayed in the king-mashal is far from being the stock image of biblical and post-biblical tradition. Since Ignaz Ziegler's monumental study of the king-mashal at the beginning of this century, it has been recognized that the features of the king portrayed in the king-mashal are modeled upon those of the Roman emperor—or if not upon the emperor himself, then upon his procurator, and later proconsul, in Palestine.[30] As Ziegler showed, the meshalim are filled with the lived realities and material details of the Greco-Roman world and its imperial courts. The king-mashal's language is suffused with terms borrowed from Greek and Latin.[31] Some meshalim use material like the story of Pandora borrowed from Greco-Roman mythology, and many allude to the political and social facts of the Greco-Roman world.[32]

Indeed, some meshalim are virtually unintelligible if the historical incidents to which their narratives allude are not understood.[33]

All these characteristics of the king-mashal pointing to the Rabbinic literary form's rootedness in the Greco-Roman world led Ziegler and other scholars after him to treat the king-mashal as essentially a historical document; Ziegler himself seemed to believe that most meshalim derived from specific, in theory identifiable, historical incidents. This conclusion is mistaken. The meshalim are fictional narratives that do not make even a rhetorical claim to be historically true. But the many references in the meshalim to the larger world in which the Rabbis lived certainly show how profoundly familiar the sages were with that world and its culture, and how creatively they were able to turn that knowledge into material for their imaginative narrative compositions.[34] In this the Rabbis were no different from any other writer of fiction: they exploited the imperial court for their narratives just as Dickens used the English law courts in writing *Bleak House*.

As we will see in the course of analyzing meshalim, it is difficult to establish a single all-encompassing rule to determine when or how a mashal reflects historical reality. Although many king-meshalim do not depend in any significant way on the fact that their protagonist is a king, it is also the case that when a king-mashal alludes to a fact or an incident that does not make sense in purely narrative terms, there is a high probability that behind the mashal there stands some kind of historical specificity—a tale about the emperor or his court that reached the Rabbis in some way, or a forgotten detail of Roman law or custom, or an anecdotal curiosity that may not have been of major historical import but nonetheless interested people, including the Rabbis. The extent and complexity with which historical reality is woven into the texture of the mashal's imaginative prose cannot be overstated.

The regularization of the mashal into the form of the king-mashal was never programmatic. Many meshalim with protagonists who are not kings are preserved in the various midrashic collections attributed to sages who lived in the Amoraic period, and there remain many parables that are not king-meshalim from the Tannaitic period as well as king-meshalim from that period that do not exhibit the other features of regularization.[35] Still, the form of the king-mashal is the normative one that the mashal's narrative takes from the Amoraic period onward. Meshalim not conforming to its patterns are exceptional. A small but revealing indication of this can be observed in a small feature of the transmission of certain meshalim that otherwise is inexplicable. In the few cases where we possess the same mashal in both Tannaitic and Amoraic versions, and where the protagonist in the earlier version of the mashal is simply called an *adam,* "a man," one commonly finds that the later version will change the *adam* into a *melekh,* "a king." This change often occurs even when the mashal's narrative does not require its protagonist to be a king.[36] In a few cases, the same phenomenon can be observed even in some Tannaitic meshalim that are repeated in other texts by a different Tanna.[37] Unless one understands the primacy of the king-mashal in the Rabbinic tradition as a matter of regularized style, this tendency to change the mashal's protagonist into a king appears all but arbitrary.

Stereotyping

The assimilation of the mashal into the form of the king-mashal is actually part of a larger phenomenon of regularization: stereotyping. By this term, I mean the use of conventionalized and recurring literary structures, narrative motifs, and nearly formulaic diction. When a *darshan,* or preacher, wished to compose a mashal, he had at his fingertips, as it were, a number of conventional structures in which to cast his narrative; he also had at hand a large vocabulary of stock phrases and terms he could draw upon to express narrative actions (known in narratology as functions), motifs and characters, and themes. These formal structures and their vocabulary constituted what we might call a thesaurus of thematic, motific, and lexical stereotypes. These stereotypes cover nearly every aspect of the mashal.

A description of these stereotypes can begin with the literary structures that determine the overall shape of the mashal. The most common structure, used in the vast majority of meshalim, is the simple past-tense narrative which follows the standard introductory formula. In its fullest form, that formula is as follows: *mashal lemah hadavar domeh le* ("A mashal: What is the matter like? It is like . . ."). In many meshalim, the complete formula is shortened to either *mashal le* or simply (and most frequently) *le.* There is no apparent significance to the different forms of the formula (other than the diligence or laziness of the scribe who happened to copy the particular manuscript).[38] The standard continuation of the formula, *lemelekh* ("it is like a king") is used, however, even when the king is not the protagonist of the narrative but only a marginal character: this fact again suggests the prominence of the king's position in the king-mashal.[39] Following this formulaic beginning comes the mashal's narrative, related in the simple past tense. The narrative, in turn, is followed by the nimshal. Like the mashal-proper, the nimshal too begins with a formula: *kakh* (translated in this book as "similarly," "likewise," or "so").

The logic behind this literary structure dictates a more or less direct parallel between the tale recounted in the mashal's narrative and the application spelled out in the nimshal. In addition to this structure, though, several others were available to a darshan. These include structures that begin with the formulae *melekh basar vadam,* "a king of flesh-and-blood" and *benohag sheba'olam,* "it is the custom of the world," and that consist of narratives told in the present tense which describe the acts or traits of a mortal, usually a human king. These descriptions tend to be less genuine narratives than extended comparisons between the human protagonist and God which stress either their similarity or dissimilarity. For an example, consider the following series from Vay. R. 18.5:

> R. Joshua of Sikhnin said in the name of R. Levi:
> A mortal *(basar vadam)* dispenses [as punishment] exile *(ekhsariyah),* and the Holy One, blessed be He, dispenses exile, [as it is written,] "Instruct the Israelites to remove from camp anyone with an eruption or discharge . . ." (Num. 5:2). A mortal can dispense incarceration in prison, and the Holy One can dispense incarceration in prison, [as it is written,] "the priest shall isolate the affected person for seven days" (Lev. 13:4) . . .

The passage continues by enumerating seven additional points of similarity between God and a human king in their respective ways of executing judgment; however, the mashal concludes with the following instance of dissimilarity.

> R. Berechiah said in the name of R. Levi:
> A mortal makes a wound with a knife and heals it by means of a plaster. But the Holy One, blessed be He, how does He make a wound and then heal it? "I will bring healing to you and

cure you by means of (literally: of) your wounds—declares the Lord" (Jer. 30:17).

This kind of antithetical comparison is not, in fact, unusual, especially in structures using the *melekh basar vadam* form, since a common rhetorical function of this structure was to condemn the Roman imperial cult and to refute its claims for the divinity of the Roman emperor.[40] Probably the most famous example of such an antithetical mashal is the following text recorded in the Mekhilta (Shirta, 1) as a comment upon Exod. 15:1:

> A king of flesh-and-blood *(melekh basar vadam)* enters a province, and everyone praises him—that he is mighty, when he really is weak; that he is wealthy, when he is poor; that he is wise, when he is foolish; that he is merciful, when he is cruel; that he is a fair judge, when he doesn't have any of these qualities *(midot)*.
>
> Nonetheless, everyone flatters him.
>
> But He who spoke and thereby created the world is not so: "I will sing to God" (Exod. 15:1)—that He is mighty, as it is said, "the great, the mighty, and the awesome God" (Deut. 10:17) . . .

The mashal's irony lies precisely in understanding that the flattery paid to the emperor in the mashal is modeled in part upon the conventional praises sung to the gods.[41]

"Custom of the world" *(benohag sheba'olam* or *minhago shel 'olam)* meshalim work in much the same way as "flesh-and-blood" comparisons, except that their analogies between the human and the divine are nearly always antithetical. In general, the overall logic and form of these meshalim is somewhat freer than in typical past-tense meshalim. On occasion, the structure of a *melekh basar vadam* mashal will overlap—formally and rhetorically—with a past-tense narrative mashal. Consider the following example from Eikh. R. 1.2 (p. 59):

> R. Levi said: It is like a hero *(mashal legibor)* who dwelled in a province, and the inhabitants of the province placed their trust in him. If enemies attacked, the hero would show them his might (literally: his right arm) and they would flee. One time the enemy attacked, and they asked the hero: Why do you not show them your might (literally: right arm)? He replied that he was ill.
>
> But here *(beram hakha):* "No, the Lord's arm is not too short to save" (Isa. 59:1). What then led to your [i.e. Israel's] defeat?

"But your iniquities have been a barrier between you and your God" (Isa. 59:2).

This mashal is narrated in the past tense and begins with the formulaic *mashal le,* but its overall structure is closer to the kind of antithetical comparison typical of *melekh basar vadam* meshalim.[42]

Stereotyping in the mashal extends far beyond the use of these larger structures; it is most evident in the specific language of the mashal, its conventional themes and narrative motifs. Since these instances of stereotyping are best discussed in specifics, let us turn to the analysis of a particular mashal.

Eikhah Rabbah 4.11

The following pages contain a series of meshalim in English translation. The first two meshalim cited in this group are variant texts of Eikh. R. 4.11, representing respectively the Ashkenazic and Sephardic recensions of Eikh. R. (hereafter noted as A and S, respectively); Hebrew texts of both recensions can be found in Appendix B. The remaining meshalim all include stereotypes that are cognate or parallel to Eikh. R. 4.11's themes, motifs, or diction.

The parts of the meshalim are keyed as follows: (1) Illustrand. (2) Introductory formula. (3) Mashal-proper. (4) Nimshal. (5) Prooftext.

I:1 Eikh. R. 4.11A
(1) "And He has kindled a fire in Zion, which has devoured the foundations thereof" (Lam. 4:11). It is written: "A song of Asaph. O God, heathens have entered Your domain" (Ps. 79:1). A song! It should have said, "A weeping"!
R. Eleazar [ben Pedat] said:
(2) It is like *(mashal le)*
(3) a king who made a bridal-chamber *(she'asah hupah)* for his son. He cemented, plastered, and decorated it *(giyyedah vesiyyedah vetsiyyerah).* One time his son angered him, and the king destroyed the bridal-chamber *(pa'am ahat hikh'iso usetarah).* The pedagogue sat down and began to sing. [People] said to him: The king has destroyed his son's bridal-chamber *(hamelekh satar hupat beno),* and you sit and sing! He said to them: For this reason *(lekakh)* I sing: For I said, Better that he poured out his anger *(sheshafakh hamato)* upon his son's bridal-chamber, and not upon his son.

(4) Similarly *(kakh)*, people said to Asaph: The Holy One, blessed be He, has destroyed His temple, and you sit and sing! He said to them: For this reason *(lekakh)* I sing: For I said, Better that the Holy One, blessed be He, poured out His anger upon wood, stones, and dirt and not upon Israel.

(5) That is what is written. "And He has kindled a fire in Zion, which has devoured the foundations thereof" (Lam. 4:11).

I:2 Eikh. R. 4.11S

(1) "And He has kindled a fire in Zion, which has devoured the foundations thereof" (Lam. 4:11). It is written, "A song of Asaph. O God, heathens have entered Your domain" (Ps. 79:1). Should not the verse have said, "A weeping of Asaph," or "a lament of Asaph," or "a dirge of Asaph"? And you say "a song of Asaph"?

(2) But it is like *(ela mashal le)*

(3) a king who made a bridal-chamber *(she'asah beit hupah)* for his son, and plastered, cemented, and decorated it *(vesiyye-dah vekiyyerah vetsiyyerah)*. The son turned to wickedness *(vey-atsa beno letarbut ra'ah)*. Immediately the king went up to the bridal-chamber, and tore its curtains, and broke its supports *(miyad 'alah hamelekh lahupah vekara' et havilaot veshiber et hakinim)*. The pedagogue took a tube of reeds *(venatal pedagog shelo iybuv shel kinim)* and began to sing. [People] said to him: The king has destroyed his son's bridal-chamber *(hamelekh hafakh hupato)*, and you sit and sing! He said to them: I sing because he has destroyed *(shehafakh)* his son's bridal-chamber, and he has not poured out his anger *(velo shafakh hamato)* upon his son.

(4) Similarly *(kakh)*, they said to Asaph: The Holy One, blessed be He, has destroyed His sanctuary and temple *(heikhal umikdash)*, and you sit and sing! He said to them: I sing because the Holy One, blessed be He, poured out his anger *(sheshafakh . . . hamato)* upon wood and stones, and did not pour out his anger upon Israel.

(5) This is what is written: "And He has kindled a fire in Zion, which has devoured the foundations thereof" (Lam. 4:11).

II:1 B. Sanhedrin 108a

(1) "And all existence on earth was blotted out" (Gen. 7:23). Man sinned, but what sins did animals commit that warranted their destruction?

A Tanna recited in the name of R. Joshua b. Karha:

(2) It is like *(mashal le)*

(3) a man *(adam)* who made a bridal-chamber *(she'asah hupah)* for his son, and prepared a banquet *(vehitkin . . . se'udah)* of every sort of food. After a few days, the son died *(leyamim meit beno)*. The man arose and destroyed *('amad uvizer)* the bridal-chamber. He said: I made this only for the sake of my son. Now that he is dead, what do I need this bridal-chamber for?

(4) Even so *(af)* the Holy One, blessed be He, said: I created animals and beasts only for the sake of man. Now that man has sinned, what do I need animals and beasts for?

II:2 Ber. R. 28.6
R. Pinhas said:

(2) It is like *(le)*

(3) a king who married off his son and built a bridal-chamber for him *(ve'asah lo hupah)*, and plastered, cemented, and decorated it *(vesiyyedah vekiyyerah vetsiyyerah)*. The king became angry at *(ka'as . . .'al)* his son, and killed him. He entered the bridal-chamber, and began to break its supports, to tear down its walls, and to rip apart its curtains *(hithil leshabeir bekinim umakhpi'a bahitsa'ot umekarei'a bavila'ot)*. He said: My son is destroyed and these things still exist!

(5) Therefore *(lefikhakh)* [Scripture says], "Both man and beast" (Gen. 6:7).

II:3 Ber. R. 10.9

(1) ["On the seventh day God finished the work . . ." (Gen. 2:2).] Geniba said:

(2) It is like *(le)*

(3) a king who built a bridal-chamber *(she'asah hupah)* for himself, and plastered, cemented, and decorated it *(siyyedah vekiyyerah vetsiyyerah)*. What was the bridal-chamber lacking? A bride to enter it.

(4) Similarly *(kakh)*, what was the world lacking? The Sabbath.

II:4 Ber. R. 9.4

(1) ["And God saw all that He had made, and found it very good" (Gen. 1:31).]
R. Yonathan said:

(2) It is like *(le)*

(3) a king who married off his daughter, and made a bridal-chamber and house *(ve-asah . . . hupah uvayit)* for her, and plastered, cemented, and decorated it *(vesiyyedah vekiyyerah*

vetsiyyerah). When he saw it, it pleased him. He said: My daughter, my daughter, if only *(halevvay)* this bridal-chamber would always please me just as it pleases me now.

(4) Similarly *(kakh),* the Holy One, blessed be He, said to His world: My world, if only you would always please Me just as you please Me now.

II:5   Eikh. R. Petihta 24

(1) [When He saw that His temple was destroyed,] the Holy One, blessed be He, said to Jeremiah:

(2) Today I am like *(ani domeh hayom le)* a man who had an only son, and who made a bridal-chamber for him *(ve'asah lo hupah).* And the son died inside the bridal-chamber.

(3) Do you not feel pain for me and for my children?

III:1   Ber. R. 28.6

R. Yudan said:

(2) It is like *(le)*

(3) a king who handed his son over to a pedagogue, and he turned the son to wickedness *(vehotsio letarbut ra'ah).* The king became angry at *(ka'as 'al)* his son, and killed him. The king said: It was this man alone who turned my son to wickedness. Yet my son is destroyed and this one still lives!

(5) Therefore *(lefikhakh)* [Scripture says], "Both man and beast" (Gen. 6:7).

III:2   Mid. Teh. 90.1

(1) "A prayer of Moses, the man of God" (Ps. 90:1). It was necessary to say only "A prayer of Moses." Why does it also say, "the man of God"?

(2) It is like *(mashal le)*

(3) a king who became angry at *(sheka'as 'al)* his son and wished to kill him. The [king's] courtier *(ohavo)* said to him: I beg you! Forgive him. Do not kill him. The king restrained himself *('amad)* and did not kill him. The next day the king began to say: If I had killed my son, I would have injured *(makhshil)* only myself. Now I should thank my courtier who begged for pity for my son. From now I will make him a father to kings *(av limelakhim).*

(4) Similarly *(kakh),* the Holy One, blessed be He, said, "Leave me alone, that I may destroy them" (Deut. 9:14). Moses said to Him, "And if You deal thus with me, kill me" (Num. 11:15). And what is written afterward? "And the Lord said: I have pardoned according to your words" (Num. 14:20).

Afterward, the Holy One, blessed be He, said to Moses: If I had killed Israel I would only have injured myself. I should therefore thank Moses who begged for pity for them—as it is said, "And Moses besought the Lord his God" (Exod. 32:11)—I will pay him honor, and call him a father of prophets, a father of angels, a father of those who pray.

(5) This is the meaning of "A prayer of Moses, the man of God."

III:3 Mid. Teh. 3.1

(1) Another interpretation of "A song of David" (Ps. 3:1). When did David recite this song? When he "went up by the ascent of Mount Olives, and wept as he went up" (2 Sam. 15:30). But if he wept, then why did he sing? And if he sang, why did he weep?
R. Abba b. Kahana said:

(2) A mashal. What is it like? It is like (mashal lemah hadavar domeh le)

(3) a king who became angry at (sheka'as 'al) his son, and banished him (uterado) from his palace. The king sent his pedagogue after him. [The pedagogue] went and found the son weeping and singing. The pedagogue asked him: Why are you weeping and singing? The son replied: I am weeping because I angered my father, and I am singing because he did not condemn me to death but only to banishment. And not only did he not execute me, but he [only] banished me to a province of commanders and prefects!

(4) R. Yudan said:
Similarly (kakh), David said: Jacob fled, as it is said, "And Jacob fled into the field of Aram" (Hos. 12:13). Moses fled, as it is said, "Moses fled from Pharoah" (Exod. 2:15). Elijah fled, as it is said, "And he went in the strength of that food forty days and nights until Horeb the mountain of God" (1 Kings 19:8). So I will flee like them. He began to say: "I remembered Your judgments of old, O Lord, and have comforted myself" (Ps. 119:52)—I remembered the principle of justice by which You led my predecessors, and You have consoled me. When did David say this? [When] "David said to all his servants who were with him in Jerusalem, Arise and let us flee; for otherwise we shall not escape from Absalom: make speed to depart, lest he overtake us suddenly, and bring evil upon us" (2 Sam. 15:14). Rav and R. Yudan [offered interpretations of this verse]. Rav said: So

that he will not judge us like a condemned city (*'ir hanidahat*). R. Yudan said: Once the owner of the cup begins to clean it, he does not stop until he has utterly cleansed it. Similarly (*kakh*), when David saw that the Holy One, blessed be He, had utterly cleansed him of his sins, he immediately began to say:

(5) "a song of David."

III:4 Mid. Teh. 79.1

(1) "A song of Asaph. O God, heathens have entered Your domain" (Ps. 79:1). Was it right for Asaph to recite a song? Should he not have recited a lament? Similarly, you also find Scripture saying, "And David went up by the ascent of Mount Olives and wept as he went up" (2 Sam. 15:30); and it is also written, "A song of David as he fled" (Ps. 3:1). This is what the verse says, "It is a joy to the just to do judgment" (Prov. 21:15). When the righteous pay for their sins, they sing to the Holy One, blessed be He. And similarly, Asaph said: "A song of Asaph. O God, heathens have entered Your domain."

(2) It is like (*mashal le*)

(3) a king who had a son who was disobedient and did not listen to his father. What did the king do? When he was filled with anger (*keyvan shenitmalei heimah*), he entered the bridal-chamber of his son and tore, ripped, and threw out the curtains until all of them had been torn, and he threw them out. The king said: Did I not act wisely by destroying the bridal-chamber of my son, for I can make a more beautiful [bridal-chamber] for him, and by not killing him in my anger, for if I had killed him, my nephew would have succeeded me, and it is better that my son succeed me.

(4) Similarly (*kakh*), Asaph said: Did not the Holy One, blessed be He, act well by pouring out His wrath upon wood and stones, and not upon His children?

(5) And so the verse says, "The Lord has accomplished His fury, and He has kindled a fire in Zion, which has devoured the foundations thereof" (Lam. 4:11). It is therefore written, "A song of Asaph."

To display the degree of stereotyping in Eikh. R. 4.11, I have arranged all the stereotyped phrases and elements of diction in the narrative in the following list. The list is divided in two columns corresponding to the two recensions.

A	S
It is like a king	It is like a king
made a bridal chamber for	made a bridal chamber for
he plastered, cemented, and decorated it	he plastered, cemented, and decorated it
[he] angered [him]	[the son] turned to wickedness
[he] destroyed . . .	the king went up to the bridal-chamber, and tore its curtains, and broke its supports
The pedagogue . . . sings	The pedagogue . . . began to sing
People said to him:	People said to him:
The king has destroyed [his house]	The king has destroyed [the bridal-chamber]
He said [to him]	He said [to them]
Better that . . .	I [sing] because . . .

As this list indicates, the two recensions differ mainly in length and detail. For example: (1) While A uses a single word to say that "he angered him" *(hikh'iso)*, S explains in several how the son did this, namely, by turning to wickedness *(veyatsa beno letarbut ra'ah)*. (2) A uses a single verb *(usetarah)* to tell us how the bridal-chamber was destroyed; S employs the more elaborate and trebled formula, "immediately he went up to the bridal-chamber, and tore its curtains, and broke its foundations." (3) To express the pedagogue's reaction, S explains that "the pedagogue took a tube made from reeds and sang." A reads solely: "the pedagogue sat down and began to sing."[43] The language in both recensions, however, is equally formulaic, and both recensions tell the same narrative; from their language alone, there is no way of determining if one version is the earlier or more original one. Finally, in both recensions, as the narrative approaches its end, the language becomes less and less stereotyped, and more identical to analogous phrases in the nimshal immediately following the narrative.

For the purposes of analysis, the mashal's narrative can be divided into two major motifs: (1) the account of the king's construction and destruction of the bridal-chamber; (2) the portrait of the pedagogue's paradoxical behavior. The first motif, in turn, can be treated as a combination of three motemes: (1) the construction of the bridal-chamber; (2) the son's provocation of his father; (3) the destruction of the bridal-chamber.

The first and the third of these motemes are explicitly attested in a mashal attributed to a Tanna, R. Joshua b. Karha, and translated above as II:1. The mashal, recorded in B. Sanhedrin 108a in connection with Gen. 7:23, appears as a response to the question, Why did God destroy both men and beasts in the Flood when it was mankind alone that sinned and deserved to be punished? Now as it happens, this Tannaitic mashal is also recorded in Ber. R. 28.6 (cited above as II:2) where it is attributed to an Amora, R. Pinhas, who uses it in connection with Gen. 6:7 but in response to the same question that Gen. 7:23 had raised for R. Joshua.[44] In nearly all respects, the two meshalim are identical—except for the fact that the Tannaitic mashal is not quite regularized while its Amoraic counterpart is.

The mashal's regularization can be observed in several features. First, while the protagonist of the Tannaitic mashal is an *adam*, "a person," this anonymous character is changed in the Amoraic version into a *melekh*, a king. This change, as already noted, epitomizes the tendency of regularization to assimilate all meshalim with anonymous protagonists into the king-mashal. Second, the narrative of the Tannaitic version, which does not explain the reason for the son's death, is less coherent than the Amoraic mashal, which does. Third, and finally, the diction of the Amoraic narrative is stereotyped in a way in which that of the Tannaitic mashal is not. Note, for example, the constant trebling of actions and phrases in the Amoraic version, which is not present in the Tannaitic mashal, and the use of such stereotyped phrases as "began to break its supports, to tear down its walls, and to rip apart its curtains" (which is virtually identical to I:2's "the king went up . . . its foundations"); and "he made a bridal canopy . . . and plastered, cemented, and decorated it" (*she'asah beit hupah . . . vesiyyedah vekiyyerah vetsiyyerah*).[45] Incidentally, this last formulaic phrase is found in all the Amoraic versions cited thus far— I:1, I:2, and II:1—as well as in II:3, II:4, and III:4 (with some variation in diction).

These two motifs—one, the image of a bridal-chamber that has been built in anticipation of the son's marriage (or the daughter's, as we shall soon see); the other, the motif describing either the actual death of the son or a premonition of his death—represent a thematic combination that is itself deeply traditional, attested numerous times in ancient Jewish literature. In addition to the examples already cited, one may note the especially unusual use of the combination in the passage cited as II:5. This passage occurs in the course of a strikingly mythological and anthropomorphic narrative in which God, stricken with inconsolable grief, uses the motif Himself—to describe His own miserable situation after the Destruction! This narrative is most probably a late Amoraic text, but the use of the two themes in combination is attested as early as the Fourth Book of Ezra, a pseudepigraphic text that was probably composed shortly after the destruction of the Second Temple, at the end of the first century. In that work, the protagonist Ezra encounters a woman in mourning who refuses to be consoled; when the prophet asks her to describe the tragedy she has suffered, she tells him her story—how she and her husband, after thirty years of marriage, were finally granted a son, whom they raised, rejoiced over, and prepared for marriage:

> But it happened that when my son entered his wedding chamber, he fell down and died. Then we all put out the lamps, and all my neighbors attempted to console me . . . (10:1–2).[46]

As Ezra subsequently learns, the woman is a symbolic apparition representing Zion in mourning over the destruction of the Temple—a symbolic meaning that we have already seen the traditional motif used for in several meshalim. In other parabolic contexts, however, the image of the son dead in his bridal-chamber can symbolize different catastrophes. In II:2 and II:3, it represents the Flood, while in still another midrashic text about the Binding of Isaac, Abraham is said to have "resembled (*hayah domeh*) a man who was building a bridal-chamber for his son" while Isaac "resembled a man who was making a bridal-chamber for himself."[47]

As a final point, we should note that the specific form the motif takes in II:3 and II:4 is especially revealing since it shows how this moteme with its formulaic diction comprises an independent unit that can be combined with other motemes and motifs to compose entirely different meshalim for distinct exegetical and rhetorical purposes. As an independent unit, the stereotype can be formulated thus:

> [It is like a king who] built/made a bridal-chamber for . . . and plastered, cemented, and decorated it.

The identity of the person for whom the king builds the bridal-chamber—be it himself, his daughter, or his son—does not affect the stereotype or its diction. Although in all the meshalim we have discussed it happens to be the king who builds the bridal-chamber, the same action could in fact be performed by another character—an instance of the independence of function (or action) and agent that was first pointed out by Propp in connection with the Russian folktale.[48]

The second moteme in Eikh. R. 4.11—describing the son's provocation of his father—is also a stereotyped motif, though its diction varies widely: *hikh'iso* (I:1); *ka'as hamelekh 'al beno* (II:2); *keyvan shenitmalei heimah* (III:4); *veyatsa beno letarbut ra'ah* (I:2; in this example, the fact that the king thereby becomes angry at his son must be inferred from the narrative). The difference between the first two of these variants may seem negligible—both use the same verb, though in the former the verb is in the causative and the son is its subject, while in the latter the verb is in the simple active and its subject is the king—but the fourth variant appears to be the one associated specifically with the character of the pedagogue. Note, for example, the mashal listed as III:1 (which in Ber. R. 28.6 immediately precedes II:2), in which the pedagogue is described as actively leading the son into wickedness *(vehotsio letarbut ra'ah)*.

A brief word must be said here about the pedagogue. As a character in the narrative, the pedagogue essentially plays the role of what narratologists call a Helper. He is neither the subject of the narrative (like the king) nor its object (the son), but a mediating figure; in this function, he resembles other figures like the *oheiv* or *philos*, the king's admirer or friend, and the *shoshbin*, the guardian or attendant, to name only two. What is more significant about the character of the pedagogue is his name, which is a Greek loan-word, and which signals, by its very presence in the narrative, the mashal's own historical rootedness in the Greco-Roman world. Despite the word's meaning in English, the pedagogue is not a mere teacher: in Late Antiquity, the figure was an identifiable social type, usually a household slave who was responsible for supervising minors and ensuring their moral as well as physical and intellectual welfare.[49] Indeed, so gravely important were his responsibilities that the pedagogue himself could be held personally guilty for the transgressions of his charge and could suffer punishment for the latter's misdeeds[50]—a fact directly reflected in R. Yudan's mashal (III:1), where the king threatens to kill the pedagogue after killing his son, and indirectly in III:2, where the pedagogue begs the king to spare his son. So, too, in Eikh. R. 4.11 it is surely significant that the character selected to react to the king's act of destruction is the pedagogue: Is his paradoxical praise of the king for not killing the son perhaps motivated by gratitude that the king did not kill him, the pedagogue, as well? In this very question, the issue of stereotyped narrative behavior in the mashal confronts the separate problem of when parabolic narrative is to be read for historical insight.

The final instance of stereotyping in our mashal that we need mention is the diction describing the king's destruction of the bridal-chamber. While Eikh. R. 4.11A uses a single verb *usetarah* to express the moteme, the verb is reminiscent of the earliest Tannaitic version's *uvizeir* (II:1). On the other hand, there exists an obvious similarity between S's "the king went up to . . . and broke its foundations" (I:2); Ber. R.'s "he entered . . . and to rip apart its curtains" (II:2); and Mid. Teh. 79.1's "he entered . . . had been torn" (III:4). All three expressions represent the moteme in phrases that describe trebled acts.

The Mashal as Traditional Literature

The presence of these stereotypes in the mashal recalls the formulaic language and themes that characterize much of ancient epic and other types of oral literature, and as in these traditions, stereotyping in the mashal may point to a mode of composition resembling those first proposed in this century by such scholars as Milman Parry, Albert Lord, and Vladimir Propp for epic poetry and folktales.[51] For the mashal, the Parry-Lord thesis is especially pertinent. As Parry and Lord suggested in their studies of Homeric and Serbo-Croatian epic, formulaic diction and narratives come into existence in response to the necessities of orally improvised performances: they directly facilitate the work of an epic poet, or a traditional singer of tales (as Parry and Lord called these poets), who must spontaneously compose narratives of fluidity and complexity. Formulaic narrative motifs and diction give the singer, in Parry's words, "his phrases all made, and made in such a way that, at the slightest bidding of the poet, they will link themselves in an unbroken pattern that will fill his verses and make his sentences."[52] Analogously, conventional motifs and narrative conventions—ways of stringing together episodes and of determining the interactions of characters—provide the oral singer with ready-made patterns and plots that he can employ in constructing his epic song.

In much the same way, we can suppose that when a darshan was called upon to compose a mashal for a particular verse or occasion, he was able to draw upon stereotyped elements—of theme and of diction—in order to improvise his composition under the pressured requirements of spontaneous performance. The total sum of these elements—all the tradition's conventions, in other words—composed a kind of ideal thesaurus which would have supplied the darshan with all the building blocks he needed for his mashal: its themes and motifs, overall patterns of structure and narrative, and stereotyped lexical expressions. Needless to say, this thesaurus was not an actual book. It is *our* metaphor for the sum total of all the strong conventions governing the mashal as its tradition came to be regularized: for everything a darshan needed to know in order to compose a mashal, and all that we can assume an experienced member of a mashal's audience—a "competent" audience (in the structuralist sense of competence)— would have known as well.[53]

The compositional theory I am proposing for the mashal should not be confused with the separate question of oral tradition in Rabbinic Judaism or with the issue of the putatively oral character of specific documents in Rabbinic literature.[54] Rather, my proposal attempts strictly to account for an exceptional, otherwise inexplicable, stylistic feature of the mashal: the formulaic stereotypes that pervade its narrative. As any casual reader of Ziegler's massive anthology will observe, its nearly one thousand king-meshalim give two opposite impressions. On the one hand, the vast majority of the meshalim resemble one another: they share rhetorical structures, narrative motifs, and elements of diction, with the same phrases and narrative functions recurring in mashal after mashal. On the other hand, as the reader will also notice, nearly every mashal in the anthology is also a singular composition, appearing as though it had been created specifically for the verse it explicates. Almost no two meshalim in the entire anthology are in fact identical.

These two seemingly contradictory impressions together constitute a kind of paradox for which, I suggest, the theory of oral
composition offers the most satisfactory resolution. It is far more
persuasive than the other available explanation, which would
attempt to describe the relationship between meshalim in terms
of an "original" mashal that was later adapted and reworked into
other, secondary or derivative meshalim. Such an explanation fails
to account for the subtle differences *and* the remarkable similarities that simultaneously exist among meshalim, and for the ways
in which both resemblance and difference are connected to the
mashal's exegetical and ideological dimensions.

My theory of oral composition does not, however, prove that
the specific meshalim preserved in the various midrashic collections were originally composed orally or were once delivered in
improvised performances. The actual history of any given mashal
is impossible to trace. For one thing, it is possible that, once
the mashal's conventions were established and regularized, any
darshan or the editor of any midrashic anthology could have composed written meshalim that would have appeared perfectly traditional simply by imitating all the conventions of oral composition.
By their very nature, traditional elements tend to persist beyond
the oral stage into the written.[55] Many of the meshalim in Ziegler's
anthology may therefore be literary creations in the literal sense,
composed by editors for readers—who may, however, have
included among their ranks darshanim who then used the
meshalim in sermons of their own, delivering them orally to live
audiences. The possible exchanges between oral and written stages
in a literary tradition are multifarious.

In post-Rabbinic Hebrew literature, the literary form of the
mashal undergoes radical transformations. But within Rabbinic
tradition itself, from the earliest Tannaitic collections to the latest
texts from the Tanhuma-Yelamdeinu tradition, it is difficult to
see any significant variations between documents or changes in
the king-mashal's literary form or rhetorical use—apart, that is,
from the differences I have already noted, which relate to the
process of regularization. Yet while stereotyping in the mashal
can be observed most clearly in meshalim attributed to Amoraim,
it is possible to observe in Tannaitic compositions the embryonic
presence of many stereotypes, and thus to see the very working of
the process of regularization, its coming into being. The only

other major difference between meshalim in these two periods is that while Tannaitic meshalim are all in Hebrew, it is common for Amoraic parables to have a mixture of Hebrew and Aramaic, the latter being used often (though not always or exclusively) for dialogue.[56]

From Narrative to Exegesis

The composition of the mashal through stereotypes should not be imagined as having been a mechanical process. For *how* the darshan actually employed the stereotypes—from choosing the motifs and language he used to deciding how to actually join and present them in a plot—was entirely his own doing, a matter of his skill as a narrator and the result of the exegetical and ideological pressures under which he composed. For example, in Eikh. R. 4.11, as we saw, the two separate motifs that make up this narrative—one, the account of the king's construction and destruction of the bridal-chamber; the other, the portrait of the pedagogue's paradoxical behavior—are both traditional elements, attested elsewhere in the mashal's tradition. What is not traditional—attested in no other meshalim—is the precise way R. Eleazar combined the separate motifs into a continuous narrative. What does their combination mean? Why did R. Eleazar make the pedagogue react as he does?

To answer these questions, let us turn back to the figure of the pedagogue. In other meshalim, as we saw, the pedagogue finds himself in a comparable situation where the king becomes angry at his charge, the king's son and the pedagogue's student, but in those meshalim he acts differently. For example, in Mid. Teh. 3.1 (III:3), the pedagogue goes as the king's emissary to the son, and finds *him* singing and weeping over his punishment—in other words, acting just as the pedagogue does in Eikh. R. 4.11. In Mid. Teh. 90.1 (III:2), the king's courtier, the *philos* or *oheiv*,[57] a Helper-figure like the pedagogue, saves the son from his father's anger, and later is rewarded by the king for having done so. As these examples show, there is nothing predetermined about the pedagogue's behavior in Eikh. R. 4.11.

If the pedagogue's behavior in Eikh. R. 4.11 is determined by anything, it is the model of Asaph in the nimshal. The precise identity of this figure is not entirely clear: in the Bible, he is one of the Levitical singers of Psalms, but our mashal does not specify who he is though elsewhere the Rabbis identified Asaph as a son of Korah who, with his brothers, survived the earthquake in which their father was swallowed alive.[58] Happily, Asaph's historical identity is less important than the role he plays in the nimshal and its exegesis. That role is a complicated one. The reply that Asaph gives to the question of why he sings after the Destruction is, first of all, a response to the question initially asked in the illustrand preceding the mashal (numbered as part 1): Why does Ps. 79—a psalm traditionally associated with the destruction of the Temple—begin "A song of Asaph," and not "a weeping" or "lament" of Asaph?[59] Asaph's answer, as we know, is that he sings and rejoices because God destroyed only the Temple, not Israel and its people. This interpretation of Ps. 79 is then applied in the nimshal to Lam. 4:11, which R. Eleazar now reinterprets in such a way that this verse also describes God's ultimate mercy to the people of Israel.[60] According to this exegesis, the verse reads, in effect, "And He has kindled a fire in Zion, which has *not* devoured Zion, but *only* the foundations thereof."

By destroying the Temple, in other words, God paradoxically spared Israel. Indeed, the mashal may even be understood as implying that the reason God destroyed the Temple—mere "wood and stones"—was that He desired to contain His wrath against Israel. The Temple was a kind of surrogate. In fact, the very image used to symbolize the Temple, the image of the bridal-chamber, which is drawn from the Greco-Roman *thalamos*, a hymeneal booth, is of a makeshift, temporary structure. This image of the Temple, as a marriage bed (for God and Israel) or as a canopied litter, appears elsewhere in Rabbinic texts, particularly in connection with the *apiryon* or palanquin of Song of Songs 3:9.[61] But in our mashal the image of the *thalamos* is used with the further suggestion that it was intentionally built this way, as an impermanent structure, so that God could easily destroy it. This remarkably ambivalent attitude toward the Temple is attested elsewhere in Rabbinic sources, and in one other text in a tradition attributed to R. Eleazar b. Pedat.[62]

As a midrashic exegesis, R. Eleazar's reading of the verse can be characterized as pointedly literalist, almost hyperliteralist; it offers a kind of radical inference or *diyyuk* based upon the verse's most restricted sense: Why does the verse mention "foundations"?

Because *only* the foundations—that is, wood and stones—were destroyed.

What has instigated this interpretation? There is no obvious lexical or syntactic difficulty in the verse that would have given rise to the exegesis, though it is possible that R. Eleazar may have understood the verb *kilah* in the sense of God "completed" His anger rather than "gave vent to it."[63] Another possibility, at least for the image of the Temple as a *thalamos,* might be a pun on the verb *kilah* and the Aramaic *kila/h,* a common word in Rabbinic texts for a booth, like a *sukkah* or a *hupah;* in fact, another midrashic text makes precisely this pun in connection with Num. 7:1.[64]

The most likely motive for the interpretation lies, however, not in any word or phrase *in* the verse but in an extra-textual factor (which nonetheless may have figured just as crucially in the reading of the verse): the accusation, frequently made against the Jews in the third and fourth centuries, and well documented in Christian polemical literature of the period, that the destruction of the Temple and the calamitous fate of the Jews in its aftermath conclusively proved that God had rejected His people. In *Adversos Judaeos,* ch. 13, for example, Tertullian claims that because the Jews "had committed these crimes, and had failed to understand that Christ 'was to be found' in 'the time of their visitation,' their land has been made 'desert, and their cities utterly burnt with fire, while strangers devour their region' in their sight: 'the daughter of Zion is derelict,'" and so on.[65] These lines are largely compounded out of verses in Isaiah (55:6,7 and 1:7,8), but to make much the same point Tertullian could have quoted Lam. 4:11. The verse's plain sense, after all, does seem to testify to God's unmitigated wrath against Israel. R. Eleazar's interpretation can be seen as a response, an apologetic reply, to precisely this kind of reading.

Indeed, it may not have been necessary to make this kind of apologetic interpretation only in response to a polemical Christian reading of the verse. Because the verse's plain sense is close enough to this reading, Jews themselves no doubt were very sensitive to its plausibility without any stimulus from the outside. Yet such a plain reading could never have been a viable one for the Rabbis. It contradicted every belief they held about the world and their place in it, and the abiding continuity of their transcenden-

tal, covenantal relationship with God (even if the sages would
have admitted that that relationship had been temporarily dis-
rupted by the destruction of the Temple). The very survival of
Judaism in the aftermath of the Destruction precluded the possibility of taking the verse in its plain sense. In the face of this
impossibility, the Rabbis used midrash. Rather than deny history,
they turned to interpretation to save the meaning of Lam. 4:11.
In a single midrashic act, they confirmed the veracity of Scripture
and countered the despair that Jews themselves must have felt
after the Destruction.[66] And by making this verse, Lam. 4:11, the
very source of their hopelessness, describe the very condition for
hope in the aftermath of the Destruction, the Rabbis salvaged a
meaning in Torah from the catastrophe they had suffered.

The overall rhetorical function of R. Eleazar's mashal can
therefore be described as apologetic. By praising the wisdom of
the king who destroyed the bridal-chamber instead of the bridegroom, R. Eleazar's mashal responds to an implied polemical
argument, either one actually made by gentiles or one feared by
Jews as a truth that might be found in the Torah. The full meaning of the mashal, however, goes beyond this apologetic interpretation. We can see this best by returning to the relationship of the
mashal's narrative to its nimshal. How does the mashal actually
join narrative and exegesis? We can begin to answer this question
by pointing out that the connection between the mashal and the
exegesis of Lam. 4:11 is actually an artificial one—or more accu-
rately, an artifice of the mashal's own rhetorical structure. For
while the mashal in its entirety is constructed so as to give the
impression that its narrative "creates" or produces the culminating
interpretation of Lam. 4:11, it will be clear to any careful reader
that the opposite is the truth. Ontologically as well as compositionally, the interpretation is prior to the narrative. Aside from this
being obvious on logical grounds, the priority of the exegesis can
be substantiated by the simple observation that the final statement
the pedagogue makes in the narrative—his response to the question of why he sings and does not weep—is directly based upon
the response of Asaph in the nimshal. And the latter is convincing
only within the context of the interpretation of Lam. 4:11.

But if the mashal's narrative does not actually produce the
interpretation of the prooftext, then what is the verse's connection
to the narrative, that allusive tale with an ulterior purpose? The

answer to this question is close to what I have just suggested: their relationship is rhetorical. The narrative is made to seem as though it produces the revisionary exegesis of Lam. 4:11, while the verse, once reinterpreted, is then exploited to authenticate the validity of the narrative—to give it the authoritative aura of Scripture. The internal hermeneutics of the mashal is therefore consciously self-reflexive, almost circular, so that, in the course of completing its hermeneutical rounds, the mashal strategically justifies itself as a rhetorical device for interpreting Scripture.

Exactly how it does this can be deduced from the pedagogue's behavior in the narrative. On one level, his behavior is a *reaction* to the king's destruction of the bridal-chamber. On another level, though, as the pedagogue explains himself, his singing is the narrative equivalent to an *interpretation* of the king's action. Within its own narrative, in other words, R. Eleazar's mashal provides a model for the activity of interpretation. Just as the pedagogue explains his paradoxical behavior, so too does R. Eleazar justify the equally paradoxical logic of the two interpretations in the mashal—first, Asaph's singing in Ps. 79:1; then, the exegesis of Lam. 4:11.

The narrative of the mashal is therefore itself about interpretation. It provides a model for the interpretive activity, and thus does more than solely fulfill a rhetorical function. The narrative assumes a cognitive value of its own, telling us something in its own right: about the inherently paradoxical character of interpretation, and about the extreme conditions under which such interpretation becomes necessary. In our mashal, those conditions are the historical events surrounding the destruction of the Temple, as symbolized in the motif of the bridal-chamber and its destruction. Yet the symbolic use made of that motif in our mashal is itself context-specific, dictated by the exegetical content of Lam. 4:11; as we saw earlier, the same motif of the destroyed bridal-chamber is used elsewhere to refer to the Flood and to the sacrifice of Isaac. An analogous ad hoc specificity characterizes the figure of the pedagogue who, in other meshalim, is used to represent personages as different as Moses, David, and the beasts destroyed in the Flood.

This last fact is significant because the pedagogue's paradoxical behavior is a traditional motif employed not solely in the mashal. The same motif is used elsewhere as an attribute of the Rabbinic sage as he is portrayed in literature. In a famous passage at the conclusion of Eikh. R., nearly identical and equally paradoxical joy over the destruction of the Temple is attributed to R. Akiba; and Akiba's behavior may itself be traced to analogous descriptions, in contemporary Greco-Roman literature, of philosophers who indulge in bizarre and shocking behavior.[67]

The figure of the pedagogue in our mashal may therefore be viewed as a symbolic representation of the figure of the darshan himself, of the sage who engages in midrash, and the pedagogue's paradoxical behavior as a figure for the paradox of the midrashic act: for the daring and the freedom with which the Rabbis used Scripture to overcome the historical trauma they had endured in the destruction of the Temple. And the astonishment felt by the anonymous bystanders in the mashal's narrative at the inappropriate behavior of the pedagogue is comparable to the surprise the audience of the mashal may have felt at the exegetical reversal of R. Eleazar's interpretation of Lam. 4:11. Simply in order to present his exegesis, R. Eleazar did not need to compose a mashal. What the mashal with its image of the pedagogue taking up his flute in song adds to the local exegesis of Lam. 4:11 is a larger meaning: a rationale for midrash as a hermeneutic of recovery and recuperation.

The Mashal and Midrashic Hermeneutics

R. Eleazar's mashal points, then, to a general hermeneutics of midrash. The nature of that hermeneutics, however, is significantly different from the hermeneutics of midrash as traditionally conceived.

Attempts to describe the hermeneutics of midrash go back to the Rabbinic period itself, when exegetical rules underlying midrash, the *middot*, or hermeneutical principles, were first enumerated. These principles include the *kal vehomer* (inference from the lighter to the heavier, or the weaker to the stronger); the *hekeish* and the *gezerah shavah* (the logical and verbal analogy); *gematria* (arithmology), and *notarikon* (anagrammatic or stenographic exegesis).[68] It is likely that these early lists of middot were compiled not as how-to manuals for "doing" midrash but for ideological purposes, as documents legitimating the methods of *particular* schools of interpretation against those of other schools; some may even have been intended to defend all of Rabbinic interpretation against sectarian attacks. Early on, however, these lists came to be treated as a virtual logic for midrash.[69]

The project to "rationalize" midrash is especially visible in the works of the classical commentators on midrash, and its culmination is the massive commentary of the MaHaRZU (Zev Wolf Einhorn, 19th c.) on Midrash Rabbah; in this work, its exceptionally learned and ingenious author, using the list of thirty-two middot ascribed to R. Eleazar b. Yose Hagelili, attempted to account for every interpretation in Midrash Rabbah by referring to a specific numbered middah.[70] The shortcomings as well as the strengths of the method are evident in the MaHaRZU's commentary, and they point to those of the classical genre of midrash-commentary as a whole. Even though their commentaries abound in suggestive and illuminating insights, the classical commentators never examine the status of the middot as a rationale for midrash. These commentators still stand wholly within the midrashic tradition.

The first modern scholar to stand back from the tradition and attempt a critical examination of the methods of midrash was the German scholar Isaac Heinemann. In his encyclopedic study *Darkhei Haaggadah* (The Methods of Aggadah), Heinemann proposed two categories of his own invention, "creative philology" and "creative historiography," to describe the singular features of midrash.[71] According to Heinemann, these categories represented the two aspects of a way of thinking that was prerational, primitive, or, as Heinemann called it, "organic," more like ancient myth and popular folk literature than the philosophical and scientific discourse of the modern age. In Heinemann's view, the Rabbis had the same ultimate interests as modern historians and philologists—the understanding of the past and of texts—but they pursued these concerns more in the manner of imaginative poets than as self-consciously reflective critical scholars.

The organicist consciousness that Heinemann ascribed to the Rabbis as authors of midrash was a product of late-nineteenth- and early-twentieth-century beliefs about symbolism, human creativity, and literary expression. It was more Romantic in character than Rabbinic. Still, Heinemann's work marked a watershed in the history of midrash scholarship. It succeeded in liberating midrash from apologetics, and legitimated the study of Rabbinic

hermeneutics. And since Heinemann, many other scholars have
made important contributions to our understanding of midrash by
pointing to its connections and shared features with Greco-Roman
legal and literary exegesis, to ancient dream-interpretation, to
hermeneutical tendencies already detectable in biblical tradition,
and the like.[72]

Still more recently, contemporary literary theorists and critics
have refocused attention on the hermeneutics of midrash itself.[73] In poststructuralist theory, midrash has been put forward
as a historical and conceptual alternative to the modes of logo-
centric interpretation that have dominated Western thought since
antiquity. Thus, where the latter forms of interpretation are said
to seek to recover a text's original or true meaning, midrash is
described as delighting in a plurality, even a plethora, of meanings
that overflow from within the text; instead of seeking meaning
"behind" the text, midrash finds meaning in the text's material
surface, in its language, and in its intertextuality; instead of seeking after metaphysical presence, midrash epitomizes "a life in
literature or in scripture that is experienced in the shuttle space
between the interpreter and the text," as a recent anthology
has characterized the common features of midrash and post-
structuralist theory.[74]

What R. Eleazar's mashal suggests, however, is that midrash
may be less a hermeneutics, a system or even stance of interpretation, than a narrative of exegesis. The nature of that narrative, as
told in the mashal, has already been related: it begins with a crisis
and is followed by an effort at recuperating or salvaging the text—
saving not only its meaning but its value, its felt importance in the
life of the reader. What makes midrash different from other kinds
of interpretation is that its subject, its text, is the Torah, and its
reader not just *a* reader but the Jew who is the recipient of the
covenant that the Torah embodies. For this kind of reader, midrash makes the Torah bearable, livable. Rather than primarily
determining the Torah's meaning, or its multiple meanings, midrashic interpretation seems often to be more concerned with
maintaining the Torah's presence in the existence of the Jew, with
bridging the gap between its words and their reader, with over-
coming the alienation, the distance of Torah, and with restoring
it to the Jew as an intimate, familiar presence.[75] The midrashic
interpreter in this sense is literally a translator: one who carries

the text across a divide, who negotiates the space between the text and its comprehension.

Other meshalim I will analyze in this book relate different versions of this narrative of interpretation. Fittingly enough, the narrative of midrash has not one but many forms, and the mashal is only one. What makes the mashal so deeply characteristic of midrash is not its narrative of interpretation alone but the highly structured, stereotyped form it lends to that narrative. However unpredictable the narrative of midrashic interpretation may sometimes be, however chaotic midrashic interpretive practice often seems to be, its deep and abiding stability—the very quality that guaranteed midrash its normative status in Rabbinic Judaism and made it identifiable as an exegetical tradition—derives from the nature of its regularized, strictly governed discourse. In this chapter, we have witnessed the form that stability in the mashal assumes on the levels of composition and exegesis. In the next three chapters, we will see equivalent patterns of stability in the mashal's rhetoric, poetics, and thematics.

2

Rhetoric

The Occasions of the Mashal

For scholars, one of the more frustrating features of Rabbinic literature is its reticence about itself—how little we are told about its making, about the circumstances surrounding the composition of its texts. In this respect, the mashal is actually quite unusual, for a good number of passages directly or indirectly describe the situations in which sages composed and recited parables. There is, for example, the mean and witty story about Bar Kappara, quoted at the beginning of Chapter 1, as well as the account in Ber. R. 64.10, also quoted in Chapter 1, relating the political circumstances in which R. Joshua b. Hananiah recited his fable of the lion and the Egyptian heron in order to dissuade the Jews of Palestine from rebelling against the Romans. Another Talmudic passage (B. Berakhot 61b) describes how R. Akiba told a fable about a fox and a fish in order to encourage the study of Torah during the period of the Hadrianic persecutions.

In both the latter instances, the mashal purportedly served a covert political purpose as an oblique means of expressing opinions that were too dangerous to be spoken openly.[1] The Rabbis were even able to gently mock those who claimed to be able to use the mashal in such politically charged situations. Commenting on the "bravery" of the patriarch Jacob as he anxiously prepared to meet his brother Esau after their long estrangement (Gen. 33:1), R. Levi recited the following fable:

> The lion got angry at the animals and the beasts. They said to each other: Who will go and conciliate the lion? The fox spoke up: I know three hundred fables *(matlin)* [with which] I'll conciliate him. The animals replied: Go! The fox went a few steps,

and stopped. They asked him: Why have you stopped? The fox replied: I forgot a hundred of the fables. They answered him: Still, two hundred are plenty. He went a few more steps, and stopped. They asked him: What is this? He answered: I forgot another hundred fables! They said to him: Still, a hundred are sufficient. But when the fox reached the lion, he said: I've forgotten all the fables. Let every one conciliate the lion by himself.

Likewise: Jacob . . . (Ber. R. 78.7).

So we are to understand Jacob's "fabled" courage.

Less bellicose situations, however, provided occasions for reciting meshalim as well. Some sages are depicted as using parables in order to respond to polemical challenges made by gentiles (not unlike the way Jesus is portrayed in the gospels as employing parables to argue with and confront the Jewish leaders who oppose him).[2] Still other anecdotes describe sages like R. Abbahu, who once used a mashal to apologize to another sage whom he feared he had insulted.[3] Another tale (in B. Ta'anit 5b) relates how R. Nahman, upon taking leave of his colleague R. Yitzhak, used a mashal as a belletristic substitute for a farewell blessing.[4] Finally, sages appear to have customarily recited parables in praise of the dead, either as eulogies or in the course of consoling the relatives of the deceased. Several sources record meshalim of this kind; one text relates how R. Yohanan b. Zakkai recited two meshalim about himself even as he lay in bed dying.[5]

The most frequent occasions for the recitation of meshalim, however, were the delivery of the sermon in the synagogue and the study of Torah in the academy. Even though there exists no explicit documentation for this claim, it is highly probable that most meshalim preserved in Rabbinic literature were at least intended to serve as material to be used in lectures or sermons.[6] Appropriately, then, the most common literary context in which meshalim are recorded in Rabbinic literature is in midrash. It was this context that determined the conventional two-part structure of the mashal, consisting of a narrative and a nimshal, and it was this exegetical setting that gave the mashal its primary raison d'être for the Rabbis as an exegetical tool.

From deathbed to pulpit, then, the mashal was an exceedingly popular, widely used literary-rhetorical form. Was there a common denominator in function and form that it shared in all these contexts? What is the mashal's rhetorical character? How, through all these differing occasions, did the mashal effectively persuade audiences of its message? What was the nature of the relationship of its literary form to its thematic messages, on the one hand, and to its audience, on the other?

Three Models for the Mashal

We can begin to answer these questions by saying that there is no single model that will comprehensively explain all meshalim in Rabbinic or classical Jewish literature. There are, in fact, at least three separate models for conceptualizing the mashal; taken together, these models constitute a kind of spectrum that encompasses virtually every use to which the mashal has been put in practice, or conceived by scholars as doing in theory.

The Mashal as Illustration

This view of the mashal sees the literary form as a device for illustrating abstract ideas or beliefs through narrative examples that are concrete, familiar, and thus more easily comprehended. Highly influential in Christian parable-scholarship since Jülicher, this conception of the mashal sees the literary form as being close to a simile, a figure of likeness.[7] And indeed, illustration is one use to which the mashal is put in Rabbinic passages, as in the following mashal about Abraham recorded in Ber. R. (39.2):

> What did Abraham resemble? A bottle of balsam with an air-tight lid that was off in a corner, and its perfume could not spread. But once it was moved, its perfume began to spread.
> Similarly, the Holy One, blessed be He, said to Abraham: Move yourself from place to place so that your name will grow great through the world. Hence: "Take yourself . . ." (Gen. 12:1).

The purpose of the likeness is clear—to illustrate the reason God commanded Abraham to leave his home: so that his sweetly aromatic fame, Abraham's "name," would waft and spread through the world. Yet while this passage has the outward form of a mashal, the narrative is so spare—it does not even say who moves the bottle of balsam—it is hardly more than a simile. Somewhat more complex as illustrations are the two well-known meshalim in

Ber. R. (1.15) attributed to the Houses of Hillel and Shammai as responses to the question of what was created first in the universe, the heavens (according to the House of Shammai) or the earth (House of Hillel).

> According to the House of Shammai, it is like a king who built a throne for himself, and then made a footstool to go with it, as it is written, ". . . The heaven is My throne and the earth is My footstool" (Isa. 66:1).
>
> According to the House of Hillel, it is like a king who built a palace; after he built the ground floor, he built the upper stories, as it is written, ". . . on the day when the Lord made earth and heaven" (Gen. 2:4).

These two illustrations initially seem very simple, but upon reflection it becomes clear that they do more than illustrate two positions on the order of creation. The meshalim actually suggest two very different conceptions of the nature of the universe, and of God's relationship to the cosmos: for the House of Shammai, the earth is God's footstool; for the House of Hillel, it is His palace.

The use of the mashal as an illustration becomes increasingly dominant in post-Rabbinic, early medieval literature, first in the ninth-century composition *Tanna de-Bei Eliyahu* (TDE) and even more so in subsequent philosophical works by such authors as Maimonides. For the vast majority of meshalim in Rabbinic literature, however, the illustrative model is inadequate, and for several reasons. First, most midrashic meshalim are far less illustrative than the examples I have cited. Second, and more important, the narratives of most meshalim, which according to this view are supposed to facilitate the understanding of their lessons, are actually far more enigmatic and difficult to understand than the nimshalim themselves. In these texts, what requires elucidation is the narrative, not the nimshal or its lesson. As illustrations, then, these meshalim are terrible failures.

The Mashal as Secret Speech

This view, the second conception of the parable, is related to the position that identifies the mashal with allegory. The conception may already be attested in the gospels, in the famous "theory" of parabolic discourse expounded in Jesus' speech to his disciples, particularly as formulated in the version in Mark 4:11–12:

> And [Jesus] said to [the disciples], "To you has been given the
> secret of the kingdom of God, but for those outside everything
> is in parables; so that they may indeed see but not perceive, and
> may indeed hear but not understand; lest they should turn
> again, and be forgiven."

Among modern scholars, the secret-speech view has been most
elegantly championed by Frank Kermode, who sees *all* narrative
as enigmatic and exclusive, as having the "property of banishing
interpreters from its secret places"; for Kermode, the parable is
only a purer or more intense instance of this general characteristic
of narrative.[8]

According to this view, the mashal is an implicitly esoteric mode
of communication, an interpretive event that separates "insiders"
from "outsiders"—those who understand from those who don't—
and that restricts its understanding to a select, or elect, few. As a
consequence, it is sometimes claimed by proponents of this conception that the parable was employed to express controversial or
dangerous beliefs that were better not articulated openly, or that
could not be for political or doctrinal reasons. We have already
mentioned two examples of parables recited in such contexts, the
meshalim attributed to R. Joshua and to R. Akiba.

The Rabbis themselves would probably have found this subver-
sive or "secretive" conception of the mashal congenial. When they
came to interpret Yotham's politically rebellious mashal in Judges
(9:7–20), they treated it as an allegory.[9] One or two passages in
the Rabbinic literature also suggest that the Rabbis understood
how the parable could be used to express controversial opinions
in less than fully explicit fashion: for example, in Ber. R. (22.10),
a mashal that in effect condemns God for having allowed Cain to
kill Abel is prefaced by the following qualification attributed to R.
Simeon b. Yohai: "It is difficult really to express [the idea behind
this mashal], and impossible to explain it."[10]

Yet this mashal and the few others like it in Rabbinic texts are
truly exceptional. The use of the mashal as a form of secret, exclusive discourse does not fully emerge until the maturing of Kabbalistic literature in the early Middle Ages. In Rabbinic tradition,
the communicational model for the mashal is exoteric, not esoteric. Even where a mashal's message is ambiguous or especially
subtle and difficult to paraphrase, that message can be "interpreted out" of the mashal by any sufficiently competent reader.

The Mashal as Rhetorical Narrative

In my view, this model is the single one adequate to explain most meshalim in Rabbinic literature. It steers a course midway between the two conceptions just discussed. According to this view, the mashal is neither a secret tale with a hidden meaning nor a transparent story with a clear-cut moral. Rather, it is a story that turns allusiveness to effect in order to persuade its audience of the value of a certain idea or approach or feeling. Unlike the two other models, which respectively conceive of the mashal as an instrument for either demonstrating or concealing the truth, this model represents the mashal's relation to meaning as oblique and indirect. While the mashal suggests its message to its audience, it requires them in the end to deduce that message for themselves.

It may help to clarify the nature of the parabolic communication through a diagram. The base model for direct communication is the following:[11]

$$\text{Sender} \longrightarrow \boxed{\text{Message}} \longrightarrow \text{Receiver}$$

In indirect communication that model is replaced by:

$$\text{Sender} \longrightarrow \boxed{\text{Story} \supset \text{Meaning}} \longrightarrow \text{Receiver}$$

where $\supset$ = implies.
And in the midrashic mashal, that model in turn becomes:

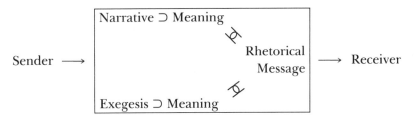

As the diagram indicates, both the narrative in the mashal-proper and the midrashic exegesis in the nimshal imply, respectively, their individual meanings, and together those two meanings contribute to the mashal's overall rhetorical message. The latter, in turn, anticipates on the compositional level both the narrative and the exegesis, corresponding in effect to a prior rhetorical intent.[12]

As an example of this communicational model, consider Eikh. R. 4.11, the mashal analyzed in Chapter 1. That mashal's rhetorical message can be described primarily as praise of God for His wisdom in destroying the Temple rather than the people of Israel. The mashal-proper communicates that message of praise in its narrative through the figure of the pedagogue and his paradoxical behavior. The nimshal, in turn, communicates the same message through its exegesis of Lam. 4:11 (as well as through the separate exegesis of Ps. 79:1). In both parts of the mashal, the act of communication is wholly accessible to the audience, even though they have to complete it themselves so as to arrive at the mashal's full meaning—at what we might call its interpretation.

That full interpretation embraces all the implications proceeding from the mashal's message of praise. These include both its apologetic argument, which rationalizes the Destruction as a surrogate punishment, and the picture the mashal provides for the interpretive act as a rhetorical construct, as an imaginative coup that transforms a historical catastrophe into a proof of God's loving care for Israel. In this last and largest sense, the mashal's meaning amounts to praise for midrash itself.

Even for a mashal, Eikh. R. 4.11 has a decidedly complex meaning. Yet most meshalim in Rabbinic literature can be described as serving a comparable rhetorical function. They express thematic messages, but those messages tend to be *phrased* in the terms of praise or blame, or as a variation upon these opposites: approbation or disapproval, appreciation or disappointment, pleasure or pain.[13] While praise and blame are not in themselves the mashal's meaning, they are its structures of signification, the modalities through which it expresses its thematic messages, either symbolically or mimetically. These messages, though in theory numberless, can in practice be named in a few categories: apologetics and polemics (both of which can be phrased as either praise or blame); consolation (often formulated as eulogy, namely, praise of the dead); complaint (blame directed against the mashal's addressee, a character usually figuring in the mashal's own narrative); and a few others.

The thematic categories and the rhetorical structures are systematically related to each other, as well as being complementary. And both are equally necessary to analyze a mashal. To describe a mashal solely in terms of its rhetoric, as either praise or blame, would obscure the truly complex ways in which it communicates ideas and feelings while eliciting the reactions of praise and blame from its audience. On the other hand, solely to thematize the mashal, to discuss it strictly in terms of its ideological message, runs the risk of turning the mashal into an exemplum, and all but eliminates its singular literary features, its qualities of literariness—in Roman Jakobson's terms, the poetic function of the mashal's message—leaving behind only its communicative side.[14]

Meshalim of Praise and Blame

The rhetorical categories and their thematic companions are best charted in examples. We can begin with a praise-mashal. The following text, from Vay. R. 2.4, appears as one among several meshalim extolling the nation of Israel. The author, R. Berechiah, is a late-fourth-century Amora.

> R. Berechiah said:
> It is like an elder who had a robe *(ma'aforet)*. He commanded his disciple, and said to him: Fold it and iron it and be careful with it. The disciple asked: My master, O elder! Of all the robes you own, why do you command me only about this one? The elder said: Because that robe is the one I wore the day I was appointed an elder!
> Likewise: Moses said before the Holy One: Master of the universe! Of all seventy independent nations that you have in the world, you command me only concerning Israel!? He replied: "For they accepted my sovereignty at Mt. Sinai and declared: 'All that the Lord has spoken we will do and we will obey'" (Exod. 24:7).

This mashal is not a king-mashal—the characters of the elder and his disciple are drawn from the Rabbinic academy rather than from the Roman imperial court—but its form is otherwise fully stereotyped. The exegetical occasion for the mashal, its prooftext, is Exod. 24:7, which here is understood literally as a statement of *kabalat 'ol malkhut shamayim*, Israel's acceptance of God's sovereignty. The mashal's main rhetorical message, however, is not praise of God but of Israel, whose status in God's eyes, we are told, is unique. Yet that uniqueness derives, in turn, from the praise, the special glory, that Israel pays God, as suggested by the central image in the mashal's narrative, the image of the robe.

This image, as Lieberman has pointed out, refers to the special ceremonial robe of office that an elder assumed upon appointment.[15] The use of the image in the mashal is extremely bold, for it implies that God was not "appointed" to His office until the children of Israel elected Him at Mt. Sinai. Theologically controversial, the mashal suggests that the relationship between God and Israel, as epitomized here in the praise they exchange, is based upon an almost dialectical reciprocity.[16]

The daring of the image only intensifies the high praise paid to Israel. And the same message informs the exegesis of Exod. 24:7, the mashal's prooftext, whose full "midrashic" meaning might be paraphrased as follows: Even though the Jews, unlike the seventy gentile nations, do not have an independent and self-ruling political state of their own (a fact that undoubtedly had a pointed and sad truth for Jews in the fourth century), they are still dearer to God than all the gentile nations. Why? Because Israel alone accepted God's sovereignty—His law—at Sinai. Inasmuch as Israel's praise is achieved indirectly through a comparison with the other nations, this mashal involves a degree of polemic. In brief, then, we might describe the mashal as an example of polemicized praise.

For an example of blame, consider the following mashal, found in Kohelet Zuta 7.16.[17]

> It is like a band of robbers who rebelled against the king. He caught them and incarcerated them in prison. What did they do? They dug a tunnel and escaped. But one among them did not flee, and in the morning the king found the man. He said to him: You enormous fool! Here was a tunnel, and yet you did not flee!? As for your friends who fled—what can I do to them?
>
> Likewise: The Holy One, blessed be He, said to the wicked: Here is repentance open to you, and you still did not repent!? This is what is written, "Escape is cut off from them" (Job 11:20).

The narrative of this mashal cleverly plays upon the unexpected, the rhetorically surprising. The fact that the king should condemn as a fool the sole prisoner who does *not* flee is initially bewildering—until the reader learns in the nimshal that the prison cell symbolizes a life of sin, and that escaping from prison is not flight from law but religious repentance. If the incarcerational imagery recalls Gnostic descriptions of the body and life in this world as a prison-house, this is less relevant for its doctrinal suggestiveness than for what it reveals about the mashal's playful rhetoric, how it subverts the audience's expectations just as the nimshal discloses its concluding message.

As in the preceding Vay. R. praise-mashal, this mashal contains a heavy dose of homily condemning the wicked man who fails to take advantage of the opportunity to repent. Yet unlike the Vay. R. mashal, whose theological content was at least slightly unorthodox, the sermonic lesson presented in this mashal is a commonplace. What is most novel about this mashal is its wit. The almost counter-intuitive relationship between the mashal and the nimshal compensates, as it were, for the routineness of the homily. Otherwise, this mashal is a fairly simple blame-mashal—or, because it warns of the consequences of not repenting, a mashal of admonition.

The two meshalim we have looked at so far are fairly straightforward examples of pure praise and blame. Many meshalim, however, combine the two rhetorical modalities. In the following example, the very point of the mashal appears to be the contrast between its dual rhetorical structures of praise and blame.

> It is like a king of flesh-and-blood who distributed royal garments to his servants. Those who were clever folded the garments and put them away in a box; those who were foolish went and did their work in them. Some days later the king asked for his garments back. The clever servants returned them all pressed and clean, while the foolish servants returned them dirty. The king was pleased with the clever servants, but he was angry with the foolish ones. Regarding the clever servants, he said: Let their garments be placed in the treasury and let them go home in peace. And regarding the foolish servants, he said: Let their garments be given to a washerman, and have them incarcerated in prison.
>
> So too the Holy One, blessed be He, says about the bodies of the righteous: "He shall yet come to peace; he shall have rest on his couch" (Isa. 57:2); and about their souls He says: ". . . the life of my lord will be bound up in the bundle of life" (1 Sam. 25:29). And about the bodies of the wicked he says: "There is no safety, said the Lord, for the wicked" (Isa. 48:22); while about their souls, He says: "But He will fling away the lives of your enemies as from the hollow of a sling" (1 Sam. 25:29). (B. Shabbat 152b)

In this mashal, the almost too obvious contrast between the clever and the foolish servants is saved from pedantry by the nimshal's witty citations of verses that match the narrative almost too perfectly; note, for example, the exegesis of the two halves of 1 Sam. 25:29 to fit the fate of the souls of the righteous and the wicked alike. In other meshalim combining praise and blame, the contrast between the two rhetorical modes is less heavy-handed, with one of the two subordinated to the other:

> It is like a king whom bandits robbed. But the king was a clever man. He said: If I rise up against them now, they will say: What stolen goods have you found in our possession? I know that in the future they will rob me three times. Afterward, I will rise against them and slay them.
> Similarly: The king is the Holy One, blessed be He, the bandits are the gentile nations . . . the place broken into is Jerusalem . . . and the Holy One, blessed be He, will emerge and battle against them, as it is said, "Then the Lord will come forth and make war on those nations . . ." (Zech. 14:3). (Mid. Teh. 118.13)

The overall message of this mashal is one of theodicy: it justifies God's behavior in permitting the gentile nations to attack Israel/Jerusalem three times before punishing them. This apologetic message is communicated, however, through joint praise and blame—praise of the king for his wisdom (in waiting for the bandits to attack the destined, hence unavoidable, three times); blame of the gentile nations for both their acts of banditry and their knavery (for thinking to deny their guilt before God when He captures them).

In still other meshalim, the rhetoric of praise and blame are combined in such a way that one modality contradicts or belies the other. In the following mashal, the narrative explicitly communicates one message of praise and simultaneously hints at a second message closer to blame.

Eikhah Rabbah 3.21

The mashal Eikh. R. 3.21 is found in several parallel sources.[18] Its author, R. Abba bar Kahana, is a third-generation Amora. I will first quote the mashal's narrative:

R. Abba bar Kahana said:

It is like a king who married a woman and wrote her a large marriage-settlement *(ketubah)*. He wrote her: So many bridal-chambers I am building for you; so much jewelry I make for you; so much gold and silver I give you. Then he left her for many years and journeyed to the provinces. Her neighbors used to taunt her and say to her: Hasn't your husband abandoned you? Go! Marry another man. She would weep and sigh, and afterward she would enter her bridal-chamber and read her marriage-settlement and sigh [with relief]. Many years and days later the king returned. He said to her: I am amazed that you have waited for me all these years! She replied: My master, O king! If not for the large wedding-settlement you wrote me, my neighbors long ago would have led me astray.

The mashal's symbolism is nearly all traditional—the king represents God, the wife the people of Israel, the hostile neighbors the gentile nations[19]—but its conventionality should not blind us to its special uses in the mashal. How many other texts in Rabbinic literature—for that matter, in all ancient literature—portray a woman who literally survives through reading, or who reads to survive?[20] The image of the marriage-settlement, though it might seem to be conventional, is in fact unique to this mashal, and as described in the narrative, is actually closer to the biblical *mohar*, or bride-price, than to the Rabbinic *ketubah* (which is only paid after divorce or the husband's death), despite its being named as such.[21]

As for its rhetoric, the mashal is a praise-mashal, but its praise is actually doubled: at first, the king praises his wife for remaining faithful during the long period of his absence; in response, she pays her own praise to the ketubah for giving her the strength to survive and await her husband's return. In the mashal's nimshal, the hapless woman's situation is further adumbrated:

Likewise: The nations of the world taunt Israel and say to them: Your God does not want you. He has left you. He has removed His presence from you. Come with us, and we will appoint you to be generals, governors, and officers.

And the people of Israel enter their synagogues and houses of study, and there they read in the Torah, "I will look with favor upon you, and make you fertile . . . I will establish My abode in your midst, and I will not spurn you" (Lev. 26:9,11), and they console themselves.

In the future, when the redemption comes,[22] the Holy One, blessed be He, will say to Israel: My children! I am amazed at how you have waited for Me all these years!

And they will say to Him: Master of the Universe! Were it not for the Torah You gave us, in which we read when we entered our synagogues and houses of study, "I will look with favor upon you . . . and I will not spurn you," the nations of the world long ago would have led us away from you.

That is what is written, "Were not your teaching my delight, I would have perished in my affliction" (Ps. 119:92). Therefore it says: "This *(zot)* I call to my mind; therefore I have hope" (Lam. 3:21).

The specific focus of the mashal's exegesis of Lam. 3:21 is the word *zot,* or "this," with which the verse begins. Now in its scriptural context, *zot* refers to the series of verses *following* Lam. 3:21. These verses list the various characteristics of God's goodness—how His mercies are not spent (3:22); how ample is His grace (3:23); how good He is to those who trust in Him (3:24); and so on—and it is these indubitable propositions about God's character that the *gever,* the "man," the unnamed protagonist-victim of the third chapter of Lamentations, recalls to himself in order to regain hope and confidence in divine mercy.

According to R. Abba's mashal, however, the word *zot* refers not to God's attributes but to the Torah. Probably implicit in this interpretation is the connection between *zot* and Torah made in Deut. 4:44, *vezot hatorah,* "and this is the Torah," a verse that is in fact explicitly quoted in parallel versions of the mashal.[23] Whatever its midrashic source, few interpretations could be more deeply characteristic of Rabbinic ideology than this one, with its shifting of meaning from God to Torah as the referent for the demonstrative. The significance of this interpretation is only heightened by the fact that Lam. 3:21, as Alan Mintz has pointed out, is the pivotal verse in its chapter, precisely the point when the gever turns from despair to hopefulness.[24] By substituting Torah for God at this very moment, the mashal virtually sums up the achievement of Rabbinic Judaism in instituting Torah-study as the practical and theoretical foundation for spiritual comfort in the time of Israel's exile.[25]

The mashal's praise of Torah-study is, however, only one of several exegetical details in the mashal. In fact, this mashal in praise of Torah and its study—midrash, in other words—is itself packed with midrash and the products of midrash, with references and allusions to other midrashim and to extrabiblical aggadot. For example, the taunting words that the nations of the world address to Israel allude to the famous midrash on Song of Songs 5:9–6:3, found both in the Mekhilta (Shirta 3, where it is attributed to R. Akiba) and in Sifre Deut. (343). Similarly, the verses from Leviticus (26:9,11) cited in the nimshal have a lengthy history of interpretation which can be traced back as early as the Tannaitic collection Sifra (Behukotai, 120a–b), where the Rabbis interpreted those verses eschatologically, as blessings that will be realized and fulfilled only at the time of the redemption. And since these verses are invoked in the nimshal to comfort the people of Israel, we can assume that R. Abba also intended the audience to understand them in the terms of the future redemption. This means, in other words, that these verses, as cited in the nimshal, are quoted already in their *interpreted* sense.

Finally, the narrative's central image, the ketubah, may itself be the product of an exegetical act. It is possible that this image derives from a pun upon the Hebrew word *vehifreiti* (Lev. 26:9), literally "I will make [you] fruitful," and the Aramaic word *parna*, based on the Greek *phernē*, a marriage-settlement.[26] This punning etymology would explain the genesis of the ketubah as an image in the mashal, and it would also suggest a reason why these specific verses from Leviticus are cited in the nimshal. And if so, the mashal may be said not only to describe exegesis as an activity but also to contain within its narrative a key to its own beginnings as a midrashic act.

The mashal's meaning, however, is not exhausted by its exegetical efforts. After all, R. Abba bar Kahana could have offered his interpretation of *zot* as referring to the Torah without using the literary form of the mashal; he could have presented it as a simple definition of the demonstrative term *zot* on the basis of Deut. 4:44. The distinctive contribution of the mashal is therefore not its interpretation of *zot* but its vivid and moving portrayal of the conditions of despair in which the poor abandoned wife of the king finds herself and in which the necessity for the eschatological-consolatory interpretation is born. In presenting this narrative of distress and consolation through Torah-study, the mashal effectively represents the history of its own composition. As we have already noted, the verses from Leviticus cited in the nimshal are meant to be read here "literally" in an eschatological sense. Yet even before the nimshal, within the narrative itself, the king's return to his wife, after his lengthy absence, may be said to anticipate the future redemption and, *in narrative terms,* actually to fulfill the promises of Scripture made in Leviticus. In the very course of its narrative, then, R. Abba's composition dramatically enacts the coming redemption before its audience's eyes, and by extension it guarantees to that audience the same consolation that the consort derives from reading her ketubah.

At this point, however, we might ask: Why should that consolation be necessary in the first place? Why must the poor matrona suffer in the king's absence? Or to put these questions in the terms of the narrative's own logic: Why must the king leave his wife in the first place? Why must he journey to the foreign provinces? If these questions are never answered in the course of the mashal, neither are a host of others: Does it ever enter the king's mind that, after he departs, the wicked neighbors will test and torment his wife? Are the lavish promises he makes to his wife in the ketubah intended in advance to console her in his absence? Or are they the actual gifts he promises to give her? But if his promises are sincere, why is the king, upon his return, so astonished at her faithfulness? Conversely, if he does not expect the ketubah to console his bereft wife, then is there any logical reason for her to remain faithful to him? Or are the promises in the ketubah actually false? Is not the king's unexplained absence really an act of unjustified and gratuitous cruelty to his hapless wife? Is the king criminally responsible for the suffering his abandoned wife undergoes during the period of his absence?

I have posed these questions not to provide answers for them but to show that the doubts they express are indeed raised by the mashal's narrative. These doubts point in the direction of a critique of the king's behavior and of the justice of his actions— which is to say, toward a critical interrogation of God and His treatment of Israel. Though never made explicit in the mashal, this critique undercuts the innocent optimism of our initial rhetorical reading of the mashal as praise and consolation. This critique leads, rather, to a second reading which understands the mashal as being closer to complaint than to consolation.

That reading is also connected to another anomalous moment

in the mashal, a tiny but significant discrepancy between the narrative and the nimshal at the point where their carefully drawn parallels diverge. The mashal's narrative, it will be recalled, is recited entirely in the past tense: the king journeyed; he returned; he and his wife were once again reunited. At the point in the nimshal corresponding to the king's return, however, there is a sudden, unanticipated leap into the future: "In the future—literally, tomorrow—when the redemption comes, the Holy One, blessed be He, will say to Israel," and so on. For the mashal's audience, this discontinuity—between pastness and futurity—can lead only to one conclusion: Genuine consolation, the true fulfillment of the promises in Scripture, will come only at the time of redemption, at the end of history. The return of the king in the mashal's narrative was possible only because narrative is by convention told in the past tense. Why? Because narrative is fiction. But in the realm of historical reality, and as long as that reality—human history—will last, the redemption will always be future. Until it comes to pass, there will exist only substitutes for the authentic redemption. Of these the foremost substitute is the study of Torah, midrash. Yet even study of Torah is not true redemption; it is only a surrogate, a palliative.

In its totality, then, this mashal appears to produce two very different readings which, taken together, produce an overall message that cannot avoid appearing ambiguous, at least on the interpretive level. To students of literature, the hermeneutical dilemma posed by this mashal's ambiguity may be reminiscent of other cases of literary ambiguity, for example that in Henry James's "The Turn of the Screw." And as in James's novella, the "solution" to the hermeneutical conundrum posed by this mashal lies not in deciding upon a univocal reading of the mashal—the explicit consolatory reading alone or the implied critique—but in reading both messages as the result of an inherent ambiguity in the narrative.

That ambiguity would seem to derive from the one statement in the narrative whose meaning is suppressed—namely, the possibility raised by the neighbors when they tell the consort that her husband, the king, has indeed abandoned her and will not return. The consort, to be sure, cannot even entertain for a moment this possibility, this "interpretation" of the meaning behind the king's sudden disappearance. Her insistence upon reading the ketubah in her husband's absence clearly indicates her desire to deny the possibility that her husband has disappeared and its implications: to insist, in other words, on not suspecting the king even of cruelty, despite all appearances to the contrary. Yet the neighbors' claim is not, in fact, solely a malicious taunting provocation. According to Roman law, a relationship between an eligible man and woman was made into legal marriage not by physical union alone, but by consent. It was necessary to display the intention to be in the married state *(maritalis affectio)*, and during marriage, that consent had to be maintained; its withdrawal by either party was grounds for unilateral divorce.[27] By leaving his wife as he did, the king might have intended to withdraw his consent, his intention to remain married—or so it might appear to an uninvolved spectator. The neighbors' taunt might thus be a perfectly accurate view of the state of the marriage, and their invitation to the consort to marry one of them a perfectly neighborly gesture.

Of course, the king *does* return in the end; as we learn in the nimshal, neither he nor God ever intended to abandon his partner. But the mashal's happy ending does not negate the fact that it was impossible for the consort ever to believe that her neighbors' interpretation of her situation might be correct, just as it is impossible for Israel to admit to the possibility that God may have severed their covenant. Still, the mashal's narrative raises both possibilities, and its power as narrative lies in its capacity to sustain both alike: to marshal its doubts about the king's treatment of his consort in order to strengthen its message of consolation. Rhetorical praise and divine critique thus jointly state this mashal's theme, which is rightly the product of the two readings together.

This is not the only way in which rhetoric can serve theme. But before we consider the other ways, which will eventually lead us to the question of thematics in the mashal, a more systematic inspection of its poetics—the narrative strategies through which the mashal communicates its message—is required.

3

Poetics

Theorizing Midrash

The main challenge involved in trying to construct a "theory" of midrash—a poetics of the mashal, for example—comes from the very recalcitrance of the subject matter, the innate resistance of Rabbinic literature to analytic discourse. For all their preoccupation with the practice of exegesis, the Rabbis showed little self-conscious awareness of its procedures, and even less interest in describing them in a systematic way. In contrast to the self-reflexivity of literary theory—critical thought turned in on its own operations—midrash tends to reflect its own workings by couching its few statements of apparently theoretical import in the language of exegesis. While those statements would seem to be the obvious place to begin to build a theory for midrash, they are often the ones that require most analysis to elucidate their meaning.

The issue most critical for understanding the poetics of the mashal is the relationship between exegesis and narrative. As it happens, the most programmatic description of the mashal in all Rabbinic literature, and possibly the most extensive statement about a literary form that the Rabbis ever made, directly deals with this very issue. The lengthy passage, found in Shir R. 1.1.8, is cited as one of several interpretations offered at the beginning of the midrash on the Song of Songs in order to explain precisely what is the meaning of the two words *shir hashirim,* "the Song of Songs," which begin the celebrated love poem.

> Another interpretation of "The song of songs." [Its meaning] is what this verse says: "And even more so: Because Koheleth was a sage, he continued to instruct the people. He trained his ears and tested the soundness of many maxims *(meshalim)*" (Eccles.

12:9). [This means:] He listened to the words of Torah; he tested the words of Torah; he made handles (*oznayim,* literally ears) for the words of Torah.

And thus you find that before Solomon, the example[1] did not exist.

R. Nahman recited two [versions or parables]: It is like a great palace that had many entrances. Everyone who entered lost his way from the entrance. A certain clever man came. He took a spool of thread and hung it at the way to the entrance; [thereafter,] everyone came and went by means of the spool of thread.

Likewise: Before Solomon lived, no one was able to comprehend the words of Torah; but after Solomon everyone began to understand Torah.

R. Nahman gave a second version: It is like a thicket of reeds, which no one was able to penetrate. A certain clever man came along. He took a scythe and cleared it; [afterward,] everyone began to enter and leave through the path he had cleared.

Likewise: Solomon.

R. Yose said: It is like a huge basket of fruit which did not have a handle *(ozen),* so no one was able to move it. A certain clever man came along. He made handles for the basket, and began to move it by its handles.

Likewise: Before Solomon lived no one could understand the words of Torah; but after Solomon, everyone began to comprehend Torah.

R. Shela said: It is like a large pot full of boiling water, but it did not have a handle with which to move it. A certain man came along, he made a handle for it, and began to use the handle to move it.

R. Hanina said: It is like a deep well full of water whose waters were cold and sweet and delicious, but no one was able to drink from it. Then a certain man came along, and supplied the well with one cord tied to another, one rope tied to another, and drew water out of the well, and drank from it. Then everyone began to draw water and drink it.

Likewise: from one matter to the next, from mashal to mashal, Solomon arrived at the secret of Torah, as it is written, "The proverbs *(meshalim)* of Solomon, the son of David, king of Israel: [For learning wisdom and discipline; for understanding words of discernment]" (Prov. 1:1–2). [This means:] By means of his meshalim, Solomon came to understand the words of Torah.

The Rabbis said: Do not look upon the mashal as a trivial

thing, for by means of the mashal a man is able to understand Torah. It is like a king who lost a gold coin or a valuable
jewel in his house. Does he not go looking for it with a penny-
candle?

Likewise: Do not look upon the mashal as a trivial thing, for
by means of the mashal a man is able to comprehend the words
of Torah. And know that this is so, for Solomon comprehended
the finest points of Torah by means of the mashal.

The exegesis offered in this passage for the phrase "the song
of songs" is a remarkable one: according to the passage, the Song
of Songs, in its entirety, is actually a mashal, and it was through
this mashal that its author, Solomon, interpreted the meaning of
Torah, for himself and for others—hence the appellation of the
Song as a supreme composition, *the* song of all songs.[2]

For our present concerns, however, more significant than the
passage's final exegesis is its method of exegesis, the structure of
the passage. The passage begins with praise of Solomon for having invented the mashal; before Solomon, we are told, the example, presumably the mashal, did not exist, and no one could
understand Torah. Yet in order to communicate this message in
praise of Solomon for having invented the mashal, the editor of
the passage uses the literary form of the mashal—in not one, but
five separate meshalim, all with parallel structures but each one
with different imagery for the Torah and for the mashal (which,
however, is never explicitly named in any of the narratives).

Thus, in R. Nahman's initial two "versions"—it is unclear
whether they are two parables or two versions of a single parable—the narratives represent Torah in spatial figures: either as a
labyrinth or maze impossible to exit or as the "other side" of the
impassible thicket of reeds; in the former, the mashal is the proverbial Ariadnean thread, in the latter, a scythe. In contrast to
these two images, the second pair of meshalim, attributed to R.
Yose and R. Shela, both conceive of the Torah as an object, not a
place, but an object that by itself cannot be moved. Where the two
meshalim differ is in their conception of Torah: in one mashal, it
is a basket of delicious fruit, an unambiguously desirable object;
in the other, a cauldron of scalding water, a dangerous and
threatening presence. In both meshalim, though, the mashal is
the "handle" that enables the object to be moved, or a student to
get ahold of Torah—an image deriving from a midrashic pun

involving the word *veizein* in Eccles. 12:9 and *ozen,* an "ear" or handle. Finally, the fifth and last mashal in the series, attributed to R. Hanina, joins the imagery for Torah in the two preceding parables, the images of the delicious fruit and the boiling water, and transforms them into an image of water that is cool and delicious, like the fruit, yet inaccessible, because it is deep within a well that has no bucket or rope. In this parable, the mashal is the bucket and the rope.

The explicit purpose of this "litany" of parables, as Gerald Bruns has aptly described it, is to give a theory of the mashal as a hermeneutic rather than as a literary form: as a tool for interpreting Torah rather than as a narrative in its own right.[3] Yet the passage itself uses the mashal as narrative in order to convey this hermeneutical theory. The concluding image of the rope—of the slender cords and short strands tied together into a single lengthy rope—is a figure that can stand not only for its explicit reference, the meshalim that Solomon used to arrive at the secrets of Torah, but also for the parables in the series itself. Following close upon one another, strung one to the next, like the rope carrying the water from the bottom of the well to the top, the meshalim in the passage transport its audience from the beginning to the end. In its full shape, the passage as a whole deliberately blurs the line distinguishing between mashal as composition and mashal as exegetical instrument. Text and commentary merge (as they do so often in midrash). Exegesis produces a seed for a figure—*izein* yields *ozen*—which then becomes material for a narrative about making idiomatic ears, *oznayim,* handles, which in turn symbolize the mashal as an exegetical device.

If the mashal is thus used in this passage to praise the mashal—typical midrashic self-reflexivity—nothing is more characteristic of its Rabbinic "theorizing" than the sudden reversal the passage makes at its conclusion. Until this point, as we have seen, the passage offers unqualified praise of Solomon for having invented the mashal and for having thereby facilitated the understanding of Torah. The final parable, however, turns directly to the mashal itself but now offers it decidedly back-handed praise. "Do not look upon the mashal as a trivial thing," the Rabbis say, suggesting that there were people who did. Indeed, according to the Rabbis' own parabolic narrative that immediately follows, the mashal is no more than a penny-candle, to be lit and blown out and discarded—just as, for example, each of the preceding meshalim in the passage made its appearance upon the midrashic stage, and then was passed over and vanished (like the proverbial rope that was used to climb through the window at night and then thrown away). According to the Rabbis, the mashal *is* a trivial thing. The reason it is trivial is that it is a fictional narrative, indeed the only type of narrative in Rabbinic literature that the Rabbis acknowledge to be fictional; it has no inherent, substantive value of its own. Whatever value the mashal does possess is determined by its utility as an exegetical device, as a means to the comprehension of Torah.

This last mashal, then, radically qualifies, even overturns, the praise that preceded it. What is the meaning of the passage in its entirety? What is its overall statement on the relationship between narrative and exegesis? If we consider it as a theoretical statement, perhaps the most interesting thing about the passage is how untheoretical, how ambiguous about its final message, it really is. The qualification behind the last mashal's message of praise only complicates, doesn't clarify, our understanding of the mashal and its value as an exegetical narrative.

What the passage is clear about, however, is its final estimation of the mashal: whatever value the mashal possesses, great or small, lies in its exegetical utility. Yet as we have already seen amply enough, this particular estimation, standing alone, is unsatisfactory. In midrash, exegesis may be the mashal's occasion, but its exegetical occasion does not exhaust the mashal's meaning, which goes far beyond both exegesis and narrative alone, lying instead in their intersection, in the rhetorical and thematic effects of the mashal's narrative and exegesis alike. That the Rabbis in their concluding mashal cannot recognize this is symptomatic only of the absolute importance they wish to attribute to midrash as mere study of Torah, not as a reflection in any way of their own ideology.

Narrative or Exegesis?

If the Rabbis' own reflections on the mashal will not help us in theorizing its meaning or constructing a poetics, what will?

To begin, recent literary criticism of ideological narrative offers some helpful insights. In genre, the mashal is of a type with the moral allegory, the exemplum, and the *roman à thèse*, all of which openly display their didactic purpose, their intention of using fictional narrative to instruct their audience. These types raise theoretical questions different from those raised by other genres of narrative. For example, where most fiction tends to conceal or obfuscate its communicative function—the fact that it is not merely an imaginative creation but a medium for transmitting a message—didactic literary forms wear their communicative identification on their sleeves; they explicitly acknowledge their rhetorical motives, their service to an idea or ideology that they seek to impress upon their audience. Where most fiction raises the question, How does narrative mean? the question posed by ideological narrative is, as Susan Rubin Suleiman has written, How can a fictional narrative communicate an unambiguous message, and especially one that bears insistently upon its audience's lives? How can narrative "demonstrate the validity of . . . doctrine"?[4]

One way the mashal does this is by pretending not to be narrative. In genre, the Rabbinic mashal can be defined as a parabolic narrative that claims to be exegesis and serves the purposes of ideology. In this, the mashal is similar to biblical narrative, which, as Meir Sternberg has shown, claims to be history and uses that claim, with an appearance of history-likeness, as a medium for impressing a world-view, an ideology, upon its reader.[5] So, too, scriptural exegesis, or exegesis-likeness, works for the Rabbis as an ideological medium.

And as with other types of ideological literature, a good part of the mashal's art lies in its capacity for obscuring its ideological purpose. Sometimes this is accomplished simply by hiding rhetoric under the cloak of exegesis; at other times, by pretending that the midrashic interpretation of the verse is indeed the necessary, inevitable meaning. This impression is achieved, in turn, by making the mashal's narrative appear to create or to produce the nimshal, which then serves as the setting for the interpretation of the mashal's prooftext, for the midrashic event of interpretation. The prooftext, once interpreted via the nimshal, then casts back upon the preceding narrative the aura of its own scriptural authority, as though to authenticate that narrative, to salvage it from the triviality of mere fictionality. Thus a whole, seamless rhetorical artifice is created inside which ideology hides.

The relationship between narrative and exegesis is not, however, always so seamless. In Chapter 1, I discussed the origins of the nimshal as a functional medium; as I explained, the nimshal originated as a device for supplying the mashal's audience with the information necessary to allow them to apply the mashal's rhetorical message to the exegetical occasion behind its composition. Yet once the nimshal became a normative part of the midrashic mashal, it was used to do more than just supply information. Whether heard in oral delivery or read on the printed page, the nimshal became a continuation of the narrative. It could be used to extend the narrative, to revise it, or to reinterpret its meaning. However the nimshal was used, it became possible for authors of meshalim to exploit the sequence of mashal-proper and nimshal for rhetorical purposes. Most often this was done by the introduction of discrepancies into the space between the mashal-proper and the nimshal; we have seen examples of this technique in the mashal in Eikh. R. 3.21.

At the same time, the nimshal also became more a narrative in its own right. As this happened, the nimshal's relationship to the mashal-proper also became less transparent. We are accustomed to looking at the nimshal as dependent upon the mashal-proper, as a kind of translation into transcendental or covenantal terms of the mashal-proper's story. Yet while the overall rhetorical strategy of the mashal is certainly intended to give the impression that the nimshal is dependent upon the mashal-proper for its narrative, the opposite is the truth. The nimshal has priority, chronologically as well as ontologically, over the mashal-proper. Before the mashal, there is always a nimshal, and even before the nimshal there already exists an exegesis which, in turn, is largely motivated by a preconceived rhetorical function or desire. From this perspective, the mashal-proper's narrative is clearly dependent upon the nimshal, as story is dependent upon meaning.

Yet the nimshal's meaning is not a static discursive presence. In fact, the nimshal is simply another narrative: typically, a single moment in the master plot, the covenantal narrative of God's relationship with His chosen people and their representatives. Which one of these narratives, then, is primary? The fictional narrative in the mashal-proper about a human king, or the exegetical narrative in the nimshal dealing with God and Israel? To answer this question, an analogy with another type of interpretive narrative, the Freudian case history, will be helpful. As Peter Brooks has shown, the narrative structure of a case history involves not one but several narratives.[6] Invoking the Russian formalist distinction between *fabula* and *sjuzhet*—*fabula* is "the order of event or chronology referred to by the narrative, whereas *sjuzhet* is the order of presentation of event in the narrative"—Brooks has suggested that if the text of the case history is viewed as the *sjuzhet*, then that text has as its *fabula* either (1) the structure of the neurosis or (2) the history of events in the past that caused the neurosis or (3) the order of the emergence of past events during the analysis. In writing case histories, Brooks suggests, Freud himself had to tell several stories at once: "the story of a person, the story of an illness, the story of an investigation, [and] the story of an explanation," while the ultimate "meaning" of the case history lay "in the effective interrelationship of all of these."[7]

An analogous relationship holds between the two narratives in the mashal. If the narrative recounted in the mashal-proper is the *sjuzhet*, then its *fabula* may be one of several other narratives. It may be an ideal narrative, a conventional *fabula*, standing behind the specific events presented in the mashal-proper. It may also be the nimshal's narrative, which one scholar has described as "a statement of a convention or code, through which the real story, the nimshal, receives its narrative and normative meanings."[8] Finally, it may be the ideal master-narrative or *fabula* of the covenantal relationship between God and Israel in its full scope, which is truly realized only in Scripture but which stands behind the nimshal's partial narrative of one moment in that relationship. The full meaning of the mashal, however, lies not in any one of these narratives alone but in their combination and their intersection within the mashal. As the members of the mashal's audience move from mashal-proper to nimshal, and back again, they must shift and redefine their understanding while negotiating between the shifting perspectives offered by each narrative and its claim to meaning.

This movement, too, can serve as a medium for the communication of an ideological message—and an especially effective one, because it gives the audience the impression that they are actually working through the process of understanding on their own. In this the mashal again resembles the analysis recounted in a case history. The relationship between narrative and exegesis in the mashal is therefore exceedingly complex and many-sided. And as we shall see, it informs not only the overall relationship between mashal-proper and nimshal but also the separate structure of the narrative alone and its poetic strategies.

Narrative Convention and Exegetical Novelty

Exegesis informs the mashal's narrative in many ways. In addition to the most obvious cases, as when a narrative incident clearly derives from a detail in the nimshal, we have seen how a detail of exegesis can "create" a narrative fact. For example, the image of the ketubah in Eikh. R. 3.21 is the product of a midrashic pun on a key word in a verse in the nimshal; a similar pun may also lie behind the image of the bridal-chamber in Eikh. R. 4.11.

In other cases, an exegetical novelty, a pun or a witticism, can also "make" a mashal by enlivening what would otherwise be an entirely conventional narrative. For example, one of the more common narrative structures in the mashal's entire tradition is based upon a comparison between two types of behavior, obedience and disobedience, and the reward and punishment that respectively follow upon them. The narrative structure derived from this comparison is a simple one:

If X obeys Y, then Y rewards X.
If X disobeys Y, then Y punishes X.

Not incidentally, this narrative structure almost perfectly exemplifies the covenantal paradigm, a fact that helps to explain why it appears in so many meshalim. The following are a few examples:

R. Simeon b. Yohai said:
It is like a king who had many children and servants whom he himself fed and supported. The key to the treasury is in his hand. When they do his will, he opens the treasury, and they eat and are satisfied. When they do not do his will, he locks the treasury and they die of starvation.
Similarly, when Israel does the will of God, "The Lord will open for you His bounteous store, the heavens" (Deut. 28:12). And when they do not do the will of God, ". . . the Lord's anger will flare up against you, and He will shut up the skies so that there will be no rain . . ." (Deut. 11:17). (Sifre Deut. 40)

Another interpretation of "Give ear, O heavens" (Deut. 32:1). R. Judah used to say:
It is like a king who had administrators *(epitropoi)* in his prov-

ince. He made an agreement with them and handed over his son to them, saying: Whenever my son does my will, be nice, refresh him, indulge and feed him, and let him drink. But when he does not do my will, do not let him touch anything of mine.

Similarly, when Israel does the will of God, what is said concerning them?—"The Lord will open for you His bounteous store, the heavens . . ." (Deut. 28:12). And when Israel does not do the will of God, what is said concerning them?—"For the Lord's anger will flare up against you, and He will shut up the skies so that there will be no rain . . ." (Deut. 11:17). (Sifre Deut. 306)

R. Samuel b. Nahman said:

It is like a king who had an orchard, and he planted it in rows of nuts, pomegranates, and apples, and he handed it over to his son. Whenever his son did his father's will, the king would travel and look for the finest fruit in the world; and he would pick it and bring it and plant it in the orchard. And whenever the son did not do his father's will, then the king would look for the finest fruit in the orchard, and uproot it.

Similarly, whenever Israel does God's will, He looks for the righteous among the nations of the world, for people like Jethro and Rahab, and He brings them and joins them to Israel. But when Israel does not do the will of the Holy One, blessed be He, He looks among them for whoever is righteous and honest and pleasing and God-fearing, and He removes them from their midst.   (Shir R. 6.6 = J. Berakhot 2.8 = Koh. R. 5.8)

It is like a king who loved his son. He made a golden necklace for him and hung it around his neck. But the son angered his father, and the king took the necklace away from him, made chains out of it, and put them on his son's legs.

Similarly the Holy One, blessed be He, made the letters of the Torah like a necklace, and hung it upon the necks of the Israelites, as it is written, "For they are a graceful wreath upon your head, a necklace about your throat" (Prov. 1:9). But Israel only abandoned the Torah, as it is written, "For they would not hearken to my words, and they rejected my Torah" (Jer. 6:19). He wrote their letters into Israel's punishment and brought upon them "Alas, lonely sits the city" (Lam. 1:1).   (PR 138a)[9]

It is like a king who loved his servant and made him a necklace of gold. The servant acted offensively, and the king took away the necklace and put chains upon him.

Similarly, God made priestly garments for Adam, but when he sinned, He removed them, as it is written, "And they sewed fig leaves together" (Gen. 3:7). (Yalkut 1.34)[10]

Each one of these meshalim, in its own way, tailors the traditional narrative structure to its particular exegetical occasion and thematic needs.

Eikh. R. 1.1B also uses the structure, and similarly adapts it to the requirements of its prooftext, Lam. 1:1:

"Lonely sits the city" (Lam. 1:1).
R. Berechiah said in the name of R. Abudimi of Haifa:
A mashal. It is like a king who had a son. Whenever he obeyed the will of his father, the king clothed him in garments of fine wool; and whenever the king was angry at him, he clothed him in an olive-presser's garments *(bigdei bedudim).*

Similarly, all the time Israel obeys the will of the Lord, He clothes them in garments of fine wool, as it is written, "I clothed you with embroidered garments" (Ezek. 16:10). R. Simlai said: it means "in purple garments," and Aquilas translated the word as *epikolithon.*[11] But once they angered Him, He clothed them in an olive-presser's garments *(bigdei bedudim).*[12]

In this mashal, the contrastive structure has been adapted to the symbolism of garments, and that symbolism, in turn, has been tailored to the mashal's exegetical context. As the Yalkut mashal and other sources show, the use of clothes-symbolism is traditional.[13] Less traditional and more context-specific are the choices of clothes. The garments of fine wool, associated with the *purpira,* the royal crimson imperial robes, derive from Ezek. 16:10 as interpreted by R. Simlai (whose gloss on the word *rikmah,* incidentally, seems to be quoted everywhere in Rabbinic literature that Ezek. 16:10 or other verses using the word *rikmah* are cited).[14] Even more interesting, though, are the olive-presser's clothes in which the king dresses his son as punishment. These clothes are also exegetically derived, the basis of the exegesis being a virtually untranslatable pun on the word *bodad,* "lonely"—in Lam. 1:1, *eikhah yashvah bodad,* "Alas, lonely sits the city"—for which R. Berechiah substitutes the very similar word *badad,* "an olive-worker." The latter may specially connote in our narrative's context a prisoner-of-war or a slave who was forced to work in an olive-press.[15]

The classical commentators on Midrash Rabbah have proposed various lexical and grammatical difficulties in Lam. 1:1 that may account for this obviously forced and artificial pun.[16] R. Berechiah's primary motivation, however, was probably less a difficulty in the verse than a desire to tailor the conventional narrative structure to its exegetical occasion as cleverly as he could. And this he did. The rhetorical message of the mashal is essentially an apologetic elaboration upon the covenantal paradigm: When Israel disobeys God, He dresses them in the clothes of a prisoner or a slave; when they obey Him, He garbs them in royal robes. Still, in this mashal, clothes do not make the man, or the divinity. Whether the people of Israel obey or disobey God, He remains their father, and they His children.[17] The punishment and the reward are no more than matters of external appearance; they do not touch upon the inner, true reality, the abiding relationship between father and child that is the human correlative for the covenant.

Consoling as it may be, what makes this apologetic argument memorable is the punning exegesis on *bodad/badad* by which the mashal "locates" its message in Scripture, giving it both a source and authority. If R. Berechiah ever recited his mashal before an audience, we can assume they would immediately have recognized its traditional narrative structure with its apologetic message. What would have held their attention would have been the desire to see how R. Berechiah would manipulate the traditional structure in order to compose a mashal for Lam. 1:1—to see, in other words, how he would give the traditional form an ad hoc application for the verse. This he does through the pun on *bodad/badad*. Without the mashal, the pun makes little sense. But without the pun, the mashal and its argument are tendentious. For the author of a mashal, the latter is by far the more grievous sin, and R. Berechiah saved himself from it by coming up with a fresh exegetical novelty.

Gaps, Ambiguities, and Narrative Conceits

Among the most distinctive characteristics of the mashal's poetics is the strategically placed point of discontinuity, technically called a gap.[18] A gap is a deliberately withheld piece of information in a narrative—(1) a missing link in a series of events; (2) an absent cause or motive; (3) a failure to offer satisfactory explanations for an occurrence in a story; (4) a contradiction in the text that challenges the audience's understanding of the narrative; (5) an unexplained departure from norms.

Since it is neither possible nor desirable for a storyteller to relate everything that happened in a given occurrence (the ideal *fabula,* in the terms of Russian formalism), every narrative (or *sjuzhet*) can be described heuristically as a system of gaps, and the process of reading a narrative as the practice of filling or closing gaps, of constructing hypotheses and solutions (often multiple systems of hypotheses, in fact) to answer the questions raised in the narrative. Yet if all narratives are characterized by gaps, no narrative utilizes the feature as an ideological tool more pervasively and effectively than does biblical narrative. As Meir Sternberg has written, specifically in reference to the story of David and Bathsheba (2 Sam. 11), though his remarks are true of any biblical narrative:

> Biblical narratives are notorious for their sparsity of detail . . . And the resultant gaps have been left open precisely at key points, central to the discourse as a dramatic progression as well as a structure of meaning and value. Hence their filling in here is not automatic but requires considerable attention to the nuances of the text, both at the level of the represented events and at the level of language; far from a luxury or option, closure becomes a necessity for any reader trying to understand the story even in the simplest terms of what happens and why.[19]

Not to mention its larger, more complex dimensions.

Like all close readers, the Rabbis were exceedingly sensitive to the gaps in the biblical narrative, and though they often brought to their reading assumptions and hypotheses that we today consider illegitimate, they were indefatigable in their efforts to fill the biblical gaps. They even used the mashal to close gaps, to solve problems in the biblical narrative by inventing fictional narratives. One example will suffice.

In verses 12–17 of the first chapter of Lamentations, the figure of Zion, personified by the hapless widow, relates the narrative of her persecution and tormenting by God: He has afflicted her on the day of His wrath (1:12); hunted her like prey (1:13); delivered her into the hands of the enemies (1:14); crushed all her young men (1:15); and removed "any comforter who might revive my spirit" (1:16). In verse 1:17, this self-portrait of victimization

reaches its conclusion. By this point, Zion has been rendered so
helpless she is no longer capable even of speaking for herself; she
can only gesture: "Zion spreads out her hands, she has no one to
comfort her." Precisely because she is dumb with pain, and there
is no one to whom she can appeal for help anyhow, the biblical
text shifts from the first person of her self-narration into third-
person exposition.

A midrashic interpretation perfectly captures Zion's despair at
this moment: "She is like a drowning man, his hands flailing in
search of something to rescue himself with."[20] In the chapter's
very next verse, however, Zion undergoes a sudden change.
Regaining her voice, she openly acknowledges her own responsibility for the terrible fate she has suffered and confesses: "The
Lord is in the right, for I have disobeyed Him."

What motivates this abrupt transformation? Why does Zion
come to this self-realization now? How is it that she reacquires
her voice precisely at this moment, when she reestablishes her
relationship with the God who, just verses before, she could
imagine as nothing other than her ruthless adversary? Now in the
biblical text of Lamentations, these unmarked shifts in speaker
and in audience addressed, unmotivated developments in character and self-understanding, and other such "transformations
of the rhetorical situation"—all of them identifiable types of
gaps—are precisely the ways in which, as one critic has recently
written, "the fundamental categories of God, Israel, and adversary
are brought into relationship, and thus, in this way, the drama of
the covenant played out."[21] In other words, gaps like the one
between Lam. 1:17 and 1:18 serve a rhetorical and ideological
purpose; they are significant precisely for the response they elicit
from the reader.

The Rabbis, however, used the gap in the biblical text differently; they filled it in their own fashion, through a mashal:

"Zion spreads out her hands" (Lam. 1:17) . . .

R. Joshua of Sikhnin said in the name of R. Levi: It is like a
king who became angry at his son. He chastised him. [The son
said:] I have sinned. Finally, the son stretched forth his two
hands and said to the king: Everything is before you. Hit me as
much as you please.

Similarly, "Zion spreads out her hands."

Through the mashal, R. Levi reads Zion's gesture of spreading out her hands as an act of contrition.[22] In effect, the verse becomes a kind of stage direction for the succeeding verse, 1:18, in which Zion confesses her sins to God and acknowledges His righteousness. The mashal anticipates this verse, and thereby eliminates the gap in the biblical text.[23]

The most outstanding indication of the mashal's continuity with biblical narrative is the use it makes of gaps in its own narrative poetics. Of these the most important are the following types:

Disparities between Narrative and Nimshal

The clearest example of this kind of gap is the discrepancy we saw in Eikh. R. 3.21, where the gap develops from the difference between the past-tense narrative of the mashal-proper and the future tense of the nimshal; as we saw, the discrepancy points to an alternative interpretation of the mashal's meaning that radically diverges from the mashal's explicit rhetoric of praise.

It is worth noting that, in the same mashal, there is an additional discrepancy between the narrative and the nimshal which is not of hermeneutic or poetic value. This kind of irrelevant discrepancy is technically known as a blank as opposed to a gap; rather than being a planned omission, a blank is the result of an inadvertent failure to supply information.[24] Thus, in this mashal's narrative, the king is portrayed as returning to his consort; in the nimshal, however, it is the redemption, not God, that arrives. Though hardly a trivial difference if considered for its theological import, the nimshal's formulation also happens to be a conventional expression for the arrival of redemption: to the extent that God is understood anthropomorphically as having *left* Israel at the time of the Destruction (at least according to some traditions), so too He is understood as returning at the end-time. Narratologically, the discrepancy is therefore trivial.

Unexplained Motives

Again, probably the best examples are in Eikh. R. 3.21: the narrator's withheld explanations for why the king leaves the consort to go abroad; for why he returns when he does; for why he does not communicate with her as his absence grows protracted; and for how he actually expects his wife to behave in his absence.

Unexplained, Improbable, or Excessive Acts

This kind of gap is close to what Alfred Hitchcock calls a "Mac-Guffin," the pretext for a plot.[25] The king suddenly gives an order for no reason. Or in Eikh. R. 4.11: What kind of transgression does the son commit that so angers the king as to make him destroy the bridal-chamber? Or in the two meshalim in Ber. R. 28.6, attributed respectively to R. Pinhas and R. Yudan (quoted in Chapter 1), what does the son do that leads his father to kill him? This type of failure to specify a deed or its motive occupies an especially significant position in the poetics of the mashal's narrative, and it dovetails with the representation of excessive behavior that is either unmotivated or far out of proportion to any reality. Nowhere is the latter type of gap used more effectively than in Jesus' parables: see, for example, Matthew's version of the parable of the Wedding Feast (22:1ff) and its hyperbolic portrayal of the reaction of the king who, finding the improperly dressed guest at his feast, commands his servants not only to throw him out but to "bind him hand and foot and throw him into the dark where there will be weeping and grinding of teeth" (22:13). Rather than being theologically significant, this motif may simply be a conventional rhetorical conceit.

These kinds of *permanent* gaps, however, should be distinguished from a *passing* or provisional one as in Eikh. R. 4.11 when, after the king destroys the bridal-chamber, the pedagogue picks up the reed-flute and begins to sing. Here the pedagogue's initially paradoxical behavior is explicitly noted in the mashal's narrative by the nameless people who ask the pedagogue to explain himself, thus leading to the nimshal's application.

Gaps in Plot

Aside from failures to specify the exact nature of a deed—as in the son's unexplained behavior in Eikh. R. 4.11—narratives in meshalim do not often omit significant parts of the plot; if they do, it is usually at the very conclusion of the mashal-proper, where the narrative is deliberately left open and unresolved. In Eikh. R. 3.1 (to be analyzed in the section on complaint in Chapter 4), the mashal's narrative gives the consort the last word, which is a triumphant challenge to the king's unjust behavior; yet the mashal does not resolve her helpless plight. This technique of withholding closure can also be used rhetorically to focus attention on the consort's position. In these cases, what is usually left out of a mashal is thought, not deed: What does the king think when he angrily slays his son? How does the king intend his wife to use their marriage-contract?

Violations of Norms

The phenomena in this category span a range of instances that deliberately violate the audience's normal expectations as to human behavior, either in the psychological, social, or religious realm. And since in the Rabbinic world social, religious, and psychological normativeness—for the individual and the community alike—is largely identified with the norms of halakhah, Rabbinic law, it is common for transgressions of norms to coincide with the violation of known halakhot. In the mashal, this kind of behavior is given special significance when the violation of halakhah is attached, via the persona of the king, to God. For when God acts contrary to halakhah, the violation violates still other theological norms. This particular type of gap is also used in some meshalim that attribute overly anthropomorphic behavior to God, as in those parables that portray His regret over past actions or His inconsolable grief, and thereby run counter to normal expectations about God's self and being.

A brief analysis of one mashal will illustrate how many of these different types of gaps can work in a single narrative:

"... for You have done it ..." (Lam. 1:21).
R. Levi said: [26]
It is like a consort to whom the king said: Do not lend anything to your neighbors, and do not borrow anything from them. One time the king became angry at her and drove her out of the palace. She went about to all her neighbors, but none of them received her, so she returned to the palace. [27] The king said to her: You have acted impudently. She said to him: You are the one who has done it! Because you told me: Do not lend

anything to your neighbors, and do not borrow anything from them. If I had lent them an article or borrowed one from them, and if one of them had seen me outside her home, would she not have received me?

Similarly at the time [following the Destruction], the gentile nations went everywhere the Israelites fled and blocked them [from fleeing]: in the east, in the west, in the north, and in the south. In the east: "Thus said the Lord: For three transgressions of Moab . . ." (Amos 2:1). In the west: "Thus said the Lord: For three transgressions of Tyre . . ." (Amos 1:9). In the north: "Thus said the Lord: For three transgressions of Damascus . . ." (Amos 1:3). In the south: "Thus said the Lord: For three transgressions of Gaza . . ." (Amos 1:6).

The Holy One, blessed be He, said to Israel: You have acted impudently! Israel said before the Holy One, blessed be He: But have You not done it?! For You told us: "You shall not intermarry with them: do not give your daughters to their sons or take their daughters for your sons" (Deut. 7:3). If we had married our daughters to their sons, or taken their daughters for our sons, and one of them had seen their daughter or their son with us, would they not have received us? That is [the meaning of]: ". . . for You have done it . . ."

The message of this mashal is a complaint: Israel protests God's abusive treatment of her when the very conditions that make her behave as she does are, she argues, the direct result of her having faithfully obeyed God's laws. "You have done it!" she tells God—decontextualizing the scriptural phrase from its home in its verse, and turning the phrase into an angry accusation of God's tyrannical, ungrateful actions.

To communicate this message, the mashal's narrative is virtually constructed out of a series of strategic gaps and omissions: (1) There is no explanation for why the king becomes angry at the consort and banishes her. (2) No motive is given for why the king initially prohibits the consort from borrowing from or lending to her neighbors. (3) There is no clarification within the narrative itself of what the prohibitions mean. (4) The king's own behavior is so beyond normal modes that without further psychological elaboration, which is of course lacking, his behavior appears grotesquely despotic. (5) The narrative's plot itself works against normal logical expectations: although the audience may initially think that the king banishes the consort from the palace because she has transgressed his prohibitions, it becomes clear that this was not the case as soon as the consort fails to find refuge among her neighbors because, as she tells the king, she previously snubbed the neighbors by faithfully following the king's order not to have anything to do with them. But why, then, should he banish her so peremptorily? (6) The lack of further explanation for this only confirms the audience's intuitive feelings of sympathy for the helpless consort, and arouses the opposite feelings about the king's unsympathetic treatment. (7) Finally, these feelings of the audience are further bolstered by the narrative's failure to resolve the consort's dilemma. The fact that she is given the last word in the narrative, along with the lack of a response from the king, serves, paradoxically, to vindicate her claim.

All these gaps work rhetorically to confirm the validity of the consort's complaint against the king—and by extension, Israel's against God. The most remarkable gap in the mashal, however, is one that may be less apparent to a modern reader though it constitutes the most damning evidence in the mashal of the king's mistreatment of the consort.

As noted already, the mashal's narrative gives no explanation for the prohibitions that the king hands down to his wife, though in the nimshal we learn that they correspond to the Deuteronomic prohibitions against intermarriage. Yet while the king's commands—as stated in the narrative—may seem to a modern reader somewhat arbitrary and meaninglessly bossy, the original Rabbinic audience of the mashal would immediately have recognized them as bearing a special meaning in addition to their symbolic value as the Deuteronomic prohibitions. These prohibitions actually quote known halakhic tradition. A *beraita,* a non-Mishnaic Tannaitic tradition, quoted in B. Ketubot 72a, states:

> If a man places his wife under a vow not to lend or not to borrow a sieve, a basket, a millstone, or an oven, he must divorce her and give her ketubah to her because he causes her to have a bad name among her neighbors.[28]

The mashal's original audience would have immediately remembered this tradition upon hearing the mashal, and they would have understood the obvious implication: the prohibitions that the king orders his wife to observe constitute an illegal command on his part. According to halakhah, not only is the king *not* able to

punish the consort for disobeying commands like these; he himself is penalized for enforcing them. The reason for this, as the
beraita explains, is that, by observing the prohibitions, the wife
will receive "a bad name among her neighbors." And this, of
course, is precisely what happens.

Translated into the nimshal's terms, this scathing critique of
the king's behavior becomes one implicitly directed against God.
His treatment of Israel is now claimed to be illegal in terms of the
very law He has authorized the Jews to live by. Yet the actual
hermeneutic of translation between narrative and nimshal here is
more complex and ambiguous than the direct transference of
meaning from one plane to the other suggests. For one thing, the
"illegal" act in the narrative is performed by the king; it is not
actually performed in the nimshal by God. Furthermore, while
the reader is deliberately enticed to tease out the analogy and
naturally extends it to God, the analogy does not quite hold up
once the king's commands are translated into the Deuteronomic
prohibitions. For the latter can hardly be said to be "against the
Law." They *are* the Law. Nonetheless, the mashal's message is
clear: God has behaved with manifest injustice toward His chosen
people.[29] He has acted against His own Law, if not against its
letter, then its spirit—the spirit of halakhah. And all the while,
Israel has faithfully obeyed His Law, and yet suffered—precisely
for her faithful obedience.

Point of View and Authorial Presence

Narrative in the mashal tends to be what Seymour Chatman has
called "non-narrated narrative"—that is, narration that presents a
bare transcription of events and narrative facts in sequence with
relatively few intrusions by the narrator.[30] Dialogue is usually
enacted in direct speech and only occasionally does the narrator
present a character's thoughts or feelings. Yet even if his presence
is unobtrusive, the mashal's narrator is not entirely invisible. Narratorial intrusions, however minimal they may be, are shrewdly
employed for rhetorical purposes, particularly for focalization,
Gerard Genette's helpful term for describing the ways in which
an author can focus the narrative upon the point of view of a
specific character and thus reorient its perspective.[31] Since the narrator's perspective in the mashal is usually quite generalized,

in fact omniscient, when focalization does occur, it tends to narrow the perspective to the point of view of a particular character.

The most common type of narratorial intrusion in the mashal is the simple rhetorical question: What did X do? (In the following meshalim, all narratorial statements are italicized.)

R. Simeon b. Lakish said: It is like a king who had a legion. That legion rebelled against him. *What did his general do?* He took the royal banner and fled.

Likewise Moses: At the time Israel did that deed [i.e., worshipped the Golden Calf], he took the Tent of Meeting and fled. Therefore it is said: "Now Moses will take the Tent" (Exod. 33:7). (Sh. R. 45.3)

Such rhetorical questions, which are usually invoked as symptoms of the mashal's oral provenance, actually do double duty in the narrative. In R. Simeon b. Lakish's mashal, for example, the rhetorical question serves as a conjunction that bridges between two moments in the narrative (the legion's rebellion and the general's reaction), and it simultaneously draws attention to the general's seemingly cowardly response, thus making him the focus of the narrative. In the following mashal, from Ber. R. 8.10, the rhetorical question is used within a more complicated narrative context.

R. Hoshayah said: At the time the Holy One, blessed be He, created Adam, the ministering angels mistook Adam [for God] and wished to recite before him "Holy, holy, holy" (Isa. 6:3).

What is this like? It is like a king and his provincial prefect who were together in a carriage. The inhabitants of the province wished to hail the king, O Dominus! but they didn't know which one he was. *What did the king do?* He pushed [the prefect] and threw him out of the carriage, *and they knew who was king.*

Likewise: At the time the Holy One, blessed be He, created Adam, the ministering angels mistook Adam [for God]. *What did the Holy One, blessed be He, do?* He cast sleep upon him, and everyone knew that he was a human. This is what is written: "Trust no more in man; he has but a breath in his nostril; how much is he worth?" (Isa. 2:22).

Here again, the rhetorical question—"What did X do?"—serves as a transition marker. But in this mashal the transition is from exposition—the entire passage from "the inhabitants . . ." until "he was"—to the narrative itself. Exposition—by which I mean scene-setting, prefatory explanations, and so on—does not generally occupy a large place in the narratives of the meshalim; indeed, the exposition in this example is uncharacteristically lengthy: the narrative does not actually begin until after the rhetorical question. Typically, the exposition is spoken by an omniscient narrator who relates matters that only he could know—the frustrated wishes of the inhabitants, their inability to recognize the king, and so on—though, as we discover later in this narrative, the king, too, is all-knowing (like God); he even knows that the provincials can't distinguish between him and his general. In contrast, the narratorial statement at the very conclusion—"and they knew who was king"—comments sardonically upon the angels' realization. Because the angels are mankind's traditional rivals for God's favor, according to Rabbinic tradition, the fact that they are incapable of distinguishing between Adam and his creator is obviously meant to be ironic.

Rhetorical questions are asked so frequently in the mashal that they nearly always raise the interpretive question of whether or not they are to be analyzed for significance. Some rhetorical questions are asked solely so that the narrator can state their answers. Not every question, though, is rhetorical. Sometimes a question makes a real interpretive point, thereby creating what I will describe shortly as an interpretive model. This is the function of the question in the following mashal.

> R. Judah b. R. Simon said:
> It is like a person who was sitting and making a crown for the king. Another person passed by and asked him: What are you doing? He replied: I am making a crown for the king. The other said to him: Everything that you can set in it, set. Set emeralds in it, set jewels in it, set pearls in it. *Why? For it is destined to be placed on the king's head.*
> So the Holy One, blessed be He, said to Moses: As much as you are able to praise Israel, praise them! to exalt them, exalt them! to glorify them, glorify them! Why? Because I am destined to be glorified through them. This is what is written: "He said to me, You are my servant Israel, in whom I shall be glorified" (Isa. 49:3). (Vay. R. 2.5)

While it is not entirely clear who utters the italicized question, "Why"—whether it is the anonymous passerby or the narrator—the more significant thing to notice is that the answer to the question is a kind of meta-narrative comment, a virtual interpretation of the preceding narrative. That interpretation, in turn, points directly to the closing exegesis of Isa. 49:3, which dwells upon the verse's own paradoxical meaning.

A final example of narratorial intrusion points to the more subtle ways in which the narrator can shape the narrative by appearing in it. The following mashal, from Ber. R. 75.10, subtly combines praise with blame; the occasion is the Rabbis' need to rationalize Jacob's embarrassing flattery of Esau in Gen. 33. Esau, of course, is by convention in Rabbinic tradition a thoroughly nasty character. The mashal comments specifically upon the moment in the biblical narrative when the two brothers finally meet after their long separation, and Jacob, manifestly terrified of Esau, prostrates himself before his brother, saying to him: ". . . for to see your face is like seeing the face of God" (Gen. 33:10). In its literal sense, Jacob's obsequious similitude, in the Rabbis' eyes, must have seemed close to blasphemy—at the least, inexcusably inappropriate.

> A mashal: What is it like? It is like a person who invited to a banquet an acquaintance *whom he knew wished to kill him.* He said to the man: The taste of this dish resembles the taste of a dish I had in the king's house. *The other person says [to himself]: So he knows the king! This makes him fearful, and he does not try to kill him.*
>
> So, too, with Jacob: Once he said to Esau: ". . . for to see your face is like seeing the face of God," that wicked man Esau said [to himself]: The Holy One, blessed be He, has brought him to this greatness. I cannot contend with him.

The ingenious interpretation offered for the Genesis verse reverses its plain-meaning by turning Jacob's problematic flattery of Esau into a double proof—of Jacob's cleverness and of Esau's cowardice. In this interpretation, the narrator's presence in the mashal-proper is felt both implicitly and explicitly. The various statements reflecting his omniscient knowledge of the characters' motives and their thoughts attest to his implicit presence, while the narrator explicitly contributes to the narrative in its final lines when he offers a psychologizing explication of the wicked character's reaction. This closing explication is unusual for providing a reason why the character should be condemned for his cowardice; more typically, focalizations of this sort are used to attract the audience's sympathies to a character, not their distaste. In this mashal, however, the nimshal turns this last focalization in a different direction by explaining Esau's reaction not as cowardice but as due to an awareness of Jacob's divine protection; hence the futility of opposing divine providence.

Point of view and authorial/narratorial manipulation need not operate only through devices of intrusion. Focalization also works through strategically placed gaps and lacunae that require the reader to fill them to narrative sense. A useful example of this technique can be seen in Eikh. R. 3.21, where the absence of an explanation for the king's departure has the dual effect of making his behavior look unfair and of making his consort's helpless plight especially worthy of sympathy. Analogously, in the same mashal, the absence of motivation for the king's return confirms the sense of *his* unfair selfishness and of *her* selfless faithfulness.

The Implied Interpreter

As Frank Kermode has reminded us, every narrative requires interpretation.[32] The mashal, however, is virtually composed of hermeneutical components: from the exegetical application in the nimshal to the various features of its narrative technique from gapping to focalization, all of which directly or indirectly elicit interpretive effort from the mashal's audience. In fact, because its audience so actively participate in the mashal's interpretation, they may be said to figure actively in its narration.

In this, too, the mashal is hardly unique. Recent writers on narrative theory have argued that readers invariably play a significant role in determining textual meaning, and they have shown the different guises in which the figure of the reader can appear within the narrative artifice. Gerald Prince's "narratee," Wolfgang Iser's "implied reader," and Naomi Schor's "interpretant" are the best-known names for this fictionalized image of the reader.[33] For our purposes, the most relevant of these is Schor's interpretant, an "interpreting character" whom she defines as a figure typically "coextensive with the first-person narrator or main protagonist of the fiction," through whom "the author is trying to tell the interpreter [the reader] something *about* interpretation."[34]

In the mashal, these theoretical constructs all coalesce into a figure whom I will call the implied interpreter: an idealized character in the mashal who serves as a model for the real interpreter/

reader and who guides the latter's acts of reading and interpretation. The implied interpreter is not identical with his or her counterpart in real life. Extending Iser's insightful remarks about the implied reader, the implied interpreter is a figure *in* the text, inscribed as part of the fictional or exegetical structure of the mashal. Unlike the fictional implied interpreter, the real addressee of the parable will always bring additional interpretive resources to his or her comprehension of the mashal: the knowledge of general models of coherence (rules of chronology, causality, and so on); of literary conventions (specifically of midrash); of hermeneutical conventions (in general as well as specifically midrashic ones, like the *kal vehomer, notarikon, gematria*). Nonetheless, the implied reader remains an ideal interpreter who possesses all the literary competence needed to understand a mashal.[35]

The implied interpreter, however, does not only supply the real interpreter/reader with exegetical direction. As a fictional character, the implied interpreter inscribes the relationship between narrative and exegesis in the mashal; the character joins fictionality and hermeneutics in his or her persona. The most obvious example of such a persona is the helpless and beleaguered matrona in Eikh. R. 3.21 who consoles herself by reading the promises her absent husband has left her in the ketubah, her marriage-contract; the act of reading the ketubah, along with the matrona's own elucidation of its effect upon her, is about as explicit a representation of interpretation as can be found in any mashal. Only slightly less explicit is the representation in Eikh. R. 4.11 of the pedagogue who picks up his reed-flute and plays joyfully upon it after the king destroys his son's marriage-canopy. As I have suggested, the pedagogue, singing and playing upon his reed-flute, is an apt figure for the darshan, his paradoxical yet triumphant behavior pointing to those very features characteristic of midrash itself.

In addition to the implied interpreter, Eikh. R. 3.21 and Eikh. R. 4.11 represent in their narratives what I will call the *event* or *scene of interpretation,* the conditions under which interpretation becomes a necessary act, sometimes almost a way of surviving. Sometimes, this scene or event is presented in the form of a recognizable hermeneutical operation. An example is the following mashal from PRK 20.6. The mashal is recorded in the course of a lengthy debate over the question—the ultimate hermeneutical question, perhaps—of what kind of tree was the Tree of Knowledge of Good and Evil. The midrashic collection records the opinions of several Rabbis, and then R. Yose's belief that it was a fig tree. To support this view, R. Joshua of Sikhnin in the name of R. Levi recites the following mashal:

> It is like a king who had a son and many maidservants. The king commanded his son, saying: My son, be careful. Do not touch any of these maidservants. What did the son do? He went and disgraced himself with one of the maidservants. Once his father became aware of this, he banished him from the palace. The son went around to all the houses of the maidservants, but not one of them would take him in. You turn out having to say the following (*nimtseita atah omer*): That one with whom he had disgraced himself—she opened her door and took him in.
>
> Similarly: Once Adam ate from that tree, all the trees could be heard saying: You thief! You thief! You tried to deceive the Creator, you tried to deceive your Master. "Let not the foot of the arrogant tread on me" (Ps. 36:12): [this means:] Let not that foot that stretched forth arrogantly come upon me! "Or the hand of the wicked drive me away" (ibid): Let not that hand shake me! Do not take my !eaves! You turn out having to say the following (*nimtseita atah omer*): That tree that gave him of its fruit also gave him leaves: ". . . and they sewed together fig leaves and made themselves loincloths" (Gen. 3:7).

Overtly a blame-mashal, this narrative has as its underlying but real subject what we might call an *implied* interpretation, an interpretive act like the logical deduction that is performed in this mashal at the end of both the narrative and the nimshal. The presence of this hermeneutical operation is signaled in the text by the phrase *nimtseita atah omer,* an idiomatic formula that is almost impossible to translate: formulated in the second-person passive, it calls upon an implied reader/interpreter to draw a necessary conclusion from the preceding narrative.

In other meshalim, the interpretive act is sometimes explicitly identified as a hermeneutical operation that any student of Rabbinic tradition would know—the *kal vehomer,* for example, the argument from the weaker case to the stronger. Consider the two following examples:

> The Rabbis say:
> It is like a king who had an orchard. He gave it to a tenant-farmer. What did that tenant-farmer do? He filled baskets of

figs from the produce of the orchard and placed them at the entrance to the orchard. When the king passed by and saw all this choice fruit *(shevah)*, he said: If there is all this choice fruit at the entrance to the orchard, then how much more must there be *('al ahat kamah vekhamah)* inside the orchard!

So in the first generations, there were the men of the Great Assembly, Hillel and Shammai, and Rabban Gamliel the Elder; in later generations, R. Yohanan b. Zakkai, R. Eliezer, R. Joshua, R. Meir, R. Akiba; and their disciples, how much [even greater] will they be! About them the verse says: "Both freshly picked and long-stored [fruit] have I kept, my beloved, for you" (Song 7:14). (Shir R. 7.18)

R. Joshua b. Levi said:
It is like a king who made a banquet, brought in his guests, and seated them at the entrance to his palace. They saw dogs coming out with pheasants in their mouths, and the heads of fattened animals and of calves. They began to say: If this is how the dogs [eat], then how much greater *('al ahat kamah vekhamah)* will be the banquet itself!

The wicked of Israel are spoken of figuratively *(nimshelu)* as dogs, as it is said, ". . . the dogs are greedy" (Isa. 56:11), and [if] they live in contentment in this world, then how much more so will Israel in the world-to-come! as it is said, "You have put joy into my heart" (Ps. 4:8). (Mid. Teh. 4.11)

In both these meshalim, we can follow the implied interpretation step by step. The phrase *'al ahat kamah vekhamah* would have been recognized by any member of the mashal's audience as the conventional term for the kal vehomer. Since this exegetical principle is among the most fundamental rules in all Rabbinic hermeneutics, the mashal's audience would have seen in these narratives not only an identifiable logical-exegetical operation but also an interpretive event conforming to the institutions of Rabbinic Judaism and its tradition of scriptural interpretation. After identifying the operation, they would have worked out the operation in their heads just as the guests do; then they would have applied the operation to its corresponding application in the nimshal, and drawn the necessary rhetorical and thematic conclusions.

However, the presence of the implied interpreter in the narratives of these last two meshalim is only hinted at. This is the case in many meshalim, and especially so when the implied interpreter's existence is not implied by a technical hermeneutical operation. For example, in Vay. R. 2.4, the praise-mashal quoted in the previous chapter, the elder creates the scene of interpretation and then becomes the implied interpreter himself, while his disciple, whom the elder commands to fold and take special care of his official robe, is the foil for the implied interpretation, an interpreter's straight man. In still other meshalim, the implied narrator does not figure at all as a character within the narrative; instead, the narrative represents the interpretive event more explicitly, as in the following mashal from Vay. R. 1.8:

> What is it like? It is like a king who entered a province with his princes, governors, and generals. We do not know which one of them was most favored (haviv). But whomever the king turned his face to and addressed—that one we know was the most favored.
> Likewise: Everyone stood around the Tent of Meeting— Moses, Aaron, Nadav, Avihu, and the seventy elders, and we do not know which of them was most favored. But from the fact that the Holy One called to Moses and spoke with him, we know that he was the most favored. Therefore it says: "And He called to Moses" (Lev. 1:1).

The implied interpreter here is identified in the text by the rhetorical "we"—even though the precise identity of that "we" is unclear: in the text I have translated, the "we" may include the provincial inhabitants, the citizens whom the king is visiting and who cannot distinguish among the members of the royal retinue; some manuscript variants, however, explicitly differentiate the "we" as narratee from the provincial inhabitants.[36] In any event, the real focus of this mashal is the scene of interpretation rather than the figure of the implied interpreter, and that scene, the interpretive event, involves a comparison: the hermeneutical challenge faced by the rhetorical "we" (as well as by the provincials) to figure out who is best, here defined as most favored.[37]

Comparative operations are among the most common techniques used to create an implied interpretation. They can be invoked more or less explicitly, for both praise and blame—for example, asking who is more or less worthy of praise or blame—as well as for comparative praise and blame. Comparisons themselves range from deciding who is best of all (as in the mashal above, Vay. R. 1.8) to distinguishing which one of two persons or things is the better (or the worse). An interesting example of the latter is the following mashal, from Vay. R. 7.4, whose narrative alone I will quote:

> R. Berechiah and R. Hanan in the name of R. Azariah of Kefar Hitya [said]:
> It is like a king who had two cooks. The first one made the king a cooked dish, and he ate it and was pleased. The second cook also made him a dish, and he ate it and was pleased. We don't know which one of them pleased him more. But from the fact that the king commands the second cook and tells him, Make me a dish like that one, we know that the second cook's dish pleased him more.

As in Vay. R. 1.8, this narrative identifies the implied interpreter as "we." Here, however, the interpretive task focuses upon the simple task of comparing and judging between the two cooks— and thus praising one while rejecting the other.

Two final meshalim will illustrate especially clever "applications" of the implied interpreter/interpretation as a narrative stratagem. The first of these examples is a mashal that appears in the Vilna edition of Ber. R. 56.8, among other places, in connection with God's command to Abraham in Gen. 22:2: "Take your son, your favored son, Isaac, whom you love, and go to the land of Moriah, and offer him up there *(veha'aleihu)* . . ."[38]

> They recited a mashal:
> It is like a king who said to his admirer: Offer up *(ha'aleih)* your son on my table. The admirer, a knife in his hand, brought his son. The king said to him: Did I tell you, Offer him up—so as to eat him!? I said to you, Offer him up—for love.
> This is what is written: ". . . it never occurred *('alah)* to me" (Jer. 19:5)—this refers to Isaac.

In this narrative, the implied interpreter, the admirer, *misunderstands* the king's command by interpreting it literally, and his misinterpretation has to be rectified by the shocked king, who thereby becomes an implied interpreter himself (of his own words). What is most revealing about this event of interpretation, however, is that it revolves around the meaning of a word, just as in midrash, with the correct interpretation being the figurative reading— another typically midrashic preference!

The second example revolves around another case of enigmatic language that is susceptible to misinterpretation. The mashal is recorded in Sifre Deut. 26 (ad Deut. 3:23):[39]

Moses said before the Lord: Master of the Universe! Let the sin which I have committed be recorded after me so that people will not say, It appears that Moses falsified the words of the Torah or proclaimed a precept which had not been commanded.

It is like a king who decreed: Whoever eats unripe figs of the Sabbatical year shall be marched around the assembly-place! A certain woman of good family went out and gathered and ate unripe figs grown during the Sabbatical year, and [after she was caught,] she was marched around the assembly-place. She said to the king: I implore you, O king! Make known my offense so that the citizens of the province will not say, It appears that she has been found guilty of an act of sexual immorality, or that she has been found guilty of some sort of witchcraft. If they see unripe figs hanging around my neck, they will know that it is because of these that I am being marched around.

Similarly: Moses said before the Lord: Let the sin which I have committed be recorded after me. The Holy One, blessed be He, said to him: Behold, I am writing that it was only in connection with the waters [of Merivah, as it says, "When you disobeyed My command] in the wilderness of Zin, when the community was contentious, to uphold My sanctity in their sight by means of the water" (Num. 27:14).

According to Rabbinic law, during the seventh year, the Sabbatical year, figs can not be picked and eaten before they have ripened. The phrase "to eat unripe figs of the seventh year" was, however, also a figurative expression the Rabbis used to refer to enjoying "the favors of an unmarried woman or even the connubium of the betrothed with her own bridegroom before they were fully married."[40] This double-entendre results in the mashal just quoted in a kind of pun the misreading of which is precisely what the mashal's protagonist, the guilty woman, fears: that her crime of material consumption (eating unripe figs in the Sabbatical year) will be misunderstood to have been a sexual offense; accordingly, she implores the king to hang *real* figs around her neck to show that her crime was literal not figurative.[41] What the mashal describes, then, is the protagonist's attempt to forestall a misinterpretation.

With this last example, we come nearly full circle, from the explicit portrayal in the mashal of the implied interpreter to a picture of an implied misinterpretation being anticipated and avoided. In all these meshalim, however, the figure of the implied interpreter or interpretation gives narrative form to the hermeneutical event within the mashal. And in the implied interpretation, the mashal's narrative reaches its highest state of self-reflexivity.

Characterization

For all its self-reflecting hermeneutical concerns, the mashal is essentially mimetic narrative. It is about events and characters, and particularly one character—the king, or God. Beyond all else, the mashal represents the greatest effort to imagine God in all Rabbinic literature. The achievement behind the mashal's characterization of God is even more extraordinary in that virtually all the other characters appearing in the mashal are what students of narrative call types or stock characters. Created to fit generic situations in the plot, these figures duly fulfill their functions as characters in the narrative, but they have little psychological or emotional depth. Their behavior is usually predictable or easily explained. They rarely contain the nuanced particularities, the conflicted intimations of flesh and soul, that inform full-bodied, vividly imagined fictional creations.

The one character in the mashal who is never a type or stock character is the king; he is the only character consistently to possess a personality—or personalities, since he can change utterly from one mashal to another—and this distinction among characters may stand, from a theological perspective, as an emblem of God's profound difference from all else in the universe. For our concerns, however, the more pressing question is the nature of God's character, the precise personality of His characterization as king. The image of God as king—ubiquitous in the Bible, and common in other ancient Near Eastern literatures—is distinct in the mashal in that the king here is a genuine character. Not only modeled upon the historical figure of the Roman emperor (or of the imperial representative in Palestine), he bears a plethora of human details and markings that are without parallel in earlier Israelite literature; and because of the nature of the analogy underlining the mashal, all those details and markings are inevitably transferred to God. The portrayal of God through the figure of the king therefore touches upon two distinct issues in the matter of narrative representation in Rabbinic literature—first, the historical quotient of the mashal's representation of God as king; second, the question of its explicitly anthropomorphic features.

In a recent study of biblical king-imagery, Marc Z. Brettler has proposed that even in the Bible the various attributes and manifestations attached to God's kingship should be considered in relation to the institutions of Israelite monarchy.[42] An analogous connection between king-imagery and historical reality is to be sought in the mashal, even though by the Rabbinic period Jewish self-rule, let alone monarchy, had long since ceased. When the Rabbis searched for a contemporary exemplar to represent God's sovereignty, the most available and familiar model was not Jewish but Roman.

Nonetheless, the Rabbis' choice of the Roman emperor as a symbol for God was a paradoxical one. Nothing was more characteristic of the Roman emperorship than the imperial cult, a fact that did not escape the Rabbis. As E. E. Urbach has shown, that cult, with its claims for the divinity of the emperor, was the form of pagan religion in Late Antiquity that the Rabbis felt necessary to oppose with the most stringent measures; they prohibited even the least actions that might hint at acquiescence to the cult and its pretensions.[43] The main function of one subgenre of meshalim, that of antithetical meshalim, as we have already seen, was to demonstrate the dissimilarity between the Roman emperor and God, and thus to explode the myth of the divine emperor. And yet, apart from this one subgenre, the Rabbis enthusiastically exploited the emperor as a symbolic figure for God; they did not even hesitate to borrow from the imperial cult some of its most singularly idolatrous features in order to use them as symbols for various subjects. The ubiquitous icons and statues of the emperor, employed in the cult as objects of worship as well as of political propaganda, were conventionally used in the king-mashal to represent the human being created in the image of God.[44]

The significance of this paradox requires a proper appreciation. The ideological and literary use to which the Rabbis put the alien, even taboo, regalia of the imperial court resembles the ways in which early Christian artists appropriated the iconography and the stylistic conventions of classical Greco-Roman art. As Ernst Kitzinger has noted, the emergence in the third century of religiously meaningful images drawn from classical tradition yet employed in identifiably Christian contexts "was part of a process of coming to terms with that way of life"—that is, of coming to terms with the greater Greco-Roman pagan world in which these early Christian artists and their audiences lived.[45]

The same process may be said to inform the analogous Rabbinic material from Late Antiquity. This material includes the substantial remains of a Jewish art in the land of Israel and the Mediterranean diaspora that freely used the imagery and symbols of Greco-Roman paganism—the famous mosaic floors in the synagogues at Hammat Tiberias and Beth-Alpha depicting the zodiac with Helios, the sun-god, at its center; the patriarchal tombs in Beth Shearim wherein mythological themes like that of Leda and the Swan adorn the sarcophagi of wealthy and aristocratic Jews; or the portrait of King David as Orpheus in the synagogue at Gaza, to name only a few of the most dramatic examples. Many of these artistic remains from Late Antique Jewish culture have been found only in this century, and they have justifiably fascinated scholars, not least because of the "contradiction" they appear to document between actual practice by Jews and what has been assumed to be the official ideological opposition of the Rabbinic authorities to such practice.

Probably the most celebrated response this "contradiction" has elicited came from Erwin Goodenough in the twelve formidable volumes of *Jewish Symbols in the Greco-Roman Period*. After collecting and reproducing all the material that had been discovered until his time, a massive achievement in its own right, Goodenough resolved the contradiction between Rabbinic halakhic ideology and apparently common practice by postulating the existence among Jews of a popular mystical religion that was closer to other types of popular, syncretic Greco-Roman religion than to "normative" Rabbinic Judaism.[46] Alas, no other evidence exists for this popular mystical Judaism, and Goodenough's theory has since been rejected by most scholars. Still, the importance of the pictorial, nonliterary material to which he called attention cannot be ignored. Nor can the major intellectual project his work initiated, a project that concerned in the largest sense the historical, spiritual, and aesthetic relationship of Late Antique Judaism, in all its aspects, to its contemporary Greco-Roman context.

In an oft-cited review essay, Elias Bickerman acknowledged both the strengths and the weaknesses of Goodenough's work. As an alternative to Goodenough's Hellenized Judaism, Bickerman proposed viewing the art as an ancient attempt to "Judaize" pagan symbolism.[47] According to Bickerman, these pagan symbols had long since ceased to hold for Jews the repugnant idolatrous meaning they originally possessed; once the symbols were emptied of their pagan meanings, Jews used them freely because they (like pagans in Late Antiquity) were aware of the difference between idols and images: the former were there for worship, the latter for representation. The same logic, I would like to propose, is at work in the king-meshalim and their use of imperial imagery. Although the Rabbis stringently opposed the practices of the imperial cult on religious grounds, the imagery and regalia of the cult, once removed from their lived context, lost their transgressive character. They could be "Judaized" in the mashal and used as a medium for symbolizing God. In the Rabbis' own minds, there was probably not an inkling of the contradiction felt by modern scholars between religious ideology and literary practice. The meaning of these images was transformed precisely at the moment they became symbols.

This approach to the significance of the mashal's imagery emphasizes its *symbolizing* character. Arguably, this is the most distinctive feature of narrative in the mashal in general. Virtually every detail in the meshalim demands interpretation. As in certain types of early Christian art, narrative representation in the mashal might be called "signitive." As Kitzinger describes the pictorial images,

> they point beyond themselves to a quite extraordinary degree. Biblical themes are represented for the most part in drastically abridged form, usually reduced to the minimum of figures and props necessary to call to mind a given text. It is not intended that the beholder should linger in contemplation of physical appearances. He is only meant to receive a signal. Furthermore, the texts to which the images refer are not invoked for their own sakes. There is no factual thread linking the various subjects together. What unites them is a common message which is of urgent concern to the beholder . . . Images are thus twice removed from an actual portrayal of sacred subject matter. They are ciphers conveying an idea.[48]

Virtually all the characteristics Kitzinger lists in this passage as typical of Late Antique art can be fruitfully applied to the description of narrative in the mashal. As in the former, the mashal also uses "irrational spatial relationships; scale and proportions determined by symbolic importance rather than laws of nature; frontality; jerky and abrupt movements; hard, sharp-edged forms brought out by deep undercutting."[49] Even "frontality," the habit of making the figures in a picture all face the beholder regardless of the logic of the event depicted in the picture, has an analogue in the mashal's constant use of rhetorical questions, authorial intrusions, and the figure of the implied interpreter, all of which tend to directly address and involve the mashal's audience in its narration, the event of its recitation.

The king-mashal, then, was very much a product of its historical environment: both in the substance of its narratives, which frequently consist of realistic details drawn from the contemporary Greco-Roman world, and in its modes of representation, through which the Rabbis drew upon and transformed the world in which they lived for their own purposes. The narratives in the king-mashal represent the literary equivalent in Rabbinic Judaism to the pictorial art of early Christianity. The narratives about the king entering his foreign provinces, judging and punishing his rebellious subjects, restoring peace and justice to the fractured provinces, even quarreling with his consort and pacifying the members of his court, are the Rabbinic analogues to the great Byzantine frescoes depicting the triumphal advent of Christ as world-ruler and judge.[50]

Anthropomorphism

The historical context for the mashal's representation of God provides a valuable background against which to consider the second issue raised by the mashal's mode of characterization: the question of anthropomorphism. Since the beginning of the century, when A. Marmorstein collected all the relevant data in a seminal monograph devoted to the Rabbinic idea of God, scholars have recognized the extent to which anthropomorphic conceptions of God pervade Rabbinic literature (although there is still considerable debate over their meaning and historical significance).[51] Unhappily, virtually all modern discussions of Rabbinic anthropomorphism have framed the problem in the terms set for it by Jewish philosophers since the time of Saadiah (if not earlier).[52] The problem of anthropomorphism has been treated by scholars either as a question of God's corporeality, hence as a problem of metaphysics, or as an issue in the semantics of religious language, an extreme instance of the question of whether any human expression can truthfully be applied to the description of God.[53] And when Rabbinic anthropomorphism has been discussed, the major question has typically been whether or not the Rabbis actually believed in the anthropomorphic and anthropopathic features they attributed to the Creator. In other words, how philosophically sophisticated were the Rabbis' ideas about God?

These discussions have all treated anthropomorphic language in Jewish sources essentially as a cipher for the negativity of human belief or language. Virtually no one has approached the question of anthropomorphism on its own terms: that is, how these expressions likening God to man are used in a positive, constructive form in order to personalize God and to affirm His presence. To consider anthropomorphism from this perspective is to view it as trope and figure, a turning of creative language to express truth (rather than to obscure or obstruct it, as the philosophical view of anthropomorphism implicitly claims). Viewed from this perspective, anthropomorphism is less a matter of metaphysics or semantics than of the construction of divinity: the intentional, conscious use of language to represent God's character.[54] This perspective is especially relevant for analyzing the mashal, whose narratives about the king and his court are implicitly anthropomorphic descriptions of God in His relationship to Israel. If, as we have suggested, the king is the only character in the mashal to possess depth, what is the nature of that depth? What is the quality of God's personality?

The figure of the king is not, of course, the only image or character type used to represent God in the mashal. Some meshalim represent Him in the figure of an unnamed person (an *adam* or *ehad*), or as a hero (*gibor*), an elder (*zakein*), a doctor (*rofei*), or a shepherd (*ro'eh*). Each of these characterizations for God points to a particular aspect of His being—as sage, or protector, or healer. The image of God as king, in turn, emphasizes His role as ruler, as wielder of power and dominion over the universe.

God as king is both beneficent and severe. But what is most exceptional about the mashal's portrayal of the king is the way he is represented as being uncomfortable with the absolute power at his disposal. The king in the mashal tends to use his power in extreme, often seemingly unreasonable ways. He is either a tyrant or a victim of circumstance. When he gives expression to his feelings, it is often in the most intense and impulsive fashion. When he is angry, he sometimes responds with violence, ruthlessly; when he is in love, he can be desperate, obsessed, almost comically jealous. In either case, one senses that he is not fully in control, that his emotions have gotten the better of him.

By extension, all these feelings of discomfort, lack of control, and insecurity are predicated of God as well, and especially in narratives that deal with God's troubled relationship to the people of Israel, who tend to be the main victims of His unease and ambivalence. Perhaps the most extraordinary example of this portrait of the ambivalent God is the following mashal, Eikh. R. 1.1C:

> Another interpretation of "She . . . is become like a widow" (Lam. 1:1) . . .
> The Rabbis said:
> It is like a king who became angry at his consort. He wrote her a bill of divorce *(get),* and gave it to her, but then he returned, and grabbed it from her. Whenever she wished to marry someone else, the king said to her: Where is the bill of divorce with which I divorced you? And whenever she claimed support from him, he said to her: I have already divorced you.
> Similarly, whenever Israel wishes to worship idolatry, the Holy One, blessed be He, says to them: "Where is the bill of divorce of your mother whom I have dismissed?" (Isa. 50:1). And whenever they ask Him to perform a miracle for them, He tells them: I have already cast you off, as it is written, "I cast her off and handed her a bill of divorce" (Jer. 3:8).

To understand this mashal's narrative, it is necessary to appreciate the significance of the *get,* the bill of divorce, in Rabbinic law.[55] As a legal document, the get has a dual nature: it both constitutes the act of divorce and serves as evidence of divorce (primarily for the woman's sake). In its first role, the get resembles a kind of "performative" utterance: it must be written specially for each divorce; it has to be deliberately handed by the husband (or his agent) to the wife (or her agent), and willingly accepted by her, and through all this, properly attested by witnesses. The document thus actually "makes" the divorce. Once it is accepted by the woman, the divorce is irrevocable; if a man gives his wife a get, then changes his mind and tries to annul the divorce by retracting the document, his attempts have no legal validity. If he wishes to remarry the woman, the two of them must repeat the entire marriage ceremony. And once she takes possession of the get, she is a free woman, whether he likes it or not; she is free to marry another man, while her former husband is no longer required to support and protect her.

In addition to this "performative" function, though, the get also serves as proof of divorce. If the woman wishes to remarry she must be able to produce the document to show that she has been legally divorced from her previous husband.

This is precisely the consort's predicament in this mashal: because the king wrested the get from her by force, she cannot prove that she is divorced when he denies it, and she therefore cannot remarry. On the other hand, whenever she asks the king to support her, he is able to produce the document and show that he did divorce her. The king's behavior is clearly against the law. He openly lies when he denies having divorced her. His possession of the get is a case of outright theft. When he refuses to support her, as he must if they are still married, he immorally exploits her helpless position.

What is the point of this bizarre narrative? In exegetical terms, the picture of the wife's helpless situation at the king's unjust hands is a bold attempt to explain the meaning of the phrase *kealmanah,* "like a widow," which modifies the portrait of Zion in Lam. 1:1. According to the mashal, Zion is "like a widow" just like the consort in the mashal: that is, she is *like* a widow inasmuch as her husband might as well be dead, since he is no good to her; but she is only "like" a widow because, alas, her husband is not dead.[56] In rhetorical terms, the mashal has features that point to a critique of God's treatment of Israel; such a critique, strangely enough, may have served an apologetic end, if only by demonstrating that God refuses to release the Jews from the covenantal bond even *after* He has divorced them, and even though *they* are willing to dissolve their union with Him. This apologetic uses God, somewhat paradoxically, to rationalize the misery of Israel's existence. In contrast to the common apologetic strategy that justifies Israel's suffering by tracing it back to her misdeeds, this mashal attributes Israel's unhappy existence to God and to the conflicts of His personality!

It is this portrait of God's personality, in all its irrationality and unfairness, that overshadows both the exegetical and the rhetorical dimensions of the mashal's meaning. The basis for the king's behavior is left unexplained—a strategic omission, as such gaps nearly always are. Does the king act as he does because he cannot make up his mind and decide what he wants? But if this is the reason behind his behavior, must his poor wife therefore live the worst of all possible lives—not married, not divorced, not widowed? Must *his* indecision, *his* ambivalence ruin her life? Or does the king possibly intend something crueler? Not content with divorcing her, does he steal the get precisely in order to make her situation still more unbearable? Is this his idea of punishment?

Whatever the answers to these questions may be, the mashal's narrative suggests that God has two distinct sides, or aspects: in one of them, He is indissolubly bound to Israel in their covenantal relationship; in the other, He is already alienated from that relationship, utterly distant and separated from His nation's travails. These two aspects point toward two separate characters of God, two extreme forms of His personality, as it were. Both inform the mashal at separate moments in its tradition. In a single mashal, usually only one aspect appears at a time, though, on occasion, as in Eikh. R. 1.1C, the two may surface simultaneously, while in other narratives in Rabbinic literature the two characters appear in still different, even more disturbing guises.[57]

The crucial fact is that these two aspects or personalities of God are closer to being two distinct and independent characters than complementary attributes of a single divine being. My point in saying this is not to make a theological assertion, but to suggest that neither characterization of God—let alone both together—can easily be reduced to a normative divine being of the sort found in most theological systems. As a character, each portrait of God is too unpredictable, too uncanny, to be anything other than a creation of the imagination. Indeed, this is the sum meaning of the anthropomorphic paradox: the Rabbis were able to portray God's full complexity only by imagining Him in the human image. Why? Because only human behavior presented the Rabbis with a model sufficiently complex to do justice to God. In the king-mashal's narratives, the anthropomorphic imagination of the Rabbis reached its greatest height of achievement.

4

Thematics

The midrashic mashal is a type of ideological narrative, which seeks to impress the truth and validity of a world-view—that of Rabbinic Judaism—upon its audience. In any particular mashal, that world-view is refracted within the mashal's specific message, its theme or thesis. Though not necessarily equivalent to the mashal's entire meaning, the message is certainly one of its significant components.

How can we define these messages in greater detail? As we have already seen, a mashal's message tends to be phrased in terms of either praise or blame, a fact that is itself a revealing index of the difficulty of distilling the mashal's message into a succinct, let alone systematic, formulation. More a modality or a gesture than a static presence like an idea, the mashal's message by nature resembles what Edgar Allan Poe called an "effect," the reaction or impression its author wishes to elicit from his audience. In Poe's famous formulation, "a skilful artist" who "has constructed a tale . . . has not fashioned his thoughts to accommodate his incidents, but having deliberately conceived a certain *single effect* to be wrought, he then invents such incidents, he then combines such events, and discusses them in such tone as may best serve him in establishing this preconceived effect."[1] To adapt this description to the mashal's composition, one would need to add only at the beginning that its author chooses the mashal's scriptural proof-text, its exegetical occasion, and determines its interpretation. But the mashal's "effect" is, in either case, not only its result and product but also its cause, its informing, guiding intention as well as the reaction it elicits from the audience.

This means, in other words, that the mashal's message is essentially a functional category rather than an abstraction or a belief.

In the course of this book, we have already noted a number of these categories—apologetics (for Eikh. R. 4.11), consolation (for Eikh. R. 3.21), complaint (for Eikh. R. 1.21)—and we have seen both their uses and their limitations in helping us understand the mashal's meaning. It remains now to investigate and describe these types of messages more systematically. I have chosen in this chapter five of the more prominent thematic functions that the mashal serves, and for each category I have selected one or two exemplary meshalim as illustrations. In each category, I will be concerned with two basic questions. First, how does the mashal use its traditional compositional, poetic, and rhetorical strategies in order to communicate its message? And second, how does the mashal's thematic function influence its shape both as narrative and as exegesis?

Apologetics

The term apologetic denotes an act of defense, particularly one made in response to an attack, and in Rabbinic literature, specifically those attempts to defend and rationalize God's behavior in relation to Israel. For the most part, these attempts defend Israel's status as God's chosen people.

The need for such apologetic efforts was particularly intense in the aftermath of the destruction of the Temple in 70 c.e. The vastness of the spiritual and material devastation that had befallen the Jewish people required justification, as did God's willingness to allow these terrible tribulations to happen. At issue simultaneously was Israel's sense of identity and the justice of God's deeds. If the Temple's destruction was not a sign of the rejection of Israel, then what was it? Either God was powerless, or He had allowed the gentiles gratuitously to inflict evil upon His obedient servants. Neither answer was satisfactory, and it was the job of apologists to offer alternative explanations.

The need for these responses was especially acute within the religious and political circumstances in which Jews lived in the second, third, and fourth centuries. Contemporaries of the Rabbis, the early Church leaders among them, did not hesitate to exploit the national sufferings of the Jews by interpreting them as proof that God had rejected Israel and that, in its place, He had chosen others—*themselves,* the early Church Fathers claimed. Even if the Rabbinic parables do not explicitly address these enemies, it is likely that the arguments of the Christians were known by Jews and had to be answered in any case. To their Jewish audiences, in turn, the Rabbis had to justify the awful state of their historical predicament, and simultaneously provide reassurance that, despite all appearances, the Jews remained God's chosen people.[2]

The Destruction was also not the sole cause for apologetics. The Rabbis used the mashal to defend any one of God's deeds whose justice appeared questionable or problematic. Many of these defenses initially appear historically innocent. Consider the following mashal, recorded in Sifre Num. 119, a comment on Num. 18:20, in which God tells the Levites, "You shall, however, have no territorial share among them [the other tribes] or own any portion in their midst; I am your portion and your share among the Israelites." To explain why the Levites alone were refused a share among the other tribes, the midrash relates the following mashal in defense of God's act.

> [God said to them:] From My table you will eat and from My table you will drink.
>
> A mashal. What is it like? It is like a king of flesh-and-blood who gave gifts to his sons. To one son, however, he gave nothing. The king said to him: Even though I have given you no gift, from my table you will eat and from my table you will drink.
>
> And thus the verse says: ". . . I have given it as their portion from My offerings by fire . . ." (Lev. 6:10). "They shall live only off the Lord's offerings by fire as their portion" (Deut. 18:1).

According to the mashal, God did not deny the Levites a portion; rather, their portion is the right they own to eat from the sacred offerings, and that privilege is actually a greater share than any other. In order to offer this defense of God's behavior, the mashal adopts the rhetorical mode of praise—not of God, however, but of the Levites who, we learn, are distinguished by being the worthy recipients of this special gift. But this praise also serves the purpose of explaining why God treats them specially. The narrative does this first by creating a situation that appears problematic, thus creating the need for an interpretation, and then by having the king, playing the role of an implied interpreter, resolve the "difficulty" in the narrative by explaining his behavior to his son.

The explicit subject of this mashal is a law relating to a situation that obtained during the division of the land of Israel in the biblical period; in the Rabbinic period, long after the Temple's destruction, the primary relevance of this verse and others like it was to affirm the continuing legal obligation to give the Levites and priests their special gifts.[3] But is it possible to take the propertyless tribe of Levites as a figure for the Jewish people as a whole? They, too, lack a "portion" in this world in the sense of being "stateless," and if so, the mashal might be read as an implicit apologetic for the political subjugation of the Jewish people. It would also offer its audience a message of consolation for their loss of national independence by suggesting that the Jews, "a kingdom of priests," enjoy a special and unique seat at God's own table even if they have no political share of their own among the nations of the world. A "purely" scriptural exegesis can easily be extended in this way, and made relevant to contemporary historical experience.[4]

The seven apologetic meshalim in Eikh. R.—Eikh. R. 1.1A, 1.1B, 1.17, 2.1A, 2.1B, 2.7, and 4.11—all address exegetical occasions whose immediate historical import is more obvious. With one exception (Eikh. R. 4.11), the other apologetic meshalim in Eikh. R. are all blame-parables, and they tend to follow one or more of three strategies: (1) condemning Israel for its sins, which they specify, thus justifying Israel's suffering as due punishment; (2) qualifying and modifying the historical catastrophe by downplaying its size and significance, thereby blunting its most painful edges and limiting its frightening immensity; (3) contextualizing the catastrophe within the larger framework of the covenantal relationship between God and Israel, thereby depriving the catastrophe of any absolute historical or theological finality.

Eikh. R. 4.11, as we saw, essentially employed the second strategy. Each of the two meshalim I will analyze in this chapter uses one of the two others. Both parables comment upon the same verse, Lam. 2:1, "He has cast down from heaven to earth the majesty of Israel." With its dramatic syntax, its grand, almost hyperbolic description of Israel's downfall, and its unusual stipulation of the object of God's wrath as Israel's "majesty," this verse offered the Rabbis a rich occasion for exegesis, and this occasion was only made more compelling by the fact that the verse, in its literal sense, invoked a historical reality that was all too threatening to the Rabbis. All these factors were sufficient cause for apologetic reinterpretation.

Eikhah Rabbah 2.1A

"He has cast down from heaven to earth the majesty of Israel" (Lam. 2:1).
R. Huna b. Aha said in the name of R. Hanina the son of R. Abbahu:[5]
It is like a king who had a son. The son wept, so he placed him upon his knees. The son wept, and the king took him in his arms. He wept again, and the king set him upon his shoulders. Then the child dirtied him, and he cast him down to the earth. His ascent was unlike his descent: his ascent was little by little, but his descent was all at once.
Similarly: "I have pampered Ephraim, taking them in My (literally: His) arms" (Hos. 11:3). And after that: "I will make Ephraim ride, Judah shall do plowing, Jacob shall do final plowing" (Hos. 10:11). And after that: "He has cast down from heaven to earth the majesty of Israel (tiferet yisrael)" (Lam. 2:1). Their ascent was unlike their descent: their ascent was little by little, but their descent was all at once.

The narrative of this mashal is quite straightforward, but its nimshal requires some explanation. Each of the three verses quoted in the nimshal refers to one of the three stages through which the child in the narrative passes—from his father's knees to his arms, from his arms to his shoulders, and from the shoulders down to the earth. The basis for these scriptural parallels actually is found in the final exegesis in the nimshal. In Lam. 2:1's closing phrase, tiferet yisrael, the second word is understood not as the nation of Israel but as the patriarch Jacob (an interpretation based on the famous renaming incident in Gen. 32:29; cf. 35:10),[6] while Jacob's "majesty" is understood as a reference to Ephraim, Joseph's younger son, whom Jacob not inadvertently blesses before his older brother Manasseh (cf. Gen. 48:12–22). The person of Ephraim is then taken as a figure for Israel as God's favored child, a symbolization also used elsewhere in Rabbinic literature.[7]

This exegetical figure is then expanded in the two opening exegeses in the nimshal of Hos. 11:3 and 10:11, in both of which Ephraim figures as the verse's primary object.[8] Thus, R. Huna, reading Hos. 11:3, takes the phrase *tirgalti* (literally "I taught them to walk") as referring to the legs *(raglayim)* of God, thus meaning, "I have taken him (Ephraim) upon My legs"—presumably meaning, His knees. Similarly, the sage takes the second half of the verse, *kaheim 'al zero'otav* ("taking them by their arms") as referring literally to God's arms, thereby reading the clause as "I took them (Ephraim) in My arms."[9] Finally, Huna interprets the phrase *arkiv ephrayim* in Hos. 10:11 ("I will make Ephraim to ride") so that it too refers to God's body: "I will take him upon My shoulders."[10]

Taken together, these playfully anthropomorphic interpretations provide perfect scriptural analogues for the mashal's narrative, the story of the unhappy child's ascent in his father's arms, stage by stage, culminating unexpectedly in the calamitous fall that is the narrative equivalent to Lam. 2:1's "He has cast him down from heaven to earth." This narrative is a variant upon a subtradition of meshalim that describe the king's love for his children and for a favorite son in particular. Perhaps the best-known mashal in this subtradition is the following Tannaitic mashal, which is preserved in several places in the Mekhilta:

"And the angel of God journeyed . . ." (Exod. 14:19).

R. Judah says: This is a verse rich in content, and is echoed in many places.

A mashal. What is this like? It is like a man who was walking on the road and was leading his son in front of him. When robbers came from in front in order to capture the son, the man took his son from in front and placed him behind. When a wolf came from behind, he took his son from behind and placed him in front. When robbers came from in front and wolves from behind, he took his son in his arms. When the son began to suffer from the sun, his father spread his cloak over him. When the son was hungry, he fed him. When he was thirsty, he gave him to drink.

The Holy One, blessed be He, acted the same way, as it is said, "I have pampered Ephraim, taking them in My arms" (Hos. 11:3). When the son began to suffer from the sun, He spread His cloak over him, as it is said, "He spread a cloud for a screen" (Ps. 105:39). When he was hungry, He fed him bread, as it is said, "Behold, I will cause bread to rain from heaven for you" (Exod. 16:4). When he was thirsty, He gave him water to drink, as it is said, "He brought streams also out of the rock" (Ps. 78:16).

Although the literary form of this mashal has not yet undergone complete regularization,[11] its resemblance to Eikh. R. 2.1A is clear. Both meshalim describe in vivid detail, nearly step by step, the king's affectionate handling of his child, the care he takes to comfort and protect his son. Even if Eikh. R. 2.1A concludes with the child suddenly dirtying his father and with the father thereupon throwing his son down, the overall feeling of the mashal is of a piece with the Mekhilta parallel. Both meshalim play upon the inherently positive nature of the father-son relationship, and this feeling of beneficence overrides even the rhetoric of blame in Eikh. R. 2.1A.[12]

As in the Mekhilta mashal, the meaning of the narrative in Eikh. R. 2.1A is also very much connected to clever exegetical parallels in the nimshal; indeed, the narrative can even be considered as a kind of pretext for the collocation of the three verses into a single unit, as providing a kind of logic for their sequence. It supplies a rationale for the child's ascent—his weeping, which unfailingly garners his father's affection—and for his sudden descent—his dirtying of his father.

What, however, does this last motif mean? It must refer in some way to Israel's transgressions against God. But how seriously? Is it merely a baby pooping in his father's arms? Is the father's reaction, his "casting-down" of the infant, really just an instinctual response? Or is the baby's act meant to symbolize a truly grave transgression, a deed of monumental disgrace and ingratitude? And if so, is the father's response one of genuine rejection?

The mashal itself does not explain the motif's meaning, but a key to it may lie in the narrative's concluding statement (also repeated at the end of the nimshal): "His ascent was unlike his descent: the ascent was little by little, but the descent was all at once." Although its genesis is unknown, the expression is doubtless a proverbial or folk saying, as both its colloquial Aramaic and its pithy comparison of rising to falling suggest. The saying calls to mind such proverbs as "To rise to a great height is difficult, but to fall is easy," or "It is a long journey from the bottom to the top, but from the top to the bottom only a step."[13] Whatever its origin, the expression functions in the mashal as a narratorial comment on the order of an epimythium (the moral or didactic lesson attached to exempla or fables, as in the Aesopic collections). Serving as a meta-commentary, the proverb offers a "universalizing generalization," in Galit Hasan-Rokem's phrase, on the preceding narrative.[14]

What this "meta-commentary" suggests is as follows: The child's fall should not be taken too grievously. Precipitous as the fall may seem, it is important to remember that falling is always swifter than ascending. Nothing falls that didn't once ascend, and one can only fall so far as the height to which one has risen.

In ideological terms, this means that Israel's fate in the aftermath of the Temple's destruction should not be interpreted in the worst possible light. By destroying the Temple, God did not intend to reject Israel, any more than the father wished to reject his child when he threw him down after being dirtied. The mashal's message is therefore an apologetic, and the two primary rhetorical strategies it uses are those of qualification and contextualization. While the narrative acknowledges Israel's responsibility for its own misfortune, it simultaneously minimizes the catastrophe and contextualizes it within the larger history of Israel's familial relationship with God. At the same time, the narrative also "interprets" the proverb: See the greatness from which Israel toppled, the mashal exhorts its audience. See how quick was their downfall in comparison to their slow climb to greatness. As a result of God's responsiveness, Israel rose to awesome heights over time, but fell in an instant by dirtying the very One who had raised the people so high. Indeed, had Israel not risen so high in God's favor, had He not taken such care to protect and nurture His people, their descent would not appear so calamitous. Even so, their downfall is only a single, temporary moment in the history of Israel's covenant with God. Sooner or later, the child Israel will cry again, and God will lift up His people, taking them in His arms once more.

Eikhah Rabbah 2.1B

"He has cast down from heaven to earth the majesty of Israel" (Lam. 2:1).

R. Joshua of Sikhnin said:[15]

It is like the inhabitants of a province who made a crown for the king. They provoked him but he bore with them; they provoked him again, but he bore with them. He said: The inhabitants of the province provoke me only because of the crown that is placed upon my head. Here, I cast it down in their faces!

Similarly, the Holy One, blessed be He, said: The Israelites anger Me only because of the image of Jacob that is sculpted on My throne. Here, I cast it down. This is what is written, "He has cast down from heaven to earth the majesty of Israel."

Like Eikh. R. 2.1A, this mashal is a blame-parable, its message stated unequivocally by the king when he angrily throws down the crown presented to him by his provincial subjects after they have repeatedly angered him. Although the mashal never says what the subjects did to anger the king, there is no question about the king's motive or his patience or the deservedness of the punishment.

The interest of this mashal lies less in its narrative shape than in the way it manipulates traditional symbols and images with exegesis to serve its rhetorical purpose. Virtually all the motifs in this mashal are traditional. The narrative's central motif, in which a character (here the provincial subjects) angers the king, appears in two other meshalim in Eikh. R. alone (2.7 and 4.11), while the initial motif, describing how the provincials make a crown for the king, is actually a variant upon a more basic function—X makes/prepares Y for the king—that in Eikh. R. appears in three meshalim (Eikh. R. 2.7, Petihta 10, Eikh. R. 3.8A).[16] The crown itself is a conventional symbol that appears in countless meshalim, and represents either an actual crown or a laurel wreath; if the former, as is most likely, the image probably derives from the *aurum coronarium*, a wreath made of solid gold, which was offered to the emperor on occasions like his accession to office, the winning of a military victory, or a visit to the provinces, as in this mashal.[17] In these various contexts, the crown symbolizes different things, but most frequently it is some kind of praise or prayer paid to God: communal prayer; a song of praise like the Song at the Sea; a specific psalm; or the trishagios that the angels recite daily before God.[18] In one instance, the crown symbolizes the people of Israel, but there the mashal explicitly describes the Israelites as the instruments through which God is glorified—that is, as a medium of praise not unlike prayer.[19]

In Eikh. R. 2.1B, the crown symbolizes something very different, "the icon of Jacob." What is this image, and what is its meaning? We can begin to answer this question with the image's genesis on the exegetical level. The icon is a playful interpretation of the phrase *tiferet yisrael*, "the majesty of Israel," which in Lam. 2:1

God hurls down from heaven to earth. As we noted earlier, that phrase may have seemed enigmatic to the Rabbis for several reasons: What is Israel's majesty? Is it something different from Israel itself? How could it fall from heaven to earth? According to the mashal's exegesis of the phrase, the name *yisrael* is again identified as the patriarch Jacob, as in Eikh. R. 2.1A, while the word *tiferet* is punned here with *pe'eir,* a crown or ornament. Taken together, these two translations yield "the icon of Jacob"—a relief-like image that, we are told, is engraved or sculpted upon the divine throne. It is this image that God now casts down from heaven to earth.

What is this icon? The peculiar image appears in several Rabbinic aggadot and may even predate them, as James Kugel has recently argued, having originated as an exegesis of Gen. 28:12: "And he dreamt, and behold there was a ladder set up on the earth, and the top of it *(rosho)* reached to heaven; and behold, the angels of God were ascending and descending upon it."[20] According to Kugel, the word *rosho* was read literally as "his head"— namely, Jacob's—which "reached to heaven," that is, was found on high, on the divine throne, in the shape of an icon.

The notion of an icon of Jacob existing in heaven may also have been conflated by the Rabbis with "the face of the man" *(pnei adam)* upon the divine throne which the prophet Ezekiel described in his famous visions of God (Ezek. 1:10, 26). But the image probably derived from something even more concrete and historically real than these verses and their interpretation. The Rabbis were certainly familiar with actual iconic images, usually in the form of medallions portraying the Roman emperor or the Roman consuls, that were used throughout the empire to decorate imperial and consular chairs. These icons are typically pictured upon consular diptychs, tablets made from ivory that were presented by consuls to their friends and relatives as souvenirs on the occasion of their appointment to office; the tablets usually represent the consul seated upon a throne, and that throne is often decorated with icons.[21]

The imperial and consular thrones decorated with iconic images were later adapted in the early Church for episcopal chairs, which contained ivory medallions engraved with biblical stories and icons of saints, as we know from early Christian illustrations.[22] Unhappily, there are no comparable Jewish objects from Late Antiquity; the few throne-like chairs that do exist, like the Seat of Moses from Khorazin, lack human figurative carvings of any kind. Even so, it is not hard to believe that the Rabbis imagined God's throne in heaven on the model of the imperial throne with all its ornate decorations. And this being the case, whose face would have been more suitable to adorn the heavenly throne than that of the patriarch Jacob? As Louis Ginzberg pointed out, "Jacob is the ideal man, and hence it is his countenance which represents the human race on the divine throne."[23]

In fact, the iconographical tradition behind Jacob's icon may be somewhat more complicated than Ginzberg proposed. As Alexander Altmann argued in his study of the Gnostic background of Rabbinic Adam legends, Jacob's image on the divine throne may have represented not an ideal but a primordial man, Adam Kadmon; and the Rabbinic accounts of Jacob's icon may actually have been part of a Rabbinic polemic against Gnostic attempts to attribute divinity or semi-divinity to the primordial Adam.[24] Whatever the icon-image's origins, though, early on it became part of the unique hagiographical tradition surrounding the patriarch, a tradition that includes belief in his immortality, his special concern for Israel, and his merits, or *zekhuyot,* and their benefits for his descendants, the children of Israel.[25] In the light of this tradition, it seems likely that Jacob would have been an ideal countenance not for Adam or for mankind in general, but for the people of Israel in particular. His icon would have perfectly represented *Israel's* presence upon God's throne. Indeed, the desire to situate a figurative representation of Israel upon the divine throne is itself a sufficient motive to explain the invention of the image of the icon—Israel's wish to be literally at God's right hand.

If these are the exegetical and symbolic meanings of the image of Jacob's icon engraved upon the divine throne, what does the mashal mean by describing God as hurling the icon out of His presence, from heaven down to earth? One scholar, A. Marmorstein, has suggested that the mashal's meaning is a polemical attack against those Jews who wished to rely upon the merits of the patriarchs to protect themselves from punishment for their sins.[26] According to Marmorstein, the icon represents Jacob's patriarchal merits, the *zekhut avot,* and the mashal itself is part of a debate that goes back to the Pharisaic period over the efficacy and power of those *zekhuyot*. Elsewhere in Rabbinic literature, this debate is reflected in a few exegeses which claim that at the time of the Destruction the Jews attempted to invoke the merits of the patriarch to avert the catastrophe, but to no avail.[27]

The problem with Marmorstein's interpretation is that it is impossible to believe that anyone in the third century—the time of R. Joshua of Sikhnin (or R. Joshua b. R. Nahman, to whom the mashal is attributed in S)—would have doubted the fact that the patriarchal merits had *failed* to avert the destruction of the Temple. Even if the mashal reflects the polemic against the doctrine of patriarchal merits, it is very unlikely that a Rabbi would have used the Temple's destruction to prove the inefficacy of the doctrine; too many other reasons could be adduced to justify the Destruction.

Rather than being a polemic, R. Joshua's parable is an apologetic mashal. By interpreting the phrase *tiferet yisrael* not as "the majesty of Israel" but as "the icon of Jacob," R. Joshua effectively defused the verse's most threatening and dangerous meaning. According to the mashal, the verse no longer describes God as rejecting Israel but only as removing an ornamental icon from the divine throne. Even if He literally hurled that icon down from heaven to earth, as the verse says, it was only an icon, a decoration. The king's angry behavior, God's violent outburst—these are no more than angry warnings to Israel to cease its provocations.

The mashal conveys this apologetic message by using the rhetorical technique of surrogacy. By substituting the icon for the people (or majesty) of Israel, the mashal transposes the horror of the catastrophe from a truly threatened subject (the people of Israel) to an innocuous object (the icon). The real threat is thereby eliminated, and its scriptural source is neutralized. Did the Rabbis honestly believe that this is what the verse meant—that *tiferet yisrael* actually referred to an icon, or that God really hurled a decorative image off His throne and down to earth? Not necessarily. But the cleverness of the exegesis, along with the rhetorical technique of surrogacy, would have been sufficiently distracting to divert the audience from the verse's more horrible implications.

Surrogacy, rhetorical substitution, is a technique commonly used for the purpose of apologetic argument precisely because it is highly adaptable to varying contexts and applications. While the narrative in Eikh. R. 2.1B specifically refers to the destruction of the

Temple, the mashal's message could be reapplied to other tragedies in Israel's history. Moreover, as an explanatory model, the
same act of substitution can be transferred to other exegetical occasions so long as they fit the same structure as the original prooftext.
Eikh. R. 2.7 comments on Lam. 2:7 through the following mashal:

> "The Lord has rejected His altar" (Lam. 2:7).
> R. Haggai said in the name of R. Isaac:
> It is like the inhabitants of a province who prepared banquets
> (literally: who set tables) for the king. They provoked him, but
> he bore with them. They provoked him but he bore with them.
> The king said: The only reason inhabitants of the province pro-
> voke me is because [they rely upon] these banquets that they
> have prepared for me. Here, it is thrown down in their faces!
> Similarly, the Holy One, blessed be He, said: The only reason
> Israel provoked Me is because [they rely upon] the sacrifice that
> they used to offer before Me. Here, it is thrown down in their
> faces!

In its narrative structure, its exegetical technique, and its rhetorical strategy, this mashal is identical to Eikh. R. 2.1B. The only
difference between the two meshalim is in the specific object that
the provincials present to the king, here a banquet or table, and
that object has obviously been determined by the mashal's prooftext and its subject, the altar *(mizbeiah)* which God rejects. Otherwise, this mashal reenacts the identical gesture of substitution made
in Eikh. R. 2.1B to the same apologetic effect. The one thing that
is remarkable about this mashal is that in it the surrogate is not
some ornamental object like an icon, but the Temple (for which
the word "altar" is clearly a synecdoche). God's own altar is transformed here into a substitute for the people of Israel. This displacement recalls the comparable substitution implied in Eikh. R. 4.11
(where Asaph praises God for destroying the Temple rather than
the people of Israel), but it is also a transformation of the conventional image for the Jewish victims of the war as sacrifices of atonement upon the altar of punishment for Israel's sins. In this mashal,
the altar literally atones for their sins in place of the victims.

Polemics

As its name suggests, the polemical rhetorical function is com-
bative in nature; it specifically designates parables whose purpose

is to attack and condemn beliefs or persons the Rabbis considered inimical.

Polemical meshalim would appear almost by definition to be blame-parables. In fact, this is not always the case, as we shall see in our analysis of Eikh. R. 3.24, a praise-mashal. But the majority of polemical meshalim are either phrased unambiguously in the language of blame or at least set in comparative terms that are weighted heavily against the party who is invariably the polemic's object of blame.

Polemical meshalim that are phrased in terms of straight blame tend to utilize the rhetoric of affect—underhanded hyperbole, mockery, invective, and sexual innuendo. A typical polemical mashal of this kind is Eikh. R. 1.10. Commenting on Lam. 1:10— "The foe has laid hands on everything dear to her; she has seen her sanctuary invaded by nations which You have denied admission into Your community"—the Rabbis identified "the foe" as the nations of Ammon and Moab. This identification was largely based on the similarity between the end of the verse and the prohibition against Ammon and Moab in Deut. 23:4, "No Ammonite or Moabite shall be admitted into the congregation of the Lord," that is, allowed to marry an Israelite.

> R. Judah b. R. Simon said in the name of R. Levi b. Parta: What were they like?
>
> It is like a fire that broke out in the house of the king. Everyone ran to plunder silver and gold, and the slave ran to plunder his deed of slavery.
>
> Similarly, when the gentile nations entered the Temple, everyone ran to plunder silver and gold, and the Ammonites and Moabites to plunder the Torah for the purpose of expunging "No Ammonite or Moabite shall be admitted into the congregation of the Lord" (Deut. 23:4).

The intent of the mashal is to ridicule Ammon and Moab: *Only* a slave thinks of looting the palace to look for his deed of slavery when everyone else is busy plundering the royal gold and silver. *Only* Ammon and Moab thought to plunder the Torah when every other gentile nation was busy stealing the Temple gold. And *only* Ammon and Moab were stupid enough to believe that by expunging the verse from the Torah they could actually remove the prohibition against Israelites' marrying them![28]

Polemical invective is not always so blunt. Some meshalim are more subtle in making their attack. Consider the following example from Tan. B. (Num., p. 81 = Bam. R. 16.23):

> It is like a consort who had a Cushite maidservant. The consort's husband went off to a foreign province. All night the maidservant said to the consort: I am more beautiful than you. The king loves me more than he loves you. The consort replied: Let morning come, and we will know who is more beautiful and whom the king loves.
>
> Similarly, the nations of the world say to Israel: Our deeds are more beautiful, and we are the ones whom the Holy One, blessed be He, desires. Therefore Israel says: Let morning come, and we will know whom the Holy One, blessed be He, desires—as it is said, "The watchman replied, Morning comes" (Isa. 21:12): Let the world-to-come, which is called morning, arrive, "and you shall come to see the difference between the righteous and the wicked" (Mal. 3:18).

The mashal's polemic has a double agenda: to refute the gentiles' claim that God loves them more than He does the Jews, and to affirm Israel's counterclaim to being God's true love. To accomplish this twofold aim, the mashal stages a kind of debate or contest between the consort and her maidservant, and this debate elicits from the audience a comparative interpretive act. This comparison, in turn, serves to disparage one party while praising its opposite.

What makes this comparative operation characteristic of polemical meshalim is that, from the outset, the comparison is predetermined in favor of one party and against the other. In this mashal, the two rivals are explicitly represented as characters of distinctly unequal status—one is the king's consort, the other *her* maidservant.[29] The former is helplessly beleaguered—no reason is given for her husband's departure, a gap that by convention makes her position more sympathetic to the audience—while the latter, the maidservant, exploits her helpless situation. The fact that the maidservant is "black" does not necessarily mean that she is ugly, physically or spiritually, but the detail is a crucial factor in the narrative inasmuch as the Cushite maidservant taunts her mistress *at night*, which is of course precisely the time when her own blackness, epidermal or figurative, cannot be discerned. Hence the irony in the consort's retort that when day comes, it will be clear that she is the more beautiful one and that the king loves her more.

Again, the characteristically polemical feature of this comparison is that it is entirely artificial, contrived solely in order to condemn what its author and audience know from the beginning is worthy of being condemned. Such is the typical character of polemic argument in the ancient world. It is usually directed at an audience of believers (here, Jews) rather than skeptics or outsiders (such as gentiles), and intended not so much to convince as to confirm what its audience already knows. As a result, novelty of presentation is a more critical factor in its success than the substance of the polemical charge.

It is therefore not surprising to find that the most common objects attacked in polemical meshalim are rather tired subjects: forms of idolatry and those who worship idols, that is, the gentile nations. The Rabbis do not always distinguish between the sin and the sinner. But these generalized attacks upon idolatry or upon the gentiles sometimes disguise more specific beliefs or persons that the Rabbis wish to condemn.[30] Although we can assume as a rule that the original audience of the mashal would have understood the particular nuances of the polemic, these nuances can be more difficult to uncover today. In the next mashal I will analyze, we will see how a polemic originally (it seems) directed at one very specific target was later generalized to fit a new exegetical occasion.

Eikhah Rabbah 3.24

"The Lord is my portion, I say with full heart" (Lam. 3:24).

R. Abbahu said in the name of R. Yohanan:

A mashal. It is like a king who entered a province, and with him were generals, captains, and military commanders. One man said: I will entertain (literally: take to myself) a general. Another said: I will entertain a commander. A certain clever man (*pikeiah*) was there, and he said: I will entertain the king himself. For they will all pass away but he will never pass away.

Similarly, among the nations of the world, some worship the sun, some the moon, some the trees, and some stone. But the Holy One, blessed be He, is the portion of Israel. That is what is written, "The Lord is my portion, I say with full heart"; and just so you say, "The Lord is my allotted share and cup" (Ps. 16:5) . . . "Therefore will I hope in Him" (Lam. 3:24): I declare the unity of His name twice a day, "Hear, O Israel, the Lord our God, the Lord alone" (Deut. 6:4).

The meaning of this mashal at first seems clear. It is a praise-mashal, and its narrative affirms Israel's decision to worship God as against the idols the gentile nations choose, the reason for Israel's choice being that the idols "will all pass away but he will never pass away," just as the *pikeiah,* the clever man, in the narrative says about his own choice of the king rather than the generals. This explanation implicitly conveys double praise: first, and most obviously, of Israel's God, who will never pass away, but also of the explanation's own speaker, the *pikeiah* himself, the wise or clever man symbolizing Israel, precisely for his wisdom in choosing the king, or God. This implied comparison between the *pikeiah*'s wisdom and the other citizens' lack of it is the basis of the mashal's narrative; it is also a traditional motif best known, perhaps, from Jesus' parable of the Wise and the Foolish Maidens (Matt. 25:1–18).[31] In this mashal, the comparison ultimately serves the purpose of praising the wisdom of the Jews and disparaging the stupidity of the gentiles.

The same polemic informs the nimshal's exegesis of Lam. 3:24. According to R. Abbahu's interpretation, the verse's key phrase, *amrah nafshi,* is understood literally as "my soul says," and the soul then is taken as a figure for the people of Israel. In its entirety, the verse voices a challenge to the gentile nations: "You may worship whomever you wish; I choose God." The identical exegetical logic underlies the interpretation of Ps. 16:5, an exegesis consistent with other Rabbinic exegeses of that verse.[32] Finally, the nimshal's concluding citation of Deut. 6:4, which Israel recites twice daily as the *shema'* prayer in the standard Rabbinic liturgy, is explicitly deployed as a gloss on the second half of Lam. 3:24, "Therefore I will hope in Him." The entire Lamentations verse is thus taken as a virtual credal statement of Israel's faith in God.

So far the mashal's polemic is clear. The complications in its analysis arise at two points. The first of these is the specific identity of the types of idolatry against which the mashal polemicizes. The nimshal explicitly names gentiles who worship the sun, moon, trees, and stones. Is it possible to specify the type of idolatrous worship being attacked here in any greater detail? Pagan worship thrived in many different forms during the third century, the time of R. Yohanan, the mashal's author. Although R. Akiba is said to have asserted in the second century that "my heart and your heart know that there is no substance to idolatry"—a claim that some scholars of Rabbinics have taken to mean that paganism had lost its vitality by the early Rabbinic period and was no longer considered a threat by the Rabbis—recent scholarship has revealed the exact opposite to be the historical reality, and our mashal is certainly strong evidence of the Rabbis' felt need to state their abiding difference from their pagan neighbors in this respect.[33] But is it possible to be more specific as to exactly what kind of idolatry R. Yohanan is condemning in his mashal?

The second problem with the mashal, which also bears upon the first question, stems from the fact that the same mashal found in Eikh. R. 3.24 appears in another Rabbinic text where it is applied to an entirely different exegetical occasion. This is a relatively rare but significant phenomenon in the tradition of the midrashic mashal. The "other" mashal in this case is found in Dev. R. 2.34, as part of a *petihta,* a midrashic proem, for Deut. 6:4; not coincidentally, the opening verse for the petihta is Lam. 3:24.

> R. Isaac recited a proem: "The Lord is my portion, I say with full heart; therefore will I hope in Him" (Lam. 3:24).
> R. Isaac said:
> What is this like? It is like a king who entered a province, and with him there came generals, captains, and military commanders. Some inhabitants of the province chose a general whom they agreed to support, others a captain, and still others a commander. But one of them who was a clever man said, I will choose only the king. Why? For they will all pass away, but the king will never pass away.
> Similarly, when the Holy One, blessed be He, descended on Mt. Sinai, bands of angels descended with Him—Michael and his band, Gabriel and his band. Some of the nations of the world chose Michael for themselves, and others chose Gabriel. But Israel chose the Holy One, blessed be He. They said: "The Lord is my portion, I say with full heart." Behold, "Hear O Israel, the Lord our God, the Lord alone" (Deut. 6:4).

In contrast to the much more generalized situation in Eikh. R. 3.24's nimshal, this version in Dev. R. applies the same narrative to a very specific circumstance: God's revelation at Sinai, where, according to the mashal, God revealed Himself to all the nations, not just to Israel. Israel alone, however, chose God; each gentile nation chose one of the angels accompanying God.

What is the relationship between these two different nimshalim? Until now in this book, I have avoided using originality as a criterion in evaluating meshalim. Because the mashal is a form of traditional literature, I have argued that features shared by meshalim—motifs, diction, themes—stem from the common use by different authors of the same traditional conventions, not from one author's borrowing from another; it is incorrect to suppose that there once existed an "original" or Ur-mashal from which others developed or were later derived. But in the case of these two meshalim—Eikh. R. 3.24 and Dev. R. 2.34—one must have been borrowed from the other. The only difference between them is in their exegetical contexts, not their narratives. It therefore seems most likely that one application was original, the other derivative, since the details in the nimshal are almost always exegetically determined, not traditionally composed.

In fact, there is another possibility. Rather than being distinct compositions, the two meshalim may represent two tradents' or disciples' separate versions of a single mashal that they both inherited from a common teacher but that they remembered differently. In the case of Eikh. R. 3.24 we are explicitly told that R. Abbahu transmitted the mashal in the name of R. Yohanan Nappaha of Caesarea; revealingly, R. Isaac, the sage named in Dev. R. as that mashal's author, was also a disciple of R. Yohanan b. Nappaha. It is therefore possible that R. Isaac was repeating a parable he had heard, in one form or another, from his famous teacher.[34]

Even so, this explanation does not answer the deeper question: Which of the two *applications* or nimshalim of the parable was the "original" or the earlier one? Although we cannot settle this question definitively, it is possible to find in the larger tradition of the mashal some clues to an answer. As attested in the tradition, the key motifs in our mashal's narrative are nearly always applied to a specific divine revelation: if not to Sinai, then to another place where God revealed Himself to Israel. Consider the following Tannaitic mashal from the Mekhilta (Shirta 3, 11.32–39), one of the earliest attributed meshalim to use the motif of a king entering a foreign province surrounded by his royal company. The mashal appears in connection with the very beginning of the Song at the Sea that Moses sings to God after the Israelites cross the Reed Sea.

"This is my God and I will glorify Him" (Exod. 15:2).

R. Eliezer ben Hyrcanus says: From this verse you deduce that a maidservant saw at the sea what Isaiah and Ezekiel and all the prophets never saw? For about the latter prophets Scripture says: "And spoke parables through the prophets" (Hos. 12:11), and it is also written, "The heavens opened and I saw visions of God" (Ezek. 1:1).

They recited a mashal. What is this like? It is like a king of flesh-and-blood who entered a province surrounded by a circle of guards; his heroes stand to his right and to his left; his soldiers are before and behind him. And everyone asks, saying: Which one is the king? [Why?] Because he is a man of flesh-and-blood just like the others.

But (*aval*) when the Holy One, blessed be He, revealed Himself at the sea, no one had to ask: Which one is the king? As soon as they saw Him, they recognized Him, and all of them opened their mouths and said: "This is my God and I will glorify Him."

This mashal is recognizably part of the same tradition as our mashal, but like the version in Dev. R., it applies the narrative to an event of divine revelation. The same is true of cognate Amoraic meshalim.[35] From this evidence, it is fair to conclude that R. Isaac's version in Dev. R. is more likely the original application of the mashal, and that R. Abbahu reapplied the mashal to Lam. 3:24, in the process universalizing the earlier polemic against angel-worship into a more general attack upon idolatry and its gentile worshippers.

This conclusion is borne out by the historical background to the mashal's central motif describing the king as he enters a province surrounded by his royal company. This motif was not an invention of the Rabbis' imaginations. It derived from a sight that must have been familiar to them—the spectacle of the Roman emperor or of his plenipotentiaries as they made their grand tours of the provinces, accompanied and surrounded by vast retinues of assistants and bureaucrats. The imperial *adventus*, the emperor's grand entrance, was an elaborate ceremonial occasion that was also a highly significant political event for the local community being visited, particularly when the visitor was "an emperor whose legitimacy was not yet established or, as in the last days of Roman rule in the Near East, a foreign conqueror," as Sabine MacCormack has remarked.[36]

For the provincial subjects, these visits were notoriously expensive, but they promised tangible rewards for those who could make the initial investment. A man of ready wit who arranged a personal encounter with the emperor or a direct petition to him could find lucrative opportunities in the imperial visits. A provincial town, particularly if it was isolated or otherwise beleaguered, could gain from its generosity to the emperor the hope of greater security and protection in the future.[37] Indeed, the fourth-century bishop of Alexandria, Athanasius, used such well-known knowledge about the profits of imperial visits as the basis for what is in effect a king-parable of his own:

> As when a great king has entered any great city and dwelt in one of the houses in it, such a city is always esteemed worthy of much honour and no longer does any enemy or bandit come against it and attack it, but it is thought worthy of the greatest esteem because of the king who has taken up residence in one of its houses.
>
> So also is the case with the Saviour of us all. For because He has come to our realm and has dwelt in a body similar to ours, now every machination of the enemy against men has ceased and the corruption of death, which formerly had power over them, has been destroyed.[38]

As in our mashal, Athanasius speaks of the benefits to be derived from entertaining in one's home a member of the imperial retinue.

This historical background to the mashal also illuminates the meaning of the polemic in R. Isaac's version of the mashal in Dev. R. In that version, as well as elsewhere in Rabbinic literature, the angelic host surrounding God are depicted expressly in the image of the imperial court. The angels were members of God's *familia* (Hebrew: *pamiliyah*), freedmen in the celestial household, the divine retinue of servants, counselors, and ministers.[39] Given this fact, and given the power and influence that the imperial freedmen often possessed, one can easily understand why the angels would have been worshipped, and why the Rabbis would actively have polemicized against them.

This polemic is attested elsewhere in Rabbinic literature, and has been connected by recent scholars with polemics against Gnostic beliefs in "two powers in Heaven."[40] Indeed, it is not incidental that two of the main protagonists in the Rabbinic polemic against "two powers" are R. Yohanan b. Nappaha and R. Isaac.[41] For these Rabbis, the transgression involved in worshipping angels was not simple idolatry, the kind of transgression in worshipping the sun or the moon as gods; rather, the mere belief that the angels shared in God's power was considered heresy as well as idolatry. Although the Rabbis did not deny every belief in angelic mediation, they warned strongly against allowing those beliefs to grow into challenges against God's power, into the idea that an angel could usurp God's sovereignty and become a divinity in its own right.[42]

This is precisely the process of misattribution narrated in R. Isaac's mashal. The error involved in the misattribution is explicitly formulated by the *pikeiah* in the statement he makes at the end of the narrative when he explains his choice of the king: "For they will all pass away, but the king will never pass away." The origins of this expression are unknown. Partly resembling a folk saying,[43] it also echoes theological and political sentiments common in ancient classical literature. Depending on the context, its key word *mithaleif* can mean "pass away" or "perish," as I have translated it, but also "change," and "be changed" or "replaced," as well as "be exchanged" and "mistaken one for the other."[44] In theological terms, the expression would then mean that God alone is immutable and unchanging; the statement recalls common Neoplatonic, Gnostic, and early Christian descriptions of the perfect and true God as "imperishable" and "unbegotten."[45] As a statement with political implications, though, it may also be a sly nod in the direction of contemporary politics in the turbulent first half of the third century. Amid the period's unending palace revolts, imperial usurpations, and military and economic crises, the idea that any holder of political office would never "pass away" would have seemed dubious indeed; some emperors rose to power one day and were deposed the next. If read within this historical context, the *pikeiah*'s statement may be a shrewd piece of political advice as much as a theological truth.[46]

Whether it is a statement with theological overtones or with political ones, the idea best fits R. Isaac's application to the angels.[47] Indeed, when R. Abbahu generalized the polemic to make it into an attack against all idolatry, he seems not to have realized that the *pikeiah*'s statement was somewhat inappropriate to its new context. For one thing, in R. Abbahu's version, the mashal never fully denies the idol's substance and reality, which would have been the correct Rabbinic view; in fact, R. Abbahu's version of the mashal even implies that the idolatrous objects— the sun, the moon, the trees and stones—are all part of God's heavenly retinue!

These are, however, quibbles. The main point of the mashal's polemic—that God is unique and Israel's choice alone—is maintained even in R. Abbahu's version. The concluding citation in its nimshal of Deut. 6:4 is especially appropriate to this message, for by the early Rabbinic period this one verse had become the virtual liturgical credo for God's unity and singularity, the *shema'*. Indeed, more than being merely a credo, the *shema'* had also become for Jews a statement acknowledging faith in God that was powerfully associated with the act of martyrdom, with affirming one's belief in God even at pain of death.[48] No situation is more intrinsically polemical.

Eulogy and Consolation

Eulogy and consolation make up the two sides of lamentation: where one praises the dead, the other comforts the mourner. Both rhetorical modes typically take the form of praise—eulogy in its radical sense—though, on rare occasions, the expression of loss can be phrased as blame, as when the mashal accuses a person of having been the cause of a loss.

As I noted in Chapter 2, several Rabbinic texts describe sages who recited parables to comfort their colleagues after deaths in their families. Sometimes, these meshalim attempt to rationalize the death, to explain, almost apologetically, why the tragic loss of a young child or the premature decease of a righteous colleague should not offend their sense of God's justice. Within the literary context of midrash, however, the mourner whom lament-meshalim most often address is God, in mourning over the destruction of the Temple or the tragic fate of His chosen people Israel.[49] Indeed, it is sometimes God Himself who uses the literary form of the mashal to express His own sorrow. We have already seen one instance of this in the lengthy aggadic narrative from Petihta 24 analyzed at the conclusion of Chapter 2, in which God, mourning the Destruction, likens Himself to a father whose only son has died, on his wedding day, inside his bridal-chamber.

Although the Destruction was the paradigmatic catastrophe in classical Judaism, it was not the only occasion in which God or the Jewish nation collectively was thrown into mourning.[50] In the following passage from Tan. B. (Deut., p. 13), God again uses a lament-mashal, though now to describe to the archangel Metatron His grief at the death of Moses. The irony lying behind the passage is that it was God Himself who decreed that Moses must die at this time; nonetheless, *after* Moses' death, God feels so bereaved by the loss that He must explain His feelings to the angel:

> What is the matter like? It is like a king who had a son. Every day the father became angry at his son and wished to kill him, for the son did not honor his father. His mother, however, repeatedly saved the son from his father's hands. After some time, the son's mother died. The king wept. His servants asked him: Our master, O king, why do you weep? He told them: Not only for my wife am I weeping, but for my son as well. For I often became angry at him and wished to kill him. But she saved him from my hands.
>
> So, too, the Holy One, blessed be He, said to Metatron: Not only for Moses alone am I weeping, but for him *and* Israel. For many times they angered Me, and I became angry at them, and Moses stood interceding before me in order to turn back My anger from destroying them.

The mashal's narrative reenacts God's own predicament including, most surprisingly of all, the need He feels to explain His grief. It is this explanation—an implied interpretation, in effect—that serves as the medium for the eulogistic praise of Moses. That eulogy, however, serves the additional purpose of emphasizing the immensity of the loss God feels—and the inconsolability of His grief.

This rhetorical strategy—using praise of the dead to elicit sympathy for the mourner—is characteristic of many lament-meshalim in which God figures as chief mourner. Yet the very idea of God as mourner is a paradox of the largest order. The idea of a divinity mourning over his nation's unhappy fate is not, of course, unique to Rabbinic literature. Parallels exist in ancient Greek epic and tragedy, and the Rabbinic aggadot have many ancestors in ancient Near Eastern laments which describe in detail the pathos of city-gods over the destruction of their city-states.[51] Like the stricken deities in these laments, God is portrayed in the Rabbinic accounts as devastated by His nation's catastrophe, as identifying Himself with the loss almost to the point of solipsism.

These narratives all demonstrate the inevitability of anthropomorphic representation: in order to portray God's grief, the Rabbis had no recourse but to draw upon their own experience of loss. Given this necessity, it is not surprising that the Rabbis resorted to the mashal that naturally "doubles" God with a human king. But the full measure of paradox involved in this need to describe God's grief in the human image goes beyond mere anthropomorphism. In a famous passage in Eikh. R., commenting on Lam. 1:1 (pp. 42–43), we are told:

> R. Nahman said: The Holy One, blessed be He, asked the ministering angels: When a king of flesh-and-blood mourns, what is it customary for him to do? They said: He hangs sackcloth over his door. He said to them: I will do likewise, as it is said, "I clothe the skies in blackness, and make their raiment sackcloth" (Isa. 50:3). He again asked them: When a king mourns, what is it customary for him to do? They said: He extinguishes the lamps. He said to them: I will do likewise, as it is said, "Sun and moon are darkened, and stars withdraw their brightness" (Joel 4:15). He again asked them: When a king mourns, what is it customary for him to do? They said: He overturns his coach. He said to them: I will do likewise, as it is said, "Thrones were set in place, and the Ancient of Days took his seat" (Dan. 7:9). He again asked them: When a king mourns, what is it customary for him to do? They said: He walks barefoot. He said to them: I will do likewise, as it is written, "He travels in whirlwind and storm, and clouds are the dust on His feet" (Nahum 1:3). They also said to Him: He rends his purple robes. He said: I will do likewise, as it is said, "The Lord has done what He purposed, He carried out the Decree" (Lam. 2:17). They also said to Him: He sits in silence. He said: I will do likewise, as it is said, "Let him sit alone and be patient" (Lam. 3:28). They said to Him again: He sits and weeps. He said to them: I will do likewise, as it is said, "My Lord God of hosts summoned on that day to weeping and lamenting, to tonsuring and girding with sackcloth" (Isa. 22:12).[52]

This passage works out the analogy between God and the human king to its fullest possible realization. Not only does God wish to follow the model of the human king in the practices of mourning; but to do so, He must seek instruction from the angels in the correct procedures. The true irony behind this request lies in what it implies about God's innocence, His need for instruction. Without the angels, God is utterly at a loss, entirely ignorant of the protocols of mourning. This picture of God may strike us, perhaps, as rather whimsical, especially given our ideas about divine omniscience. Yet, in fact, how could God know how to mourn? He Himself is untouched by death. And if the Destruction was indeed the unprecedented catastrophe that the Rabbis believed it to be, God Himself must have been as unprepared for its devastation as were its human victims.

The real power of this passage lies not only in its depiction of God as a human-like mourner but in the ultimate reality it confers upon the human tragedy by making even God its mourner. In Rabbinic literature (or in the Bible) God never dismisses human suffering or loss as being merely mankind's lot. He never views human tragedy *sub specie eternitatis,* treating it as a cosmic triviality. In His hands, the lives of men and women are never playthings, toys. Rather than diminish human suffering, the Rabbis were more willing to have God descend to the human level—even at the price of appearing somewhat comic or grotesque—in order to establish the absolute seriousness of the horrible experience that His chosen nation had endured.[53]

The lament-meshalim in which God figures as chief mourner share this "serious realism." Inevitably, too, these parables involve a dimension of apologetic in addition to their main function as lament. For by showing that God actually participates with His nation in the sorrow of their tragedy, these meshalim actively negate the claim that in destroying the Temple God rejected Israel forever, and simultaneously, they console their audiences by asking them, representatives of Israel, to comfort God; indeed, not infrequently it is God Himself who directly insists upon and demands this comfort. He needs His creatures as much as they need Him. The single best example of all these features is in the three parables that together make up Petihta 2(2), and which I will analyze in detail in the next chapter. For the present section, I have selected another mashal, also found in a petihta, which illustrates the rhetoric of eulogy in a somewhat subtler fashion.

Petihta 25

> [The Shekhinah departed from the Temple in ten stages: . . . It
> went] from the platform of the House to the Cherubs, as it is
> written, "Then the Presence of the Lord left the platform of the
> House and stopped above the cherubs" (Ezek. 10:18). "Then
> [it] left . . ."! Scripture only had to say, "Then [it] came . . ." And
> yet you say, "Then [it] left . . ."! What does "Then [it] left . . ."
> mean?
> R. Aha said:
> It is like a king who departed from his palace in anger. But
> once he departed, he went back, and embraced and kissed the
> palace's walls and the palace's columns, and wept, saying:
> Farewell my palace, farewell my kingdom's home, farewell my
> precious house, farewell from now, farewell.
> Similarly, when the Shekhinah was departing from the Tem-
> ple, it went back, and embraced and kissed the Temple's walls
> and the Temple's columns, and it wept, saying: Farewell my
> Temple, farewell my kingdom's home, farewell my precious
> house, farewell from now, farewell.

The literary and exegetical contexts for this mashal require
some explanation. First, the term Shekhinah is the Rabbinic name
for God's immanent presence in the world, especially as He is
present amid the nation of Israel, and particularly in the Temple. This proem, Petihta 25, enumerates ten stages *(masa'ot)* that
the Shekhinah journeyed in the course of leaving the Temple at
the Destruction.[54] This theme of the *histalkut hashekhinah*, "the
departure of the Shekhinah," for which this passage is perhaps
the locus classicus, is among the most famous responses of the
Rabbis to the theological crisis provoked by the Destruction,
but its precise meaning was also the subject of debate among the
Rabbis.[55] According to some opinions, the Shekhinah went into
exile with the people of Israel, accompanying them throughout the Diaspora. According to others, the Shekhinah did not
actually accompany the Jews into exile but ascended from earth
to heaven to await the restoration of the Temple at the time of
the final redemption. Our mashal does not state which one of
these two views it follows, nor does it identify the Shekhinah's
destination, but the petihta as a whole appears to follow the first
view, at least from the evidence of another opinion preserved in
its discussion.[56]

The mashal's overall concern, however, lies less with the She-khinah's destination than with the pain, the hesitation, and the sheer difficulty it encountered in departing. All of this is suggested by the list of the ten stages. Explicitly based upon an exegesis of Ezek. 8–10, the list may be connected to other lists in Rabbinic literature relating to the Temple and its sanctity: the most famous of these is the list in M. Kelim 1.6–9 of the ten degrees of holiness, culminating in the holiness of the Holy of Holies, and the corresponding list of ten ascending degrees of impurity which pollute the Temple and its holy cult.[57] Whatever its precise origins, though, the list of ten stages and the idea behind it lend a heightened sense of ceremony to the Shekhinah's departure—the spectacle of a formal royal exit rather than of a panicked retreat.

Our mashal takes its occasion from a specific moment in that process of withdrawal which is connected to the exegesis of Ezek. 10:18. This verse, part of the prophet's awesome theophanic vision enacting the punishment of Jerusalem, is problematic on several counts.[58] In the first place, the verse is actually a continuation not of the verses immediately preceding it but of the narrative begun earlier in the chapter in verse 4. In that verse, we are first told that the Presence of the Lord—here identified with the Shekhinah[59]—moved from the cherubs to the platform. The prophet's vision thereupon digresses—first, with the mysterious command to the man dressed in linen to take fire from the cherubs, then with a lengthy description of the cherubs (7–17)—until finally, in 10:18, it resumes the account of the departure of the Lord's Presence from the platform so as to return, once again, to the cherubs. Hence the midrash's opening question: "What does '[It] left . . .' mean?" The verse should say, "The Lord's presence came."

In response, our mashal takes the verb "it left" figuratively, as an indication of the difficulty the Shekhinah had in leaving—as though it left, then returned, then left again, and so on, exactly in the manner of the regretful hesitant king described in the narrative. Although the king initially leaves in anger—why, we are never told—his love for the palace immediately stops him in his tracks, and he cannot leave without the repeated farewells, which thereupon become his medium for praising the very same palace he seems so intent upon leaving in his anger.

As a lament-mashal, this narrative is an almost pure example of praise-eulogy. Its most remarkable feature, though, is that it laments not a deceased person but a lost thing—the king's palace, the Temple; indeed, it is not just the idea of the Temple, but the Temple building, its walls, its columns, its sheer physical presence, that the king embraces and kisses and to which he finally bids his endless farewells just as he would to a beloved consort.[60] Although one effect of all this is to suggest that the king will eventually return to the palace—the phrase "farewell from now" may mean "for the time being"—its other result is to implicitly personify the building. The king's personification of the palace, like God's personification of the Temple, complements the mashal's personification of the Shekhinah and its grief. It is this personified God to which Israel also bids farewell "for now"—and He is a God like the king in the narrative who is unhappily caught between anger and love, between doing what He must and what He desires.

Complaint

Complaint is a specialized form of blame in which the mashal accuses a specific party of having acted unfairly or unjustly. What distinguishes the complaint from other types of blame-meshalim is that the figure, implied or real, to whom the complaint is addressed is also the subject of the complaint, the one being blamed. The reason this feature of the complaint is so noteworthy is that, in Rabbinic literature, this figure most commonly is God. He is both the complaint's addressee *and* its subject, and He is not only complained about but also asked to redress the injustice He has committed. These features are so characteristic of the complaint-mashal as a subgenre that it can virtually be defined as a parable in which blame is assigned to God.

The idea of addressing blame to God and contesting His justice may seem blasphemous. Yet "the quarrel with God" is a lengthy tradition in classical Jewish literature, whose history begins with the Book of Genesis.[61] Before Sodom and Gomorrah are destroyed, Abraham fearlessly challenges God, "Shall not the Judge of all the earth deal justly?" (Gen. 18:25)—clearly implying that God's planned course of action is unjust. Moses, too, questions God's actions, not quite as brazenly as Abraham, but also to persuade God to reconsider His decrees in the name of a higher justice. And in later times, classical prophets like Jeremiah share their ancestors' quarrelsome nature; these prophets appear frequently in the dual roles of Israel's defenders and their advocates in the face of divine adversity. The quarrel with God continues to inform such later biblical books as Job and Jonah, and it persists in subsequent Jewish literature. In Rabbinic tradition, it takes the specific form of the complaint.

With its deep roots in Jewish tradition, the complaint against God indicates neither lack of faith nor a feeling of improper disrespect; rather, the right to complain, to question the justice of God's actions, should be understood as a corollary to the covenantal ideal. Just as God has legitimate claims upon the people of Israel—obedience to His law, the right to punish the Israelites for their transgressions, absolute loyalty on their parts to His sovereignty, and so on—so too the Israelites hold legitimate claims upon God. These are, primarily, that He treat them with the justice they deserve or merit; that He be sensitive to their plight; and that, if He has been insensitive, His own justice can be appealed to in complaint (even though God Himself is the one responsible for the injustice). The existence of the complaint thus serves as an almost paradoxical guarantee of the covenantal bond.

This character of the complaint is typified in its language and diction, which is imbued with the frankness, even the intimacy, of the covenant. When Israel and God speak to each other in complaints, they speak as familiars, and this familiarity points to the closeness of the relationship between God and Israel, to its abiding solidity.

Not surprisingly, the mashal was one of the Rabbis' favorite literary modes for the expression of complaint. Some scholars have explained this phenomenon by suggesting that the mashal, with its oblique, concealing nature, offered a convenient disguise for the complaint's more scandalous aspects.[62] In fact, there is nothing hidden or obscure about most complaint-meshalim; if anything, their messages are too loud and clear. Rather, the probable reason the mashal was so frequently employed for the complaint was that its familiarizing, representational narratives about human behavior provided the best index of standards by which to measure God's deeds. The complaint-mashal inevitably shows how unjustly God has acted *even* in terms of human norms; and it is precisely God's shameless violations of those norms that gives the complaint its credibility.

The norms that God is most frequently portrayed as violating typically involve the unfair exercise of power, usually through the victimization of Israel. In my survey of the mashal's narrative poetics, I have already discussed these types of violations under the category of gaps. More than nearly any other subgenre of the mashal, the complaint exploits gapping and gap-filling as a rhetorical device, and in such a consistent way that it is generically recognizable. The same consistent poetics is true of the subgenre's other features. While complaint-meshalim are among the most powerful and memorable parables in all Rabbinic tradition, they also tend to be the most generically identifiable group.

This can be seen even in the way certain complaint-meshalim use traditional motifs. For example, two complaint-meshalim in Eikh. R.—1.21 and 3.1—begin by describing how a king became angry at his consort and banished her from the palace. This motif of banishment is a very common one in the mashal's tradition, from the Tannaitic period onward, and it almost invariably is used together with a companion motif describing how the king and consort are, in one way or another, reconciled in the end; typically, the motifs in combination appear in apologetic meshalim.[63] In the complaint-mashal, however, the motif of reconciliation is pointedly absent: indeed, it is precisely the motif's absence that generates the complaint. Other complaint-meshalim, or meshalim with aspects of complaint in them, analogously violate parallel modes of closure. This tendency is so prevalent that we can assume that a sophisticated audience familiar with the mashal's conventions would have recognized and felt these violations as part of the complaint-mashal's generic style.

The same is true of the complaint-mashal's exceptional techniques of characterization. The complaint's king is not just an all-powerful ruler; he is a tyrant singularly abusive in his exercise of power. Although the immediate model here is the Roman emperor (or one of his representatives), as usual, the complaint-mashal's king is especially tyrannical even for an emperor; he acts more like an oriental despot than a beneficent paterfamilias, as the Roman emperor liked to fancy himself. And next to the king, the other characters in the mashal are invariably powerless, helpless creatures.

Narratologically, one effect of this inequity between the characters is to focus the narrative upon the least powerful characters, usually the victims of the king's despotism; rhetorically, the focus turns the audience's sympathies toward these characters. The intensity of focus is often increased by the use of certain types of gaps in the narrative: the failure to motivate the king's behavior, to supply reasons for his sudden changes of mind or his abrupt decisions, or even to allow access to his state of mind. Finally, the last word in the narrative is almost always given to the victim, and that last word is often the explicit complaint itself. By making the complaint into the mashal's literal climax, the absence of a response from the king constitutes still another gap; this has the effect of further emphasizing the complaint, and gaining still more sympathy for the victim. A small consolation, perhaps, but still something—since the injustice about which he or she complains is rarely corrected in the narrative itself.

Complaint-meshalim address various subjects in midrash.[64] No event or deed, however, elicited more intense complaint than did the painful and formative experiences of the Jews from the time of the Destruction through the Bar Kokhba Rebellion and the Hadrianic persecutions. While the general thrust of the Rabbinic response to this extended historical ordeal was acceptance of its justice, as deserved punishment for Israel's transgressions, there remained an excess of suffering and pain that resisted the rhetoric of apologetic assuagement. The unprecedented severity of the punishment; the enemy's gratuitous cruelty to the victims; above all, the seemingly endless persistence of their horrible situation— all these agonies and humiliations, all of them condoned by a silent God if not directly instigated by Him—seemed to the Jews to exceed by far anything they had done to deserve them.[65]

The result is a sense of excessive, irreparable hurt expressed in a number of passages in Eikh. R.[66] Perhaps the most revealing of all these passages is a mashal that the Congregation of Israel recites before God about its own predicament. The mashal is recorded as part of a proem to Lam. 5:1, "Remember, O Lord, what has befallen us!" (p. 154):

> The Congregation of Israel said before the Holy One, blessed be He:
> Master of the universe! It is the usual case *(benohag sheba'olam)* that if a man owns two gladiators, the one stronger, the other weaker, he makes the stronger one submit to the weaker, so that the one will not arise and kill the other— because he, their owner, cares about his property.

And yet, You! You do not seem to care about Your nation.
You leave them among the nations . . .

This mashal inverts the normal structure of the *benohag
sheba'olam,* "it is the custom of the world," pattern. Typically, this
pattern draws a *positive* analogy between human behavior and
divine; here, the analogy is profoundly negative. Not only is God
implored to learn from a human model, but the model is a
gladiator-owner! On the other side of the analogy, the relationship between Israel and the nations of the world is figured in
almost Hobbesian terms as a contest among gladiators; and
though it may seem quaint to see Israel likened to a gladiator
(albeit not a very strong one), the point of the analogy is not at all
whimsical. In the ancient world, gladiators were notoriously
expensive to own; to maintain and support a company of gladiators required serious wealth, on account of which their owners
were understandably cautious and did not permit the gladiators
to kill one another needlessly.[67] There is, accordingly, nothing
fatuous about the mashal's closing remark that a gladiator-owner
is more protective of his property than God is of the children of
Israel.

This mashal registers a particularly angry and bitter note, but
the voice is typical of the genre. Complaint-meshalim express
their authors' feelings of having been betrayed by God. Exactly
what sort of betrayal is the subject of each particular mashal, but
the complaint against God they all share is one of the most complex and difficult themes that the mashal is used to communicate.
The two following examples illustrate this perfectly.

Eikhah Rabbah 3.1

"I am the man" (Lam. 3:1).
   R. Joshua b. Levi said:[68]
   The Community of Israel said before the Holy One, blessed
be He: I am that one, and I am accustomed to suffer whatever
You bring upon me.[69]
   It is like a consort at whom the king got angry, and whom
He banished from the palace. What did she do? She went and
covered her face [so as to humble herself],[70] and went behind a
column. When the king passed by, [S adds: he said to her: You
have acted impudently!], she said to him: My lord! O king! So

it is seemly for me [to do], and fine for me, and proper for me. For no woman would accept you except for me. The king said to her: That is not so. I disqualified all the women on account of you. She answered him: That is not so! They are the ones who did not accept you.

Similarly, the Community of Israel said before the Holy One, blessed be He: Master of the Universe! So it is proper for me. For no nation accepted Your Torah except for me. The Holy One, blessed be He, said: That is not so! I disqualified all the nations for your sake. Israel said to Him: That is not so! They are the ones who did not accept You. For what reason did You go to Mt. Seir? Was it not to offer the Torah to the children of Esau, and they did not accept it? And similarly to the desert of Paran? Was it not to offer the Torah to the children of Ishmael, and they did not accept it? Why did You go to the Ammonites and the Moabites? Was it not to offer the Torah to the children of Lot, and they did not accept it?

That is what is written: "He said: The Lord came from Sinai; He shone upon them from Seir; He appeared from Mount Paran, and approached from Ribeboth-kodesh (or: with holy myriads). Lightning (or: a fiery law) flashed at them from His right" (Deut. 33:2). In the beginning He took Himself to Esau at Mt. Seir, and said to them: Do you accept the Torah? They asked Him: What is written in it? He said to them: "You shall not kill" (Exod. 20:13). They said to Him: That is the blessing our father blessed us with—"Yet by your sword you shall live" (Gen. 27:40). We cannot live without it. And so they did not accept it.

He went to the desert of Paran, to the children of Ishmael, and asked them: Do you accept the Torah? They asked Him: What is written in it? He replied: "You shall not steal" (Exod. 20:15). They replied to Him: But that is our inheritance from our father—"His hand against everyone, and everyone's hand against him" (Gen. 16:12). We cannot live without it. And they did not accept it.

He went to the Ammonites and the Moabites, and said to them: Do you accept the Torah? They asked Him: What is written in it? He said to them: "You shall not commit adultery" (Exod. 20:14). They said to him: But the origins of all those men [i.e., our ancestors] is precisely from the category of such illegitimate offspring, as it is said, "Thus the two daughters of Lot came to be with child by their father" (Gen. 19:36). We cannot live without it. And they did not accept it.

He came to Israel, and said to them: Do you accept the

Torah? They said to Him: Yes, yes! "All that the Lord has said
we will faithfully do" (Exod. 24:7).[71]

After all this praise, Israel said: "I am the man that has seen
affliction" (Lam. 3:1).

In the Yalkut (Lam. 1:28), the conclusion of the nimshal is
recorded in the following, expanded form:

And how many more good deeds have I done for Your sake—I
sanctified Your name at the sea and sang a song for You; I
accepted Your Torah unlike all the other nations, and after all
this praise . . .

The narrative of this mashal is characteristic of the complaint.
Its structures resemble both Eikh. R. 1.21 (discussed in Chapter
2) and Eikh. R. 2.1C (analyzed next in this chapter).[72] In all three
parables, the king is angered by the other main character in the
narrative (either the consort or the king's subjects); he banishes
the character; but the character refuses to accept banishment and
instead complains about the treatment he or she has received.
This structure is typical of the complaint. The first two motifs are
both deeply traditional, while the third motif, which embodies the
complaint and is most closely determined by the nimshal, also violates the more expected motif of reconciliation.

Equally characteristic of the complaint subgenre are the
mashal's poetic and rhetorical strategies. These include frequent
use of gaps (particularly concerning the king's motivation: What
makes him so angry at the consort? Why does he punish her so
severely? Why is he angered by her continued presence?); and
focalization upon the consort, who is the victim in the narrative
and the real hero of the complaint. At the same time, the mashal
intentionally shifts the audience's sympathy toward the consort
(by giving her, among other things, the final statement in the
dialogue), and thus consolidates the legitimacy of her complaint.

Compositionally, rhetorically, and poetically, then, this mashal
is a virtually classic example of its subgenre. The mashal obtains
its unique features, however, from its exegetical application. The
mashal's scriptural occasion is a verse that furnished the Rabbis
with a rich opportunity for exegesis, and especially so in its opening declaration, "I am the man who has seen affliction." This
announcement posed several questions to the Rabbis. For one
thing, who is this "man," the *gever*? Why must he announce his

presence so boldly? And what special significance does this announcement hold by virtue of being placed at the very beginning of the first verse of Chapter 3 of Lamentations? Finally, as anyone who has read Lamentations knows, Zion, the Community of Israel, is personified in the first two chapters by the figure of the *almanah*, the forlorn widow. Why does she disappear after the second chapter? Why is her place taken by the male *gever*? The word *gever* itself, as the Rabbis would have felt, also happens to be an unusually intensive word for "man." To what does Scripture mean to call our attention by using this word?

The Rabbis did not provide answers to all these questions, but their multiple interpretations in Eikh. R. do suggest several possibilities for the identity of the *gever*—among others, that he is the prophet Jeremiah (according to tradition, the author of Lamentations), or the Community of Israel (which, we are told, identified its own tribulations with those of Job, the suffering Everyman, who once referred to himself as a *gever*—Job 34:7).[73] Our mashal takes off from a third interpretation of the meaning of *gever*: though this interpretation again identifies the speaker as the Community of Israel, it reads the word *gever* as *gibor*, "a hero," thus making the initial part of the verse mean "I am that hero"— namely, the one who accepted the Torah at Sinai even before he had heard the commandments, as explicated in the famous aggadah associated with Exod. 24:7.[74] The same exegesis continues with the second phrase in the verse, *raah 'oni*—in context, a clause modifying *hagever*, "who has seen affliction"—which it now reads as an imperative to God: "Behold my affliction" *(reei 'oni)*.

The precise meaning of this imperative is then unfolded in the mashal. As we learn by the nimshal's conclusion, the words *ani hagever, reei 'oni* in Lam. 3:1 are the substance of Israel's complaint to God. As the consort herself explains, her sufferings are manifestly unfair. Why? Because she was the only woman willing to marry the king. As translated in the nimshal, the latter claim directly refers to the famous aggadah about how God unsuccessfully offered the Torah to all the gentile nations before He finally found Israel, who alone was willing to accept it.

The history of this aggadah has been masterfully studied by Joseph Heinemann in a classic analysis tracing its evolution, its separate by-forms, and the history of its transmission.[75] As Heinemann has shown, the aggadah probably originated out of two distinct impulses or motivations. One was as an answer to the question, frequently asked in the ancient (particularly Hellenistic) world, Why did God give the Torah only to the small and insignificant nation of Israel, and not to all mankind? The answer offered by the aggadah is that God *did* offer the Torah to the gentile nations but they refused to accept it. This motive for the aggadah's origin was therefore a functional, probably apologetic one.[76] The other originating impulse was more strictly exegetical. Deut. 33:2, the aggadah's prooftext, is a famously enigmatic verse, and the aggadah offered an interpretation of its meaning by explaining through its narrative what God had been doing in Seir and Mt. Paran before He came "from Sinai"; as the aggadah tells us, He was there trying to persuade the Edomites (that is, the Romans) and the Ishmaelites (the Arabs) to accept the Torah.

We need not trace the precise path the aggadah followed from these two separate points of origin to appreciate how revisionist is the use to which the mashal in Eikh. R. 3.1 puts the aggadah.[77] As it appears in the nimshal, Israel invokes the aggadah not to defend God's wisdom in giving the Torah solely to Israel, but to prove its own worthiness and thus to buttress its protest against God's behavior. The aggadah becomes in the nimshal the very basis of Israel's complaint against God: the reason Israel claims *not* to deserve its punishment is precisely because it was the sole nation willing to accept God's Torah. Yet in order to make the aggadah serve this rhetorical function, R. Joshua had to reinterpret the legend's meaning in much the same way that he reinterprets the mashal's prooftext, Lam. 3:1; indeed, the virtual plasticity that the aggadah assumes in the sage's hands is not all that different from the nature of Scripture as it is handled by the Rabbis in midrash. In both Written and Oral Torah, meaning is dictated by rhetoric and ideology as much as by textual requirements. R. Joshua's contemporary audience would doubtless have appreciated his reinterpretation of the aggadah as much as they would have admired his midrashic virtuosity. Both are exegetical tours de force.

With this in mind, we can turn back to R. Joshua's interpretation of *ani hagever* in Lam. 3:1. While the opinion immediately preceding the mashal focuses on the noun *gever*, the burden of the mashal's interpretation rests more on the pronoun *ani*, "I."

This pronoun becomes the nub of the quarrel between the king and his consort. Although the two words *ani hagever* are never incorporated in full into the narrative, one can hear their echo in the angry dialogue between the king and the consort: "*Ani,* 'I,' was the one who first chose you!" "No, *I* was the one who chose you!" and so on. King and consort both claim to have initiated their relationship. Each one wishes to be its real *ani*—the I, the ego, as it were.

Their argument alludes as well to a significant theological debate in Rabbinic Judaism over the election of Israel, the meaning of the covenant, and the question of ultimate, or primary, authority in the covenantal relationship: Who initiated that relationship, God or Israel? And who is truly responsible for its continued existence?[78] As the mashal's original audience listened to the domestic squabble between the consort and the king, they surely were sensitive to its theological reverberations. And though the mashal itself never explicitly takes a position in the argument, it nonetheless supports Israel's claim implicitly—if only by locating a source for Israel's complaint in Lam. 3:1.

R. Joshua's interpretation of this verse is impressive for its subtlety. He does not alter the scriptural phrase in the least, nor does he reattribute the verse to a new speaker or even recontextualize it; rather, his interpretation derives simply from a new tone, a subtle recasting of intonation, that he gives to the two words, *ani hagever.* These words now assume a nuanced indignation, perhaps even a slight undertone of sarcasm: "And after I have shown such faith in You, O God, am I now the person who must bear all these tribulations of Yours!?"

The anger that R. Joshua thereby assigns to the scriptural phrase is not an invention of his own. Lamentations 3, the chapter that this verse begins, consists of three sections or movements.[79] In the first of these sections, verses 1–20, the gever describes his sufferings in gruesome and relentless detail; he relates how his torturer, God (whom the gever cannot even bring himself to name), has hunted him down, how he has trapped him like prey, and how he has physically subdued him. In verse 21, however, the gever abruptly changes the course of his monologue, embarking in the subsequent twenty verses upon an ambitious journey to discover the theological meaning of his painful ordeal; this movement concludes when he finally affirms God's justice and acknowledges his own sins. At this point (verse 41), the gever turns back to God, but now he reminds Him that although "we have transgressed and rebelled, You have not forgiven"; instead, the gever boldly tells God, You have only "slain without pity" (42–43). And in the subsequent verses, he goes on to complain further about God's silence and His failure to heed the gever's prayers for help.

R. Joshua's interpretation of *ani hagever* directly anticipates these verses. One might even say that R. Joshua's reading of the phrase helps to uncover a meaning that is latent in Lam. 3:1, in the chapter's opening phrase, but that in Scripture itself does not explicitly surface until the conclusion of the chapter, in the verses I have just mentioned when the gever openly complains on behalf of his nation that the sufferings they have endured deserve greater mercy from God. At this point, the rhetorical function of the mashal and its exegetical occasion coincide almost perfectly.

To restate this last point differently: If one looks at R. Joshua's interpretation of Lam. 3:1 strictly from a simplistic exegetical perspective, from the viewpoint of the "literal" meaning, the complaint that the sage finds in Lam. 3:1 may seem to take an outrageous exegetical liberty with the verse. But from the perspective of the mashal, its exegesis of Lam. 3:1 solely amplifies, makes explicit, a sense that is already present in Scripture—even if the reader discovers it only verses later. By seeing how the mashal's rhetorical message anticipates those later verses, one understands what the Rabbis may have meant when they described the mashal as an indispensable tool in revealing the secrets of Torah.

Eikhah Rabbah 2.1C

"He did not remember His Footstool" (Lam. 2:1) . . .[80]
R. Yudan said:
It is like a king who captured his enemies and slew them. The inhabitants of the province painted themselves[81] with the enemies' blood. One time they provoked the king and he banished them from the palace.[82] They said: The king does not remember in our favor (literally: for our sake) that blood—when we painted ourselves with the blood of his enemies.

Similarly, Israel said before the Holy One: You do not remember in our favor that blood which was in Egypt, as it is said, "They shall take some of the blood and put it on the two doorposts and the lintel . . ." (Exod. 12:7).

Formally and poetically, this mashal resembles the other complaint-meshalim I have discussed. Its basic rhetorical message—the subjects' complaint that the king has not remembered their past loyalty to him—is clear. What is less clear is the precise meaning of the "blood in Egypt" that the Israelites say the Holy One does not remember, and what is entirely puzzling, even bizarre, is the motif in the narrative relating how the provincial inhabitants painted themselves with the blood of the king's enemies, and how they later boasted of having done this.

At first glance, this motif would seem to be artificially derived from the mashal's exegetical base, specifically the word *hadom* in Lam. 2:1. In its plain sense a "footstool," the word *hadom* here is used as a figure for the Temple.[83] In this mashal, however, *hadom* is revocalized so as to read *hadam,* "the blood," and then that blood is identified as the ritual blood of the Passover sacrifice which the Israelites in Egypt were commanded to sprinkle on their doorposts and lintels on the night of the Exodus.[84]

In the biblical narrative, the presence of this blood on the Israelites' doorposts has an apotropaic power; it averts the plague of the first-born sons from their homes. In Rabbinic tradition, additional powers came to be attributed to this blood, the powers of *zekhut* (pl. *zekhuyot*) or ancestral merit, from which the people of Israel are said to have derived various benefits in the past—including the redemption from Egypt itself.[85] According to a famous passage in Mekhilta Pisha 5, commenting upon Exod. 12:6, the Israelites were required to purchase the Paschal lamb four days before its slaughtering on the fourteenth of Nisan precisely because they needed "religious duties to perform by which to merit redemption." Consequently,

> The Holy One, blessed be He, assigned them two duties, the duty of the Paschal sacrifice and the duty of circumcision, which they should perform so as to be worthy of redemption . . . For one cannot obtain rewards except for deeds.

The same tradition is elaborated and amplified in later midrashim: In PRE (chap. 29), for example, God Himself announces (according to R. Eleazar) that the *zekhuyot* of circumcision and of the Paschal sacrifice not only merited Israel's past deliverance from Egypt but will also merit the final redemption "at the end of the fourth kingdom." And other midrashic sources stipulate still more benefits that stemmed from the merits of "the two bloods."[86]

In several passages in Eikh. R., these merits play a role significantly different from their role in other Rabbinic sources. Typically, the *zekhuyot* afford *positive* benefits like the redemption from Egypt. In the mashal in Eikh. R. 2.1C, however, the merits of the Passover sacrifice (and, in another opinion in Eikh. R., of the blood of circumcision) are invoked *negatively:* as having *failed* to prevent what was, in effect, the eschatological opposite to the redemption—the destruction of the Temple and the exile Israel suffered in its aftermath. This is a virtually unique occurrence, to the best of my knowledge.[87]

This negative use of *zekhut* in Eikh. R. 2.1C is, of course, the substance of Israel's complaint against God: He "forgot" the blood's merit when He allowed the Temple to be destroyed. Yet this complaint is about more than just the mechanical failure of the *zekhuyot* to operate in Israel's behalf. Behind the exegeses of Exod. 12:7 there lies an additional allusion to an aggadic tradition that must be understood in order to appreciate the mashal, and specifically its blood-painting motif.

This aggadah originates from the fact that the Egyptians worshipped the lamb as a sacred animal. The Egyptian belief in the lamb's sacredness was well-known in the ancient world as a kind of religious curiosity; it was frequently commented upon by ancient authors, and it also did not escape the Rabbis' notice when they attempted to explain why the lamb, and not another animal, was expressly ordained by God for the Passover sacrifice *in Egypt.*[88] According to one Rabbinic tradition, the reason God commanded the Israelites to offer up the lamb was to test whether the Israelites had abandoned the idolatry of the Egyptians (to which they had succumbed in the course of their subjection); thereby they were meant to prove their undivided loyalty to God.[89] A related tradition, even more relevant to Eikh. R. 2.1C, carries this theme still further. According to this tradition, the reason the Jews were commanded to select their lambs *four* days before sacrificing them was to publicly show the Egyptians that they no longer stood in awe of their former masters' religious beliefs; indeed, the purpose here may even have been to provoke the Egyptians and taunt them by committing a sacrilege against their sacred animal.[90]

This interpretation of the commandment in Exod. 12:7—as an act intended to defy the Egyptians as well as to prove Israel's loyalty to God—is certainly the reason for its citation in the nimshal. The substance of the Israelites' complaint to God is not only that He failed to remember the merit of the Passover blood; their real complaint is that He did not remember the *danger* to which they exposed themselves in publicly defiling the Egyptians' religious taboos in order to prove their obedience to God. Instead of remembering their past loyalty and courage, He ruthlessly banished them from home at a mere provocation.

Yet the mashal may have an even more historically rooted meaning than this. The narrative relates that the provincial inhabitants showed their loyalty to the king by *painting* themselves with the blood of his enemies. This particular behavior, about which the provincials boast so proudly, may seem rather bizarre to us today, but such acts of atrocity were far from rare in the ancient world. Comparable if not more horrendous deeds of sacrilege, mutilation, and cannibalism are reported in classical sources with sufficient frequency as to make the actions described in the mashal appear perfectly credible in historical terms.[91] The particular motif of the subjects painting themselves with their enemies' blood may, however, have an even more specific historical source.

In the years 114–117 c.e., roughly forty years after the defeat in the Great War and about twenty years before the Bar Kokhba Rebellion, the Jewish communities in Egypt, Cyrene, and Cyprus all rebelled against Trajan, the Roman emperor. In Xiphilinus's epitome of Cassius Dio's *Roman History* (Bk. 68.32), the "barbaric" behavior of the Jews during these revolts is described as follows:

> Meanwhile the Jews in the region of Cyrene had put a certain Andreas at their head, and were destroying both the Romans and the Greeks. They would eat the flesh of their victims, make belts for themselves of their entrails, anoint themselves with their blood (*tō te haimati āleiphonto*) and wear their skins for clothing; many they sawed in two, from the head downwards; others they gave to wild beasts, and still others they forced to fight as gladiators. In all two hundred and twenty thousand persons perished. In Egypt, too, they perpetrated many similar outrages, and in Cyprus, under the leadership of a certain Artemion. There, also, two hundred and forty thousand perished . . .[92]

Xiphilinus explicitly tells us that one atrocity the Jews committed against the gentiles consisted of "anointing themselves with [the enemy's] blood," an atrocity nearly identical to the act of "painting themselves" described in the Eikh. R. 2.1C mashal. Although some modern scholars argue that Xiphilinus invented this and the other atrocities in the passage, or that he drew them from the arsenal of Alexandrian anti-Semitic literature, it is perfectly likely that Jews themselves would have heard of these reports, of the atrocities *attributed* to them and to their co-religionists, and it is not unlikely that they would have proudly accepted the reports and believed them.[93] Many Jews, inspired by zealotic nationalism and anti-Romanism, were deeply sympathetic to the causes of the rebellion. Furthermore, even if the rebellious Jews in Cyrene and Egypt did not really eat gentiles or make their skins into garments, their behavior was reportedly ferocious. Archaeological evidence suggests that the Jewish rebels desecrated pagan temples and images with special avidity.[94]

For understanding Eikh. R. 2.1C, it is no less significant that the atrocities described in Xiphilinus's account occurred in the locale of Egypt and northern Africa. After all, this is the same geographical area associated with the mashal's exegesis, which also has an Egyptian locale. We need not read the mashal's narrative as a contemporary political allegory in order to entertain the possibility that R. Yudan may have identified the acts of the rebellious Jews in Egypt and Cyrene with the legendary deeds of the Jews' biblical ancestors. By their acts of defiance, both groups of Jews protested their political-religious subjugation, and both times, the rebels deliberately provoked violence. R. Yudan may even have conflated the report of the behavior of the rebellious Jews in Cyrene and Egypt with the aggadah connected to Exod. 12:7 (about smearing the blood on the doorposts to taunt the Egyptians), and thus used the (more or less) historically contemporary events as material for the fictional narrative in the mashal.

If read this way, the complaint of the inhabitants of the province (that is, the Jews) to their king (God) might be paraphrased as follows:

> To prove our loyalty to You, O God, we rebelled against the Romans in Egypt. We even painted ourselves with their blood (just as You commanded us in Exodus to sacrilegiously paint the lintels of our houses with the blood of the Egyptians' holy

animals). Yet You still have refused to remember our acts of loyalty! And instead, You have punished us and exiled us unjustly!

If the background to Eikh. R. 2.1C does lie in these North African rebellions, then the complaint in R. Yudan's mashal possesses a very contemporary meaning. Not only did God overlook the various *zekhuyot* accrued in the biblical past. He did not even remember that, nearly in the Rabbis' own time, the Jews had publicly declared their loyalty to God when they dared to rebel against the Romans and to outrage the bodies of their enemy as a show of their faith. More than nearly any other mashal, Eikh. R. 2.1C offers us a window with a direct view into the Rabbinic imagination.

Regret and Warning

Mashals of regret and warning share the feature of being conflicted, as it were, about their messages. A regret-mashal typically represents its protagonist as doing or saying something, and then reconsidering it. A mashal of warning, in contrast, implicitly expresses a wish not to have to act upon its own message; it says, in effect, "If you do this or that, then I will have to punish you in such a way; therefore please do not do it." In either case, the mashal's overall message is radically qualified: praise, but with hesitation or second thoughts; blame, but with qualms, and a longing for what might have been a happier resolution under different circumstances.

Eikh. R. does not record any warning-meshalim, but many examples exist in other Rabbinic sources. The following mashal is from Sifre Deut. 48 (= ARN A, chap. 24), and occurs in the course of a passage about the importance of "guarding" one's learning—that is, repeating and remembering the words of Torah one has been taught.

R. Ishmael said:
"But take utmost care and watch yourself *(nafshekha)* scrupulously" (Deut. 4:9). A mashal:
It is like a king who trapped a bird and handed it to his servant. He said to him: Take great care with this bird which is my son's. For if you lose it, do not think that you have merely lost a bird worth a penny. But it will be as though you have lost your own self.

Although this mashal lacks a formal nimshal, its overall message of warning can be deduced from the surrounding literary context: one must be very careful to preserve what one has learned even if it seems insignificant.

But the mashal's warning goes beyond this simple admonition to diligence. The narrative actually revolves around a pun on the two senses of the word *nefesh* (the noun in *nafshekha*) in Deut. 4:9. In biblical Hebrew, *nefesh* refers to a "person" or "self"; by the Rabbinic period, however, the word had come primarily to designate the soul of a person (as opposed to the body), which here is identified as the seat of learning and wisdom.

R. Ishmael's message of warning in the mashal plays upon these two senses through the image of the bird. On the most obvious level, the king warns the servant to take great care of the bird because its real value is greater than what it appears to be ("a penny"); if the servant loses the bird, the king warns him, it will be *as if* the servant has lost his own self. But this warning is itself ambiguous, for it can mean two things: either that the servant should watch the bird as carefully as he would guard his own soul; or that if the servant loses the bird, he will actually lose his soul—be executed, in other words. This ambiguity is enhanced by the fact that the bird is a conventional symbol for the *nefesh*, the soul. Thus, when the king warns the servant about losing the bird, he may also be understood as telling him that he, the servant, will perish spiritually—indeed, that he will "lose" his soul—if he loses the bird. Losing one's life therefore means perishing spiritually in this world or the next. It is this eventuality against which the mashal truly warns.[95]

In contrast to warning, regret is a rhetorical function for which the mashal is employed much less frequently in Rabbinic literature. One of the more remarkable examples of the function is an anonymous mashal that appears twice in Ber. R. (5.1, in reference to Gen. 1:9; 28.2, in reference to Gen. 6:7), as well as in Eikh. R. where it is quoted within a problematic passage commenting on Lam. 1:16.[96] In both passages in Ber. R., the mashal is preceded by the following opinion:

> R. Abba b. Kahana said in the name of R. Levi: It is written, "And God said, Let the waters be gathered (*yikavvu*)" (Gen. 1:9). [This means] the Holy One, blessed be He, said: Let the waters await me (*yikavvu li*) for what I will do with them in the future.

It is like a king who built a palace, and placed in it residents who were mutes. They used to arise and salute the king—by [pointing their] fingers, by [making] gestures, and by [waving their] handkerchiefs.[97] The king said: Now if these people who are mutes salute me with their fingers, with gestures, and with handkerchiefs, how much more [lavishly] would normal people [salute me]! The king settled normal residents [in the palace], but they rebelled and seized it, saying: This is not the king's palace, it is our palace! The king said: Let the palace return to what it was.

So, at the beginning of the creation of the world, the praise of the Holy One, blessed be He, ascended only from the waters; this is what is written: "From the voices of many waters" (Ps. 93:4). And what did they say? "The Lord is majestic on high" (Ps. 93:4). The Holy One, blessed be He, said: Now if these waters that possess no mouth or power of speech praise Me so, how much more [will I be praised] after I create mankind! But the generation of Enosh arose and rebelled against Him, the generation of the Flood arose and rebelled against Him. At that point, the Holy One, blessed be He, said: Remove them, and let the waters return. That is: "The rain fell on the earth forty days and forty nights" (Gen. 7:12).

The thrust of the mashal is clear: the creation of mankind is represented in the narrative as the result of the king's vanity, his desire to be praised ever more lavishly; and as the narrative proceeds, we see how the king learns the hard way to regret his vain desire. So, too, we are meant to understand that God, after creating mankind, wished that He had been satisfied with the praise the primordial waters originally paid Him. Indeed, we are told that, at the very beginning of Creation, God foresaw the need He would have of those waters at the time of the Flood, but He apparently did not foresee the disappointment that lay ahead of Him when He created man. The creation of mankind was an act of bad judgment on God's part—so the mashal suggests.

To be sure, this mashal resists a fully satisfying analysis; I suspect that its rather enigmatic narrative (why, after all, should a king ever place mutes in a palace to salute him with handkerchiefs?) alludes to some historical reality that has unfortunately been lost to us.[98] But the mashal is nonetheless memorable for its highly anthropomorphized portrait of God as a vain, somewhat fumbling and unlucky king whose eventual expression of regret at his vanity is, perhaps, his most sympathetic feature. To express this message, the narrative utilizes a simple rhetorical strategy. It focuses upon the character of the king, who, in response to a crisis in the narrative, almost unwittingly states his longing for time past, before his own actions brought about the crisis he now faces.

The notion of divine regret was not an invention of the Rabbis. The Bible relates that the Lord, after seeing how great was man's wickedness on earth, "regretted that He had made man on earth . . ." (Gen. 6:6), and in their exegetical comments on this verse, the Rabbis elaborated upon its characterization of God's feelings.[99] As an instance of anthropomorphization, the representation of divine regret in the mashal parallels the portrayal of God in mourning. In the mashal I will presently analyze, as in the lament-meshalim, we will again see how little the Rabbis were troubled by the anthropomorphization of God so long as it enabled them to express their feelings about His treatment of Israel. However theologically paradoxical these representational strategies may seem to us, they serve the ultimate purpose of familiarizing God: of making Him share the same doubts and conflicts as His chosen people.

Eikhah Rabbah 3.20

"When I thought of them I was bowed low" (Lam. 3:20).

R. Hiyya taught:

It is like a king who went to Hammat-Gader [S: to war][100] and took his sons with him. One time they angered him and he swore that he would no longer take them with him. But when he remembered them, he used to weep and say: I wish my sons were with me even though they anger me!

Similarly: "Oh, to be in the desert, at an encampment for wayfarers!" (Jer. 9:1). The Holy One, blessed be He, said: I wish my sons were with Me as they were in the wilderness even though they complain against Me. And similar to that: "O mortal, when the House of Israel dwelt on their own soil, they defiled it . . ." (Ezek. 36:17). The Holy One, blessed be He, said: I wish my sons were with Me in the land of Israel even though they defile it.

This unusual mashal combines blame with regret. The emphasis, however, clearly falls on the latter feeling, especially as the mashal adumbrates the king's feelings in the openly artificial exegeses of the nimshal. The two verses from Jeremiah and Ezekiel are understood by R. Hiyya as identically voicing God's sorrow over His separation from Israel. Both verses, in their plain contextual senses, are (direct or indirect) condemnations of Israel; as R. Hiyya interprets them, though, they become statements of divine regret. Thus, the first half of Jer. 9:1—the sole part of the verse that R. Hiyya interprets—is taken in a concessive sense, so that the final phrase in the verse, *melon orhim,* "an encampment for wayfarers," is reread as meaning in effect, "that place where their custom *(orhat)* was to complain *(malin)* against me"; "that place" in turn is identified, on the basis of the word *bamidbar,* with the Sinai wilderness *(midbar sinai)* where Israel complained against God ten times. The key to this interpretation is the opening phrase in the verse, *mi yitneini,* literally "who might place me [in the desert, etc.]," which R. Hiyya understands, in a kind of phonetic pun, as *mi yitein banai 'imi,* "who might set my children with me"—as once we were together in the Sinai wilderness.

Similarly, Ezek. 36:17's plain sense—a prophecy of Israel's doom—is reversed by R. Hiyya into a concessive statement of divine regret. In reading the verse this way, the sage may have meant to exploit the apparent switch in tense in the verse from the present participial *(hayoshvim)* to the future tense *(vayetamu).* As in his exegesis of Jer. 9:1, R. Hiyya ignores the continuation of the verse (in which Israel in exile is likened to a menstruating woman who must be separated from her husband for reasons of ritual impurity); taking the phrase out of context, he makes it express God's desire to be reunited with Israel in their homeland *despite* the fact that they have polluted it.[101]

R. Hiyya thus interprets both verses as expressions of God's disappointment with history. Simultaneously nostalgic and anxious, the verses express His regret over the unhappy turn His relationship with Israel has taken, and His longing for an idealized past, either in the desert or in the land of Israel, when He and Israel dwelled together in peace. These feelings about Israel are, in turn, understood by R. Hiyya as the references of Lam. 3:20, "When I thought of them, I was bowed low." This verse is now interpreted by R. Hiyya to mean: "When I, God, thought of Israel, my absent nation, I was bowed low with regret and disappointment and longing for their presence."

This reading is, of course, a wholesale departure from the verse's contextual meaning. In Scripture, Lam. 3:20 is spoken not by God but by the gever, the anonymous victimized man who is the chapter's speaker and its protagonist; the verse comes at the very conclusion of the gever's relentless account of the harrowing ordeal he has undergone at the hands of his pitiless victimizer, God. In context, Lam. 3:20 is an expression of the gever's despair, his utter hopelessness: the mere thought of his past misery overwhelms him with depression. R. Hiyya does not really change the verse's substance; he simply—radically—changes its subject, from the gever to God.

In doing this, R. Hiyya was not impelled by any outright textual or semantic problems in the verse, but solely by what we may call interpretive will: the desire to reattribute the verse to God in order to compel Him to express regret over His treatment of Israel. Other interpretations in the midrash take the verse differently, as a plea Israel addresses to God: "Please remember me, because I am so terribly bowed low by suffering."[102] But there can be no question about R. Hiyya's intention in making God the verse's speaker. By joining Lam. 3:20 with Jer. 9:1 and Ezek. 36:17, the mashal's author simultaneously decontextualized the prooftext and placed it in a new literary context consisting of other verses that in their interpreted senses also express the same divine regret. By doing this, R. Hiyya showed that Lam. 3:20 was not a unique or anomalous verse. To the contrary: the three verses that he brings together comprise what is, in effect, a testimony-list to divine regret.[103]

Revealingly, each verse in this list refers to a different stage in the history of God's relationship with Israel: Jer. 9:1 alludes to the period of Israel's wanderings through the wilderness on their way to Canaan; Ezek. 36:17 speaks of the period when Israel dwelt in their homeland; while Lam. 3:20 is spoken either in the course of, or in anticipation of, its exile from that land. As a group, then, the three verses effectively span Israel's entire history, from the period of the desert-wanderings until the exile. And yet, as God confesses regretfully, He would willingly tolerate Israel's sinning if He could return to any of these earlier moments in the covenantal history—if only He could.

The brunt of the narrative falls upon its characterization of the king, which, spare as it is, successfully climaxes in his one-line confession of regret (and is later extensively elaborated in the nimshal). This remarkable confession undoubtedly carries apologetic implications as well. Far from having abandoned Israel, God is now shown not only to regret the ruin of His people; even more astoundingly, He expresses His willingness to live with them despite their habitually sinful nature. The mashal does not deny the fact that Israel sinned or that God punished His nation (by no longer allowing them to accompany him to war).[104] Yet this apologetic dimension of the mashal is subordinated to the portrayal of God's regret. His conflicted feelings, His longing for the people of Israel in their absence, His regret over the course history has taken—all these offer sufficient consolation. With this mashal, one begins to understand how the various functional rhetorical-thematic categories overlap and coincide—not because the categories are inadequate but because a good mashal, like any true fictional artifact, is more complex than a theoretical category will ever allow.

5

The Mashal in Context

The Problem of Context in Midrash

Unlike the fables of Aesop, which early on were collected into anthologies, or the New Testament parables, which were incorporated into the gospel narratives as part of the life and teachings of Jesus, the meshalim of the Rabbis are preserved solely in the larger documents of Rabbinic literature, in the Talmud and various midrashic collections. In these works, particularly in the midrashic collections, meshalim are recorded indiscriminately along with the rest of the content, sometimes as isolated comments, at other times as units in more ambitious, elaborately orchestrated discussions. Some verses have a mashal, others two or three, and most none—but for no discernible logic or reason.

In their seemingly haphazard positions in these collections, the meshalim are no different from the rest of the contents. The structure and composition of these documents are famously difficult to identify. Despite a few recent attempts to demonstrate the "integrity"—the formal and thematic coherence—of the various midrashic collections, they remain to all appearances more like anthologies of traditional Rabbinic interpretations that an anonymous editor selected and recorded than like self-contained, logically structured books in their own right.[1] Consisting of running commentaries on Scripture—either on entire books or on selected passages from the Bible that were read on holidays and special Sabbaths—the exegetical opinions and traditions in the various collections are organized according to the order of the verses they comment upon, but with hardly any other discernible principle of organization. The midrashic collections give the impression of being at best semi-edited transcripts of the academic and casual conversations held by sages over countless generations.

Opinions are juxtaposed for no obvious reason; traditions contradict one another; and the same comments are sometimes repeated two or three times on different verses.

To be sure, it is possible to observe occasional redactional efforts at structuring their contents into sections with formal beginnings and (more commonly) endings.[2] Some collections, like Eikh. R., contain units of narrative material that may once have formed small story collections before they were absorbed *en bloc* into the anthologies.[3] *Petihtaot,* midrashic proems, are sometimes organized into mini-anthologies; in Eikh. R., there is a group of thirty-six petihtaot to the first verse of Lamentations. But these units are exceptional. For example, Eikh. R. is divided into five chapters, each of which corresponds to one of the five chapters in Lamentations; but these chapters are purely artificial divisions in the collection. None has a formal beginning or end, nor does the collection in its entirety. In fact, the two separate recensions of Eikh. R. that have come down to us organize their opinions in chapters somewhat differently, but without major consequence.[4]

Within collections, it is of course possible on occasion to discern thematic unities between different opinions; some of these thematic connections are inevitable, others may be more programmatic, the results of exegetical "schools" or specific ideological tendencies. These thematic unities are perhaps more pronounced in Eikh. R. than in other midrashic collections, if only because the Rabbis used the study and interpretation of Lamentations as the primary medium through which they responded to the destruction of the Second Temple and to the catastrophes that followed in its aftermath.[5] But these unities are not reliable keys to the midrashic collection's identity as a literary document, and not even to the meaning of a problematic passage, since what appears to be the context for a particular statement may in fact be entirely unrelated to it. In selecting the passages for his anthology, the anonymous editor(s) of Eikh. R. primarily used exegetical, not thematic, criteria.

As a result of all these factors, the "contextual" interpretation of midrash—reading a midrashic passage in its literary, documentary context—is a very problematic venture. The larger literary units that we most comfortably use in reading and interpreting the meaning of literary works—the document as a whole, chapters, even subsections in chapters, or discrete narrative or legal sections in a work like the Bible—do not constitute significant units of meaning for midrash. Just as midrashic exegesis tends to be, in James Kugel's felicitous phrase, "verso-centric"—that is, oriented to interpreting the meaning of verses (or parts of verses) in isolation from their larger contexts *in situ*—so, too, midrash itself needs to be read in its native literary and rhetorical units, even though the units are by definition more fragmentary, miscellaneous, and atomistic in makeup.

These units include the mashal, the petihta, the enumeration, the aggadic narrative, the homily, even the exegetical miscellany. The majority of meshalim from Eikh. R. that I have analyzed thus far are recorded in the collection as independent units commenting upon their prooftexts; in some cases, the mashal is one of several literary units offering an interpretation for a verse's meaning, but even in these cases, the separate units together tend to compose simple exegetical miscellanies with no significant superstructure. There are, however, several meshalim in Eikh. R. that are embedded and preserved in more complex contexts, where they are joined with other literary-rhetorical structures and forms, or are presented as episodic parts of lengthier passages. These meshalim offer us an opportunity to investigate the problem of context in midrash: to see how a typical literary-rhetorical unit like the mashal relates to other typical units, and to consider the generic and hermeneutic questions that arise from these combinations. These questions relate directly to the definition of midrash. By situating the mashal within the larger order of midrash, we will be able to understand the meaning of midrash itself as discourse.

The Mashal and the Homily

A homily is a brief passage whose express purpose is the teaching of a lesson or law; in itself, the teaching is usually not strictly exegetical, but the homily often enlists exegeses to prove its point. Homilies of this kind are ubiquitous in Rabbinic literature. Some preserve lessons that were probably once actually delivered; others are editorial constructs, intended perhaps to serve as aids for preachers in need of material for their own sermons. The following brief homily in Eikh. R. 3.8, a comment on Lam. 3:8, consists of two meshalim.[6]

"And when I cry and plead, He shuts out my prayer" (Lam. 3:8).

R. Aha and the Rabbis [offer interpretations].

R. Aha said: Whoever prays in a congregation—what is it like?

It is like men who made a crown for the king. A certain poor man came and gave a contribution. What does the king say? On account of this poor man, shall I not accept it?! [No!] The king accepts it immediately and places it on his head.

Similarly: If ten righteous men were standing in prayer, and a wicked man stood among them, what does the Holy One, blessed be He, say? Because of this wicked man, shall I not accept their prayers?

The Rabbis say: If a person comes [to pray] after the congregation [has completed the prayer-service], his actions are scrutinized in detail.

What is this like? It is like a king whose tenants and household members gathered to honor him. One man came last. The king said: Let his wine bottle be shut up.[7] And what caused this? The fact that he came last.

Similarly, whoever prays after the congregation, his actions are scrutinized. Therefore it is written, "And when I cry and plead, He shuts out *(satam)* my prayer." It is written *s-t-m* [with the letter *sin*, which can also be read as *shin*] because the congregation has completed *(shetamu)* their prayers.

The two meshalim in the passage complement each other nicely on both the thematic and the formal levels. Although their respective narratives actually derive from separate compositional and rhetorical traditions—R. Aha's is a praise-mashal drawing upon the motif of the royal subjects who make a crown for the king, while the Rabbis' mashal, a blame-parable, derives from a tradition based upon the historical institution of *salutatio*, the honorific greeting paid to the emperor by his subjects[8]—both meshalim are about honoring the king. Similarly, their rhetorical messages both emphasize, albeit from separate directions, the importance of participation in *tefillah betsibur*, communal prayer as recited in a *minyan*, a quorum of ten adult males. R. Aha's mashal stresses the efficacy of communal prayer, particularly for a person whose own character does not make him or his prayers worthy of being heard by God. The Rabbis' mashal teaches the importance of prompt attendance at communal worship, presumably in synagogue, with the implication that the person who is habitually tardy will be found out to be wicked and accordingly punished.

Both these messages are commendable, albeit unexceptional. The particular novelty of the passage as a whole, and of the two meshalim in particular, lies in the exegetical connection to Lam. 3:8—a connection that is, to say the least, artful if not artificial. R. Aha's mashal lacks any scriptural prooftext or exegetical connection whatsoever, a fact that has troubled at least one classical commentator, although the phenomenon is not entirely unusual when multiple meshalim are found in extended passages.[9] The Rabbis' opinion, in turn, is based upon a punning exegesis of Lam. 3:8 and its key word *sin-t-m*. In its scriptural context, this word appears to be simply an orthographic variant to *samekh-t-m*, "to close off" or "shut out." Nonetheless, its orthography here is unique, a fact that the Rabbis doubly exploited—first, by having the word appear in the mashal's narrative in the king's angry command to his attendants to have the latecomer's wine bottle shut up *(tisateim havito);* second, in the nimshal, by repointing the word and reading it as *shetam[u],* "that was completed," making the verse mean, in effect: "Even though *(gam)* I cry and plead, [my prayers are not heard] because [the congregation's] prayers have been completed."

This exegesis is so self-consciously clever it probably would not have passed muster if its purpose, its ideological intent, were not so halakhically correct; indeed, one classical commentator appears to have been so impressed by its judicial authority that he treated the fictional narratives in the two meshalim as actual legal precedents.[10] The meshalim's striking halakhic character only reminds us, however, of their utter lack of connection to the larger themes that dominate Eikh. R.—the response to the Destruction, the existence of Israel in a state of spiritual exile, and so on. This lack of connection is so outstanding that were Lam. 3:8 not explicitly cited in the nimshal to the Rabbis' mashal, it is doubtful that anyone would ever situate the passage in Eikh. R.

My reason for pointing this out is not to question the passage's place in the midrashic collection. Rather, the fact that this passage was preserved in Eikh. R. shows that verses from Lamentations were interpreted for homiletical or ideological points entirely unconnected to the Destruction, and that the editor of Eikh. R.

used exegetical criteria, rather than thematic considerations, as his standard in deciding what to include in the collection. Although we will never know the real origins of these meshalim, it is perfectly likely that they originated in a Sabbath-morning sermon urging punctuality—a theme that preachers doubtless found pertinent in the third century just as Rabbis do today.

But are the two meshalim and their homiletical messages entirely unconnected to themes relating to the Destruction? My reason for raising this question a second time is another exegesis for Lam. 3:8 that is recorded in a famous passage in B. Berakhot 32b. The opinion is offered in the name of R. Eleazar b. Pedat (the author of the mashal on Lam. 4:11 analyzed in Chapter 1).

> R. Eleazar said: From the day the Temple was destroyed, the gates of prayer have been locked, as it is said, "And when I cry and plead, He shuts out my prayer" (Lam. 3:8). But even if the gates of prayer are locked, the gates of tears are not locked, as it is said, "Hear my prayer, O Lord; give ear to my cry, do not disregard my tears" (Ps. 39:13).

Scholars have disputed the precise import of R. Eleazar's statement in this passage. Some have understood him as denying altogether the efficacy of prayer after the Destruction—a very pessimistic observation indeed.[11] Others have proposed, rather more optimistically, that R. Eleazar's initial interpretation of Lam. 3:8 is to be understood as it is qualified by his second exegesis of Ps. 39:13; according to this view, the passage in its entirety asserts that prayer remains effective after the Destruction, but only if it is "like tears"—that is, heartrending and genuinely remorseful.[12]

Even the latter view implies, however, that the verse Lam. 3:8, if read in isolation, could be understood as meaning that after the Destruction God ceased to listen to the prayers of Jews. This possibility, that God could actually shut out Israel's prayers, must have seemed especially threatening to Jews in the post-destruction era. Did not God appear to have acquiesced in shutting out Israel's sacrifices? And if sacrifices, why not prayers? R. Eleazar's exegesis of Lam. 3:8, though radical, was not a historical impossibility. In fact, verses similar to Lam. 3:8—Isa. 1:15, for example—were exploited by early Church Fathers to prove that God had rejected the prayers of Jews.[13] Nor was R. Eleazar the only Rabbinic sage to voice such a despairing opinion. In B. Berakhot 8a,

R. Aha, the author of the first of these two meshalim, is himself reported to have said that when men pray in groups God does not despise their prayers—suggesting that when they pray alone, He does.

R. Aha's statement in Berakhot is consistent with the message of his mashal here. If his mashal and the Rabbis' are now viewed against the background I have just sketched, their strictly halakhic messages take on a radically different coloring. According to R. Aha, *tefillah betsibur* will profit even the wicked man, while the Rabbis' exegesis of Lam. 3:8 now can be heard as an affirmation of the importance of communal prayer for maintaining God's attentiveness to Israel's prayers—even after the Destruction. Revealingly, neither mashal explicitly denies the *sentiment* behind R. Eleazar's almost literal interpretation of Lam. 3:8: the fear that God no longer hears prayer. Instead, the meshalim defuse the more volatile aspects of this reading of the verse by shifting its force onto the prayers of an individual who does not participate as he should in the Rabbinic institution of communal prayer. In this way, the homily accomplishes two purposes at once. The verse's "unacceptable" plain sense is countered, while the threatening occasion is in turn transformed into a positive opportunity for sermonizing about the great benefits to be derived from a distinctly Rabbinic institution. This is only one place in Eikh. R. that uses a two-pronged apologetic strategy of this sort—wherein a negative moment of scriptural exegesis is deflected by being transformed into a positive occasion for homily—in connection with prayer and repentance.[14]

Read this way, the homily on Lam. 3:8 with its two meshalim turns out to be far more relevant to the overall thematic concerns of Eikh. R. It would be a mistake, however, to see the passage's inclusion in Eikh. R. as necessarily a result of this reading. If these meshalim are "primarily" about any one thing, it is the importance of participating in communal prayer, not the efficacy of prayer in the aftermath of the Destruction. But by looking at the meshalim from the perspective of the Rabbinic response to the Destruction, we see them in a sharper light—and understand how a seemingly strictly halakhic homily might actually be part of a larger ideological program, and serve two masters at once.

The Mashal and the Petihta

As its name suggests, the *petihta* or midrashic proem is an introductory sermon. Probably the single most characteristic literary form in all Amoraic midrash, the petihta may have originated, as Joseph Heinemann suggested, in a short sermon that was delivered in the synagogue immediately before the weekly reading of the Torah.[15] This *Sitz im leben* for the form would explain its distinct structure, which, as Heinemann remarked, is nearly the opposite of that of most other midrashic literary forms: instead of beginning with its prooftext, the petihta concludes with it. While the prooftext is typically the initial verse in the weekly Torah reading, the verse with which the petihta itself begins is usually one taken from another book in Scripture, and it is chosen for its apparent lack of connection to the concluding prooftext. This "opening" verse is explicated and interpreted in the petihta, phrase by phrase, opinion by opinion, until the preacher has constructed an exegetical bridge culminating in the final prooftext. The formal structure of the petihta is equivalent to a journey from the one verse to the other.

Heinemann's hypothesis regarding the petihta's origins offers a compelling rationale for its unusual shape. It is more doubtful, though, if the petihtaot preserved in the existing midrashic collections were once actually delivered in synagogue services, as Heinemann suggested. Recent studies have argued that many of the existing compositions may have been composed by anonymous editors who used the petihta-form as a way of organizing traditional exegeses.[16] An equally plausible theory for the numerous petihtaot preserved in the midrashic collections (and for the unusual fact that multiple petihtaot for the same prooftext are regularly recorded in the collections) is that the petihtaot are not transcripts of sermons delivered in the past, but sketches for future sermons—"model" petihtaot prepared by an editor for preachers to use in preparing their own sermons. In any case, it is clear that the petihta should be treated as a coherent literary structure with rhetorical and poetic conventions of its own. Foremost among these are the twin requirements a preacher must fulfill to compose a successful petihta: on the one hand, he must carry his audience forward along the exegetical journey he makes from the opening verse to the concluding prooftext, the so-called lectionary (weekly Torah reading) verse; on the other, he must also maintain his audience's attention by making them wonder how he will connect to the lectionary verse. The actual composition of every petihta can be viewed as an attempt to consolidate these opposite rhetorical desires—attention and suspense—at once.

The petihta's overall structure exemplifies the fundamental midrashic project to unify Scripture, to reveal the hidden connections between the most dissimilar verses, and thus to demonstrate the unity of the divine will as expressed in the Bible. Thus, in addition to serving as a synagogue sermon, the petihta-form is employed in many places in midrash, in the form of *pseudo-petihtaot*, solely as a frame for organizing scriptural exegeses and traditions. We can recognize these pseudo-petihtaot by their concluding prooftexts, which could never have been lectionary verses for real petihtaot in the synagogue. One such passage we have already encountered is Eikh. R. 4.11, which begins as a comment on Ps. 79:1, and via the mashal about the pedagogue, culminates in the prooftext, Lam. 4:11. Eikh. R. 1.16, a more problematic passage, also reflects the pseudo-petihta structure.

In both these passages, the mashal is incorporated into the petihta as a bridge between verses or interpretations. At other times, a mashal, or a group of meshalim, can even constitute a petihta in its entirety. One example of this phenomenon is the famous passage about Solomon's invention of the mashal in Shir R. 1.8 (cited and discussed at the beginning of Chapter 3), the conclusion (not the entirety) of a lengthy petihta, which presents a litany of parables in praise of the mashal as a device for revealing the secrets of Torah. As we saw, the chain of meshalim in the passage transports the reader to those very secrets whose discovery via the mashal's literary form is the subject of the petihta's praise.

The following petihta, Petihta 2(2),[17] presents a similar series of meshalim. Its prooftext is Lam. 1:1 (the prooftext for nearly all the petihtaot in Eikh. R.), while the "opening" verse is Jer. 9:16. As the reader will see, the petihta journeys from the opening verse to the prooftext by means of three meshalim and their successive interpretations. This petihta was probably an editorial construct, but we have no way of knowing for certain. The authors of two of the three meshalim in the petihta, R. Yohanan b. Nappaha and R. Simeon b. Lakish, both early-third-century sages, were brothers-in-law, and their traditions were often transmitted together; we do not know who were the anonymous "Rabbis," the authors of the final mashal in the petihta.

"Thus said the Lord of Hosts: Listen! Summon the dirge-singers, let them come" (Jer. 9:16). R. Yohanan, R. Simeon b. Lakish, and the Rabbis offer interpretations of this verse.

R. Yohanan said:
   It is like a king who had two sons. He became angry at the first one, took a stick, thrashed him, and banished him. The king said: Woe to this one! From what comfort has he been banished! He became angry at his second son, took a stick, thrashed him, and banished him. The king said: The fault is mine. The education I gave him was bad.
   Similarly, the Ten Tribes were exiled, and the Holy One, blessed be He, began to proclaim the following verse: "Woe to them for straying from Me" (Hos. 7:13). And once Judah and Benjamin were exiled, the Holy One, blessed be He, said—as it were *(keveyakhol)*—"Woe unto Me for My hurt" (Jer. 10:19).

R. Simeon b. Lakish said:
   It is like a king who had two sons. He became angry at the first one, took a stick, and thrashed him, and he writhed in agony[18] and died. The king began to sing a dirge over him. He became angry at the second son, took a stick, and thrashed him, and he writhed in agony and died. The king said: I no longer have the strength to sing a dirge over them. Summon the dirge-singers and let them sing dirges over them.
   Similarly, when the Ten Tribes were exiled, He began to sing dirges over them, "Hear this word which I intone as a dirge over you, O House of Israel" (Amos 5:1). And once Judah and Benjamin were exiled, the Holy One, blessed be He, declared—as it were—I no longer have the strength to lament over them. But "summon the dirge-singers and let them come . . . Let them quickly start a wailing for us" (Jer. 9:16–17). It is not written here "for them" but "for us"—namely, for Me and them. "That our eyes may run with tears" (Jer. 9:17). It is not written "their eyes" but "our eyes"—namely, Mine and theirs. "Our pupils run with water." It is not written "their pupils" but "our pupils"—namely, Mine and theirs.

The Rabbis say:

It is like a king who had twelve sons. Two died, and he began
to console himself with the ten. Two more died, and he began
to console himself with eight. Two more died, and he began to
console himself with six. Two more died, and he began to console himself with four. Two more died, and he began to console
himself with two. But when they had all died, he began to
lament over them, "Alas! lonely sits . . ." (Lam. 1:1).

These three meshalim offer a nearly perfect example of traditional composition at work. All three use the same three or four
motifs and functions, but each one combines them differently so
as to create a distinct narrative. Thus, all begin with the common
stereotype, "It is like a king who had X number of sons,"[19] and
then construct parallel narratives that artfully use repetition (of
the same motifs and of the same or similar diction) and gradually
diverge on their own plots. The interested reader can compare
the three narratives motif by motif, line by line, to follow this
spiraling design.

The purpose of this design is to fit the rhetoric of the petihta.
By joining in sequence these three similar meshalim, the petihta's
author or editor created a kind of meta-narrative that effectively
carries his audience from the opening prooftext to the lectionary
verse. And by the petihta's conclusion, one discovers that the latter verse has been radically reinterpreted: the subject of Lam. 1:1,
"Alas! lonely sits . . ." is no longer the personified figure of Zion,
but God.

The meta-narrative that leads to this exegesis is, fittingly, a narrative of exegesis rather than of human deed, and it builds upon
the rhetoric of repetition and accentuation. The second motif in
each narrative duplicates the preceding one, but carries it one
step further; that step, in turn, nearly always coincides with a
more intense focusing—not upon the victim, though, the son or
child who is punished or who dies as punishment, but upon the
figure and reactions of the king, as parent and mourner.

Thus, in R. Yohanan's mashal, the king banishes his first son,
blaming the child for having made him do this, but after banishing the second son, the king blames himself. In R. Simeon b.
Lakish's mashal, the king gets angry at his sons (as he did in R.
Yohanan's mashal), but instead of banishing them, he now beats
them to death. After the first son dies, the king himself laments,

but after the second dies, the king is too weakened by grief to lament by himself, and he must call for professional dirge-singers. Finally, in the Rabbis' last mashal, the sons die once again (though now we are not told how or why; they simply expire), until finally, the king alone is left, "lamenting." At this point, the petihta concludes with Lam. 1:1, which now, we learn, describes God Himself. He is the one who sits solitary, mourning the tragedy of His people.[20]

It will help us to appreciate the full meaning, theological and literary, of this concluding exegesis if we look at the other exegeses in the petihta, beginning with the "opening" verse, Jer. 9:16. The first thing to remark about the petihta's structure is that it does not actually begin with exegesis of Jer. 9:16. As the classical commentators noted, somewhat to their dismay, R. Yohanan's mashal does not explicitly treat either Jer. 9:16 or Lam. 1:1, but two entirely different verses, Hos. 7:13 and Jer. 10:19.[21] In fact, this is not an uncommon phenomenon in the petihta as a literary tradition: very frequently, the first section of a petihta will set up the thematic or rhetorical design for the remainder of the composition without directly treating its main prooftexts. In any case, the two verses that R. Yohanan's mashal does treat have obvious thematic relevance to the petihta as a whole. The Hosea verse in context is a lament spoken by the prophet in God's name about the Northern Kingdom of Israel, known euphemistically as "Ephraim," which has "fled" *(nodedu)* from God by turning to foreign alliances with Egypt and Assyria; this lament anticipates the destruction of the northern kingdom by the neo-Assyrians in 722 B.C.E. The Jeremiah verse, in turn, describes the Jews of the Judaean, southern, kingdom in their exile after the destruction of the Temple; in the verse's lament, the prophet Jeremiah identifies his own plight with his nation's suffering.

Taken together, then, the two verses bewail the separate downfalls of the two kingdoms of Israel. For the midrash, however, the verses epitomize not the two prophets' reactions to the catastrophes, but *God's*. And His reaction changes, as the mashal narrates. After the first son dies, the king, while bewailing his son's lost happiness, pointedly says that it was the son's own wicked behavior that brought his punishment upon him; as translated in the nimshal, this blame becomes an indictment of the Israelites for their unfaithfulness. In the narrative's second motif, though, the king blames *himself* for his son's unhappy fate: the fault, he says, lies in the education or upbringing he gave his child.[22] Presumably, this self-recrimination refers to the Torah that God gave the Israelites—a shocking confession on God's part, not only in its own right but also because the charge, that the Torah failed as a pedagogical instrument to make the Jews righteous, was a standard part of the early Christian polemic against Judaism and the "Old Law."[23] One hardly expects to find the charge in a Rabbinic text. In our mashal's narrative, it almost appears as if the Rabbis were responding to the Christian polemic by having God acknowledge the failure as His, not Israel's. In the mashal's nimshal, though, this particular motif is translated into something rather different from what it is in the narrative. In the nimshal, it becomes a lament that God voices over His own misfortune, and for which He now seeks commiseration: "Woe unto Me for My own hurt" (Jer. 10:19).

The second mashal in the petihta turns from blame to eulogy. The king unambivalently and unambiguously laments the deaths of his two sons. What is less clear in this narrative is precisely what happens when the king beats his sons with his staff. Does he mean for them to die? Or are their deaths accidental? If the latter, does the motif suggest that the punishment God inflicted upon Israel was excessive, its terrible consequences unintended, and that God never truly wished Israel to be exiled or the Temple to be destroyed? Is this, then, the reason the king laments the tragedies that have befallen his sons? Or are these meshalim actually narratives about contradictory, albeit divine, behavior? About how God, like a human king, can both inflict punishment and lament its destructiveness?

The nimshal of R. Simeon b. Lakish's mashal never answers these questions. As in the preceding mashal, R. Simeon invokes the separate downfalls of the Northern and the Southern Kingdoms, of the Ten Tribes and Judah/Benjamin, by contrasting Amos 5:1 with Jer. 9:16–17. In his exegeses of both verses, R. Simeon reverses the relationship of catastrophe to prophecy. The first verse, in its scriptural context, is a lament over the Israelite kingdom's *approaching* destruction. The two verses from Jeremiah, which in context are addressed to the inhabitants of Judah and Benjamin, are also spoken as warnings *before* the historical catastrophes they foretell. In all these cases, however, R. Simeon reads the verses as though the respective catastrophes had already tran-spired in the past. And in the case of Jer. 9:16–17, he proposes an exegesis that is even more radical, taking the summons as addressed not to the Judaean kingdom but to God's own dirge-singers. These singers—possibly they are the angels, though their identity is never made clear [24]—are called by God to mourn in His place because He has already exhausted Himself mourning over the destruction of the Israelite kingdom.

The boldness of R. Simeon's exegesis, its daring to attribute utter exhaustion to God, is only punctuated by its use of the term *keveyakhol,* "as it were" (or in the fuller though clumsier translation that Wilhelm Bächer proposed, "if the utterance were about one about whom you could say this").[25] This expression typically appears in Rabbinic texts as a qualifier of anthropomorphic state-ments about God. Its actual effect, however, is not to diminish but to intensify the anthropomorphic exegesis. In R. Simeon's mashal, the audacity of the anthropomorphism has a tripled force: not only does God lament over Israel, not only does He have to call upon dirge-singers to lament on His behalf, but He is so wearied by suffering as to lack the strength to lament. It is hard to say at which point the anthropomorphic imagery becomes excessive. Certainly, though, the phrase *keveyakhol* does nothing to soften its shock.

The phrase *keveyakhol* does not appear in the petihta's third and final mashal, the parable of the Rabbis, but its absence there does not diminish the radically anthropomorphic character of the exegesis offered for Lam. 1:1. The classical commentators have pointed to the fact that the historical narrative implied in the mashal, as to how the Ten Tribes of Israel were exiled in five groups of two tribes each, is not attested elsewhere in Rabbinic literature.[26] The real novelty in the mashal, however, is less its historiography than its exegesis: the portrait of God sitting and mourning *alone.* In His divine isolation, with no one to comfort or console Him, God has truly become Israel's heavenly counterpart. He is depicted in the mashal in nearly the same way as the widow Zion is pictured in the book of Lamentations: bereft of children, abandoned by all others. Israel is thereby provided with a God who is His nation's mirror-image, sharing the same fate as His chosen people.

From the first mashal to the last, then, this petihta observes

God as He passes from being the catastrophe's author, its maker and inflicter, to become instead its stunned victim, at once mourner and dirge-singer. This change of character—from victimizer to victim—epitomizes the core ambiguity in the Rabbis' conception of God: the sense of Him as being simultaneously His nation's judge and the sharer of its sufferings. By having God lament the Destruction, the Rabbis were able to represent His response to their own laments, and to discover an empathetic God in the text of Lamentations, not simply one who would respond to Israel's misfortune but a God who actually participated in it with them. The Rabbis thus endowed their own tragedy with the most absolute reality. The Destruction became an event of transcendent significance. Even God suffered.

This message eventually served the purpose of apologetics as well, for it implies not only that God has not abandoned Israel but that He too suffered in the Destruction and continues to lament it, even after everyone else has perished. Indeed, the mashal may even suggest that it is God Himself who most needs consolation. By utilizing the literary form of the mashal, the petihta's author was able to draw upon all the narrative's representational strengths, and by using the petihta-form, he simultaneously prepared his audience with a dramatic backdrop against which to begin their own reading of Lamentations. In this one example, we see how effectively two midrashic literary forms, the petihta and the mashal, can complement each other and serve a common rhetorical and ideological purpose.

The Mashal and the Aggadic Narrative

One of the contexts in which the mashal most frequently appears as a subordinate unit is within aggadic narratives. In Appendix A, I have briefly described the many types of aggadic narratives found in Rabbinic literature, and the mashal appears with all of them, often as a kind of appendage or appendix, sometimes even constructed in the image of the preceding aggadot. These passages in particular raise questions like these: What does the mashal add to the aggadah and to its rhetorical and ideological dimensions? What purpose does the mashal serve by its presence?

Each passage of this sort requires its own analysis, but the following example can serve as a worthy illustration of the challenges involved in analyzing parables found in these embedded contexts. Eikh. R. 1.9 is about as complex a passage as can be found in midrash. It begins as a miscellany of interpretations; then it introduces a pseudo-historical aggadah, which is followed first by an exemplum, and then by a mashal. To facilitate discussion, I have divided the passage into its different sections.

"Her uncleanness clings upon her skirts . . ." (Lam. 1:9).

I

(1) [This means that it clings] to the very bottoms, as it is said, "Upon the skirts of the robe" (Exod. 28:34): to the hems of the skirts.

(2) Another interpretation of "Her uncleanness clings to her skirts": R. Berechiah said in the name of R. Abba b. Kahana: You find that all those priests who officiated in the days of Zedekiah were uncircumcised, as it is written, "[Too long, O House of Israel, have you committed all your abominations] admitting aliens, uncircumcised of spirit and uncircumcised of flesh, to be in My sanctuary and profane My very Temple . . ." (Ezek. 44:6–7).

(3) Another interpretation of "Her uncleanness clings to her skirts." There was a place below Jerusalem called Tofet. Why was it called Tofet? R. Yudan said: Because seduction [to idolatry] was there.[27] R. Yose said: Why was it called the valley of Hinnom? Because [the Targum translates it as] the valley of Hinnom.[28] The Rabbis say: Because from there could be heard the shriekings of their children [as they passed through the fire].[29]

II

For a hollow idol was placed there, in the innermost of seven chambers, and a copper furnace was beneath it, and a copper box was in its hand. If a man brought an offering of fine meal he was admitted to the first enclosure; doves and pigeons admitted a man to the second; a lamb to the third; a ram to the fourth; a calf to the fifth; a bull to the sixth; a human offering to the seventh. The priest received the offering and put it in the copper box; he lit the fire beneath it, and they sang praises to the idol: May the sacrifice be pleasing to you! May it be sweet to you! For what reason? So that they would not hear the shriekings of their children and change their minds.

III

A heathen priest once came to a man[30] who had many sons, and said to him: The idol tells me that you have many sons.

Will you not give at least one of them as a sacrifice? The man said to him: But they are not under my control. One is a gold-worker, one a silver-worker, one a shepherd, and another raises cattle. The priest said to him: If I appear before the idol with this answer, he will be angry with you. The man then said to him: I have a young son who is now at school.[31] Wait until he comes home from school, and I will give him to you, and you can sacrifice him. The Holy One, blessed be He, said to the man: Of all your sons, must you dedicate to idolatry the single one who is dedicated as a holy thing to heaven?![32]

IV

R. Judah b. R. Simon said in the name of R. Levi b. Perata: It is like a consort whose lover[33] said to her: Make me something hot. She took the king's laurel-wreath,[34] [made a fire with it,] and made him something hot. The king said to her: Of all the objects[35] that you had in the palace, did you have to make something hot for your lover with my laurel-wreath in which I warm myself?![36]

Similarly, the Holy One, blessed be He, said to Israel: Of all your sons, you have taken that one alone who was sanctified to My name, as it is written, "You even took the sons and daughters that you bore to Me, and sacrificed them to those [images] as food . . ." (Ezek. 16:20).[37]

In its entirety, this passage explicates a two-word phrase, *tum'atah beshuleiha*, "her uncleanness [clings] upon her skirts," in Lam. 1:9. This phrase, which is simultaneously enigmatic and suggestive, is one of the few statements in the entire Book of Lamentations even to hint at the sins Zion may have committed to bring upon herself her terrible punishment. Since such hints at Zion's culpability are so rare, it is not surprising that the Rabbis seized upon the two words in the verse as an occasion to delineate the transgressions that Zion must have committed in order to deserve her immense punishment.

The phrase's central image—"uncleanness upon a skirt"— refers to the ruling figure in the first chapter of Lamentations of the beleaguered woman, the fallen widow, who personifies Zion. Precisely what the "uncleanness" is, however, is not specified. The word *tum'atah* would have connoted to the Rabbis specific notions of impurity that disqualify a person from participating in Temple worship. In its biblical context, the description of the impurity as being "upon the woman's *skirts*" also suggests a sexual transgression, but revealingly, this is one line of interpretation the Rabbis do *not* pursue.[38] Instead, the three interpretations in the passage (in Part I) appear in the following order:

1. The first interpretation takes the phrase "upon her skirts" as a reference to the skirt-like robes worn by the priests—hence, it seems, to some unspecified transgressions committed by the priests.

2. The second opinion, like the first, also understands the transgressions as belonging to the priests, but it takes the phrase "upon her skirts" somewhat less literally, as referring to uncircumcised priests who illicitly offered sacrifices and thereby polluted the Temple—hence, Ezekiel's condemnation.

3. The third interpretation offers a figurative reading of "upon her skirts": as the "outskirts" of Jerusalem, that is, the place Tofet, in the valley of Hinnom located beneath the city of Jerusalem where, according to many Rabbinic traditions, a cult of child-sacrifice, probably to the god Moloch, was located in the period preceding the destruction of the First Temple.

To corroborate this last opinion, three etymological explanations for the names Tofet and Hinnom are given. The last of these, attributed to the Rabbis, leads into the detailed and vivid description of the idolatrous cult (Part II). As one study of this passage has proposed, its description of the cult may very well have been borrowed from Greco-Roman traditions about Carthaginian (Punic-Phoenician) sacrificial cults.[39] Whatever its sources, though, the passage is narrated with enormous skill, and bespeaks both the Rabbis' horror of the Moloch-cult and their fascination with it as an embodiment of absolute evil. The description of the cult charts a veritable descent through seven consecutive chambers into the idol's innermost sanctuary, a kind of infernal opposite to the Holy of Holies.[40] This Dantesque journey yields, in turn, to the horrifying *ma'aseh* about the father with many sons who is compelled by the pagan priest to hand over his youngest child to be sacrificed (Part III). This story, part exemplum and part villain-tale, concludes with God's suddenly appearing in the narrative to condemn the man, and this condemnation prefaces the mashal (Part IV).

God's condemnation of the man for handing over the one son "dedicated to heaven"—that is, engaged in the study of Torah—is the key to the story's ideological message, and its real object of blame, which is not merely the evil of idolatry, and not only the sacrifice of children, but, specifically, the sacrifice to idolatry of young students of Torah. This message of blame is also the message of R. Judah's mashal whose nimshal ends with nearly the identical statement found at the conclusion of the *ma'aseh;* however, in the nimshal the statement is explicitly connected to Ezek. 16:20.

This verse is perhaps the most famous biblical source for the condemnation of child-sacrifice as practiced in Moloch-worship. In its scriptural context, the verse is the culmination of a long tirade wherein God describes how He first rescued Israel as a young maiden, then raised her, and finally took her to be His wife, and how, after all this, she betrayed Him by "whoring" after other lovers; "whoring" denotes both the political allegiances Israel made with gentile nations (Ezek. 16:26) and her idolatrous practices (16:17). From verse 16 on, however, God's tirade changes. Although He continues to condemn Israel, it is not for harlotry in itself, but for using her harlotry to abuse and violate the very objects with which He had shown her His love—most horribly of all, the children she bore Him, and whom she now has sacrificed to pagan idols.

Modern scholars have debated the historical question whether or not Israelites actually practiced the kind of child-sacrifice Ezekiel condemns; and if they did, whether this worship was connected to the cult of Moloch.[41] Whatever the historical truth, we can be certain the Rabbis took Ezekiel's condemnation as fact, and believed their ancestors had practiced idolatrous child-sacrifice.[42] Indeed, as our aggadah suggests, the ancient practice of child-sacrifice was anything but fiction for the Rabbis. It embodied in their imaginations the most heinous, loathsome evils of gentile culture: not just idolatry, but idolatry plus murder; and more than mere murder alone, the slaughter of helpless young children with the consent of their parents.

In its exegesis of Ezek. 16:20, the mashal, coming at the end of this passage, simultaneously extends the verse's meaning in literal and figurative directions at once. For R. Judah's exegesis in the nimshal, the crucial words in the verse are *asher yaledet li,* "whom you have borne to Me," a phrase he interprets figuratively as "sanctified to My name" *(mekudash lishmi).*[43] Yet the mashal's narrative also plays upon the literal meaning of the prooftext's conclusion, *vatizbahim lahem leekhol*, "and these you sacrificed to them to be eaten," by reading the words almost hyperliterally, via the narrative's action, as: "and these you sacrificed to them so that they could eat"—referring, that is, to the hot food or drink the consort prepares for her lover. At the same time, by using the persona of the adulterous consort to portray Israel's idolatry, the mashal also exploits the allegorical figure expressed in the conclusion of Ezek. 16:20, *hame'at mitaznutayikh*, "Is this the least of your whorings?"

The allusion to adultery reflects, of course, the stock image found throughout the Bible for Israel's faithlessness to God through idolatry.[44] The character of the unfaithful consort also appears in many meshalim.[45] No other mashal, however, uses imagery quite like ours, and though a number of meshalim describe the abuse of the king's property, it is almost always his statue or portrait that is misused, never (so far as I know) one of his personal belongings, an item like the laurel-wreath. Indeed, the idea behind the narrative—that the consort should burn the king's laurel-wreath in order to heat food or drink for her lover—may seem at first singularly contrived, even silly. The king's abusive condemnation also sounds somewhat incongruous: Why does he take the consort to task for burning his laurel-wreath, but not for committing adultery?[46]

In fact, understanding the meaning of the mashal's narrative— and a key to its role within the passage in its entirety—lies in knowing certain ancient beliefs and practices connected to the laurel and the laurel-wreath. As the visible sign of the imperial office, the laurel-wreath possessed in the Greco-Roman world a uniquely sacred status within the imperial cult, where it was an object of worship symbolizing the emperor. Yet in addition to this special sanctity, the laurel, along with the olive, was also considered a sacrosanct plant in its own right. Among other things, its use for profane ends was strictly prohibited. Moreover, as Pliny relates, the laurel

> must not be employed even for kindling a fire at altars and shrines in propitiating the deities. The laurel indeed manifestly expresses objection to the application of fire by crackling and making a solemn protest, the timber actually giving a twist to the cracks in its interstices and sinews.[47]

Once this information about the laurel is known, the mashal's narrative suddenly comes into focus. Like Isaac Deutscher,

Trotsky's great biographer, who reputedly broke with his Ortho-
dox Jewish upbringing by eating a buttered ham sandwich while
standing atop his father's grave at midnight on Yom Kippur eve,
our mashal indulges in overdetermined transgression. When she
burns her husband's laurel-wreath to heat up her lover's hot food
or drink, the consort commits multiple sins: in one blow, she commits adultery, wantonly destroys the imperial insignia, and abuses
a sacred tree. And as it is applied in the nimshal, this multiple
transgression becomes a perfect correlative for the transgressions
of the hapless father who simultaneously pays worship to the idol,
murders his young child, and abuses a student of Torah
"sanctified to God's name."

We can now say precisely what it is the mashal adds to its
aggadic context. Through the image of the consort burning the
laurel-wreath, the mashal offers a concrete, *familiarizing* illustration for the triple condemnation with which God had attacked
the nameless father in the preceding *ma'aseh*. Through its paradigmatic character, the mashal extends the condemnation from
an individual to all Israel, and simultaneously it intensifies the
condemnation by suggesting the casual manner in which Israel
committed this heinous triple transgression, sacrificing children
to Moloch as casually as the consort burned the king's laurel-
wreath to heat up her lover's refreshments. Finally, by using
the motif of the laurel-wreath in connection with the consort's
infidelity, the mashal actually manages to suggest that Israel, in
addition to committing the two cardinal sins of idolatry and
bloodshed, also committed the third by sinning sexually. And
to these three sins, the mashal adds still another: murder of the
students of Torah, of God's own "sanctified" disciples. For the
Rabbis, this last crime arguably surpassed all the others, as the
following passage in Eikh. R. (p. 2) implies:

R. Huna and R. Jeremiah said in the name of R. Samuel b. R.
Isaac:
    We find that the Holy One, blessed be He, overlooks idolatry,
sexual license, and bloodshed, but He does not overlook rejection of the Torah, as it is said, "Why is the land in ruins . . . ?
The Lord replied: Because they forsook the Teaching I had set
before them" (Jer. 9:11–12). It is not written here "because of
idolatry, sexual license, or bloodshed" but "because they have
forsaken My law."

In sum, the mashal, coming at the conclusion of this lengthy passage describing Israel's "uncleanness upon her skirts," manages to suggest within a single fictional construct every conceivable transgression that Israel could ever have committed: idolatry, sexual license, bloodshed, and, worst of all, the abuse of Torah and its students. One can hardly imagine a more sweeping, more scathing condemnation.

This hyperbolic attack, a literal polemic, has a clear apologetic dimension as well: by inventing so immense a corpus of transgressions that the Israelites supposedly committed, the Rabbis were able to justify the immensity of the Destruction as a deserved punishment. Yet the emphasis that the mashal places on the violation of the young students "sanctified to God's name"—children who epitomize in their persons the highest values of Rabbinic Judaism—may carry an additional, more contemporary burden of meaning. Through its hyperbole, the mashal condemns all fathers who allow their children to be led away from the study of Torah *for whatever reason;* according to the mashal's logic, such behavior is equivalent to sacrificing a child to Moloch.

Thus, in response to our original question—What does the mashal's presence add to the passage?—we can answer that it contributes both substance and rhetoric. In addition to focusing, intensifying, and familiarizing the aggadah's condemnation of an antiquarian transgression, the mashal discovers in the phrase "the uncleanness that clings upon her skirts" a key to a more immediately relevant sin. The mashal's polemic is against the Rabbis' contemporaries as much as against their ancestors—perhaps even more so.

The Mashal and the Exegetical Enumeration

As its name states, the enumeration is a list that counts examples. Found throughout ancient Near Eastern literature, the enumeration may once have been a rudimentary medium for organizing knowledge about the world; but early on, it proved to be a highly serviceable vessel for homiletical moralizing as well as for clever riddling. Both uses are attested in the Book of Proverbs, in passages like Prov. 6:16–19 ("There are six things which the Lord hates; seven which are an abomination to him . . .") and 30:24–28 ("Four are among the tiniest on earth, yet they are the wisest of

the wise . . ."). Precisely this plasticity and flexibility, its easy adapt-
ability, were the critical factors in making the enumeration, a
seemingly tedious and pedantic literary form, so popular a literary
form in ancient Jewish literature.

Rabbinic literature abounds in lists of all sorts, including the
enumeration. In midrash, however, the Rabbis characteristically
turned the enumeration into a device of exegesis, the exegetical
enumeration, as W. Sibley Towner calls the form in an exemplary
study of its development and use.[48] Instead of counting things or
phenomena in the world, the exegetical enumeration lists scriptural "facts": instances of unusual or otherwise noteworthy syntac-
tical constructions, of particular types of narratives or motifs or
patterns of behavior, or even of special modes of interpretation.
A typical example is the following enumeration, which is found at
the very beginning of Eikh. R.:

> Three prophets prophesied with the language of *eikhah*. And
> these are: Moses, Isaiah, and Jeremiah. Moses said: "How
> *(eikhah)* can I bear you alone . . ." (Deut. 1:12). Isaiah said: "Alas
> *(eikhah)*, she has become a harlot" (Isa. 1:21). Jeremiah said:
> "How *(eikhah)* she sits solitary" (Lam. 1:1).

This brief passage contains the two salient features of the
exegetical enumeration: one, an exegetical opinion stating a fact
and the number of its occurrences; two, a list of verses illustrating
the opening statement. The subject of this enumeration is a word,
eikhah, usually translated as "alas," though it is simply an elongated form of the more typical *eikh* (usually translated as "how").
This word, according to the exegetical opinion, was used by three
prophets. While the word *eikhah* appears some sixteen times in
the Bible, its morphology was sufficiently unusual to provoke the
Rabbis' attention. If nothing else, its position in Lamentations as
the very first word in the book must have been a signal of a special
exegetical opportunity. First words are often looked upon as keys
to a secret or hidden meaning, and no book in the Bible deserved
a key more than the Book of Lamentations with its grim and
tragic contents.

To explore the special meaning of *eikhah* in Lamentations, the
enumeration proceeds to list the three prophets who used the
word: Moses who, in Deut. 1:12, praised Israel's populousness in
a verse beginning *eikhah;* Isaiah who, in Isa. 1:21, used the word

to begin a condemnation of Israel for its harlotry and unfaithfulness to God; and finally, Jeremiah, who began his lament in Lam. 1:1 with *eikhah*. In all three cases, as the classical commentators have suggested, the word signals astonishment: at Israel's greatness, her sins, and her downfall.[49] The enumeration itself, however, does not explain the word's meaning or that of the list.

It is therefore significant that the enumeration is immediately followed by a mashal. Here, again, the question to be answered is, What does the mashal add to the passage? The mashal, Eikh. R. 1.1A, is attributed to R. Levi.

> It is like a certain consort who had three counselors. One saw her in her glory. One saw her in her wantonness. And one saw her in her disgrace.
> Moses saw [the children of Israel] in their glory, and said: "How *(eikhah)* can I bear you alone . . ." (Deut. 1:12). Isaiah saw them in their wantonness, and said: "Alas *(eikhah)*, she has become a harlot" (Isa. 1:21). Jeremiah saw them in their disgrace, and said: "How *(eikhah)* she sits solitary" (Lam. 1:1).

The nimshal virtually repeats the preceding enumeration verbatim, adding only the conditions—of glory, wantonness, and disgrace—in which the three prophets saw Israel when they exclaimed *eikhah*. The mashal's real contribution to the passage is in its narrative: the word *eikhah*'s elongated, feminized form is transformed into the character of the *matrona,* the consort, a conventional symbol for the community of Israel but here a certain reference as well to the figure of the unhappy widow, the fallen woman, personifying Zion, who dominates the first two chapters of the biblical book of Lamentations. At the same time, the three prophets who used *eikhah* are changed into the consort's special attendants or counselors.[50] Each witnesses her at a different period in her career, from the time of her greatest success to her final disgrace and downfall. In the nimshal, these three periods, in the form of the three verses, together come to make up a kind of encapsulated history of Israel's career, from prosperity through sin to disgrace.

What the mashal, with its narrative of the consort's career, adds to the passage as an exegetical unit is, first of all, a rationale for taking the verses together.[51] That rationale, however, is narrative rather than discursive: a story that explains why the word *eikhah* appears in the three verses—because, as the mashal tells us, all three verses describe the career of a single person, the consort, who was described by her different counselors at varying moments in her lifetime. This narrative rationale may also serve an apologetic function: the consort's career shows that the word *eikhah* in Lamentations is to be read in conjunction with the two other instances of the word in the Bible, and that the word itself may have other meanings than strictly a catastrophic "alas." In this way, R. Levi situates both the biblical book and its subject, the Destruction, within a recognizable pattern, the covenantal paradigm of sin and punishment. As the paradigm teaches, Israel's downfall, like the consort's, was not accidental or gratuitous; it was caused by sinning. As the consort declines from greatness, her metaphorical presence in the word *eikhah* also anticipates Zion's career in the second half of Lam. 1:1: the one "great among nations," "the princess among states," who becomes "a slave."

We should hesitate, however, before placing too weighty an ideological or theological burden upon this passage. The enumeration is a subgenre of wisdom-literature, and like other types of wisdom it thrives on wit and cleverness, the ingenious, even prodigious, display of knowledge. When it is combined with the enumeration, the mashal too partakes of this cleverness and its intrinsic desire to be remembered for being clever. The memorable narrative rationale that the mashal provides for the enumeration is sufficient reason for its presence in the passage.

Series of Meshalim

Meshalim are sometimes found in groups or series, in which case they also tend to have parallel narratives and nimshalim. There are no examples of this phenomenon in Eikh. R., but it can be observed in a well-known passage in Ber. R. 8.3, where four parables are cited in succession in order to illustrate different figures with whom God consulted before creating Adam. Probably the best example of a series, however, is Vay. R. 2.4–5, in which five meshalim are cited as comments on the phrase "Speak to the children of Israel . . ." in Lev. 1:1.

> R. Yudan said in the name of R. Samuel b. Nahman:
> It is like a king who had a mantle. He commanded his servant and said to him: Fold and iron it and be careful with it. The

servant said to him: My lord, O king! Of all the mantles you own, why do you command me only about this one? The king said: Because it clings to my body!

So Moses said before the Holy One, blessed be He: Master of the universe! Of all seventy independent nations that you have in the world, why do you command me only concerning Israel!?—"Command the children of Israel" (Num. 28:2); "Say to the children of Israel" (Exod. 33:5); "Speak to the children of Israel" (Lev. 1:1). He said: Because they cling to Me. This is what is written: "For as the loincloth clings close to the loins of a man, so I made the whole House of Israel cling to me . . ." (Jer. 13:11).

R. Abin said:

It is like a king who had a purple robe. He commanded his servant and said to him: Fold and iron it and be careful with it. The servant said to him: My lord, O king! Of all the purple robes you own, why do you command me only about this one? The king said: Because that is the one I wore the day of my coronation!

So Moses said before the Holy One, blessed be He: Master of the universe! Of all seventy independent nations that you have in the world, why do you command me only concerning Israel!?—"Command the children of Israel" (Num. 28:2); "Say to the children of Israel" (Exod. 33:5); "Speak to the children of Israel" (Lev. 1:1). He said: Because they crowned Me as king at the sea, and said, "The Lord will reign for ever and ever!" (Exod. 15:18).

R. Berechiah said:

It is like an elder who had a robe. He commanded his disciple and said to him: Fold and iron it and be careful with it. The disciple said to him: My master, O elder! Of all the robes you own, why do you command me only about this one? The elder said: Because that robe is the one I wore the day I was appointed an elder!

So Moses said before the Holy One, blessed be He: Master of the universe! Of all seventy independent nations that you have in the world, why do you command me only concerning Israel!? He said: Because they accepted My sovereignty at Mt. Sinai and declared, "All that the Lord has spoken we will do and we will obey" (Exod. 24:7).

R. Yudan said: Come and behold how much the Holy One, blessed be He, loved Israel: In one verse He mentioned their name five times!—"And from among the Israelites," etc. (Num. 8:13).

R. Simeon b. Yohai said:

It is like a king who had an only son. He used to command his freedman, saying: Give my son food, Give my son drink, Take my son to school, Take my son home from school.[52]

So the Holy One, blessed be He, used to command Moses: "Command the children of Israel" (Num. 28:2); "Say to the children of Israel" (Exod. 33:5); "Speak to the children of Israel" (Lev. 1:1).

R. Judah said in the name of R. Simon:

It is like a person who was sitting and making a crown for the king. A man passed by, and said to him: What are you doing? He answered: I am making a crown for the king. The man said: Then set in it as many things as you can! Set in it emeralds. Set in it fine stones and jewels. Why? Because it is destined to be placed on the king's head!

So the Holy One, blessed be He, said to Moses: Praise Israel as much as you can! Exalt them! Glorify them! Why? Because I am destined to be glorified through them! This is what is written: "And He said to me, You are My servant, Israel in whom I glory" (Isa. 49:3).

All five meshalim in the passage share the same message praising Israel, and use a similarly self-reflexive rhetoric to do so. The first three meshalim directly parallel one another, differing only in the identity of their characters and the object of clothing they speak about; although this is not conveyed in the translation, it is worth noting that, in each parable, the garment mentioned is designated by highly specific terminology relating to actual offices. The fourth parable, which follows R. Yudan's exegesis of Num. 8:13, continues the basic narrative structure used in the first three parables describing the king commanding his servant (in this case, his freedman), though now in regard to the king's son, not an object; while the fifth mashal returns to the garment imagery (here in the form of a crown).

What is the purpose of this collection of parables? Almost certainly the series is an editorial construction. But did the editor intend to create a mini-anthology of meshalim in praise of Israel—possibly in order to provide preachers with a choice of parables they might select for their sermons? Or did the editor wish his readers to note the subtle differences between the meshalim in the series by reading them in sequence—the way, for example, the chains of parallel meshalim in Shir R. 1.8 (about the invention of the mashal) or in Petihta 2(2) are clearly meant to be read together for their combined effect? If so, the details in each mashal clearly bear a significance they do not warrant if they are not meant to be read as a group.

I have no answers to these questions. But they do suggest some of the important consequences for interpretation that a mashal's context holds, even the problems that are raised by considering the ambiguous status of context in midrash. Until these ambiguities are fully acknowledged and investigated, we will be unable to plumb the full depths of midrash and its meaning.

The Mashal in Midrash

The passages just discussed all show how midrashic discourse is organized: in recognizable units of discourse, in literary forms like the petihta, the mashal, the enumeration, the series. These forms comprise the genres or subgenres of midrash. They constitute its language, and they maintain themselves in midrashic literature, formally and rhetorically, even when they combine with one another. The combinatory pattern of these units is essentially additive. The petihta-form provides a frame for the mashal, which in turn is made to serve the special rhetoric of the petihta; but neither form is required to surrender its distinctive structure or formal identity when it joins with the other. Similarly, a mashal can be constructed in the image of an aggadic narrative or ma'aseh, with its own lesson or homily, but it can simultaneously be employed so as to exploit its own parabolic strengths as a paradigmatic, representational narrative.

The primacy of these literary forms in midrashic discourse is significant because it shows that midrash is not simply exegesis, nor an exegetical stance, but the discourse *of* exegesis.[53] As midrash is preserved in Rabbinic literature, it does not only interpret Scripture, but already organizes and exploits exegesis—smaller, independent, often local interpretive traditions—for larger ideological purposes that have increasingly sophisticated and polyvalent meanings of their own. Midrash thus *deploys* scriptural exegesis for its own ends.

How this happens can be seen most easily by studying one passage and identifying its successive exegetical moments or layers. A midrashic passage is inevitably a palimpsest of exegeses, one level of interpretations covering another. Consider Eikh. R. 3.21 (analyzed in detail in Chapter 2).

> R. Abba bar Kahana said:
>
> It is like a king who married a woman and wrote her a large marriage-settlement. He wrote her: So many bridal-chambers I am building for you; so much jewelry I make for you; so much gold and silver I give you. Then he left her for many years and journeyed to the provinces. Her neighbors used to taunt her and say to her: Hasn't your husband abandoned you? Go! Marry another man. She would weep and sigh, and afterward she would enter her bridal-chamber and read her marriage-settlement and sigh [with relief]. Many years and days later the king returned. He said to her: I am amazed that you have waited for me all these years! She replied: My master, O king! If not for the large wedding-settlement you wrote me, my neighbors long ago would have led me astray.
>
> Likewise: The nations of the world taunt Israel and say to them: Your God does not want you. He has left you. He has removed His presence from you. Come with us, and we will appoint you to be generals, governors, and officers.
>
> And the people of Israel enter their synagogues and houses of study, and there they read in the Torah, "I will look with favor upon you, and make you fertile . . . I will establish My abode in your midst, and I will not spurn you" (Lev. 26:9,11), and they console themselves. In the future, when the redemption comes, the Holy One, blessed be He, will say to Israel: My children! I am amazed at how you have waited for Me all these years! And they will say to Him: Master of the Universe! Were it not for the Torah You gave us, in which we read when we entered our synagogues and houses of study, "I will look with favor upon you . . . and I will not spurn you," the nations of the world long ago would have led us away from you.
>
> That is what is written, "Were not your teaching my delight, I would have perished in my affliction" (Ps. 119:92). Therefore it says: "This I call to my mind; therefore I have hope" (Lam. 3:21).

In this mashal, we can identify at least seven distinct exegetical levels or "events":

1. The interpretation of Lam. 3:21, the mashal's prooftext, at the conclusion of the nimshal, the specific focus of the exegesis being the demonstrative *zot* ("this") as referring not to God, its antecedent in context, but to Torah. This interpretation is the mashal's main exegetical occasion.

2. The interpretation of Ps. 119:92 (and possibly, 119:93a), which is only slightly less explicit than the preceding exegesis of Lam. 3:21. This interpretation serves as a kind of bridge from the nimshal to the exegesis of Lam. 3:21. What is less clear is precisely how Ps. 119:92 is being interpreted; possibly, the word *'onyi*, "my affliction," is being understood as the *'inuyyim*, the persecutions, of the gentile nations.

3. The exegeses of Lev. 26:9,11 earlier in the nimshal as divine promises that are to be realized only in the eschatological period. In the mashal, these verses are understood "literally" in their already-interpreted eschatological sense; for sources, see Sifra Behukotai 1.2.5, 1.3.3.

4. The taunts of the gentiles in the nimshal echo the taunts in the well-known exegeses of Song of Songs 5:9–6:3, attributed to R. Akiba in Mekhilta Shirta 3, and recorded anonymously in Sifre Deut. 343. With these echoes, the gentiles' taunts can be considered intertextual allusions, not to Scripture but to Rabbinic exegeses of Scripture and to traditions that emerge from exegesis.

5. The image of the marriage-document in the narrative may be the product of a pun on the word *vehifreiti*, "I will make you fruitful," in Lev. 26:9, and the Aramaic *parna*, a loan-word from the Greek *phernē*, "a marriage-settlement." This implied, even concealed, exegesis would explain why the verses in Lev. 26:9,11 in particular were selected as the referents for the image of the marriage-document.

6. Point #1 above is based as well on a "buried," implicit exegesis—the identification of the demonstrative *zot* with the Torah on the basis of Deut. 4:44 (*vezot hatorah*). S's text makes this exegetical event explicit.

7. The mashal's overall "interpretation" of Lam. 3:21, which not only reinterprets the verse's meaning but enacts it in the narrative, which dramatizes the process through which "calling Torah to mind" brings hope and makes midrashic reading a path to consolation. At the same time, the narrative also depicts the conditions in which such interpretive activity becomes necessary.

This interpretation comes closest to the "full" meaning of the mashal.

This mashal is about as complex an exegetical object as can be found in midrash. Its seven exegetical moments cover nearly the entire spectrum of exegetical possibilities, from those most on the surface of the text to others buried far beneath the narrative and its imagery. For all their singular features, these possibilities can be divided, however, into two separate categories or orders of exegetical discourse.

The first of these orders consists of the local exegetical operations that lie behind nearly every midrashic passage. This order includes virtually all of the first six exegetical moments listed above for Lam. 3:21. Most of these moments can be described through the *middot,* the traditional hermeneutical principles of Rabbinic interpretation, or through comparable exegetical techniques that provide a "logic" for midrash.[54] Sometimes these local exegetical operations are embedded in the language of midrash so deeply that they are buried in its narrative; at other times they must be deduced by implication from the nimshal's interpretation of additional verses. In either case, they provide the raw material for midrashic discourse, the stuff out of which everything else is made. In their sum, they form a kind of exegetical substructure for midrash.

This substructure must be distinguished from the second order of exegesis in midrash, an order largely identical with the literary-rhetorical units I have characterized as the subgenres of midrash—the mashal, the petihta, and so on. These units constitute the macrostructure of midrashic discourse. In my list of exegetical events in Lam. 3:21, this order is represented in number 7, the final exegetical "event" in the mashal. The exegesis performed in this event goes beyond all the local exegetical operations within the mashal, but it nonetheless conveys an interpretation of the mashal's prooftext, Lam. 3:21. And as macrostructure, this exegetical event also communicates a message more complex than any of the local exegeses. It exists precisely at the point where exegesis and ideology intersect.

The macrostructures of midrashic discourse, its genres and subgenres, are characterized most obviously by their high degree of formal and rhetorical organization. The identifiable literary shapes of the macrostructures stand in sharp contrast to the amorphous and sprawling structures of the various midrashic collections (like Eikh. R.) in their entirety, on the one hand, and to the atomistic, fragmentary, and seemingly unconstrained movements of the local exegetical operations, on the other. In either case, the macrostructures lend midrashic discourse its stability. Even the most scattered local exegetical operations presented independently tend to organize themselves into larger units— dispute-forms, lists, and the like—all of which are characterized by the patterned language and structured composition that we have seen in the mashal and the other generic units of midrash. Given this fact, it is entirely justified to say that these literary-rhetorical forms constitute the primary units of meaning in midrash, its true building blocks, and its fundamental objects of analysis.

Finally, the mashal's stereotyped, regularized form—its bipartite structure of narrative with nimshal and exegesis—is one that the mashal assumes *in* midrash. While parables and parable-like narratives are found in many other literatures, nowhere else does there exist a literary form truly identical to the Rabbinic mashal, a form that draws equally upon exegesis and narrative in the rhetorical service of a particular ideology. Conversely, the precise form that the Rabbinic mashal historically assumed in midrash is inexplicable outside of its context. To this extent, then, we can speak of the mashal and the other literary-rhetorical forms like the petihta, the enumeration, and so on, as the products of midrash. These forms *are* midrash. Their presence defines its discourse.

Midrash is only one type of exegetical discourse upon the Bible that existed in Late Antiquity and in the early Middle Ages. Different groups of Jews interpreted the Bible in many diverse ways in the course of these centuries, ranging from Hellenistic allegory and Qumranic pesher to the interpretations contained in the various Aramaic Targumim and the techniques used in the "Rewritten Bible" genre; in the later Middle Ages, still more exegetical traditions emerged, including the various forms of philosophical, grammatical, and kabbalistic exegesis as well as plain-sense interpretation *(peshat)*. And just as midrash is defined by its literary-rhetorical forms, so, too, each one of these other types of exeget-

184 · Parables in Midrash

ical discourse, to a greater or lesser extent, also possesses its own literary-rhetorical forms. None of these distinct traditions can be understood solely in terms of its hermeneutics. In each tradition, the "correct" understanding of the Bible is communicated through a mode of discourse that expresses both exegetical practice and ideological program.

6

The Mashal in Hebrew Literature

This book has focused upon the mashal in midrash during the Rabbinic period. The Rabbinic mashal, however, represents only one moment in the mashal's history, which can be traced in Hebrew literature from the Bible to the modern period. In this historical continuum, we can fully appreciate the achievement of one moment, like that of the midrashic mashal, only if we understand its antecedent literary forms. Just as the midrashic mashal adapted earlier forms and acquired its singular shape so as to meet the needs of midrash, so too the mashal's literary descendants in subsequent generations transformed the midrashic form to satisfy the ideological and cultural needs of their own generations. The midrashic king-mashal therefore holds a crucially influential position in the history of Hebrew literature. To follow the mashal's history, through all its devolutions and metamorphoses, from one literary period to the next, across nearly every conceivable genre, is tantamount to tracking the history of Hebrew literature itself—and perhaps, even of Judaism.

From the Ancient Near East to Late Antiquity

The origins of the mashal lie in the ancient Near East. According to one anonymous Rabbinic saying, King Solomon invented parabolic discourse.[1] Although we need not take this statement literally, its basic claim cannot be doubted. The mashal derives from the ancient Near Eastern tradition of wisdom literature, and this tradition was identified closely with King Solomon and the period of his rule.[2] Even before Solomon's time, though, Akkadian and Sumerian wisdom texts preserve a number of compositions known in modern scholarship as contest-fables or *Streit-*

fabeln.[3] In these contests, talking—highly articulate—plants or animals, like the Tamarisk and the Palm, compete in debates over their respective strengths and virtues. These debates anticipate the literary fable, and illuminate a rhetorical connection that can be seen most clearly in two fables found in the Bible, Yotham's in Judg. 9:8–15 and Jehoash's in 2 Kings 14:9–10. Both these compositions contain the embryonic shape of the literary debate within their respective narratives, though they have already transformed it to suit their own purposes.

In contrast to the early history of animal and plant fables, it is more difficult to trace the lineage of parabolic narratives having *human* characters in ancient Near Eastern literature. In fact, the earliest full-fledged fictional narratives of this sort that we know of are those found in the Bible: the story of the poor man and his ewe-lamb which Nathan recites to King David in order to condemn the king, to his face, for his unjust behavior (2 Sam. 12:1–14); the presumably fictitious tale about her son that the woman of Tekoah is enlisted to tell David in order to bring about the return of Absalom (2 Sam. 14:1–20); and the parable of the escaped captive that the nameless prophet addresses to Ahab after the king disobeys God by sparing the life of Ben-hadad (1 Kings 20:35–43). Finally, Isaiah's "song" of the vineyard (5:1–7) combines aspects of a "human" parable with a plant-fable. These narratives all happen to have messages of blame as their rhetorical function and operate much like the blame-mashal in Rabbinic literature. Modern scholars have noted how, in the Bible, parables are employed by their speakers as legal stratagems; they remind us of the fictitious narratives used as test-cases in legal literature.[4]

The ancient Greek form of the *ainos* similarly uses fictional narrative, and comparable parabolic and fable-like forms can be found in nearly every world literature.[5] Yet it is surprising how few fables and parables are actually preserved in ancient Near Eastern and early Hebrew literature. The total number of parables and fables in the Bible is very small—I have mentioned nearly all the examples—and in postbiblical Jewish literature there are only a handful of fables: the Conflict between the Forest and the Sea in 4 Esdras (4:13); the Lion and the Cub in Pseudo-Philo (47:3–8); and several short fables in the Aramaic text of Ahikar. In all apocryphal and pseudepigraphic literature, it is questionable if there is a single parable with human characters.[6]

The dearth of parables and fables in postbiblical literature has elicited a number of scholarly responses. Some scholars have argued that the literary form did not exist in Jewish literature before Late Antiquity when it was imported into Palestinian literature from Hellenistic sources, probably through the channel of popular Greco-Roman philosophy in the form of Cynic and Stoic diatribes.[7] As even the little biblical evidence demonstrates, however, this argument is untenable. The same evidence also argues against the claim, often advanced in Christian New Testament scholarship, that Jesus invented the literary form of the parable and that the Rabbis borrowed it from him only much later.[8]

A more convincing explanation for the scarcity of parables and fables in early postbiblical literature may be based upon the social status of the literary form. Parables and fables most probably were types of popular literature that were delivered orally in sermons or in public contexts, much as the gospel narratives describe Jesus telling parables when he preached to the masses. Unhappily, aside from the gospels, we have few literary testimonies to popular Jewish preaching in Late Antiquity. Most postbiblical Jewish literature is far more "highbrow," aimed at a very literate audience, which was more exclusive and sophisticated than the masses to whom a preacher would have preached. Even a work like Ahikar, which has often been considered a mine of folklore, seems in its redacted form and setting to be connected with an aristocratic and sophisticated scribal tradition.[9] Indeed, it may be that Jewish scribes in Late Antiquity did not consider the mashal to be a literary form worthy of being recorded and preserved for posterity. As the Rabbis remarked, the mashal in itself is worth only a penny-candle—hardly an estimation of "high" or "important" literature.[10]

The very popularity parables and fables enjoyed may have diminished their value in the eyes of scribes. Whatever the reason for the scarcity of parables and fables preserved in ancient literature, the result is that little can be said about their literary history between the biblical period and Late Antiquity. Indeed, the parables attributed to Jesus in the synoptic gospels are the earliest extensive evidence for the tradition that eventually came to fruition in Rabbinic literature centuries later.

The Parables in the Synoptic Gospels

The place of the New Testament parables in the tradition of the mashal has been a subject of intense scholarly debate for the past century.[11] Unhappily, much of that scholarship has been tainted by theological polemics, on the Jewish as well as on the Christian side, with scholars in both camps claiming that their respective religious tradition discovered the literary form and brought it to the height of aesthetic achievement. In the last decade, however, with the large-scale reevaluation of the historical and theological connections between early Christianity and Rabbinic Judaism, there has also come a new understanding of the literary issues involved in the question of the relationship of the New Testament parables to the mashal. The Israeli New Testament scholar David Flusser has in particular advanced our understanding of the question by showing that Jesus' parables and the Rabbinic meshalim share compositional similarities—formulaic elements of diction, stereotyped themes, and motifs—which indicate that they were both part of a single genre of traditional narrative.[12] Flusser's conclusions are supported by my own work on the Rabbinic mashal and by the compositional, rhetorical, and poetic features I have described in the earlier chapters of this book. As a result, we can now discuss with greater confidence the common background and traits shared by the New Testament parables and the Rabbinic meshalim.

To be sure, comparative study of this sort faces a formidable number of methodological caveats. In the first place, there is the problem of language: while most scholars assume that Jesus spoke either Aramaic or Hebrew, the only language in which the parables are preserved is the Greek of the New Testament, and in order to compare the parables to the Rabbinic mashal, one must first translate them back into Hebrew.[13] Second, any attempt to use the Rabbinic evidence as background to the New Testament runs the obvious risk of importing anachronistic ideas into the earlier texts.[14] Third, both the Rabbinic collections and the gospel texts are famously problematic documents in their own rights, and the problems involved in studying them separately are only made more complicated when the two groups are compared with each other. Fourth, the study of the New Testament parables and of their place in the synoptic gospels raises still another set of scholarly challenges, which make comparative study still more problematic.

Finally, modern parable-research, since its inception, has proceeded from the assumption that the gospel parables reflect traditions that are probably closest to Jesus' own beliefs, if not *ipsissima verba*.[15] The same scholarship, however, has also assumed that the parables nearly all underwent extensive revision at the hands of the authors or editors of the separate gospels who revised the narratives and reinterpreted their meanings to fit the needs of the early Church. As a result, most modern parable-scholarship typically begins by attempting to recover the "original" parables from the texts preserved in the New Testament in order to restore their "original" meaning. Yet inasmuch as this project involves both the restoration of the "original" text and the restitution of its "original" meaning, its efforts at recovering the parables in their earliest forms are inherently problematic. Not unpredictably, the answers to the question of what the parables must once have been have often been predisposed if not altogether predetermined by modern scholars' beliefs as to what the parables must have meant. At the same time, these attempts to restore the "original" parables have been shaped by doubtful presuppositions about the literary nature of the parable, like the nonallegorical character of authentic parables.

In the present context, I cannot do more than acknowledge these methodological challenges. Here, I wish to concentrate exclusively on one question: the place of the New Testament narrative-parables in the literary history of the mashal, and in particular their status as parables preserved in narrative or semi-narrative contexts.[16] To treat this question, I will discuss the parables as they are preserved in the New Testament gospels, without attempting to reconstruct the "original" parables that Jesus may once have delivered; and I will focus my argument upon the analysis of one parable, the parable of the Wicked Husbandmen. This is one of the two narrative parables that are preserved in all three synoptic gospels (Mark 12:1–12; Matt. 21:33–46; Luke 20:9–19) as well as in the Gospel of Thomas (65). (The other parable is the Sower: Mark 4:3–9; Matt. 13:4–9; Luke 8:5–8.) Present-day New Testament scholars continue to dispute the literary relationships among the different gospels; in the following discussion I will follow the scholarly consensus in assigning priority to the Marcan version, and assume that Matthew and Luke were in one way or another using Mark.[17] The differences among the three versions are, in any case, relatively minor.[18] The following is Mark's version of the parable:

> And he began to speak to them in parables: "A man planted a vineyard, and set a hedge around it, and dug a pit for the winepress, and built a tower, and let it out to tenants, and went into another country. When the time came, he sent a servant to the tenants, to get from them some of the fruit of the vineyard. And they took him and beat him, and sent him away empty-handed. Again he sent to them another servant, and they wounded him in the head, and treated him shamefully. And he sent another, and him they killed; and so with many others, some they beat and some they killed. He had still one other, a beloved son; finally he sent him to them, saying, 'They will respect my son.' But those tenants said to one another, 'This is the heir; come, let us kill him, and the inheritance will be ours.' And they took him and killed him, and cast him out of the vineyard. What will the owner of the vineyard do? He will come and destroy the tenants, and give the vineyard to others."

Flusser has discussed in detail the composition of this parable's narrative.[19] Most of the motifs and images used in the narrative have parallels among later Rabbinic meshalim, and so it is especially easy to discuss this parable as part of the mashal's tradition. Our discussion will begin with the history of the parable's interpretation. Perhaps the earliest attempts at offering an explicit interpretation for its meaning can be seen within the synoptic tradition itself, in which, it seems, the parable was already interpreted as an allegory of the Church's relationship to the Jews. Thus, at the conclusion of the parable's narrative (in all three synoptic versions), Jesus asks his audience of Jewish priests, scribes, and elders:

> Have you not read this scripture: "The very stone which the builders rejected has become the head of the corner; this was the Lord's doing, and it is marvelous in our eyes" (Ps. 118:22–23)?[20]

In Matthew the following statement is added following the quotation from Psalms:

"Therefore I tell you, the kingdom of God will be taken away from you and given to a nation producing the fruits of it." And he who falls on this stone will be broken to pieces; but when it falls on anyone, it will crush him.

This last statement, in effect an anti-Jewish interpretation of the Psalms verse, assumes that the son in the parable is Jesus, and that the narrative as a whole and the murder of the son in particular point (for Matthew at least) to Jesus' death. His murder in turn will be cause for God's rejection of the Jews (as represented in the parable by the characters of the Wicked Husbandmen) and for the election of the Church as the New Israel (the "others" mentioned at the parable's very conclusion). And indeed, this christological anti-Jewish interpretation early on became the standard reading of the parable's meaning. Thus, the second-century Church Father Irenaeus writes: "For inasmuch as the former [the Jews] have rejected the Son of God, and cast Him out of the vineyard when they slew Him, God has justly rejected them, and given to the Gentiles outside the vineyard the fruits of cultivation."[21]

Nearly all modern interpretations of the Wicked Husbandmen begin, like much else in modern parable-research, with the work of the late-nineteenth-century German scholar Adolph Jülicher.[22] Jülicher's critical study of the parables was predicated upon the assumption that an authentic parable never contains allegorical elements. As a result, Jülicher rejected the authenticity of the entire parable of the Wicked Husbandmen, dismissing it as an invention of the early Church, mainly because its text appears in the gospels themselves in such heavily allegorized form.

Jülicher's difficulty with the parable was with its allegorical mode, not its meaning per se, and this attitude has continued to characterize more recent scholarship. Joachim Jeremias, for example, finds the parable problematic because it exhibits "an allegorical character which is unique among the parables of Jesus."[23] As Jeremias notes, the opening description of the vineyard is drawn from Isa. 5:1–7, while the other images in the parable have according to him essentially the same values and meanings as Matthew and the early Church Fathers attributed to them. "There can be no doubt," Jeremias writes, "that in the sending of the son Jesus himself had his own sending in mind" (although Jeremias concedes that it cannot be assumed that Jesus' Jewish audience would have recognized the symbolism).[24] Although Jeremias's ultimate assessment of the parable is not as extreme as was Jülicher's—Jeremias does not reject the parable as inauthentic—his interpretation of its meaning diverges from traditional views. For Jeremias, the parable vindicates the offer of the gospel to the poor, and reflects in its narrative the historical resentment felt by Galilean tenant farmers toward their absentee foreign landowners.[25]

As Frank Kermode has noted, Jeremias's interpretation is simply a "more rationalistic allegory" than the medieval readings of the parable; it is an allegory that turns the narrative into a "somewhat ridiculous fable of current affairs."[26] Yet whether or not the parable can escape allegorical reading—I do not think it can, nor that it matters—it is noteworthy that all the interpretations of its meaning, from Matthew through Jeremias, share a common Christology and read the parable as an implicitly prophetic text: according to the interpretations, Jesus used the narrative to foretell his own death, as well as God's eventual rejection of the Jews for the crime they were about to commit. The parable, in other words, is about Jesus' fate, and that fate is portrayed in the parable as the outcome of his prophetic mission.

It should be emphasized that these interpretations of the parable's meaning all claim to be its *original* meaning, the one Jesus intended, not a meaning the parable was later given by the redactors of the gospel narratives. Yet these christological interpretations pose several common difficulties. To accept them, the contemporary reader must assume, first, that Jesus either did or was able to prophesy his own death; second, that he understood his death as part of a larger divine schema, the election of the Church; and finally, that we today can know these things from the evidence of the gospels. But if we cannot accept these assumptions, the readings we have mentioned are far less compelling. Indeed, all the readings appear to be predicated upon a single, never-questioned point: that the son in the narrative is Jesus. While the imagery of sonship in the synoptics, and in Mark especially, is typically used to symbolize Jesus, that fact does not prove that the son in the parable's narrative must be Christ. The strongest reason for believing that the son must be Jesus remains the unshaken certainty of christological faith. Yet without that certainty, which Jesus himself may have lacked, the belief that the son must be Jesus is far less sure. The evidence of later Rabbinic meshalim shows that the figure of the son can represent many different personages and things, and may already have in Jesus' own time.[27] And this possibility is especially important to keep in mind because there is nothing in the Wicked Husbandmen's narrative or in its context in the gospel narrative that inevitably leads to the christological reading.

In fact, the narrative context surrounding the Wicked Husbandmen suggests a very different reading for the parable. Surprisingly, the narrative context has rarely been consulted as a key to the parable's meaning, not even by scholars who acknowledge the possibility that the situation described in it is close to the one in which Jesus may have actually delivered the parable.[28] As the gospel accounts tell us, in one form or another,[29] Jesus is on his way to Jerusalem when he is met by various Jewish leaders—in Mark, the chief priests, the scribes, and the elders; in Luke, the scribes and high priests; in Matthew, the Pharisees and high priests.[30] The text in Mark continues (11:28–33) as follows:

> And they said to him, "By what authority are you doing these things, or who gave you this authority to do them?" Jesus said to them, "I will ask you a question; answer me, and I will tell you by what authority I do these things. Was the baptism of John from heaven or from men? Answer me." And they argued with one another, "If we say, 'From Heaven,' he will say, 'Why then did you not believe him?' But shall we say, 'From men'?— they were afraid of the people, for all held that John was a real prophet. So they answered Jesus, "We do not know." And Jesus said to them, "Neither will I tell you by what authority I do these things." And he began to speak to them in parables . . .

Jesus then relates the parable of the Wicked Husbandmen, after which the narrative continues:

> And they tried to arrest him, but feared the multitude, for they perceived that he had told the parable against them; so they left him and went away. (Mark 12:12)

According to this narrative, the historical figures symbolized in the parable's characters can easily be identified. The parable's protagonists, the wicked husbandmen, correspond to the Jewish leaders whom the parable condemns for having attempted to usurp the vineyard; the owner is God; and his messengers are the various biblical prophets. But who is the son? If the wicked husbandmen are the contemporary Jewish leaders, then the narrative context dictates that the son should symbolize John the Baptist. His death is the crime for which the parable condemns the Jewish leaders.

To be sure, Mark knew that the Jewish leaders were not the ones who killed John. As Mark himself writes earlier in the gospel (6:17–29), it was Herod who ordered John to be executed at the request of his daughter, Herodias. Nonetheless, the Marcan gospel here represents Jesus as condemning the Jewish leaders for murdering John, in much the same way that Matthew later on almost explicitly condemns the Jewish leaders for crucifying Jesus. The unanswered question here is not whether Jesus had himself in mind when he condemned the Jews for John's death, but whether Mark believed that he did. This is a question we will probably never be able to answer; however, it would seem irrefutable that the evangelist wished *the reader* to draw a parallel between the fates of the two men. Indeed, to underscore this parallel, the evangelist tells the reader, immediately following Jesus' narration of the parable, that the Jewish leaders do understand the parable's point, and that they wish to arrest Jesus—to do to Jesus, in other words, precisely what they have already done to John. The Jews' fear of the multitude, however, prevents them from carrying out their wish.

Viewed from this perspective, the parable's message of blame can be read on at least two levels. As Donald Juel has written, it is a "double-narrative" whose "real point . . . can be found only at a deeper level, at a level of understanding accessible only to the reader and not to the characters in the story."[31] Because the implied reader of the parable is expected to understand its message more deeply than do the characters in the narrative, these different levels of meaning can be characterized by their irony, which progressively increases from level to level. Thus, on the least ironic level, the parable's blame is directed at the Jewish leaders for their treatment of John the Baptist. On a slightly more ironic plane, the blame is attached to the Jews for their past treatment of John *and* their present abuse of Jesus. And finally, on the most ironic level of all, blame is attached to the Jews in the parable for all the crimes previously mentioned *plus* their future murder of Jesus as Christ and Messiah.

Whether or not Jesus himself identified John's death with his own predicament is, again, a question we will never be able to answer for certain (at least from the gospel evidence). But Mark (and his fellow evangelists), as I have suggested, clearly intended *their* audiences, the readers of the gospels, to see the fates of the two men as parallel. In Matthew, the parallel is made nearly explicit. In Mark, it remains at the level of irony. In either case, the Jewish leaders in the narrative may understand the parable as condemning them for one crime, but the narrative's reader is meant to see that the Jews are being condemned for at least two sins—the execution of John *and* the far more horrible crime they are about to commit against the son of God.[32]

The double level of meaning implied in this message of blame appears to be intimated as well in the prooftext from Ps. 118:22–23 with which Jesus concludes the parable when he rhetorically asks his audience, "Have you not read this scripture: 'The very stone *(even)* which the builders *(habonim)* rejected has become the head of the corner; this was the Lord's doing, and it is marvelous in our eyes'?" As Jesus employs it, the verse appears to hold at least two meanings. On the one hand, it clearly refers to the persecution of John, with the irregular stone symbolizing the Baptist. In this respect, the key words in the verse are *rosh pinah*, a phrase usually translated as "the head of the corner" or as a cornerstone, but one that Jesus may have understood in the sense with which it appears translated in the LXX, as *kephalē gonias,* that is, the capstone or keystone in an arch, which must be irregularly shaped in order to fit its strategic position at the apex of the arch.[33] In other words: the stone the builders initially rejected because it seemed misshapen proved in the end to be the perfect shape for the capstone. Only their stupidity and/or their wickedness prevented the builders, the Jews, from recognizing its true value.

The exegesis, however, does not stop here; it continues with the next verse: "This was the Lord's doing, and it is marvelous in our eyes." Which is, in effect, interpreted thus: This is the Lord's doing *even though* it is marvelous in our eyes—marvelous being taken in the sense of being beyond human comprehension. This interpretation comes almost as if it were a response to the following question: If God indeed planned to vindicate John's authority, why did He send him to be persecuted and eventually killed? The answer is given by the verse's double assertion: even though it may baffle our understanding, and though it certainly exceeded the understanding of the Jewish leaders, the very ones whom the parable condemns, John's rejection and his eventual vindication are both the work of God. The marvel here is precisely the same perplexity that has been expressed by scholars who have pointed out how irrational the vineyard owner's behavior seems to be when he sends his son to the husbandmen after they have already mistreated his servants.[34] The man's behavior may be irrational— or paradoxical (in the literal sense of being inconsistent with common belief or experience). But paradoxical behavior is hardly an impossibility for God.[35]

Moreover, the message implied by this interpretation of the parable is consistent with other teachings of Jesus that stress the sudden reversals and overturnings of normal expectations that will attend the advent of the kingdom of heaven—"Many that are first will be last, and the last first" (Matt. 19:30, 20:16; Mark 10:31; Luke 13:30), to give only one example. On all these grounds, then, the interpretation agrees with what we know about Jesus' teachings. Yet the hermeneutical principle used in this exegesis—which applies a verse's description of an essentially ahistorical process (here, reversal) to the career and fate of a quasi-historical or biblical personage—also accords with what we know about the history of the interpretation of the verse in early Jewish exegesis; in contrast, the messianic-christological application (accepted by most New Testament scholars) becomes common only later, in early Christian exegesis.[36] Furthermore, an additional, more pointed reference to Jesus' Jewish opponents may also be present in the verse's exegesis: the word *habonim* in Ps. 118:22, literally "builders" (from the root *bnh*), may have been interpreted by Jesus as though it derived from the root *bun*, "to understand" or "to think," and therefore as a reference to "the thinkers" or "the wise," that is, the Jewish scribes and scholars whom Jesus is condemning.[37] And if this is true, the interpretation of Ps. 118:22 constitutes a pointed indictment of the Jewish leaders. The exegesis reflects the same rhetorical message of blame that the narrative directs against them.

Within the gospel narrative itself, these verses from Psalms are spoken by Jesus as a concluding retort to his Jewish interlocutors. Viewed from the (admittedly later) perspective of the Rabbinic mashal, however, the verses might also be considered part of the parable itself, part of a hypothetical nimshal, as it were. In the light of Rabbinic practice, the possibility that Jesus would have used Scripture in reciting a mashal cannot be ruled out. The Wicked Husbandmen, however, is the sole parable in the gospels to use and to interpret a scriptural prooftext in this way; the only other parable even to allude to Scripture is the parable of the Sower (Mark 4:3–20; Matt. 13:3–23; Luke 8:5–15), and there the verses involved, Isa. 6:9–10, are actually part of the so-called theory of parabolic speech that Jesus proceeds to expound to the disciples. Moreover, what is most revealing about the use of Scripture in the Wicked Husbandmen is that the Psalms verses do not serve as an "explanation" for the narrative but as a way of confirming the rhetorical message that the parabolic narrative itself bears. The verse gives the parable's rhetorical message the stamp of scriptural authority. Yet as I proposed earlier, this is the actual function that scriptural exegesis serves in the Rabbinic mashal. The Wicked Husbandmen may then be one of the earliest testimonies to the inherently rhetorical use of scriptural exegesis in a narrative parable.

Whatever the exegetical dimension of this parable, however, it is certain that Jesus was not an exegete of the same sort as the later Rabbis. The main features that demonstrate a connection between the New Testament parables and the tradition of the mashal are rhetorical and compositional, not exegetical. The same connection can be seen in the eleven other parables attributed to Jesus in the three synoptic gospels. While I cannot analyze these texts in the detail with which I have discussed the parable of the Wicked Husbandmen, a brief characterization of each parable is worth presenting.

1. *The Sower* (Mark 4:3–20; Matt. 13:3–23; Luke 8:5–15). The parable offers comparative praise/blame of the various types of audiences who hear Jesus preach and their responses. In each of the three gospels, the parable appears within an identical narrative in which Jesus preaches to the crowd along with his disciples; after reciting the parable, Jesus is asked about parables, and he responds with the so-called theory of parabolic speech, to which we will return shortly. Following the theoretical statement, Jesus explains the parable in what appears as a virtually explicit nimshal.

2. *Children in the Marketplace* (Matt. 11:7–19; Luke 7:24–35). A blame-mashal condemning "the masses" for not listening to the

warnings of John the Baptist or to the teachings of Jesus, the parable is presented within a narrative context that specifies its audience, and has an explicit nimshal in the text delivered by Jesus himself.

3. *The Marriage-Feast or Banquet* (Matt. 22:1–14; Luke 14:15–24). The context for the parable is different in the two gospels. In Matthew, the parable is presented immediately after the Wicked Husbandmen; in Luke, Jesus delivers it at a banquet given by a Pharisee. In both cases, though, the message of the parable is clearly blame/condemnation of those guests invited to the feast who refuse to come (= Jewish leaders to whom Jesus preaches), along with the announcement (= praise) of the others whom the host will invite to take their place. In Matthew, the parable has a second part, about a guest who appears at the feast in inappropriate dress; again, this narrative's message is quite clearly blame, but the referent is less clear. There is no explicit nimshal for the parable; its application must be adduced from the narrative context.

4. *The Talents or Pounds* (Matt. 25:14–27; Luke 19:12–27). In Matthew, this parable is part of the eschatological discourse, and appears among a series of parabolic and figurative utterances; it follows immediately after the extended simile about the conscientious steward, and comes right before the parable of the Ten Bridesmaids. Its narrative communicates comparative praise and blame, with its emphasis falling decidedly upon the latter, condemning the man who fails to take the necessary risks in preparing for the coming redemption. A brief nimshal is presented in the form of an epimythium.

In Luke's version, which differs in details from Matthew's, the parable is delivered in a narrative context, after Jesus is condemned for staying at the house of Zacchaeus the tax collector in Jericho and because the people suppose "that the kingdom of God was to appear immediately."

5. *The Weeds Sown by the Enemy* (Matt. 13:24–30). This parable, which is prefaced by the formulaic "the kingdom of heaven is like . . . ," follows immediately upon the Sower, and is accompanied by an explicit nimshal (36–43). The parable's message defends God's justice in deferring the punishment of the wicked

and the reward of the righteous until the end of time. Such theodicy is a common secondary application of the rhetorical function of praise in many Rabbinic meshalim; in this parable, theodicy also serves to defend the behavior of those who wait for the end.

6. *The Wicked Servant and His Debtor* (Matt. 18:23–35). Also prefaced by the "kingdom of heaven" formula, this parable is a blame-mashal directed against those who do not practice proper charity and forgiveness; the punishment such persons will receive at the end of time is used to confirm the message of condemnation. Although the parable has a nimshal in the form of an epimythium, it is told in response to Peter's question as to how often he is required to forgive his brother who has sinned against him.

7. *The Laborers in the Vineyard* (Matt. 20:1–16). This parable, an example of apologetic praise, justifies the behavior of the vineyard owner who pays the last workmen he hires in the day as much as he pays those who have worked for him all day. The parable, however, is accompanied by an epimythium, "the last will be first, and the first, last," which is also Jesus' response to Peter's question as to whether those who have sacrificed much to follow Jesus will enjoy a more privileged position than those who have not. Within this context, the apologetic in praise of the owner's paradoxical behavior also contains a message of blame against the workmen who complain about the owner's behavior (namely, those who have sacrificed much and who might therefore believe they should have a greater reward on that count).

8. *The Two Sons* (Matt. 21:28–32). This parable is recited immediately before the Wicked Husbandmen as part of the confrontation between Jesus and the Jewish leaders who challenge his authority. The parable presents comparative blame (of the Jewish leaders) and praise (of the tax collectors and harlots who heeded the teachings of John). The parable's nimshal is presented in a rhetorical exchange between Jesus and his opponents.

9. *The Wise and Foolish Maidens* (Matt. 25:1–18). Prefaced by the "kingdom-of-heaven" formula, this parable is presented within the eschatological discourse, immediately before the parable of the Talents, and contains comparative praise (of those who prepare for the arrival of the kingdom) and blame (of those who don't).

The parable has a brief epimythium, but its nimshal might also be contained in the extended trope preceding the parable (24:45–51) that compares the wise servant with the wicked one.

10. *The Rich Man and His Storehouse* (Luke 12:13–21). This parable has an explicit nimshal and is also told in response to a request a nameless man makes to Jesus to ask the man's brother to divide his inheritance with him. The parable condemns the man who wishes to store up material possessions as being covetous, and thus implicitly blames the man for making his request for help to Jesus.

11. *The Fig Tree Owner and His Steward* (Luke 13:6–9). The parable has no nimshal, but it is told in the context of a sermon urging repentance. The parable is primarily praise, and appears to urge its audience to repent even after long delay; this positive message is then used secondarily to justify God's waiting for man to repent and the deferral of punishment of the wicked in the hope that they will eventually repent of their wicked ways.

Brief as it is, this survey demonstrates that virtually all eleven narrative parables in the synoptic gospels can be categorized in terms of their rhetorical functions, as either praise, blame, or a subcategory of praise or blame. As might be expected, the rhetorical functions of several parables overlap categories, as in number 7. In nearly all the parables, though, one of the following four topics dominates the rhetorical praise or blame: the nature of Jesus' audience and their reception of his teachings and/or those of John the Baptist (parables 1, 2, 3, 8); the correct preparation for the kingdom of heaven (4 and 9); justification of God's behavior in rewarding those who have hearkened to Jesus' teachings and in punishing those who have refused to listen (5 and 7); and the proper religious behavior to be practiced (6, 10, 11).

Finally, all the New Testament evidence I have gathered suggests that Jesus used the parable (insofar as the gospel narratives tell us) in essentially the same way as the Rabbis employed the mashal—in public contexts (sermons or preaching), and as an instrument for praise and blame, often directed at the persons present in the audience. Neither the Rabbinic meshalim nor the parables attributed to Jesus serve primarily as mediums of doctrinal instruction or as literary devices for concealing the true teaching from unwanted "outsiders." Although the parable is by its literary nature an allusive narrative with an unspoken ulterior message, Jesus' parables, like the later Rabbinic meshalim, are distinctly exoteric narratives whose messages could have been comprehended by their audiences without difficulty.

This last fact may require some defense, since it appears to contradict a passage in the New Testament that has frequently been interpreted as saying the opposite. This passage, found in all three synoptic gospels, is the famous theory of parabolic discourse that accompanies the parable of the Sower, the very first parable Jesus is depicted as reciting, as he sits in a boat on the Sea of Galilee and preaches to the large crowd gathered on the nearby shore. After he tells the parables, "those who are about him with the twelve [disciples]" ask Jesus "concerning the parables."[38] Jesus responds as follows (in Mark's text):

> To you has been given the secret of the kingdom of God, but to those outside everything is in parables; so that *(hina)* they may indeed see but not perceive, and may indeed hear but not understand; lest they should turn again, and be forgiven.   (4:11–12)

After which Jesus turns to his uncomprehending disciples and asks them how, if they can't understand this parable, will they ever be able to understand the others? Yet after this rebuke, Jesus proceeds to explain the parable's meaning to them!

Jesus' impatient behavior in this instance seems contradictory, but it is not this feature of the passage that has aroused some of the greatest controversy in all New Testament scholarship.[39] As described in the passage, the literary form of the parable is represented as a kind of allegory intentionally composed to baffle its audience. The last part of the theory—the purpose clause beginning with *hina* ("so that")—is, in fact, an allusion to, if not a quotation of, Isa. 6:9–10.[40] As Frank Kermode has remarked, Mark's conception of the parable is "a bit like a riddle in a folktale, where to get the answer wrong means perdition."[41] Indeed, the harsh exclusivity of the Marcan formulation appears to have so bothered Matthew (13:11–13) that he revised the saying by changing the causal *hina* to the conjunction *hoti*, "because," thereby making the statement less a prescriptive theory of parabolic discourse than a description of the current state of the audience's members. Even after Matthew's change, however, we are still left with a theory of implicitly secret speech. As Kermode notes, Mark "says the stories are obscure on purpose to damn the outsiders," while Matthew's parables "are not necessarily impenetrable, but that the outsiders, being what they are, will misunderstand them anyway."[42]

For New Testament scholars, both the Marcan and the Matthean versions of the passage have been almost equally unacceptable. Some scholars, like Albert Schweitzer, have found Mark's theory of parabolic discourse simply "repellent"; others, like Jülicher, have dismissed the passage as inauthentic, as a self-serving ideological fiction the early Church invented under Hellenistic influence to justify its exclusion of the Jews from salvation; and still others, like Jeremias, have more liberally suggested that the saying either is misplaced in its present context or was misunderstood by Mark.[43]

In general, the passage has been especially troublesome to those who have promoted the view of Jesus as a preacher who, desiring to instruct the masses, used the parable as an illustrational form. Yet the view supported by the passage, that the parable is a form of secret or concealing speech, is not an impossibility. It accords with one conception of the parable's literary nature, and has clear parallels, a few of them in Rabbinic texts, and many in later medieval Jewish esoteric and mystical traditions. It may be possible, however, to understand both the Marcan and the Matthean formulations of the theory in a slightly more nuanced fashion by considering an aspect of the mashal as an instrument for social self-identification. One of the earliest sages to whom parables, or proto-parabolic sayings, are attributed in Rabbinic literature is the legendary Pharisee Hillel, a near contemporary of Jesus. The most famous of Hillel's sayings is preserved within ARN A 15.3, a passage that compares Hillel with his rival, Shammai.[44]

It once happened that a certain heathen passed behind the synagogue and he heard a child reading [the passage in Scripture beginning with] "These are the [priestly] vestments they are to make . . ." (Exod. 28:4). The gentile came before Shammai, and said to him: My teacher! All this honor, whom is it for? Replied Shammai: For the High Priest who stands and serves at the altar. Said the gentile: Convert me on the condition that you make me High Priest and I will serve at the altar. Shammai responded: Is there no priest in Israel? And do we not have High Priests who can stand and officiate upon the altar, that this paltry convert who has come with only his staff and bag should go and serve in the high priesthood! He rebuked him, and dismissed him in a huff.

The heathen then came to Hillel and said to him: Master, convert me on condition that you appoint me High Priest, so that I might stand and serve at the altar. Sit down, Hillel said to him, and I will tell you something. If one wishes to greet a king of flesh-and-blood, is it not right that he learn how to make his entrances and exits? Indeed, the heathen replied. [Said Hillel:] You wish to greet the King of Kings, the Holy One, blessed be He: is it not right that you learn how to enter the Holy of Holies, how to fix the lights, how to approach the altar, how to set the table, how to prepare the row of wood? The heathen replied: Do what seems best in your eyes.

First Hillel wrote out the alphabet for him, and taught it to him. Then he taught him the book of Leviticus. And the heathen went on studying until he got to the verse, "Any outsider who encroaches shall be put to death" (Num. 1:51). Immediately, of his own accord, the heathen reasoned by inference as follows: If Israel, who were called children of God and of whom the Shekhinah said, "But you shall be to Me a kingdom of priests and a holy nation" (Exod. 19:6), were nevertheless warned by Scripture, "Any outsider who encroaches shall be put to death," all the more I, a paltry proselyte, who come only with my bag! Thereupon the proselyte was reconciled of his own accord.

He came to Hillel the Elder and said to him: May all the blessings of the Torah rest upon your head. For if you had been like Shammai the Elder I might never have entered the community of Israel. The impatience of Shammai the Elder nearly caused me to perish in this world and the world-to-come. Your patience has brought me to the life of this world and the one to come.[45]

Hillel's analogy between the heathen and a man who wishes to approach a king of flesh-and-blood stands just on the verge of *not* being a parable; taken in isolation, it is barely a narrative. The story in its entirety, however, does narrate a hermeneutical act closely resembling the kind of interpretive response that parabolic narrative elicits. As in the New Testament narrative surrounding Jesus' theory of parable, a connection is made in the Hillel narrative between initiation into the community of the elect and the ability to understand the parabolic saying. In the Hillel story, after the sage draws his analogy for the heathen, Hillel explains its most obvious meaning to the heathen: before he can become High Priest, he must study Torah and the priestly laws. The heathen thereupon begins studying—first, the Hebrew alphabet; then, the Bible, until eventually he comes to Num. 1:51, the verse that prohibits *hazar*, the lay person or nonpriest, from performing the priestly tasks. At that moment, the gentile—now in fact a proselyte (as we learn shortly later)—reasons "of his own powers" *(be'atsmo):* If the Israelites, who are the children of God and who are called a kingdom of priests, are nonetheless prohibited from performing those cultic duties permitted solely to a genuine priest by birth, then certainly he, a mere proselyte, cannot perform these tasks! Not only would he be guilty of a capital transgression, but he would also lose his place in the world-to-come!

At this point, a deeper meaning to the analogy begins to emerge: what Hillel first meant to tell the heathen was not only that he would have to learn royal etiquette—the laws of priesthood—before he could become High Priest. He also intended him to understand that once he had learned the laws—once he had learned enough to understand Num. 1:51 on his own—he would appreciate the fact that he is forbidden by law to serve as a priest: that he must literally not approach the King of Kings in the Temple service. By the end of this narrative, in other words, Num. 1:51 itself has become a quintessential statement of what it means to be inside the community rather than outside: the scriptural verse may prohibit the "outsider" from offering sacrifice at the pain of death, but by the time the heathen has converted and learned to understand the verse for himself, the scriptural prohibition has become his *personal* key for entering the world-to-come. Why? Because he has joined the community of Israel, God's "kingdom of priests."

The explicit point of this narrative (and of the others in the ARN A passage) is, as the proselyte himself says at the conclusion, to praise Hillel's generosity and patience, and to denigrate Shammai's lack of both. Nonetheless, this particular story of Hillel and the heathen/proselyte is a narrative about the relationship between interpretive capacity and communal identification. To understand correctly, one must be a member of the community—a speaker of its language. If you do understand correctly, it proves that you are a speaker, and that you are therefore part of the community.

To be sure, this circular argument is a kind of literary conceit. But such a conceit of communal hermeneutical competence may also lie behind the parabolic theory enunciated in the gospels. Whether that passage is formulated in Mark's harsher language or in Matthew's slightly gentler tones, it is less a theory than a nod to the disciples on Jesus' part: "You are among the elect and therefore you are capable of understanding the parable. And here is the meaning of the parable of the Sower, anyhow. As for the others, they do not understand and never will, not because they can't understand parabolic discourse but because they aren't members of the community."

According to this reading of the Marcan passage, its key lies in the word "mystery," *mustērion,* which is not a secret or concealed truth but rather "something which can be well known, but only to those to whom God chooses to give that knowledge," as John Bowker has aptly written in connection with both Mark's and the Rabbis' use of the word.[46] According to Bowker's investigation of the term's meaning, possession or knowledge of the *mustērion* is a mark of social identity: in Rabbinic literature, the term refers to "that which constitutes or identifies Israel in its special relation to God."[47] The same sense is its meaning in the Marcan passage which defines parabolic narrative as the communicative medium for such "mystery," not a way of hiding or obfuscating it.

For both Jesus' and Hillel's audiences, the hermeneutical conceit associated with understanding parabolic narrative points to their common historical situation: to the period when Palestinian Judaism had not yet crystallized into a single homogeneous society or religious group, when both Jesus' and Hillel's audiences would have included disciples and "others," followers of the particular sage who were "inside" his community, and others who were "outside" it. For both groups the parable as the bearer of the *mustērion* would have been especially appropriate.[48] In this historical situation, most people were of course neither fully inside nor entirely outside the community: the average member of the preacher's audience would have been somewhere in between: certainly knowledgeable enough to understand being called an outsider and sensitive to what an insider might appreciate.

In the subsequent history of the mashal, from the beginning of the Rabbinic period to the time of the editing of the collections of midrash in which most Rabbinic meshalim are preserved, the audience of any particular parabolic narrative would have been far more homogeneous, less divided or sectarian in its makeup, and therefore less likely to appreciate the hermeneutical conceit. For by this period, Rabbinic Judaism had already passed its formative stages and attained its mature social identity. It is no accident that, in this period, the Rabbinic mashal also attained its distinct and mature shape.

From the Tannaim to the Amoraim

In tracing the history of the mashal in the early Rabbinic period, we encounter the many textual, philological, and historical problems associated with Rabbinic literature: the authorship and attribution of individual opinions; the dating of the various Rabbinic documents, many of them anthologies of traditions attributed to sages who lived much earlier; the redaction of these documents and their transmission; and the historical and literary interpretation of the documents and their contents.[49] Because the various Tannaitic collections (called after the Tannaim, the sages quoted therein, who lived between the years 70 c.e. and 220 c.e.) and the Amoraic collections (called after the Palestinian Amoraim, who lived between 220 c.e. and 500 c.e.) were all edited at different times *after* the close of their respective periods, both collections are known to have been "contaminated" by the stylistic features of the later period in which they were redacted.[50] As a result, it is often difficult to base clear historical judgments on particular texts.

Nonetheless, the literary history of the mashal during the Rabbinic period can be approached through the process of regularization. As I described that process in Chapter 1, it determined the composition of the mashal in its fully mature state in Amoraic literature according to the following main features:

1. The literary-rhetorical form of the mashal, which was previously a popular form of teaching and preaching, was adapted by the Rabbis for midrash, the study of Scripture, and thus became a regularly used device with a normative shape.

2. That shape consisted of the two-part structure of narrative, or mashal-proper, and nimshal. The mashal-proper and the nim-

shal are both introduced by conventional formulas that are in effect generic markers; the nimshal regularly concludes with the citation of a verse from Scripture, usually the mashal's prooftext.

3. The narrative in the mashal-proper was assimilated to the literary form of the king-mashal.

4. The narratives of meshalim consist of motifs and themes that are expressed in language and diction that, from the Tannaitic to the Amoraic periods, becomes increasingly stereotyped, almost formulaic, in style.

These features of regularization are based upon observations of the tradition in its entirety. The process of regularization was never programmatic, and there remain many meshalim, both Tannaitic and Amoraic, that were never regularized, fully or partially. The vast majority of meshalim recorded in Amoraic collections, however, bear the features of regularization; in contrast, more meshalim recorded in Tannaitic collections appear not to have undergone the kinds of stylistic and thematic stylization that is typical of the process. Needless to say, it is an entirely separate question whether or not the *absence* of these stereotyped features in a mashal attributed to an *early* sage can be taken as sufficient evidence to *prove* that the mashal under study is a *historically* veracious example of an early mashal prior to regularization.

A good example of the difficulties encountered in analyzing meshalim from the early Rabbinic period, before the process of regularization took hold, can be found in the following passage from Semahot de R. Hiyya (4.1). According to its modern editor, this brief work was probably compiled in the seventh century, but it preserves many traditions attributed to very early sages.[51] The following two meshalim are attributed to Yohanan ben Zakkai, the late-first-century sage who is most famous as the founder of Yavneh.

> When Rabban Yohanan b. Zakkai was about to die, he wept. His students asked him: Yohanan our teacher! You are a great man, a great scholar! You have taught much Torah in Israel. You have seen your students and your students' students sit in the academy before you. And yet you now weep!
>
> He said to them: I will tell you a mashal (*emshol lekhem mashal*). What is [my present] situation like? It is like a person who was on his way to appear [in judgment] before a procurator (*egemon*), before whom there are many intercessors. [His court

is] a place where money is exchanged [in return for favors], where people deceive each other, where you can swindle some-one with words, and bribe them. And lo, that man weeps, for he doesn't know whether or not he is about to be condemned to death. Now if that is how a man [feels as he goes to face a ruler] of flesh-and-blood, when he can do all these deeds [to save him-self], then how much the more should I feel it necessary to weep and to be grieved—I, who am on my way to face the King of Kings, the Holy One, blessed be He, in a place where there are no intercessors, where no money is exchanged, where there is no deception, where you can't deceive Him with words, and where you can't bribe Him, and when I don't know whether or not I am to be condemned to death.

I will tell you another mashal. What is [my] situation like? It is like a man who was traveling all day on a highway. Toward dusk he reached a crossroads, with one road leading to a settle-ment, the other to the wilderness, but he did not know which road to take.

So with me *(kakh ani):* All my life I traveled upon one road, and now I stand at a crossroads: One road leads to life in the world-to-come, the other to shame and everlasting contempt, and I do not know where they are leading me—whether to life in the world-to-come, or to shame and everlasting contempt.

R. Yohanan recites these meshalim in order to justify his per-turbed state of mind to his students; indeed, their highly personal tone, the voice of a man fearful of death, and no less so despite his greatness, makes these parables sound especially vivid and ring with authenticity. In rhetorical terms, the meshalim can be categorized as apologetic praise, but that categorization does little justice to their dramatization of R. Yohanan's dilemma. In the first mashal, the sage imagines the terror of a man who must stand to be judged before a corrupt Roman procurator.[52] Despite all the illicit means he can enlist to save himself, the man still feels utterly powerless, without redress; thus, the sage reasons, how powerless he will feel when he stands before God in the heavenly court where it is impossible to procure acquittal through any under-handed means.

In the second mashal, R. Yohanan offers what seems to be an even more straightforward illustration of his predicament through the conventional image of a man who stands at a crossroads and must decide which of the two roads to take. Yet at the conclusion of the nimshal a significant discrepancy between the mashal's narrative and R. Yohanan's fate emerges: in the former the beleaguered traveler may not know which one of the two roads to choose, but the choice is his; as R. Yohanan depicts his situation, however, he is led passively along one of the two roads; the decision has been made for him (presumably on the basis of the life he has lived); hence his present feeling of helplessness, even desperation.

Both these meshalim are in formal terms nonregularized. Their protagonists are nameless men, not kings, and though the first mashal operates along the familiar lines of the analogy between God and an earthly ruler, the latter in this narrative is a general *(egemon)* rather than a king *(melekh).* A further indication of their nonregularized state is that neither mashal cites a scriptural verse or serves an explicit exegetical function.[53] In this respect, as well as in their very personal tone of voice, R. Yohanan's meshalim recall features usually associated with Jesus' parables. These features may themselves be additional indications of the premidrashic character of the mashal's tradition. Note, too, that in his first mashal, R. Yohanan applies the parable to himself through the form of a *kal vehomer,* an argument from the weaker case to the stronger, thus recalling Hillel's practice in the anecdote discussed at the conclusion of the last section.[54]

All these characteristics point to the reasonable likelihood that these meshalim are examples of the preregularized mashal in the early Rabbinic period. There is, however, no proof for this, nor that these meshalim are the "original" meshalim of R. Yohanan, and not later inventions anachronistically attributed to him. One modern biographer of R. Yohanan, for example, dismisses the various elements in the passage, what we could call its motifs, as "late inventions" that were not original even to the period in which Yohanan lived.[55]

An example of another kind of problem that arises in discussing nonregularized or preregularized meshalim in Rabbinic collections can be gleaned from the following text recorded in the Mekhilta, the Tannaitic midrash on Exodus. R. Yehudah, the sage to whom the mashal is attributed, is a third-generation Tanna.

"And the angel of God, going before the camp of Israel, moved and went behind them. And the pillar of cloud moved from before them and went after them" (Exod. 14:19). R. Yehudah said: This is a verse [whose meaning] is enriched from many places. He recited a mashal: What is this like? It is like a king who was going on his way, and his son went before him. Brigands came from in front to kidnap [the boy], [so the king] took him from in front and placed him behind. A wolf came from behind, [so] he took him from behind and placed him in front. Brigands [came] from the front and a wolf from the back—[so] he took him and placed him in his arms, as it is said, "I taught Ephraim to walk, taking them in My arms" (Hos. 11:3). The son began to suffer, [so] he took him on his shoulders, as it is said, "in the desert which you saw, where the Lord your God carried you" (Deut. 1:31). The son began to suffer from the sun, [so] he spread a cloak over him, as it is said, "He has spread a cloud as a curtain" (Ps. 105:39). [The son] became hungry, [so] he fed him, as it is said, "Behold I send bread, like rain, from the sky" (Exod. 16:4). He became thirsty, [so] he gave him drink, as it is said, "He brought streams out of the rock" (Ps. 78:16).

This king-mashal in praise of God and His care for Israel has nearly all the features of regularization—except that its nimshal has been collapsed into the mashal-proper so as to appear almost interwoven into the narrative. Because the symbolic references of the characters in the narrative, God and Israel, are so absolutely conventional, the collapsed nimshal consists solely of the scriptural verses which are cited to offer a cumulative elaboration of Exod. 14:19. If we wished to regularize the mashal, we could do so simply by completing the narrative about the king and his son without introducing verses, and then having a nimshal which would simply list the pertinent scriptural phrases.

The fact that the form of this mashal is nonregularized would then appear to be trivial. But is it? Another scholar has argued that the mashal's nonregularized form is more indicative than the regularized form of the mashal's authentic function, which, in his view, is to offer a narrative rationale for organizing verses into new relationships and structures.[56] The truth of the matter is that we know too little about the editorial practice of the redactors of midrashic collections and about the history of midrashic literary forms to say definitively what is most authentic or revealing in many cases; this is especially so with Tannaitic texts. Precisely what is considered a mashal in the very early Rabbinic period is not even agreed upon by all scholars.[57]

What deserves to be emphasized most is not the exceptions to regularization or the small changes that ensued in the course of the process, but the overall constancy of form and function that the mashal maintains throughout the period of classical midrash, from the earliest Tannaitic collections like the Mekhilta through the last—that is, latest—collections of the Tanhuma-Yelamdenu school, the final major efflorescence of midrashic literature. Through this entire lengthy period of literary history, it is difficult to see in the existing literary documents of Rabbinic Judaism a single major change that the mashal undergoes. Even in the various medieval "encyclopaediae" of midrashic traditions—the great anthologies like Midrash Hagadol (12th c.) and Yalkut Shim'oni (13th c.)—or in the midrashim attributed to Moses Hadarshan (11th c.), perhaps the last known master of a midrashic "school," the mashal appears hardly changed from the classical Rabbinic form it first assumed centuries earlier.[58]

Tanna de-Bei Eliyahu

The midrashic mashal first undergoes significant changes only in post-Rabbinic, early medieval Jewish literature. These changes appear when literary works begin to be composed which use the literary conventions of classical midrash for purposes other than midrashic exegesis. Examples of meshalim from two such works will serve to illustrate these changes. The first of these works, Tanna de-Bei Eliyahu (TDE), known also as Seder Elijah (Rabbah and Zuta), was probably composed in the ninth century.[59] Written by a single person who unfortunately is unknown, TDE is an unusual text that has been described by one scholar as standing midway between two genres, the homiletical midrash and the ethical treatise.[60] Its author appears to have wished to compose a book that would be more unified and self-contained than a conventional midrashic collection, but he also seems to have wanted to preserve the traditional exegetical frame of midrash. The result is a kind of transitional work: an exposition of themes and ideas, but one whose coherent presentation is always being sidetracked by the lure of exegesis.

Among the literary-rhetorical forms that TDE's author borrowed from classical midrash and altered to suit his own purposes, the mashal holds a prominent place. A good illustration of how he did this can be found in the following mashal, which is partly cognate to the meshalim discussed in Chapter 1 in connection with Eikh. R. 4.11, and with which we can fairly assume TDE's author was familiar. In TDE, as in Eikh. R., the mashal is cited in connection with a discussion of the destruction of the Temple; as in Eikh. R. as well, TDE casts its discussion in the form of a very digressive exposition of Ps. 79:1, a psalm, as the reader will recall, to Asaph. In Eikh. R. 4.11, the figure of Asaph, who is represented in the mashal's narrative through the character of the pedagogue, is never identified; for TDE's author, though, Asaph was a descendant of Korah the Levite, who led the famous revolt against Moses and Aaron and was consequently punished by God by being swallowed alive in an earthquake (Num. 16). In TDE, the mashal is prefaced by a passage that relates how Asaph and other prophets beseeched God not to hand the Israelites over to the Babylonians who, they foresaw, would cruelly persecute them. The passage then returns to Ps. 79:11.

> But should it not be a "weeping" of Asaph, or a "lament" of Asaph, or an "elegy" of Asaph? What does the verse teach us when it says "a song of Asaph"? It teaches us that Asaph and the prophets were rejoicing over something.
>
> They propounded a mashal. What is this like? It is like (*mashlu mashal lemah hadavar domeh le*) the daughter of poor people who went to draw water from a well, and her clay bucket came loose and fell into the well. The daughter of the poor people began to cry and weep. Then the king's daughter came to draw water from the well and her golden bucket came loose and fell into the well. The poor daughter rejoiced and began to dance. People asked her: Until now you were weeping and crying, yet now you are rejoicing and dancing? She replied: The one who will retrieve the golden bucket will also retrieve my clay bucket.
>
> Likewise (*kakh*): When Asaph and the prophets saw that the gates of Jerusalem would be rebuilt in the future—as it is said, "Her gates are sunk into the ground" (Lam. 2:9)—they immediately began to rejoice. Asaph said: The one who will rebuild Jerusalem will also raise my father from the earth. (TDE, ch. 28, pp. 150–151)

Like Eikh. R. 4.11, TDE's mashal begins by asking why Ps. 79:1 says a "song" of Asaph and not a "weeping" or a "lament." TDE's answer, however, differs from that of the classical midrash, and that difference, in turn, points to still others. For our present concerns, these differences are more significant than the similarities between the two parables (like their common use of the motif of paradoxical behavior). For one thing, TDE's mashal is not a king-mashal. Its narrative does not refer symbolically to the destruction of the Temple, as does Eikh. R. 4.11, nor does the TDE mashal formulate a response to the Destruction. Although the parable appears in TDE within an exegetical context, it does not offer an interpretation for a verse so much as an illustration of what Asaph and the other prophets were rejoicing over. And while the parable's narrative adds a certain charm to the passage, it most resembles a quaint folktale. It lacks the kind of "surplus meaning" that the Eikh. R. mashal adds to the exegesis of Lam. 4:11, with its implied representation of the scene of interpretation, and of the *darshan,* the preacher-interpreter.

In TDE, narrative and exegesis fail to intersect as they do in classical mashal. Nothing in TDE's mashal's narrative points to the scriptural occasion of the parable. If the figure of the poor girl represents Asaph, it is not clear whom the princess symbolizes (is she Israel at large or simply a narrative foil for the poor girl?). Finally, even the motif of paradoxical behavior in the TDE mashal has been altered to appear less paradoxical, less strange: unlike the pedagogue in Eikh. R. 4.11, who never weeps but only rejoices when he should be weeping, the poor girl in TDE *first* weeps, and *then* rejoices. Her behavior changes in the course of the narrative, and when she must explain herself to the audience she introduces an additional temporal element by invoking the time of redemption when the Temple will be rebuilt, its gates recovered from the depths of the earth, and Asaph's forefather Korah unburied. Unlike Eikh. R. 4.11, which focuses its narrative upon the pedagogue's reaction, the mashal in TDE is less concentrated and increasingly romance-like—more of a story, or a miniature novella, if you wish.

These two features—the use of the mashal as an illustrative rather than a rhetorical instrument, and the tendency to "novelization," to extending the narrative through its own logic rather than concentrating it upon a single rhetorical message—mark the major shifts in the development of the mashal in TDE. The meshalim in TDE are far more stylized but less formulaic than their Rabbinic models: baroque or classicistic rather than classical. As E. E. Urbach has insightfully shown, this is generally true of TDE's Hebrew.[61] "What do the words of Torah resemble?" TDE asks at one point, answering: "A hide that is given to a man who tans it, smoothes it out, and stretches it until it becomes a work of beauty" (ch. 5, p. 15). As Urbach notes, whether or not this is true of all words of Torah, it is an apt characterization of TDE's own language. Most of the Greek and Latin loan-words and the imperial terminology so common in Amoraic king-meshalim have disappeared from TDE; so have the historical specifics, the everyday allusions, and the unstudied down-to-earth spontaneity of earlier midrashic parables. In striking contrast to Rabbinic texts, which often seem to have been written in a kind of scribal shorthand, nearly all the meshalim in TDE leisurely begin with the complete form of the standard formula *mashlu mashal lemah hadavar domeh le*. In TDE, this formula effectively acquires the meaning of "Once upon a time . . ."

A second mashal from TDE will exemplify still other changes that the Rabbinic literary form undergoes in this composition. This mashal is cited in the course of an involved discussion whose major themes are God's concern for justice and His generosity to those who obey Him. To illustrate these themes, TDE cites Exod. 21:1–3 and then Deut. 15:14,18. These two verses are understood as teaching the following lesson: the reason a Jew is sold into slavery is to atone for transgressions he has committed; accordingly, once he has completed his act of atonement and goes free, having finished the set period of enslavement, his owner must reward him by furnishing him with property. The latter commandment is then offered as a prooftext for the following argument: if persons who were once wicked, like this manumitted Hebrew slave, are rewarded in this world by their former masters, then "all the more so will the righteous of the world, who perform God's will every day," be rewarded in the world-to-come by God. At this point, TDE relates the following mashal:

> They recited a mashal: What is it like? It is like a king of flesh-and-blood who had a large palace with a locked entrance, from which there projected a shelf (*ziz*). On the shelf there were figs, grapes, pomegranates, and every type of fine fruits. Next to it there was [another] shelf, and on it there were silks, combed flax, and all kinds of dyed garments. And next to it there was a

shelf, and food, drink, victuals, and every type of provision upon it. All the people who stood outside came and satisfied themselves from the king's palace. And what did people say as they passed by? [They said:] From what goes out of the king's palace, you can deduce what is inside the palace of the king.

Likewise *(kakh):* from the chastisements of the righteous [in this world], you may learn the measure of punishment of the wicked in Gehennom, and from the prosperity of the wicked [in this world] you can learn of the reward of the righteous in the world-to-come, as it is said, "How abundant is the good that You have in store for those who fear You" (Ps. 31:20); and it says, "Such things had never been heard or noted" (Isa. 64:3). (TDE, ch. 20 (22), p. 120)

The double lesson of the nimshal is not quite identical to the introductory thesis preceding the mashal, which it is supposed to illustrate, but the two teachings are similar enough that TDE's author may not have distinguished between them, or he may have intended the mashal to serve as a bridge between them—a technique that can be observed elsewhere in TDE.[62] In either case, the points of confusion in this overdetermined passage are symptomatic of the problems that arise once the mashal is used primarily as an illustration. Any good storyteller knows that narratives do not faithfully exemplify ideas without losing some of their interest as narratives. As the illustrative function of the mashal becomes increasingly dominant in TDE, its parabolic narratives lose their more symbolic features and simultaneously become less plausible as narratives. For example, the various delights found on the shelves—the fruits, the garments, the provisions—are not symbols at all; they are literally the pleasures that will be enjoyed by the wicked in this world. On the other hand, other details in the narrative—the locked door, for one—have no symbolic value whatsoever. And most problematically of all: What is this narrative really about? What kind of door is this with shelves filled with goodies for everyone to take as he or she passes by? Has any king ever placed a shelf like this outside the door to his palace?

The artificial, implausible character of the narrative in this mashal, which is not untypical of TDE's meshalim, can be appreciated better if compared with an analogous mashal from the classical tradition. The following mashal is to be found in Mid. Teh. 4.11:

R. Joshua b. Levi said:

It is like a king who made a banquet and brought in guests,
and seated them at the entrance to his palace. [The guests] saw
the dogs as they left with pheasants in their mouths and the
heads of fattened calves. They said: If [this is what is eaten by]
the dogs, then how much more [lavish] will our banquet be!

The wicked of Israel are likened to dogs, as it is said, "the
dogs are [the] greedy" (Isa. 56:11), and they prosper in this
world. All the more so will [the righteous of] Israel therefore
[prosper] in the world-to-come, as it says, "You will put joy into
my heart" (Ps. 4:8).

The form of the nimshal in this mashal is slightly irregular, but
one can easily compare its directness and liveliness with the
stylized and contrived narrative in TDE. Where the mashal in
TDE begs for a lesson or an idea that will justify its imagery, the
midrashic mashal's narrative dramatizes its own exegetical act
through the characters of the guests who play the role of implied
interpreters as they observe the king's well-fed dogs.

It is dangerous to generalize about all the meshalim in TDE.
The collection contains more than a hundred examples, and some
are almost perfectly classical in form and function.[63] But the
majority of meshalim in TDE resemble the two examples just discussed and share the more idiosyncratic features of the work as a
whole. In these meshalim, we can see the classical mashal in the
process of its transformation into a didactic medium, and we can
also witness the expense of that transformation—as exacted in
the mashal's narrative-art as well as through its changed function
and meaning.

Sefer Habahir

An analogous though very different change in the mashal can be
seen in a second medieval work that consciously transforms the
midrashic literary form for its own purposes. That work is *Sefer
Habahir,* the "Book of Brilliance."

The earliest composition to exhibit the mystical concepts and
symbolism characteristic of medieval theosophic Kabbalah, *Sefer
Habahir* first appeared in southern France in the twelfth century
and exerted enormous influence upon subsequent Jewish mystical
writings.[64] Composed in the form of a classical midrash with

homiletical expositions of scriptural verses, *Sefer Habahir* employs nearly all the techniques of classical midrashic exegesis—puns and word-plays, interpretations of verses through other verses, gematriot, and anagrams. Among these, the mashal holds an especially prominent position in *Sefer Habahir*.[65] Its relatively short text contains forty-five parables, and these meshalim touch upon the most profound and original aspects of *Sefer Habahir*'s mystical universe.

We can best understand *Sefer Habahir*'s metamorphosis of the classical midrashic mashal into a literary vessel of esoteric doctrine by attending to what it does to the nimshal. As we have seen, the nimshal originated as the literary product of the "midrashization" of the mashal, wherein it became the conventional device for conveying to the audience of the classical Rabbinic mashal the information required to understand the mashal's rhetorical message and to apply it to the mashal's exegetical context. *Sefer Habahir*, an esoteric document that hesitates to divulge its meaning explicitly, simply leaves the nimshal out, dropping it from the mashal's form. As a result of this omission, the meshalim in *Sefer Habahir* are not necessarily entirely mysterious or incoherent. On many occasions, the mashal is preceded by a homily or a statement that helps to create some kind of context for the mashal; in other cases, clues to the mashal's meaning are supplied by its context. But *Sefer Habahir*'s reader is always left partly in the dark, and intentionally so. The absence of a nimshal spreads a kind of occluding patina over the mashal's ulterior meaning, further darkening what is already hidden.

As a result, *Sefer Habahir*'s audience, its reader or adept, is placed in a hermeneutical predicament. One variant of that predicament can be seen in the following passage, one of the few sections of *Sefer Habahir* to offer an approximate narrative context for the recitation of a mashal. The section's subject is the doctrine of the transmigration of souls, one of the book's more controversial contributions to Jewish mysticism, and its main speaker is a certain R. Rahmai, one of a group of pseudonymous fictional sages who figure in *Sefer Habahir*'s midrashic discussions. When the passage begins, R. Rahmai is being questioned by his colleagues about the question of theodicy.

Why does the wicked man[66] prosper, and the righteous man suffer? [R. Rahmai replied:] Because this righteous man was once a wicked man in the past, and is now being punished. [They asked him:] But is a man punished for [the sins of] his youth? Did not R. Simon say that the heavenly court only punishes a man for the [sins he commits from the time he is] twenty years old!? [R. Rahmai] replied: I do not speak of the [same] life; I speak of the fact that he was already there in the past. His colleagues said to him: How long will you speak enigmatically?

He said to them: Go forth and see! A mashal: What is the matter like (lemah hadavar domeh le)? It is like a man who planted a vineyard in his garden, and he hoped it would grow grapes, but it grew wild grapes. He saw that his planting did not succeed, so he cut down the vineyard, tore it out, and cleaned the good grapes from the wild ones, and planted it a second time. When he saw that that [planting] did not succeed, he tore it down, and planted it after he had cleaned it. When he saw that [the third planting also] was not successful, he tore it out and planted it. And how many times [will he replant it]? He said: Until the thousandth generation, as it is written, "The promise (davar, literally: word) He gave for a thousandth generation" (Ps. 105:8). And that is what they say: 974 generations were missing, so the Holy One, blessed be He, arose and implanted them in every generation (B. Hagigah 13b–14a). (par. 195)

This mashal, a good example of the literary form in *Sefer Habahir*, looks much simpler than it actually is, and uses a number of conventions that would have been recognized by *Sefer Habahir*'s original audience. At its beginning, the mashal alludes to Isa. 5:1ff., an allegory that, in its biblical context, portrays the failed career of Israel; the subsequent parts of the parable, describing the owner's repeated attempts to replant the vineyard after it goes bad, also use traditional motifs found in earlier Rabbinic meshalim.[67] To be sure, no classical mashal deals with the doctrine of the transmigration of souls; but the fact that this doctrine is the subject of the present mashal is also not obvious from the mashal's narrative. Little that is explicit in the mashal helps the reader who is not already initiated into *Sefer Habahir*'s doctrines to decode the mashal's meaning. If you are not familiar with the doctrine of transmigration, the citations of Ps. 105:8 and of the Hagigah passage will not enlighten you. At other points, the mashal seems intentionally to use conventions from classical midrash in a misleading way, as though to confuse the mystically innocent reader.

For example, the word *davar* in Ps. 105:8, which in classical midrash is often understood as referring to the Torah, here means something entirely different: the soul, which God appears to be willing to replant in a different human body for up to one thousand generations. Similarly, the Rabbinic dictum quoted from Hagigah has an altogether different meaning in its original context from the one in *Sefer Habahir*.[68] Consequently, even though the two scriptural and Rabbinic sources give the appearance of being nimshal-like, they actually don't give the mashal's audience any information useful for understanding its true meaning.

In fact, for all the seriousness of its subject, the entire passage, including the parable and its narrative frame, seems artfully playful. As Scholem notes, the doctrine of transmigration "is taught as a mystery, accessible to initiates only, yet at the same time the author also takes it so much for granted that he does not consider it as requiring a special justification."[69] When R. Rahmai, responding to his colleagues' question about theodicy, first mentions the doctrine to his colleagues, they appear to be wholly ignorant of it; yet when they accuse Rahmai of speaking obscurely, he responds by telling them a mashal. This parable would be no less obscure to them than his earlier remarks if they did not *already* know about transmigration of souls. Certainly an uninitiated reader could never figure out the mashal's meaning for himself. To be sure, *Sefer Habahir*'s intended reader, unlike Rahmai's colleagues, *is* expected to be acquainted with the doctrine of transmigration, and thus to be capable of understanding the parable's meaning. So the strategy of hermeneutical concealment in this passage may be a kind of mystic's joke.

But it is more than just a joke. As a strategy, it recalls the passage in the New Testament gospels that relates how Jesus first preached the parable of the Sower and then propounded a "theory" of parables that seemed to limit the understanding of the parable to a select group; the passage concludes, however, with Jesus explaining the meaning of the parable of the Sower to his uncomprehending disciples. As I suggested earlier, Jesus' theory of parables should be read and understood within the context of the surrounding narrative; from that literary perspective, the theory propounds a view of parabolic discourse that is not truly concealing or excluding; rather, it comprises a kind of hermeneutical conceit, a view of the relationship between social identification and interpretive capability, which is also implied in the Rabbinic anecdote about Hillel. In both passages, the ability to understand the parable is considered to be a sign of membership in the hermeneutical community: if you understand the parable, then ipso facto you are inside the group and a member.

As *Sefer Habahir* uses the parable, in contrast, the uninitiated reader is genuinely excluded from its meaning. This is no game; at stake are the ultimate truths of esoteric knowledge. But the act of exclusion is achieved in *Sefer Habahir* only by the transformation of the parable from an exoteric into an esoteric literary form, from an allusive narrative with an ulterior message (but one capable of being understood by any person with the necessary interpretive abilities) into a secret code, a private discourse with a hidden meaning (to be disclosed solely to a member of the sect).

The disappearance of the nimshal is the most obvious indication of the transformation that the mashal undergoes in *Sefer Habahir,* but it is not the only sign. The mashal's imagery, its symbolism, and its plot lines all become increasingly enigmatic and bizarre. Consider the following parable, which appears within a narrative context that resembles that of the previous text, and which is also used as a deliberately obscuring, rather than elucidating, instrument. The theme of this passage is the mystical meaning of the vowel *a,* called in Hebrew the *patah,* a word that (in a slightly different vocalization) also means an "opening," hence an entrance or door.

> What is a *patah?* An entrance. And which entrance? It is the one on the north, which is the entrance for the entire world: From the gate through which evil goes forth, good goes forth. And what is good? [R. Akiba] scoffed at them: Didn't I tell you? The small *patah.* They said to him: We forgot. Repeat it to us. He said: What is it like? It is like a king who had a throne. Sometimes he took it in his arms, sometimes he [placed it] on his head. They asked him: Why? [He replied:] Because it was beautiful, and it saddened him to sit upon it. They asked him: And where on his head does he place it? He said to them: In the open [letter] *mem,* as it is said, "Truth springs up from the earth; justice looks down from heaven" (Ps. 85:12). (par. 37)

Much of the imagery in this truly strange parable is, surprisingly enough, traditional. The king's throne is a common motif

used in the Rabbinic mashal; the gesture describing the king taking a fond object in his arms and placing it upon his head has
parallels elsewhere as a motif demonstrating affection; the placing
of the throne upon the king's head is modeled upon the ritual
practice of donning *tefillin,* the phylacteries worn on the forehead
during daily prayer; as used in the mashal, the motif recalls the
Talmudic legend that God wears tefillin.[70]

Yet even with all these traditional associations, the parable's
meaning, as Scholem writes, is "utterly enigmatic."[71] Even though
the open letter *mem* is a symbol of the feminine, a fact that
suggests that the parable should be understood in connection with
mystical sexuality and that the throne is probably a symbol for the
Shekhinah, the narrative still makes little sense.[72] While the king's
answer to why he does not sit on the throne and instead places it
upon his head—because the throne is so beautiful it saddens him
to sit on it—expresses real, recognizably human pathos, it is
impossible to read the narrative solely on a literal or nonsymbolic
plane without having recourse to a symbolic interpretation.
Indeed, it is no exaggeration to say that in this parable, its symbolic dimension has entirely overwhelmed its representational
power.

Reading this parable and others like it in *Sefer Habahir,* it is
possible to appreciate how truly mimetic—of the familiar world
of human reality—Rabbinic meshalim are. In *Sefer Habahir,* that
mimetic familiarity has been entirely left behind for the sake of
entering the world of gnostic speculation. As its speculations come
closer to the ineffable, *Sefer Habahir's* parabolic symbolism also
becomes more recondite, alien, self-contradictory. These tendencies are most evident in the many meshalim in *Sefer Habahir* that
use the feminine as a symbol and that touch upon explicitly gnostic
themes. Here, again, the symbolism frequently appears "traditional." For example, the figure of Wisdom is conventionally identified in Rabbinic literature as Torah; in *Sefer Habahir,* though,
Torah means Gnosis. And while in classical midrash, the Torah is
frequently symbolized either as God's daughter or as His bride, in
Sefer Habahir she becomes the figure of Sophia, who has been
exiled to this world from the *Plērōma,* the realm of "fullness." Consider *Sefer Habahir's* use of these traditional figures in the following parable, presented on its "explicit" level as an exegesis of
1 Kings 5:26, "And God gave wisdom to Solomon."

It is like a king who gave his daughter in marriage to his son, and gave her to him as a gift,[73] and said to him: Do with her as you wish.

Unlike the first *Sefer Habahir* parable we looked at, which was more mysterious than it initially appeared, this one is less enigmatic than it seems at first. The daughter of the king is Sophia, the figure of wisdom/Torah, whom God, the king, gives to Solomon, his son, as bride. Sophia, however, has a second function: she is also the feminine principle of God, and as such the partner of the masculine principle in the divinity, to whom she is already "married." As a result, the king can give her to his son, Solomon, "only as a gift."[74]

On the esoteric level, its meaning, which I have just summarized, is not out of the ordinary. On the purely literal plane, however, the narrative is extraordinary for its unembarrassed use of the imagery of incest. Though obviously not meant to be understood by the initiated reader in any literal sense, a fact that helps to explain why *Sefer Habahir*'s author does not hesitate to use a quintessentially forbidden sexual relationship to represent a matter as sublime as gnosis, it is still hard not to believe that the author used this imagery precisely for its shock value—in order to startle his intended reader into the bafflement of mystical paradox, and perhaps also to embarrass the uninitiated reader, an intruder into the text, by the outrageous implications that the imagery of incest holds if taken on a plainer level of meaning.

These transformations that the classical mashal undergoes in *Sefer Habahir* are not fundamentally different from the changes worked on it in TDE, even though the two documents are about as different as can be imagined, one of them an exoterically moralistic treatise, the other an esoterically gnostic pseudo-midrash. In both works, the mashal becomes an essentially ideational instrument, a tool for bearing a concept or idea, which is either openly illustrated or deliberately obscured through the mashal. What sets *Sefer Habahir*'s parables off from TDE's is a quality that, for lack of a better term, we might call their modernity. Consider the following two meshalim, which are cited in interpretation of Ezek. 3:12, "Blessed be the glory of God from its place."

And what is this "glory of God"? It is like a king who kept a great queen *(matronita)* in his chambers, and all his troops delighted in her, and she had sons. They came every day to greet the king, and they would bless him. They said to him: Our mother, where is she? He said to them: You cannot see her now. They said: Blessed is she wherever she is.   (par. 131)

And what is [the meaning of] what is written, "from its place"? Because no one knows its place. It is like the daughter of a king who came from afar, and nobody knew where she came from. When they saw that she was a woman of strength, that she was beautiful and dignified in all her deeds, they said: She undoubtedly was taken from the side of the light, for her deeds enlighten the world. They asked her: Where are you from? She said: From my place. They replied: If so, the inhabitants of your place must be great men. Blessed are you, and blessed is your place!   (par. 132)

Both these parables are about the pleroma, that realm of divine presence and fullness that is the ultimate object of all gnosis.[75] What is modernist about these parables, though, is precisely their relationship to the pleroma and its gnosis: their narratives do not function as mediums for the instruction *of* wisdom so much as they are *about* wisdom. Wisdom itself is ultimately unknowable, no longer a source of instruction. In the first parable quoted, the female figure representing Sophia is depicted as being literally absent; she can only be blessed in her absence, "wherever she is." In the second parable, she is present in this world, but what most interests the unnamed people in the parable—and perhaps *Sefer Habahir*'s author as well—is the place of her origin, "from afar," from which she is now absent by virtue of being in this world. In both parables, their emphasis falls on the absent, the negative.

These features of *Sefer Habahir*'s parables should not mislead us into mistaking them for authentically modern compositions. When a writer like Kafka takes up the literary form of the parable, it is consciously as an archaic form of ancient wisdom, which he employs specifically in order to express the futility of understanding, the hopelessness of our interpretive efforts. The path to wisdom cannot be regained. As Walter Benjamin noted, for Kafka that wisdom has been lost to us in everything save for its form, its "transmissibility."[76] In *Sefer Habahir*, in contrast, wisdom's absence, once acknowledged, is given, by virtue of its gnostic revisionism, a positive value; it thereby comes to hold a dream-like promise of absolute presence. In Kafka, that promise has become more like a disturbing omen of an equally absolute absence. The difference between *Sefer Habahir*'s transformation of the Rabbinic mashal and the modern appropriation of the literary form virtually sums up the literary history of the mashal. It composes, one might say, the parable of parables.

Maimonides and Other Philosophers

Beginning with the Geonic age in the eighth and ninth centuries, the imaginative energies that formerly had gone into composing midrash were channeled into other genres of Jewish literature. At the same time, the mashal gradually yielded its status as the preeminent type of fictional narrative in Hebrew to other forms like the exemplum.[77] A striking example of this change is the collection of stories known as "The Meshalim of Solomon": despite its title, this book consists entirely of exempla, without a single parable in it.[78] The same tendency is illustrated in *Sefer Hasidim*, "The Book of the Pious," the famous late-twelfth- or early-thirteenth-century pietistic treatise: though nearly every page of the book is filled with exempla, some of which are among the most original narratives in all medieval Hebrew literature, the treatise has hardly a mashal in it, while the few that do appear tend to turn into exempla by their conclusions.[79] The fable, however, unlike the mashal, remained a popular presence in Hebrew literature throughout the Middle Ages, both in story collections and in *maqamat,* the Hebrew rhymed-prose narratives that first appeared in Spain in the early twelfth century.[80]

Virtually the only authors to use the mashal with human characters in medieval Jewish literature are philosophers and mystics. These authors carry forward the tendencies initiated in TDE and *Sefer Habahir,* and complete the transformation of the narrative mashal into a form of allegory used almost exclusively as a medium for ideational illustration.[81] In the Hebrew of the later Middle Ages, the word mashal itself becomes a virtual terminus technicus for allegoresis, joining other rhetorical and philosophical terms that entered the language at this time (even though precedents for this use of the word mashal can be found in classical Rabbinic literature and the Bible).[82]

The allegorical transformation of the mashal was not solely a Jewish phenomenon. Medieval Arabic philosophers like Avicenna and Averroës used parables in their writings in much the same way, as did early Jewish philosophers like David al-Muqammis (ca. 10th c.) who wrote his works in Arabic, not Hebrew. When subsequent Jewish philosophers (many of whom originally wrote in Judaeo-Arabic, their works being translated into Hebrew only later) used the parable, it is therefore likely that they were drawing upon the philosophical rather than the Rabbinic tradition.[83] Even so, the Jewish philosophers could not have been unaware of the ubiquitous meshalim in Rabbinic literature, and their (at least) external resemblance to philosophical parables.

The philosophical parable, too, was not a one-dimensional, simplistic narrative form (though in the hands of some it could deteriorate into tendentious predictability). Bahya Ibn Pequdah, the twelfth-century author of the classic ethical treatise *The Duties of the Heart* (ca. 1180), employed meshalim to great effect, borrowing some parables from earlier sources and inventing many others himself. As Joseph Dan has suggested, Bahya used the mashal to express in the form of narrative certain radical philosophical and religious ideas that he did not wish to spell out in explicit discursive form; however, he clearly expected the attentive reader to derive those ideas and the implications of his more guarded statements from the allegorical details left unexplained in the texts of the parabolic narratives.[84]

In the case of Maimonides (1135–1203), one finds a similar use of the mashal that is, however, more interesting in its theory than in its practice. Maimonides' main significance in the history of the mashal as a narrative form lies in the way he joined the separate acts of interpretation and composition under the common rubric of allegory. One of the main purposes of the *Guide of the Perplexed*, he writes in his introduction to Part I of that book, is "the explanation of very obscure parables occurring in the books of the prophets, but not explicitly identified there as such." What Maimonides means by parables—Arabic *amthila* (singular *mithal*) or Hebrew meshalim (in Ibn Tibbon's Hebrew translation from the original Judaeo-Arabic)—are figurative sayings or passages that pose difficulties for a reader who insists upon taking them in their literal or plain sense. For Maimonides, these parables are to be likened to "apples of gold in settings of silver," to use the phrase from Prov. 25:11 that Maimonides himself invokes as his prooftext: that is, sayings whose "external meaning contains wisdom that is useful in many respects" while their internal meaning "contains wisdom that is useful for beliefs concerned with the truth as it is."[85] While Maimonides proceeds to distinguish between two types of allegorical discourse that are found in Scripture—those in which every word in the parable holds a special meaning, and others in which solely the parable in its entirety indicates the whole of the intended meaning—the parables that Maimonides himself employs in the *Guide* are closer to the former than to the latter type.

The most famous of these is surely the Parable of the Palace (part 3, ch. 51). In this parable, Maimonides uses the imagery of a palace, of its ruler, who lives in the palace, and of his subjects, who are outside the building, to describe the different ranks of mankind in terms of their attainment to complete wisdom as culminating in the perfect knowledge of God:

> The ruler is in his palace, and all his subjects are partly within the city and partly outside the city. Of those who are within the city, some have turned their backs upon the ruler's habitation, their faces being turned another way. Others seek to reach the ruler's habitation, turn toward it, and desire to enter it and to stand before him, but up to now they have not yet seen the wall of the habitation. Some of those who seek to reach it have come up to the habitation and walk around it searching for its gate. Some of them have entered the gate and walk about in the antechambers. Some of them have entered the inner court of the habitation and have come to be with the king, in one and the same place with him, namely, in the ruler's habitation. But their having come into the inner part of the habitation does not mean that they see the ruler or speak to him. For after their coming into the inner part of the habitation, it is indispensable that they should make another effort; then they will be in the presence of the ruler, see him from afar or from nearby, or hear the ruler's speech or speak to him.

In the explanation following the parable, Maimonides identifies the various ranks of mankind in the parable's groups of subjects by their distance from the king; as the explanation concludes, it is only the philosopher—that person who has come close to certainty in those divine matters "in which one can only come close"—who "has come to be with the ruler in the inner part of the habitation."[86]

Later medieval Jewish philosophers as well as modern scholars have debated the precise meaning of the palace parable within its context in the *Guide*.[87] Whatever the parable *means*, however, its description of the palace *as an image* is certainly very memorable; as Frank Talmadge has suggested, Maimonides may have modeled its imagined architecture upon that of a real royal palace like the Alhambra in Granada, with its "open designs without beginning, end, or repose, in pursuit of unattainable being, alternating between 'inner' and 'outer,'" in the words of the Spanish historian Americo Castro.[88] As a narrative, though, the parable is little more than an extended, essentially static image. The important details in it are all spatial: the design of the palace, the positions of the different subjects in it, their respective distances from the king, and so on. None relates to factors like character or plot that would be crucial in a genuine narrative.

The same is true of Maimonides' other parables, and those of most other medieval Jewish philosophers who employ the mashal.[89] While these compositions have a superficial similarity to the midrashic king-mashal, they are really entirely different literary forms. Still, it is likely that one reason philosophers like Maimonides and Bahya found the parable so attractive a literary form was precisely its presence in the classics of Jewish literature. These philosophers were well aware of the radically innovative and untraditional nature of their intellectualized approach to Judaism. As they searched for exemplars in the past to invoke as predecessors in their own defense, literary forms like the mashal helped to give their works the appearance of tradition—that is to say, the aura of antiquity.

Zohar and Other Mystical Texts

Aside from philosophy, the other major literary genre in which the mashal appears in medieval Jewish literature is the literature of Kabbalah, or Jewish mysticism, as it developed in Spain in the thirteenth century. We have already seen how the author of *Sefer Habahir* transformed the midrashic mashal into an esoteric form which he used for conveying his gnostic views. In the Zohar, the seminal work of Spanish Kabbalah and arguably the greatest imaginative composition in all medieval Jewish literature, the midrashic mashal is used once again for esoteric purposes.

At first glance, the Zohar's meshalim appear to be less paradoxical and obscure as literary objects than their predecessors in *Sefer Habahir*. In formal respects, they are more similar to the classical Rabbinic mashal. For example, like its midrashic model, the mashal in the Zohar typically appears within a homiletical—that is, mystically homiletical—context. Reversing *Sefer Habahir's* unclassical practice, the Zohar restores the standard nimshal (beginning with the formulaic *kakh*) to the mashal's literary form; and many of these nimshalim conclude "midrashically," with the citation and exegesis of a scriptural verse. These classical midrashic features all fit the Zohar's literary persona. Although the composition of the book in its entirety is extremely complex, with different literary (probably authorial) strata, the Zohar's overall ambition might be described as a vast imaginative effort to recreate the world of Rabbinic Judaism in the image of Kabbalah, replete with all its sages and the literary-rhetorical forms that characterized their discourse.[90]

Yet despite all its intentional similarities to midrash, the Zohar differs from its classical model in one crucial aspect. It is all in Aramaic, specifically in the Zohar's Aramaic—an artificial but exceedingly vital literary language which Moses de Leon, the likely author of much of the Zohar, invented for his book, energetically improvising it out of diverse sources with an almost Joycean linguistic zest.[91] In the case of the Zohar's meshalim, this difference is very striking, since Rabbinic meshalim are nearly all in Hebrew (though they often contain some Aramaic lines, usually dialogue, within them). Whatever Moses de Leon had in mind when he created the literary language for his pseudonymous work, which he claimed after all merely to have discovered in manuscript—the work having been composed, he said, by the second-century sage Simeon bar Yohai—the difference in language between the Zohar's meshalim and their midrashic predecessors produces a kind of paradoxical situation. On the one hand, the Zohar's parables seem rigorously to imitate the Rabbinic meshalim in order to maintain the pretense of their authenticity as ancient parables; on the other, their anachronistic, unmidrashic language belies their belatedness and fictionality in the plainest sense. It is almost as though we can see the Zohar's author winking at us in silent acknowledgment of the game he was playing with the hallowed literary conventions of Rabbinic tradition.

The same self-aware playfulness informing the Zohar on its linguistic plane characterizes its deployment of allegory. Scholars have long discussed the influence of Maimonides and other medieval Jewish philosophers upon Moses de Leon, and the philosopher's transformation of the mashal into a form of allegory is also reflected in the Zohar.[92] Yet unlike the philosophers, for whom parabolic narrative was essentially pictorial, employed at most to hint at a philosophical thesis buried beneath the mashal's surface, the Zohar's author used the mashal to play upon one of his favorite themes: the elusive distinction between the inner and the outer sense, appearance and reality, being and meaning. In a famous passage in the Zohar, Simeon bar Yohai, the book's pseudonymous protagonist, decries those people "who say that the Torah presents mere stories and ordinary words" and who do not recognize that "the story of Torah" is merely "a garment" for its spirit and true essence.[93] While the point of this statement in context is to disparage those persons who fail to recognize the mystical meaning of Torah, what is more revealing for our present concerns is the disparagement of narrative—as "mere stories and ordinary words"—that the statement also evinces. Yet the Zohar's own meshalim actively belie this contempt for narrative by showing how deeply revealing such "mere stories" and "ordinary words" can be.

Unlike the philosophers' parables, the narratives in the Zohar's meshalim, their characters, and their imagery, are not simply cloaks for the divine truth, or "essence," contained in the nimshal. Very often the imagery in the narratives is to be taken "literally"— that is, at face value, or nearly so, since the meaning of a literal or manifest sense, "the face value," is itself transvalued within the Zohar's self-mirroring epistemology. In one mashal, for example, Moses is represented in the narrative as the husband of the king's daughter. In itself this characterization is not surprising, and has precedents in the classical tradition. Yet within the Zohar's theosophy, with its system of *sephirot*, or aspects of God's personality, Moses "mystically" *is* the husband of the king's daughter, since he also represents the *sephirah* of Tiferet, which is actually joined in marriage with the Shekhinah, the feminine principle in God.[94] Similarly, another mashal tells of a person who loved his friend so much he brought his bed to the friend's house so they could live together. On one level, the bed represents the *mishkan*, the Tabernacle, in which God promises He will dwell in the midst of Israel; on another level, though, the *mishkan* is the Shekhinah, who herself is called in the Zohar by the name of Bed on account of her intimate relationship with Tiferet, the Holy One.[95]

Even more paradoxically, the Zohar plays with the distinction between appearance and reality, inner and outer meaning, by framing its meshalim within larger narratives. One of the most delightful of all the sections in the Zohar, that of the Sava (or Old Man) de-Mishpatim, tells of an elderly donkey-driver whom the Zohar's sages meet while traveling, and whom they ridicule until he suddenly reveals himself to be a great master of mystical truths. The Old Man, who virtually personifies the deceptiveness of external appearance, mercilessly puts the sages to shame for their haughtiness and pretensions, and then proceeds to tell them what is probably the most celebrated parable in the entire Zohar, the parable of the Princess in the Palace.

> For the Torah resembles a beautiful and stately damsel, who is hidden in a secluded chamber of her palace and who has a secret lover, unknown to all others. For love of her he keeps passing the gate of her house, looking this way and that in search of her. She knows that her lover haunts the gate of her house. What does she do? She opens the door of her hidden chamber ever so little, and for a moment reveals her face to her lover, but hides it again forthwith. Were anyone with her lover, he would see nothing and perceive nothing. He alone sees it, and he is drawn to her with his heart and soul and his whole being, and he knows that for love of him she disclosed herself to him for one moment, aflame with love for him.
>
> So is it with the word of the Torah, which reveals herself only to those who love her . . .[96]

And yet, as the Old Man relates the parable's nimshal, his own speech cannot escape the parable's highly figured language. As he describes it, the Torah is not only feminine, a grammatical if not ontological truth; but *her* manner resembles the way of personification, the oblique path of parable.

> The Torah knows that the mystic haunts the gate of her house. What does she do? From within her hidden palace she discloses her face and beckons to him and returns forthwith to her place and hides . . . Only then, when he has become familiar with her, does she reveal herself to him face to face and speak to him of

all her hidden secrets and all her hidden ways, which have been in her heart from the beginning. Such a man is then termed perfect, a "master," that is to say, a "bridegroom of the Torah" in the strictest sense, the master of the house, to whom she discloses all her secrets, concealing nothing.

The emphasis upon the mystic student of the Torah being the "'bridegroom of the Torah' *in the strictest sense*" (italics added) collapses all easy distinctions between the outer and the inner sense, the literal and the allegorical. The mystic's own relationship to Torah becomes a virtual mashal in its own right, and the figured language of the mashal's narrative is, by the parable's end, intricately woven into the texture of the Zohar's own "literal" discourse.

The Zohar's mashal recalls Maimonides' palace parable, which, though hardly a mystical text, similarly speaks of esoteric knowledge (in the form of philosophy).[97] And both meshalim hearken back to a Rabbinic mashal preserved in Tanhuma (Pekudei 4), which interprets the word "testimony" in Exod. 38:21 ("the tabernacle of testimony") as referring to the Torah. I will quote only the narrative of this mashal:

It is like a king who had a daughter and built her a palace. He set her within seven chambers, and proclaimed: Whoever trespasses upon my daughter will be considered to have trespassed against me.

It is possible that this midrashic mashal is the source for the central image in both the Zohar's and Maimonides' parables, the image of the palace as a symbol for Torah. It is also possible, however, that the two later "esoteric" parables derive from a separate tradition attested in a still earlier mashal, which, though not preserved within any extant Rabbinic text, is mentioned by Origen. In his commentary on Psalms, Origen quotes "a Hebrew scholar" as saying that Scripture is like a large house with many rooms in it, each one locked, and that outside each locked door is a key—but it is not the right key for that door; only the experienced can read the signs on the key indicating which door it will open.[98]

If the Zohar's palace parable derives from the parable mentioned by Origen, even indirectly, it may be possible to speak of a kind of esoteric subtradition of the mashal. Whether or not that tradition existed *before* the Zohar, it certainly existed afterward.

We know of at least one parable (recorded by Moses ben Makhir in his *Seder Hayom,* published in 1793, a post-Lurianic, Kabbalah-influenced guide to Jewish liturgy and ritual) that conflates several motifs from the earlier palace-meshalim—the princess locked in the tower, the locked rooms with the wrong keys, the challenge of the king, the hapless but devoted lover in search of the princess—in order to make out of them a new parable.[99]

Ben Makhir's *Seder Hayom,* along with other quasi-popular ethical treatises like it, many of them influenced by later Kabbalah, served as conduits for the mashal and its literary transmission into the early modern period.[100] Throughout this period, the parable remained a mainstay of popular preachers, as one can see in the collections of the early Hasidic masters, in works like *Shivhei Habesht* (In Praise of the Ba'al Shem Tov, published in 1814) and the *Toledot Yaakov Yosef* of Yaakov Yosef of Polnoy (published in 1780).[101] Nor was the parable used only by Hasidim. Probably the most celebrated of all eighteenth-century parabolists was the Maggid of Dubnow, Yaakov ben Ze'ev Kranz (1741–1804), a close friend of Elijah, the Gaon of Vilna. According to one account, the Vilna Gaon once asked the Maggid how he invented his parables, and the Maggid replied by telling the Gaon the following parable: A master archer was once asked by a prince how he managed always to shoot his arrow into the bull's-eye. The archer replied, "First I take aim at the target, and when the arrow sticks I outline the circles round that point, and then color them in."[102] That more or less sums up the Maggid's theory of parables.

In strictly formal terms, the parables of the Ba'al Shem Tov and of the Maggid of Dubnow bear only a tangential relationship to the midrashic king-mashal: they do not consciously employ its linguistic or thematic conventions, nor do they carry forward the project of joining exegesis and narrative that is at the very heart of the classical form. They also lack the Rabbinic mashal's anthropomorphic boldness in imagining God. Still, these late meshalim, preserved in the canons of Jewish religious literature at the dawn of the modern age, testify to the abiding impression left by the classical mashal, to its status in Jewish tradition as the exemplary form of narrative. A similar homage to the classical mashal is paid by Nahman of Bratslav (1722–1810) in his celebrated Tales. Although they are not parables in any strict sense, these tales have often—and not unreasonably—been understood by modern readers as evoking the mashal simply by virtue of their explicit intention to capture through narrative the most profound and elusive ultimate truths.[103]

Modern Hebrew Literature

The complicated relationship of modern Hebrew literature to classical Jewish literary tradition is a topic in literary history that is frequently discussed though its problematics are rarely demonstrated in practice. The points of dissimilarity and discontinuity between the two are too well known to need repeating here. The example of the mashal, however, may provide an unusual window through which to view a rare instance of continuity in modern Jewish writing. Not that the classical mashal is revived as a vibrant literary form in any major way, but the form does appear in the writings of many of the early masters of modern Hebrew,[104] usually as a piece of ornamental rhetoric, though in one writer the mashal is employed for a truly revealing rhetorical purpose.

That writer is, predictably, S. Y. Agnon (1888–1970). Like Nahman's Tales, many of Agnon's stories can be called parabolic in the loosest sense of the word.[105] But traditional parables in their classical form (though they are nearly always Agnon's own inventions) are also found in Agnon's work, where they are preserved almost as quotations of the past. Beginning with his first published story, "Agunot," Agnon used the classical mashal as a self-conscious device within his larger narratives in order to invoke the stable universe of meaning that characterized traditional Judaism and its world.[106]

The complexity, the irony, and the ambivalence with which Agnon enlists the mashal in these narratives can be illustrated by their presence in one story, "Agadat Hasofer" (The Tale of a Scribe). The scribe of the title is one Rafael, and his wife is Miriam.[107] Almost stereotypically pious, the couple are also childless, and their story, which Agnon ironically calls the *toledot* (literally, "generations") of Rafael, an allusion to Gen. 25:19 ("These are the generations of Isaac . . ."), is in fact a tale of barren piety, of the spiritual failure of generation. In the Tale, Agnon uses several meshalim at crucial moments in the narrative.

The first parable appears at the Tale's very beginning, which tells us that Rafael is often commissioned by bereaved widowers to write Torah-scrolls in memory of wives who have not borne their husbands children. In a mashal that immediately follows, the narrator uses the parable to explain how the Torah-scrolls literally take the place of children and good deeds by testifying in heaven to the deceased's piety. This message of symbolic substitution sets the logic for the rest of the Tale's narrative. When the childless Miriam herself dies a short time later, Rafael undertakes to write a Torah-scroll on her behalf, but instead of becoming a memorial to his wife's memory, or even a surrogate for the children they never had, the Torah Rafael writes becomes the instrument of his own self-immolation. Whether that immolation is literal or figurative the narrator never makes entirely clear, but at the story's conclusion, in a moment of ecstatic celebration, Rafael and Miriam are finally reunited as together they collapse to the ground with the Torah the scribe has written in his wife's memory.

Through the course of this story, a complex allegory of art as a self-consuming act of erotic fulfillment, Agnon inserts three additional meshalim into the narrative. Each of these meshalim almost perfectly imitates the classical form of the mashal. Thus, in describing how Rafael works, Agnon tells us that the scribe took great care never to write the name of God without immersing himself in a ritual bath; accordingly, he would often write an entire section of the Torah, leaving empty spaces where the name of God would appear; later, after immersing himself, he would fill the spaces in. To this anecdote, Agnon adds the following mashal:

> It is like an artisan who was making a crown for a king. Does he not first make the crown, and after that, set in it fine gems and jewels?
>
> And so [Rafael] used to sit and write until the sun set and knocked on his window, calling to him, The time for the afternoon prayer has arrived.[108]

In composing this mashal, Agnon, who was celebrated for his encyclopedic knowledge of classical Hebrew literature, certainly had in mind several meshalim about making crowns that are found in earlier Jewish texts, in Rabbinic literature, early mystical writing, and Hasidic texts.[109] The mashal is an obvious attempt at imitation, and it appears within the narrative as a kind of narratorial aperçu. Yet even though the parable's function in the Tale is primarily ornamental, lending a traditional aura to the story's language, it comes to serve a deeper purpose for Agnon. As a mode of discourse to which the narrator repeatedly returns in his narration of Rafael's history, the mashal becomes for Agnon a kind of touchstone, an occasion for returning to the equation between fiction and truth that is encapsulated in the relationship of mashal to nimshal. The literary form of the mashal becomes in this way a guarantee of meaning and stability that also lies behind the story's ideal equation between Torah-scroll and child, or art and life.

The story as a whole, however, utterly collapses these equations and confutes their truth. Its very last paragraph reads almost like an attempt to reverse the stable order of a typical mashal. The paragraph begins with what might otherwise be a nimshal: a description of the Holy One, blessed be He, removing His robe of light while the world stands in silent evening prayer. But this divine scene, a scene of devout repose, immediately gives way to its human analogue—the mashal-proper, as it were—in which Rafael the scribe is described as he lies collapsed upon the ground with his wife's wedding dress spread out over him and the Torah-scroll as a shroud.

Agnon's use of the mashal is characteristic of his treatment of tradition in general.[110] Traditional Jewish language and themes appear in Agnon's fiction almost as purely formal channels or mediums for expressing messages concerned with the doubtful presence of faith, if not its actual absence. This use of the mashal—as a traditional form that negates tradition—brings our brief history nearly full circle. In Agnon the mashal's literary form becomes its message, which is a lesson of emptiness, of nonpresence. Yet Agnon's highly deliberate and accomplished use of the mashal, his masterful recovery of the classical form, is also our strongest proof for the mashal's persistence in Hebrew literature, a powerful instance of the lines of continuity and discontinuity that govern the history of that literature. Even in periods of the greatest discontinuity, moments of surprising continuity emerge unpredictably.

Nonparabolic Narratives in Rabbinic Literature

Apart from the mashal, most narratives in Rabbinic literature belong to one of two other genres: the homiletical-exegetical narrative and the *ma'aseh*.[1] Like the mashal, these other genres are didactic in function: they always serve, directly or indirectly, to teach something. The essential criteria distinguishing them are their claim to historicity and their "history-likeness." The mashal, the only narrative form in Rabbinic literature openly to acknowledge its fictionality, does not pretend to any historical reality; it justifies its status as fiction by its utility as an exegetical tool. The homiletical-exegetical narrative claims for itself the same historicity as is attributed to the biblical narrative that is its primary subject. Finally, the ma'aseh claims to be fully historical.

Apart from this basic generic difference between them, the homiletical-exegetical narrative and the ma'aseh possess the following distinctive structural and formal features.

The Homiletical-Exegetical Narrative

This genre includes the narratives in Rabbinic literature that are associated most closely with midrash. Also called the extra-biblical legend, the genre of the homiletical-exegetical narrative consists of stories that elaborate upon the biblical text, either in the form of commentary or as independent, autonomous narratives.[2] Some of these stories explicitly respond to actual difficulties in the scriptural text, or first originated in this way and later became independent legends.[3] Others appear to have originated independently of the biblical text, to which they were later attached artificially.[4] Many examples of the extra-biblical legend tend, however, to collapse the distinction between the two categories just mentioned:

initially seeming to have only a slight relationship to the biblical text, the narrative suddenly surprises the reader by elucidating or seizing upon a real feature in it. In any case, the characters in these legends are nearly always biblical figures, often minor personages who emerge in these narratives as major players in the retold version of the Bible.

As discourse, these narratives mingle narrative and exegesis so as to create a single weave of language in which, as Ophra Meir has noted, homiletical and interpretive asides constantly interrupt and punctuate the act of narration.[5] The stories often take off from a homily or an exegesis and, after being narrated, return to their scriptural base. Consider the following passage from Eikh. R. (pp. 75–76), which relates not only a homiletical narrative but the full context for its recitation. R. Ami and R. Samuel b. Nahman were both third-generation Palestinian Amoraim.

> R. Ami asked R. Samuel b. Nahman: Since I have heard that you are a master of aggadah, what does the following verse mean: "Your charity (tzidkatekha) [is] high as the heavens, O God" (Ps. 71:19)?
>
> R. Samuel said: [It means that] just as mortal creatures need to perform charity (tzedakah) for each other, so too the heavenly creatures need to perform charity for each other.
>
> This is what is written: "He spoke to the man clothed in linen and said, 'Step inside the wheelwork, under the cherubs, and fill your hands with glowing coals from among the cherubs, and scatter them over the city'" (Ezek. 10:2). The reason the verse repeats itself by saying, "He spoke" and "[he] said," is to teach us that [first] the Holy One, blessed be He, spoke to the angel, and [then] the angel said to the cherub: The Holy One, blessed be He, said to me, "Step inside the wheelwork, under the cherubs, and fill your hands with glowing coals." But I can't enter behind your curtain; I'll be burned. Perform an act of charity for me, and give me two coals. What is written there? "And a cherub . . . took some and put it into the hands of him who was clothed in linen" (Ezek. 10:7). R. Pinhas said: The phrases "took some" and "put it" teach that the cherub let the coals cool off before he gave them to the angel.
>
> R. Joshua of Sikhnin said in the name of R. Levi: For three years those burning coals lay smoldering in Gabriel's palms because he hoped that Israel would repent. But they did not. And when they did not, Gabriel was going to hurl down the coals in fury and crush the testicles of Israel, but the Holy One,

blessed be He, said: Gabriel! Gabriel! Easy, easy! Some of them perform acts of charity for each other. That is what is written: "And there appeared to the cherubs the form of a man's hand under their wings" (Ezek. 10:8).

R. Abba bar Kahana said in the name of R. Levi: On account of what do the upper and the lower worlds stand? On account of the charity that the people of Israel do for each other.

[R. Samuel continued his exposition of Ps. 71:19:] "You who have done great things"—this refers to the two luminaries in the heavens, as it is written, "And God made the two great lights" (Gen. 1:16).

"O God, who is Your peer!" (Ps. 71:19)—Who is like You among the heavenly creatures? Who is like You among the mortal creatures? Who is like You in extending Your anger in the face of the Principle of Justice?

At that moment, the Principle of Justice leaped up before the Holy One, blessed be He, and said to Him: Master of the universe! Is this fitting Your honor? That they should say that a creature of flesh-and-blood has burned the Sanctuary?! Does this fit Your honor that a villain should boast and say: I have burned down God's House?! If so, let fire fall from on high and burn it! Replied the Holy One, blessed be He: You have offered a good argument in My defense. And immediately, the fire descended, as it is said, "From above He sent a fire" (Lam. 1:13).

I have quoted this lengthy passage in its entirety because it demonstrates the complexity with which a homiletical-exegetical narrative can shuttle back and forth among exegesis, homily, and story. What begins as a straightforward homiletical interpretation of Ps. 71:19, a small sermon in praise of charity, turns into a highly mythical narrative recounting the heavenly drama that ensued in the heavenly court before the Temple's destruction. Yet this narrative is phrased as an exegesis of Ezek. 10:2–8, itself a deeply enigmatic vision which is made only more mythical as it is retold. And while this narrative appears at first to offer an appropriate illustration for the opening homily on charity—which is the occasion for its telling—the narrative's full meaning becomes far more complex by the passage's conclusion. For, after completing the exegesis of Ezek. 10:8, R. Nahman returns to the exposition of Ps. 71:19, but that exegesis—in praise of God's charity toward Israel—itself turns into the narrative that began earlier with the Ezekiel verses; now, however, the narrative, no less mythic than before, shows how God's own charity surrenders to the Principle of Justice (charity's opposite, as it were); the narrative ends with God sanctioning the Destruction, allowing fire to descend from heaven to consume the Temple.

The full effect of the passage is something like that of an origami-strip: it folds back upon itself, reversing the difference between narrative and exegesis into a kind of illusion of discourse. Homily turns into exegesis, then into narrative, and finally back into exegetical homily until suddenly it switches into narrative once more, yet only to conclude with an exegesis of Lam. 1:13. This elaborate series of metamorphoses only distracts, however, from the passage's most remarkable feature. The conventional piety of the homily "frames" a truly unconventional picture of the divine court, which is portrayed as a kind of Byzantine bureaucracy in which even the angels seem to be subjected to union-like rules prohibiting them from trespassing beyond their strict functions while God's own honor needs to be looked after by His divine servants.

This particular example is somewhat unusual inasmuch as it presents an extended narrative more or less in its entirety. Homiletical-exegetical narratives are characteristically preserved in a more fragmentary form, telling just enough to respond to the exegetical difficulty at hand or to the immediate homiletical occasion. Frequently, too, these narratives appear in combination with other literary forms like the mashal: for one example, see Eikh. R. 3.1.

The Ma'aseh

The primary generic characteristic of the *ma'aseh*, literally "a deed" or "an occurrence," is the claim to historicity, to having once taken place. This claim, of course, has nothing to do with the separate, historical question of whether or not the ma'aseh actually did occur. Nor does the claim to historicity entail a claim to naturalism: very frequently, ma'asim contain supernatural or miraculous elements.

Perhaps the best-known type of ma'aseh is the exemplum, the story with a moral, which I discussed briefly in Chapter 1. In addition to the exemplum, the genre of the ma'aseh includes several other types of brief "historical" or "history-like" narratives.

Sage-Stories

As its name suggests, this category consists of anecdotes and tales that deal with the lives and deeds of known Rabbis who lived from the Pharisaic period on. The following story about Rabba bar Bar Hana, a fourth-century sage, is a typical example of the form; the narrative is recorded in B. Berakhot 53b immediately after the anecdote about the two disciples who did not say Grace, discussed in Chapter 1. Rabba's story picks up several themes from the preceding anecdote and the larger passage.

> Rabba bar Bar Hana was traveling in a caravan. He ate but he forgot to bless Grace. [Later he remembered], and asked himself: What shall I do? If I tell [the gentile leaders of the caravan] that I forgot to say Grace, they will tell me, Say the blessing here. Wherever you bless the Merciful One, you bless Him. It will therefore be better if I tell them that I forgot a golden dove [in the place where I ate].
>
> So he said to them: Wait for me, for I forgot a golden dove back there.
>
> He returned [to the place], said Grace, and found a golden dove there.
>
> And what was special about a dove? For the community of Israel is likened to a dove, as it is written, "The wings of the dove are covered with silver, and her pinions with the shimmer of gold" (Ps. 68:14). Just as the dove is saved only by means of its wings, so Israel is saved only by means of the commandments.

As it happens, Rabba bar Bar Hana is the protagonist of a number of fantastic travel stories resembling tall tales that are recorded in the Talmud (Baba Batra 73a–74b). On some of these journeys, Rabba claimed to have seen antelopes the size of mountains, birds as tall as heavens, Israelites who had died while wandering in the wilderness after the Exodus, and members of the rebellious company of Korah who were swallowed in the famous earthquake. The present story is a tall tale in its own right—it resembles the exotic adventures recounted in works like Lucian's *True History*—and it is also an exemplum as well as being a sage-story.

The clever novelty in Rabba's story is that the sage's reward, the golden dove, is identical to the white lie he tells the gentile caravan-leaders. The story's most remarkable feature, though, is in its final passage where the "meaning" of the golden dove is expounded as a symbol for the community of Israel. This small and fanciful narrative detail in the sage-story is treated in precisely the same way as details in Scripture are treated in midrash: not only as necessarily meaningful, but as holding a meaning that is crucial to the community of Israel in its relationship to God and His law. "Reading" Rabba's golden dove this way lends both the sage's life and everything connected to it, even this golden dove, an authority and significance equivalent to those of Torah itself. This assumption about the absolute significance of the events narrated in the sage-tale is the subgenre's underlying rationale.

As in the Greco-Roman *chreia,* the purpose of these stories is didactic emulation: to extol a certain kind of behavior and existence as exemplified in the life of the sage. Perhaps the best-known sage-stories are the many anecdotes preserved in ARN, among them the stories about Hillel and Shammai in chs. 14 and 15 (one of which I quoted and discussed in Chapter 6). That these stories should be read as ideological statements rather than as historiographical or even hagiographical documents is now accepted by most scholars, though there remain differences of opinion over the specific perspective to use in approaching the narratives. According to some scholars, the sage is to be understood as a social-political type; according to others, he is an exemplar of the religious and psychological struggles that the life of piety (as conceived by the Rabbis) requires.[6] In either case, the life of the sage is a model of ideal behavior. The form, however, can also be parodied; see the stories about R. Joshua and children in Eikh. R. (pp. 54–56).

Because it is so prevalent a category in Rabbinic literature, the sage-story can be subdivided into several more specific types:

1. *Example-stories,* in which the sage performs symbolic or parabolic deeds, or where his smallest actions, like Rabba bar Bar Hana's above, are treated as deeply meaningful, often with halakhic repercussions. Such stories are often quoted both in the Mishna and in the Talmud as legal precedents.[7]

2. *Miracle-stories,* in which the sage performs a supernatural deed—causing rain to fall through his prayers or through fasting, for example—or in which he becomes involved in a miraculous situation.[8]

3. *Pronouncement-stories,* or anecdotes that typically culminate in a clever remark that is highly quotable in addition to being wise. A famous example is the story in Eikh. R. (p. 159) describing how Akiba and the Rabbis journeyed to Rome and heard the gentile throngs rejoicing in the distance; while the Rabbis broke into tears at the sound, Akiba laughed, and when he was asked to explain his odd behavior he remarked: "If those who anger God rejoice this way in this world, then think how much more so will those who obey God rejoice in the world-to-come!"[9]

4. *Martyrologies,* or other such stories devoted to the sacrifices and sufferings that the sages undergo in their selfless devotion to the law, particularly under conditions of persecution. These stories tend to overlap with the romance, another subgenre of the ma'aseh. For examples, see the stories in Eikh. R. (pp. 78–87), especially the story of the mother and her seven sons (pp. 84–85); or the story of R. Akiba's death (B. Berakhot 61b), which also has the characteristics of a pronouncement-story.[10]

5. *Education-narratives,* detailing the training and great struggles that known sages undergo to achieve their stations of learning and piety. This category includes the famous stories about the educations of Hillel (B. Yomah 35b) and Akiba and Eliezer ben Hyrcanus (in ARN A, ch. 6), each of whom represents a different model of training for a sage.[11]

6. *Anti-sage stories,* narratives that relate the deeds of a sage that are *not* to be emulated. Probably the best example of this type is the story of Kamza and Bar Kamza with its protagonist, the otherwise unknown R. Zechariah b. Evkolos, whose "modesty," the narrative's euphemism for moral cowardice, ultimately brings about the destruction of the Temple (Eikh. R., pp. 142–143). The stories about Shammai and his notorious impatience (presented in ARN A, ch. 15 together with the stories in praise of Hillel's fabled patience—a case of comparative exempla) also fall in this category.

Although most sage-stories are anecdotal, a few are more extensively developed. These include a number of the education-narratives as well as such tales as the story of R. Yohanan b. Zakkai's flight from Jerusalem and his founding of the academy at

Yavneh, which exists in numerous versions and which became a kind of "foundation-myth" of Rabbinic Judaism.[12] These stories are complex inasmuch as they combine a variety of the subtypes listed above within their single narratives. For example, the story of R. Yohanan combines elements of the example-, miracle-, and pronouncement-stories. Most of all, however, the narrative is about the power of Torah and of midrash, for it is by virtue of his uncommon, virtually supernatural exegetical abilities that R. Yohanan is ultimately able to save himself, to prophesy Vespasian's ascent to the imperial crown, and thus to win from the new emperor a promise to allow the sages to establish an academy at Yavneh.

Villain-Stories

This genre is defined primarily by its protagonist(s), who is an out-and-out villain, like the emperor Titus in the famous story of Titus and the Gnat (B. Gittin 56b) or the evil daughters of Israel (Eikh. R., pp. 150–151). Unlike the anti-sage story, whose main purpose is a kind of negative didacticism (inasmuch as they encourage the reader not to imitate the behavior of their protagonists), the underlying subject of the villain-story is the punishment of the wicked and the vindication of God. The logic of punishment is often talionic—in the language of the Rabbis, a case of *midah keneged midah*—but the stories themselves tend to stress their historicity.

Romances

Literally an adventure story, this genre appears to have been imported into Jewish literature from popular Greco-Roman sources that circulated throughout the Late Antique worlds; it appears as early as the stories of Susanna and Bel the Dragon in the last chapters of the Book of Daniel as well as in other apocryphal and pseudepigraphic works.[13] The narratives in this subgenre that are found in Rabbinic literature tend to fall into one of three categories:

1. *Fantastica,* like the tall tales and travel stories of Rabba bar Bar Hana.

2. *Tales of sexual ordeals,* in which the chastity of the righteous is tested.

3. *Hagiographical tales* celebrating other ordeals that their righteous heroes undergo and that ultimately prove God's providence.

The last two types are distinguished by their protagonists, who represent a type of character—the saint—that is otherwise not found in Rabbinic literature. This type, which seems to have made its way into Jewish literature from non-Jewish sources like the Greco-Roman romance, has characters for whom their bodies are merely hindrances, objects to be tested and tortured, while their heads are already in heaven. Along with these identifiable character-features, the romance in Rabbinic literature also shares certain scene types and motifs that are generically distinctive, like trials of temptation that essentially serve to titillate the romance's audience. On the other hand, unlike Greco-Roman romances, which tend to take the form of novellas or lengthier prose narratives, the romances in Rabbinic literature are all fragmentary, at best sketches that recall the genre in its fuller shape. For an example, see the story of the two children of R. Tzadok the High Priest in Eikh. R. (pp. 83–84).

Fulfillment-Narratives

Historicity is the virtual raison d'être of these narratives, which are related explicitly to demonstrate the timely fulfillment and historical realization of biblical prophecies. As an example, consider the following story in Eikh. R. (p. 117), which is told in order to "fulfill" the tragic situation described in Lam. 2:12, a verse that was understood by the Rabbis as a prophecy: "They keep asking their mothers, 'Where is bread and wine?' as they languish like the battle-wounded in the squares of the town, as their life runs out in their mothers' bosoms."

It happened to (*ma'aseh be*) a certain woman who told her husband: This money is not doing me any good. Take it, and go to the marketplace and buy me something to eat so that we won't die. He did this. He took money from her and went to the market and tried to buy something, but he could not find anything to buy, and he languished and expired. They came and told her elder son: Aren't you going to go and see what happened to

your father? The son went, and he found his father dead in the
marketplace. He began to weep over him, and then he too languished and expired there. The youngest child wished to be
suckled, but he found nothing in his mother's breast, and he
too languished and expired.

[All this happened] in order to fulfill what is said, "as they
languish like the battle-wounded in the squares of the town"—
this refers to the woman's husband and her elder son; "as their
life runs out in their mothers' bosoms"—this refers to her little
child.

The object of the narrative is to show how every detail in the
scriptural verse was concretely—almost hyperliterally—realized in
the terrible catastrophe. In hermeneutical terms, this claim to historicity implies that the prophetic potential of the verse was
"exhausted," as it were, in its historical realization, in the event
that fulfilled the prophecy.[14] Indeed, this is precisely how the form
is used in the synoptic gospels, in Matthew particularly, where
various events in Jesus' life are said to have explicitly fulfilled the
messianic prophecies in the Hebrew Bible.[15] Whether or not this
is the same intention behind the fulfillment-narratives in Rabbinic midrash, the form points to the Rabbis' conviction that
hyperbolic verses, like those in Lamentations, are not to be taken
solely in a figurative sense. For an especially inventive use of the
form in a story that explicitly makes this point, see the famous
account of R. Akiba and the other sages as they ascend to
Jerusalem and see a fox on the Temple Mount (Eikh. R., pp. 159–
160). For a possibly parodic, certainly playful use of the form, see
Sifra 121b.

In addition to the fulfillment form, which typically ends with
the formulaic "in order to fulfill (lekayeim) [a verse]," there is a
second similar form in which an anecdote is related concerning
the fate of an individual, and at its conclusion a sage (or other
person) "applies" (kara 'al) a verse to the occasion. The effect
is both to ennoble the otherwise trivial life of the individual by
giving it the timeless authority of Scripture, and to demonstrate
the veracity of scriptural promise. For examples of the form,
see the pathetic stories of Martha bat Boethus and Miriam bat
Nakdimon in Eikh. R. (pp. 86–87). For a striking parody of the
form, see Vay. R. 12.1, where Prov. 23:28–29 is applied to the
story of a ridiculous drunkard.

Appendix B

Hebrew Texts of the Meshalim from Eikhah Rabbah

Eikhah Rabbah or Rabbati, (Eikh. R.), the collection from which the twenty-four meshalim analyzed in detail in this book are drawn, is the classical midrash on the Book of Lamentations. Redacted in Palestine, probably near the end of the fifth century C.E., it belongs to what is generally considered by modern scholars to be the first stratum of classical Amoraic midrash, thus being contemporaneous with the other early Amoraic midrashic collections, Ber. R., Vay. R., and PRK.[1]

Like Dev. R.,[2] Eikh. R. has been preserved in two separate recensions, known respectively as the Ashkenazic (heretofore referred to as A) and the Sephardic (S), after the geographical origins of the two major families of manuscripts—one from Germany and France (Ashkenaz in Jewish tradition), the other from Spain and North Africa (Sepharad). The existence of these two recensions was first proposed by Alexander Marx upon the appearance of Buber's edition of Eikh. R. in 1899.[3] Before this time, the only edition available was the one printed in the large folio volumes of the Romm Vilna Midrash Rabbah (MR), itself based on the 1587 Cracow edition. In comparing Buber's text with MR's, Marx realized that they represented two separate recensions. This hypothesis has now been fully confirmed by Paul Mandel, who is in the process of completing a critical edition of Eikh. R.[4] In his exhaustive studies of Eikh. R.'s manuscript tradition, Mandel has shown that all existing manuscripts can be identified with one or the other of the two geographical families, and he has also identified different patterns characterizing each recension.

The following texts of the meshalim in Eikh. R. follow Mandel's division of the manuscripts into three families. The first of these, Family A, represents the Sephardic recension, which includes

both manuscripts and the earliest printed editions of Midrash
Rabbah. The other two families, B and C, are subtypes of the
Ashkenazic recension. Family B includes Rome-Casanatense 3112
(B), the manuscript upon which Buber based his edition of Eikh.
R. My text for the Ashkenazic recension of the meshalim also follows *B*, except for cases in which all other testimonies in the same
family have been against *B*'s reading. My text for the Sephardic
recension is based upon *D*, the earliest printed edition of Midrash
Rabbah (Constantinople, 1520), though again with the same rule
for exceptions. The several meshalim taken from the petihtaot to
Eikh. R. are represented with a single text since I did not find any
difference between the two recensions for them. In general I have
not recorded orthographic variants. The punctuation and line-
marking in the texts are my own, intended solely to facilitate comparison and cross-referencing of the two recensions. In the following discussion, functions, motifs, and diction are identified by the
line in the mashal in which they appear.

In comparing the meshalim as they appear in the two recensions, one notices several types of differences that are frequently
found, and others that are not. Differences in the mashal-proper
or narratives of the meshalim fall into two types:

1. *Differences in plot.* There are no cases where the two recensions prefer versions of the same mashal that have genuinely
important differences in their respective plots. The closest one
comes to such a case is in 1.17, where S triplicates the main narrative motif (l. 4), but lacks the opening and closing functions that
are found in A (lines 3b and 6). 1.21 S omits the motif describing
the consort going around to and seeking refuge among her neighbors (l. 5) but that omission seems to parallel the different placing
of the aggadah about the nations in the mashal's context. Similarly, A's version of 2.1C lacks l. 6.

2. *Differences in diction.* These are by far the most common differences, and include several distinct kinds of which the following
meshalim are examples:

a. Differences in specific wording though the words tend to be
synonyms. In 1.1A, A has *bikhvodah*, S has *beshalvatah* (l. 4). 1.10
l. 3 has *beveito shel melekh* (A) and *letokh palatin shel melekh* (S). In
3.21 l. 9, A has *hite'u oti*, S has *ibeduni*. In 2.1C, 1.21, and 3.1—all
of which are complaint-meshalim with similar structures—their

versions in A all use the word *tarad* to describe the act of banish-ment, while the versions in S all use the verb *hotsi* (and 1.21 and 3.1 both use *dehafah vehotsiah*). These parallels seem to suggest recensional patterns.

b. Differences in language used. In 3.21 l. 6, A has the neigh-bors' speech in Aramaic, S has it in Hebrew.

c. Differences in voice and mode. In 2.1B l. 5, S has the king address the inhabitants in direct speech, while in A he speaks about them in the third person. Revealingly, this difference between the recensions is repeated verbatim in 2.7 (which uses the same structure and motifs as 2.1B)—again, a possible recensional pattern. Finally, one finds differences like the following in 1.1C l. 6: in A, the statement *kevar geirashtikh* is in the declarative; in S, *veloh kevar geirashtikh* is phrased as a negative rhetorical question.

Aside from these differences in the mashal-proper, the nim-shalim of the meshalim often differ in the two recensions in matters of specific diction and wording, and frequently in ways parallel to those in their respective meshalim-proper. In addition to those differences, there are also the following:

1. *Differences in overall structure.* In 3.20, S's version is far fuller and quotes all three verses as a testimony list; A simply has two verses with paraphrastic interpretations.

2. *Different verses quoted.* See 2.1C, in which A has Exod. 12:22, while S has Exod. 12:7. In 3.24, S lacks Ps. 16:5 (while in general its nimshal is briefer in S than in A, though its narrative in the mashal-proper is somewhat fuller).

3. *Different versions of aggadic traditions.* In 3.1, A and S preserve separate versions of the aggadah about God offering the Torah to the gentiles, and each version corresponds to one of the two recensions Joseph Heinemann identified, respectively in Targum Ps. Jonathan (S) and in Targum Yerushalmi (A).[5]

4. *Differences in placement.* In l. 21, S has the aggadah (l. 9 in A's nimshal) before the mashal, almost as an independent unit.

In concluding this brief survey of the differences between them, I can offer two general comments. First, it is difficult to identify consistent types of differences between the two recen-sions; except for a few instances, it is hard to say if A or S presents a better text. Second, for all their differences in details, most commonly in specific elements of diction, the versions recorded in the two recensions are, for all purposes, the same meshalim. This results in a kind of paradoxical dilemma for the reader: even where the versions have distinctly different wording, they present the same narratives. So that, while literary analysis is generally based upon close study of specific words in context, the specific wording in these cases seems to be of negligible importance. One can only suggest in response that this state of affairs reveals the precedence and greater importance that plot and narrative function take in the mashal over that of diction. The emphasis is on what happens, more than on how it is said.

The following critical texts of the twenty-four meshalim in Eikh. R. were prepared at the Institute of Microfilmed Hebrew Manuscripts at the Jewish National and University Library in Jerusalem, whose staff I wish to thank for their generosity and help. I wish also to express my gratitude to Paul Mandel for his generous help in reviewing these texts and for sharing with me his extensive knowledge of the manuscripts and their background.

Sigla and Manuscripts

BU	בו	Midrash Echa Rabbati, ed. Salomon Buber, Vilna, 1899
MR	מר	Midrash Rabbah, Cracow, 1587
MK	מכ	Matanot Kehunah, commentary of Issachar Baer b. Naftali Katz Cohen, Cracow, 1587

Family A

D	ד	Midrash Rabbah of the Five Megillot, Constantinople, 1520 (1514–19)
M	מ	Munich Codex Heb. 229, pp. 1–93
C	ק	Cambridge Add. 495, pp. 2a–73a

Family B

B	ב	Rome-Casanatense (3112)—Cat. no. 63.2, pp. 74–133
P	פ	Parma-Palatine 2559—De Rossi 1400

Family C

O	א	Oxford-Bodleian 164 Seld A sup. 102 (Neubauer no. 154), pp. 118a–174a
H	ה	Parma-Palatina 3293—De Rossi 1408, pp. 45b–97b
L	ל	London British Library Add. 27089—Cat. no. 1076, 4, pp. 10a–61b

שטרן/קובץ 1.1

Proem 2(2)　　　　　　　　פתיחתא 2(2)
Ashkenaz and Sepharad　　אשכנז וספרד

1) כה אמר ה׳ צבאות התבוננו וקראו למקוננות ותבואנה

1a) ר׳ יוחנן ור׳ שמעון בן לקיש ורבנן

A)　2) ר׳ יוחנן אמר:

3) למלך שהיו לו שני בנים

4) כעס על הראשון, נטל את המקל, וחבטו והגלהו. אמר: אוי לזה מאיזה שלוה
נגלה!

5) כעס על השני ונטל את המקל וחבטו והגלהו, אמר: אנא הוא דתרבותי
בישא.

6) כך גלו עשרת השבטים, והתחיל הקב״ה אומר להם את הפסוק הזה, אוי להם
כי נדדו ממני (הושע ז:יג), וכיון שגלו יהודה ובנימין כביכול אמר הקב״ה,
אוי לי על שברי (ירמיה י:יט)

B)　7) ר׳ שמעון בן לקיש אמר:

8) למלך שהיה לו שני בנים

9) כעס על הראשון ונטל את המקל וחבטו ופרפר ומת. התחיל מקונן עליו.

10) כעס על השני ונטל את המקל וחבטו ופרפר ומת. אמר: מעתה אין בי כח
לקונן עליהם אלא קראו למקוננות ותקוננו עליהם.

11) כך כשגלו עשרת השבטים התחיל מקונן עליהם, שמעו את הדבר הזה אשר
אנכי נושא עליכם קינה בית ישראל (עמוס ה:א), וכיון שגלו יהודה ובנימין
כביכול אמר הקב״ה: מעתה אין בי כח לקונן עליהם, אלא קראו למקוננות
ותבואינה וגו׳ ותמהרנה ותשאנה עליו נהי (ירמיה ט: טז, יז). עליהם אין
כתיב כאן, אלא עלינו, דידי ודידהון, ותשאנה עיניהם דמעה אין כתיב כאן
אלא עינינו, דידי ודידיהון, ועפעפיהם יזלו מים אין כתיב כאן אלא ועפעפינו,
דידי ודידיהון.

C) 12) רבנן אמרין:

13) למלך שהיו לו שנים עשר בנים

14) ומתו שנים. התחיל מתנחם בעשרה

15) מתו עוד שנים התחיל מתנחם בשמונה

16) מתו עוד שנים התחיל מתנחם בששה

17) מתו עוד שנים התחיל מתנחם בארבעה

18) מתו עוד שנים התחיל מתנחם בשנים

19) וכיון שמתו כולם התחיל מקונן עליהם

20) איכה ישבה בדד

Proem 25
Ashkenaz and Sepharad

פתיחתא כה
אשכנז וספרד

1) אמר ר' אחא

2) למלך שהיה יוצא מפלטין שלו בכעס

3) שהיה יוצא היה חוזר ומגפף ומנשק בכותלי פלטין ובעמודי פלטין ובוכה
ואומר:

4) הוי שלום פלטין שלי, הוי שלום בית מלכותי, הוי שלום בית יקרי, הוי שלום
מן כדון, הוי שלום.

5) כך משהיתה שכינה יוצאת מבית המקדש, היתה חוזרת ומגפפת ומנשקת
בכותלי בית המקדש ובעמודי בית המקדש, ובוכה ואומרת:

6) הוי שלום בית מקדשי, הוי שלום בית מלכותי, הוי שלום בית יקרי, הוי שלום
מן כדון, הוי שלום.

---

3) ובעמודי פלטין] ל ה ה ח'

4) פלטין] מ א בית פלטין|| בית מלכותין] ל בית מלכותי שלי

5) משהיתה — יוצאת] ל משהיתה יוצאת השכינה|| שכינה] מ השכינה

ER 1:1A — Ashkenaz א״ר א:א (א) — אשכנז

1) איכה ישבה בדד (איכה א:א)...

2) אמר ר׳ לוי

3) משל למטרונה אחת שהיו לה שלושה שושבינין

4) אחד ראה אותה בכבודה

5) ואחד ראה אותה בפוחזה

6) ואחד ראה אותה בניוולה

7) משה ראה אותן בכבודן. אמר: איכא אשא לבדי (דברים א:יב)

8) ישעיה ראה אותן בפוחזן. אמר: איכה היתה לזונה (ישעיה א:כא)

9) ירמיה ראה אותן בניוולן. אמר: איכה ישבה בדד (איכה א:א)

---

3) משל] כך ב פ; א ל ח׳ ‖ אחת] כך ב א; פ ל ח׳

4) בכבודה] כך ב פ ל; א בשלוותה

6) בניוולה] כך פ א ל; ב בניוולה בפחדה, בו בפחדה (אבל ראה הערתו)

7) משה] ל מוסיף כך משה ‖ בכבודן] א בשלוותן

ER 1:1A — Sepharad א״ר א:א (א) — ספרד

1) איכה ישבה בדד (איכה א:א)...

2) אמר ר׳ לוי

3) למטרונה שהיו לה שלשה שושבינין

4) אחד ראה אותה בשלוותה

5) ואחד ראה אותה בפחזה

6) ואחד ראה אותה בניוולה

7) כך משה ראה את ישראל בכבודם ובשלוותם ואמר: איכה אשא לבדי (דברים א:יב)

8) ישעיה ראה אותם בפחזותם ואמר: איכה היתה לזונה (ישעיה א:כא)

9) ירמיה ראה אותם בניוולם ואמר: איכה ישבה בדד (איכה א:א)

---

3) למטרונה] ק משל למטרונה

ER 1:1B — Ashkenaz

א״ר א:א (ב) — אשכנז

1) ישבה בדד

2) ר׳ ברכיה בשם ר׳ אבדימי דחיפה

3) משל למלך שהיה לו בן

4) כל זמן שהוא עושה רצונו של אביו היה מלבישו בגדי מילתין

5) וכל זמן שהיה כועס עליו היה מלבישו בגדי בדודין

6) כך כל זמן שישראל עושים רצונו של מקום מלבישן כלי מילת הה״ד
ואלבישך רקמה (יחזקאל טז:י). ר׳ סמאי אומר פורפירא תירגם עקילס
אפיקוליטון

7) וכיון שהכעיסוהו הלבישום בגדים בדודים.

___

2) ר׳ ברכיה] ב ח׳ ובו הוסיף

3) משל] כך ב; פ א ל ח׳

4) בגדי מילתין] כך א ה ומוסיפים כאן (מן הנמשל) הה״ד ואלבישך —
אפיקלטורין; ב פ ל בגדים בדודים; וכך בו אבל ראה הערתו; ל מוסיף כאן
(מן הנמשל) כל שעה שישראל עושים רצונו וכו׳.

5) וכל-מלבישו] כך ב פ ל; א ה וכיון שהכעיסוהו הלבישו ‖ בגדי בדודין] כך א
ה ב פ בגדים סמרטוטים; ל בגדי מילתין בדודין.

6) כלי מילת] כך ב; פ בגדים מילתים

ER 1:1B — Sepharad   א״ר א:א (ב) — ספרד

1) ישבה בדד

2) ר׳ ברכיה בשם ר׳ אבדימי דמן חיפה

3) למלך שהיה לו בן

4) בזמן שעושה רצונו של אביו היה מלבישו בגדי מילתין

5) ובזמן שאינו עושה רצונו מלבישו בגדי בדד

6) כך ישראל: כל זמן שהיו עושין רצונו של הקב״ה כתיב ואלבישך רקמה
(יחזקאל טז:י), ר׳ סימאי אמר: פורפירא תרגם אונקלס אפקלטורין פליקטא

7) ובזמן שאין עושין רצונו של הקב״ה מלבישן בגדי בדדין

8) הה״ד איכה ישבה בדד

---

3) למלך] ק משל למלך

4) ק] של אביו ח׳

Lam. 1:1C — Ashkenaz   א״ר א:א (ג) — אשכנז

1) ד״א היתה כאלמנה

2) ר׳ חמא בר עוקבא אמר: למה ישראל דומין? לשומרת יבם שתבעה מזונותיה
ולא תבעה כתובתה.

3) ורבנן אמרי:

4) משל למלך שכעס על מטרונה וכתב לה גיטה ונתן לה וחזר וחטפו ממנה.

5) כל זמן שהיא מבקשת להינשא לאחר אומר לה: היכן גיטין גירשתיך?

6) וכל זמן שהיא תובעת צרכיה הוא אומר לה: כבר גירשתיך.

7) כך כל זמן שישראל מבקשים לעבד עבודה זרה אומר להם הקב״ה: אי זה
ספר כריתות אמכם אשר שלחתיה (ישעיה נ:א)

8) וכל זמן שהם מבקשים שיעשה עמהם נס, אומר להם: כבר שילחתיה, דכתיב
שילחתיה ואתן את ספר כריתותיה אליה (ירמיה ג:ח)

---

1) כאלמנה] א מוסיף ר׳ חמא בר עוקבא ורבנן

2) למה — דומין] פ ל ה ח׳

4) משל] כך ב; פ א ל ח׳ || וכתב-גיטה] א ל ח׳ || ונתן לה] א ל ונתן לה גיטה; פ
ח׳

5) שהיא] פ שהייתה || אומר] פ היה אומר

6) שהיא — לה] פ שהייתה מבקשת לתבע צרכיה ממנו היה אומר לה || צרכיה]
כך ב פ א ל; ובו החליף במזונותיה

7) וכל נס] א ל וכל זמן שהם תובעין צרכיהם ממנו || שילחתיה] כך ב א ל פ בו
גרשתי אתכם

ER 1:1C — Sepharad   א״ר א:א (ג) — ספרד

1) ד״א היתה כאלמנה : ר' חמא בר עוקבא ורבנן

2) ר' חמא בר עוקבא אמר : לשומרת יבם שהיתה תובעת מזונותיה ולא היתה
תובעת כתובתה

3) ורבנן אמרין :

4) למלך שכעס על מטרונה וכתב לה גיטה ועמד וחטפה ממנה

5) וכל זמן שהיתה מבקשת לינשא לאחר היה אומר לה : היכן גיטיך ?

6) וכל זמן שהיתה תובעת מזונותיה היה אומר לה : ולא כבר גרשתיך ?

7) כך כל זמן שישראל מבקשים לעבוד עבודת זרה אומר להם הקב״ה : אי זה
ספר כריתות אמכם (ישעיה נ:א) ?

8) וכל זמן שמבקשים לעשות להם נסים כבתחלה אומר להם הקב״ה : כבר
גרשתי אתכם. הה״ד שלחתיה ואתן את ספר כריתותיה אליה (ירמיה ג:ח)

---

2) לשומרת יבם] כך ד ק מ ; מתנות כהונה (מדרש רבה קראקא שמ״ז) תיקן
לאלמנה.

5) גיטין] ק מוסיף שגירשתיך

ER 1:9 — Ashkenaz

א״ר א:ט — אשכנז

1) טומאתה בשוליה...

2) ר׳ יהודה ב״ר סימון בשם ר׳ לוי בן פרטא

3) משל למטרונא שאמר לה אוהבה: עשה לי חמין

4) נטלה לברנטין של מלך ועשתה לו חמין

5) אמר לה המלך: מכל כלים שהיו לך בפלטין לא היה ליך לעשות חמין לאוהבך אלא בלברנטין שלי שאני מתחמם בו !

6) כך אמר הקב״ה לישראל: מכל בנים שהיו לכם לא לקחתם אלא אותו שהיה מקודש לשמי

7) הה״ד ותקחי את בניך ואת בנותיך אשר ילדת לי ותזבחם להם לאכול (יחזקאל טז:כ).

———

3) משל] פ א ל ח׳ || אוהבה] ילקוט שמעוני (יחזקאל שנו) אהובה

4) לברנטין] כך פ א ה; ל ברנטין; ב לברנטין וכך ל אבל ראה הערתו.

5) בלברנטין] כך ב א ה; ל בברנטין; ב ובו בלברטנין || שאני מתחמם בו] ל ילקוט ח׳

6) לא לקחתם] פ לא היה לכם להקריב לעבודה זרה שלכם

ER 1:9 — Sepharad

א״ר א:ט — ספרד

1) וטומאתה בשוליה...

2) ר׳ יודן בר׳ סימון בשם ר׳ לוי בן פרטא

3) למטרונא שאמר לה אוהבה: עשי לי חמין.

4) ונטלה לורטיא של מלך ועשתה לו חמין.

5) אמר לה המלך: מכל עצים שיש ליך בבית זה לא היה ליך לעשות חמין לאוהבך אלא בלורטיא שלי !

6) כך אמר הקב״ה לאותו רשע: מכל בנים שיש לך לא היה לך להפילו לעבודה שרה אלא זה שמקודש לשמי.

7) הה״ד ותקחי את בניך וגו׳ (יחזקאל טז:כ).

———

5) לא היה ליך] ד מוסיף חמין לעשות חמין

ER 1:10 — Ashkenaz

א״ר א:י — אשכנז

1) ידו פרש צר...

2) ר׳ יהודה ב״ר סימון בשם ר׳ לוי בר פרטא למה היו דומין?

3) לדליקה שנפלה בביתו של מלך

4) והיו הכל רצים לבוז כסף וזהב

5) והעבד רץ לבוז את אוניתו

6) כך בשעה שנכנסו גויים לבית המקדש היו הכל רצים לבוז כסף וזהב, ועמון ומואב לבוז ספר תורה, כדי לעקור לא יבא עמוני ומואבי בקהל ה׳ (דברים כג:ד)

_____

2) בשם — דומין] א ח׳

3) בביתו] א לפלטין; ל בפלטין

5) אוניתו] כך פ א ל; ב אשתו, וכך בו אבל ראה הערתו.

ER 1:10 — Sepharad

א״ר א:י — ספרד

1) ידו פרש צר...

2) ר׳ יהודה בר׳ סימון בשם ר׳ לוי בר פרטא

3) לדליקה שנפלה לתוך פלטין של מלך

4) והיו הכל רצין לבוז כסף וזהב

5) ועבד רץ לבוז את אוניתו

6) כך בשעה שנכנסו שונאים לבית המקדש נכנסו עמונים ומואבים עמהם. והיו הכל רצין לבוז כסף וזהב, ועמונים ומואבים רצין לבוז את התורה כדי לעקור לא יבא עמוני ומואבי בקהל ה׳ (דברים כג:ד).

ER 1:16 A & B Ashkenaz

1) מי יתן ראשי מים וכו' (ירמיה ח:כג) ...

(A   2) אמר ר' חגי בשם ר' יצחק

3) משל למלך שבנה פלטין על גבי ביברין של מים והושיב בהן דיורין אילמין
והיו משכימין ושואלין בשלומו של מלך באצבע וברמיזה ובסודרים.

4) אמר המלך: מה אם אלו שהם אלמים הם משכימים ושואלים בשלומי,
באצבע וברמיזה ובסודרים, ואילו היו פקחין על אחת כמה וכמה !

5) חזר והושיב בהן דיורין פקחים

6) כיון שאחזו בה אמרו: שלנו היא הפלטין ואינה של מלך !

7) באותה שעה אמר המלך: תחזור הפלטין לכמות שהיה.

8) כך העולם: מתחילה לא היה אלא מים, והיה קילוסו של הקב״ה עולה מהם,
הה״ד מקולות מים רבים (תהלים צג:ד), ומה היו אומרים ? אדיר במרום ה'
(שם, שם). אמר הקב״ה: מה אם אלו שאין להם פה ולא אמירה ולא דיבור
וקילוסו עולה מהם, לכשאברא בו נפשות שלימות ומשובחות על אחת כמה
וכמה ! חזר וברא דור אנוש ומרד בו, דור המבול ומרד בו. באותה שעה אמר
הקב״ה: יחזור העולם לכמות שהיה. הה״ד ויהיה הגשם על הארץ ארבעים
יום וארבעים לילה (בראשית ז:יב).

(B   9) ר' ברכיה בשם ר' סימון אמר

10) משל לרועה שהיה לו מקל וצניף

11) עמד וסיגל צאן

12) פעם אחת נכנסו זאבים בתוך עדרו וביקּרעו

13) אמר: אחזור למקל ולצניף.

14) כך רועה — זה הקב״ה, שנאמר רועה ישראל האזינה (תהלים פ:ב), צאן
— אלו ישראל, שנאמר ואתן צאני צאן מרעיתי (יחזקאל לד:לא), וכיון
שנכנסו שונאים לירושלים והרגום, אמר הקב״ה: מי יתן ראשי מים (ירמיהו
ח:כג).

2) ר׳ חגי-יצחק] כך **פ ל**; **א** א״ר חנינא בשם ר׳ יצחק; **ב** ובו א״ר יצחק בשם ר׳ חגי, אבל ראה הערת בובר.

3) משל] כך **ב**; **פ א ל ח׳**║דיורין אילמין] **ב** דיורין ביברין║באצבע-ובסודרים] ל באצבע ובמנוולם

4) בשלומי — ובסודרים] ל בשלום המלך ובמנוולם וברמיזה.

7) לכמות שהיה] **א** למה שהיתה; **ל** לכמות שהיתה

8) וקילוסו] **ל** וקילוסי║לכמות שהיה] **א** למה שהיה

9) ר׳ ברכיה — ר׳ סימון] כך **ב א בו**; **פ** ר׳ ברכיה בשם ר׳ יהודה בר׳ סימון; **ל** ר׳ ברכיה בשם ר׳ שמעון║משל] **פ א ל ח׳**.

14) שונאים] **א** גויים

ER 1:16 A & B — Sepharad
א״ר א:טז (א+ב) — ספרד

1) מי יתן ראשי מים ועיני מקור דמעה (ירמיה ח:כג)... ר׳ אבא בר כהנא בשם ר׳
לוי אמר: כתיב ויאמר אלקים יקוו המים (בראשית א:ט). אמר הקב״ה יקוו
לי המים מה שאני עתיד לעשות בהן.

(A   2) ר׳ חגי בשם ר׳ יצחק אמר

3) משל למלך שבנה לו פלטירין על גבי ביברין של מים והושיב בהן דיורין
אלמים ובכל יום ויום היו משכימין ושואלין בשלום המלך ומקלסין אותו
ברמיזה ובאצבע

4) אמר המלך: ומה אלו שהן אלמים כך מקלסין אותי, אם היו פקחין על אחת
כמה וכמה!

5) מה עשה? הושיב בהן דיורין פקחין

6) עמדו והחזיקו בפלטין ואמרו: אין זו פלטין של מלך אלא שלנו!

7) באותה שעה אמר המלך: תחזור פלטין לכמות שהיתה!

8) כך מתחלת ברייתו של עולם לא היה קילוסו עולה אלא מן המים, הה״ד
מקולות מים רבים אדירים משברי ים (תהלים צג:ד). ומה היו אומרים? אדיר
במרום ה׳ (שם, שם). באותה שעה אמר הקב״ה: ומה אם אלו שאין להם לא
פה ולא לשון לא אמירה ולא דיבור כך מקלסין אותי, לכשאברא בני אדם על
אחת כמה וכמה! וכיון שברא בני אדם עמדו דור אנוש ודור המבול ומרדו
בו. באותה שעה אמר הקב״ה: יחזור העולם לכמות שהיה, שנאמר ויהי
הגשם על הארץ (בראשית ז:יג)

(B‏ 9) ר׳ יהודה בר׳ סימון אמר

10) לאחד שהיה לו מקל וצנית

11) עמד וסיגל וקנה לו צאן

12) ונכנסו זאבים ובקעום.

13) אמר אותו הרועה: אחזור לאותו מקל ולאותה צנית.

14) כך רועה — זה הקב״ה, שנאמר רועה ישראל האזינה וכו׳ (תהלים פ:ב). צאן
— אלו ישראל, שנאמר ואתן צאני צאן מרעיתי (יחזקאל לד:לא). נכנסו
זאבין לתוך עדרו ובקעום — אלו השונאים שנכנסו לבית המקדש. באותה
שעה אמר הקב״ה: מי יתן ראשי מים (ירמיה ח:כג).

---

3) משל] ק ח׳

4) אם היו] ק אלו שהיו

6) בפלטין] ד ק מ בפלטין של מלך || של מלך] כך ק; ד מ ח׳.

ER 1:17 — Ashkenaz

א"ר א:יז — אשכנז

1) פרשה ציון בידיה (איכה א:יז)

2) ר' יהושע דסכנין בשם ר' לוי

3) משל למלך שכעס על בנו

4) הוה מחי ליה והוה סרחית

5) בסוף פשט ב' ידיו לפניו

6) אמר לו: כוליה קדמך. מחי כל דהני לך !

7) כך פרשה ציון בידיה.

---

1) בידיה] ב ובו מוסיף [כאדם] שטובע בנהר ופורש ידיו למצוא דבר להנצל בו

3) משל] פ א ח'

ER 1:17 — Sepharad

א"ר א:יז — ספרד

1) ד"א פרשה ציון בידיה

2) ר' יהושע דסיכנין בשם ר' לוי אמר

3) למלך שהיה לו בן

4a) הוי מחי ליה ואמר: חטית

4b) הוי מחי ליה ואמר: חטית וסיכלת

4c) ועוד הוי מחי ליה

5) עד דפשט עשר אצבעוי קודמוי

6) ───────────────

7) כך הקב"ה הוה מייסר לירושלים, והות אמרה: חטית, עד פרשה ציון בידיה

2b) ואמר] ק ח'

5) קודמוי] מ קומוי

ER 1:21 — Ashkenaz　　　　　　　　　　א״ר א:כא — אשכנז

1) כי אתה עשית

2) אמר ר׳ לוי

3) משל למטרונא שאמר לה המלך: אל תשאלי כלום לשכנותיך ואל תשאלי
מהם כלום.

4) פעם אחת כעס עליה המלך טרדה חוץ לפלטין.

5) חזרה על כל שכינותיה ולא קבלוה

6) וחזרה לפלטין אצל המלך

7) אמר לה המלך: אקישטון אפיך !

8) אמרה לו: אתה הוא שעשית ! שאמרת אל תשאלי לשכינותיך ואל תשאלי
מהם כלום. אילו הווינא משאלה להון ושאלה מנייהו הוה חדא מנהון חמי
יתי יתי בגו ביתיה והות מקבלה יתי.

9) כך בשעה ששילחו אומות העולם בכל מקום שברחו בו סגרום: במזרח,
במערב, בצפון ובדרום. במזרח — כה אמר ה׳ על שלשה פשעי מואב (עמוס
ב:א). במערב — כה אמר ה׳ על שלשה פשעי צר (שם א:ט). בצפון — כה
אמר ה׳ על שלשה פשעי דמשק (שם א:ג). בדרום — כה אמר ה׳ על שלשה
פשעי עזה (שם א:ו).

10) אמר הקב״ה לישראל: אקישטון אפיכון ! אמרו ישראל לפני הקב״ה: ולא
אתה עשית ! שאמרת לנו לא תתחתן בם בתך לא תתן לבנו ובתו לא תקח
לבנך (דברים ז:ג). אילו הווין מנסבין בנתין לבניהון, או נסבין מבנתהון
לבנין, הוין מנהון מחמי ברתא או חד מינן מחמי ברתן גביה, ולא הוה מקביל
ליה? הוי — כי אתה עשית !

———————————————————

2) א״ר לוי] א א״ר יודן ; ל א״ר יוחנן

3) משל] פ א ח׳ || אל] פ לא

4) פעם אחת] ל לימים || טרדה] ל וטרדה ; א ה והוציאה

6‾7) וחזרה — אפיך] כך פ א ; ב ח׳ ובו הוסיף וראה הערתו

8) שעשית] א ח׳ ; שאמרת] א שאמרת לי || והות‾יתין] א ולא הות מקבלה יתי ; ל
ולא הות מקבלה יתי בגו ביתא.

9) במזרח — צר] כך ב פ א ל || בצפון — עזה] כך פ א ; פ בדרום כה אמר ה׳ על
שלשה פשעי עזה בצפון כה אמר ה׳ על שלשה פשעי דמשק ; ב ל בדרום כה
אמר ה׳ על שלשה פשעי דמשק (וצפון ח׳)

ER 1:21 — Sepharad

א״ר א:כא — ספרד

1) שמעו כי נאנחה אני... ורבנן פתרין קרייה בחורבן בית המקדש.

9) את מוצא שכל מקום שבקשו ישראל לברוח היו מסגירין אותן. ביקשו לברוח
כלפי דרום ולא הניחום, הה״ד על שלשה פשעי עזה וכו' (עמוס א:ו). בקשו
לברוח כלפי מזרח ולא הניחום, הה״ד על שלשה פשעי צר וכו' (שם, א:ט).
בקשו לברוח כלפי מערב ולא הניחום דכתיב משא בערב ביער בערב תלינו
ארחות (ישעיה כא:יג)

——————— (2

3) משל למלך שנשא למטרונה. אמר לה: אל תשיחי עם חברותיך ואל תשאילי
מהן ואל תשאילי להן.

4) פעם הקניטתו ודחפה והוציאה חוץ לפלטין שלו.

——————— (5

6) הלכה היא וצמצמה פניה אחר העמוד.

7) נמצא המלך עובר ורואה אותה. אמר לה: אקישתין אפיך!

8) אמרה המטרונה למלך: אדני! אילולי הייתי משאילה להן ושואלת מהן מנא
והוה עבידתי גבה או עבידתה גבי, לא הוון מקבלין לי?

10) כך אמר הקב״ה לשראל: אקשיתון אפיכון! אמרו לפניו: רבון העולמים! לא
כתבת בתורתך ולא תתחתן בם בתך לא תתן לבנו ובתו לא תקח לבנך (דברים
ז:ג). אילולא הוינן משאלין להון, ונסבין מינהון ואינון מינן מנא והוית
ברתיה גבי או ברתי גביה, לא הוו מקבלים לי? הוי — כי אתה עשית!

———————

2-4) פעם — אפיך] ד מ ח', והשלמתי ע״פ ק; מכ (קראקא שמ״ז/ח) לימים כעס
עליה המלך וטרדה חוץ לפלטין וחזרה על כל שכינותיה ולא קבלו אותה
וחזרה לפלטין אמר לה המלך אקשית אפיך.

8) המטרונה למלך] ק לו|| אדנין] ק אדני המלך לא כך אמרת לי לא תשיחי עם
חברותיך אל תשאילי להן ואל תשאלי מהן.

ER 2:1 A — Ashkenaz   א״ר ב:א (א) — אשכנז

1) השליך משמים ארץ תפארת ישראל

2) ר' הונא בר אחא בשם ר' חנינא בריה דר' אבהו.

3) משל למלך שהיה לו בן

4) בכה ונתנו על ארכובתיו

5) בכה ונתנו על זרועותיו

6) בכה עוד והרכיבו על כתפיו

7) טינף עליו והשליכו לארץ

8) לא הוה מסוקתיה כמחותיה: מסוקיתיה ציבחר, מחותיתיה כולא
כחדא

9) כך ואנכי תרגלתי לאפרים קחם על זרועותיו (הושע יא:ג), ואח״כ ארכיב
אפרים יחרוש יהודה ושדד לו יעקב (שם י:יא), ואח״כ השליך משמים ארץ
תפארת ישראל. לא הוה מסוקיתהון כמחותיתהון: מסוקיתהון ציבחר
ציבחר, מחותיתהון כולא כחדא.

---

2) ר' הונא־אבהו] א ר' חייא ור' אחא בשם בריה דר' אבהו אמרו; ל ר' הונא ור'
אחא בשם ר' אבהו.

3) משל] פ א ל ח'

5) בכה — זרועותיו] כך פ א ל; ב ח'

6) בכה — כתפיו] כך ב פ; א ל בכה ונתנו על כתפיו

8) ציבחר ציבחר] כך פ א ל; ב ציבחר

9) לאפרים] פ ל ואח״כ קחם על זרועותיו

ER 2:1 A — Sepharad

א״ר ב:א (א) — ספרד

1) השליך משמים ארץ תפארת ישראל

2) רב הונא ור׳ אחא ב״ר בשם ר׳ חנינא בריה דר׳ אבהו.

3) משל למלך שהיה לו בן

4) בכה ונתנו על ארכובותיו

5) בכה ונתנו על זרועותיו

6) בכה והרכיבו על כתפו

7) טינף עליו ומיד השליכו לארץ

8) ולא הות מחותיתיה כמסוקיתיה: מסוקיתיה ציבחר ציבחר ומחותיתיה כולא חדא

9) כך ואנכי תרגלתי לאפרים קחם על זרועותיו (הושע יא:ג), ואחר כך ארכיב אפרים יחרשו יהודה ישדד לו יעקב (שם י:יא), ואחר כך השליך משמים ארץ תפארת ישראל.

ER 2:1 B — Ashkenaz　　　　　　　　　א״ר ב:א (ב) — אשכנז

1) ר׳ יהושע דסכנין אמר

2) משל לבני מדינה שעשו עטרה למלך

3) הקניטוהו וקיבל עליו

4) הקניטוהו עוד וקיבל עליו

5) אמר: כלום בני המדינה מקניטים אותי אלא בשביל העטרה הזאת שהיא
נתונה על ראשי. הא מקלקלא לאפיהון !

6) כך אמר הקב״ה: כלום ישראל מכעיסים אותי אלא בשביל איקונין של יעקב
שהיא חקוקה בכסאי. הא מקלקלא לאפיהון !

7) הה״ד השליך משמים ארץ תפארת ישראל.

---

1) ר׳ יהושע דסכנין] פ א ר׳ יהושע דסכנין בשם ר׳ לוי; ל ר׳ יהושע בן לוי.

2) משל] כך ב פ; א ל ח׳

4) הקניטוהו — עליו] ל ח׳ || עוד] פ א ח׳

5) הזאת] ל ח׳ || הא — לאפיהון]] א הא היא מקלקלא לאפיהון; ל אנא
מקלקלה לאפיהון

6) ישראל] ל ח׳ || של יעקב] פ א ל של יעקב אביהם || הא — לאפיהון] כך פ; ב
לאפיהון ח׳; א הא היא מקלקלא לאפיהון; ל אנא מקלקלה לאפיהון.

ER 2:1 B — Sepharad　　　　　　　　א״ר ב:א (ב) — ספרד

1) אמר ר׳ יהושע בר׳ נחמן

2) משל לבני מדינה שעשו עטרה למלך

3) הקניטוהו וסבלן

4) הקניטוהו וסבלן

5) אחר כך אמר להם המלך: כלום אתם מקניטין אותי אלא בעבור עטרה
שעטרתם לי. הא לכון טרון באפיכון!

6) כך אמר הקב״ה לישראל: כלום אתם מקניטין אותי אלא בשביל איקונין של
יעקב שחקוקה על כסאי. הא לכון טרון באפיכון!

7) הוי — השליך משמים ארץ תפארת ישראל.

_____

4) הקניטוהו] ק ועוד הקניטוהו

6) יעקב] ק יעקב אביכם

ER 2:1 C — Ashkenaz

א״ר ב:א (ג) — אשכנז

1) ולא זכר הדום רגליו... ורבנן אמרי לא זכר לנו הקב״ה אותו הדם שבארץ
מצרים.

2) אמר ר׳ יודן

3) למלך שעמד על שונאו והרגו

4) והיו בני המדינה שלו מפרקסין בדמו

5) פעם אחת הקניטו את המלך וטרדן חוץ למדינה

6) ─────────────

7) כך אמרו ישראל: לא זכר את הדם שבארץ מצרים, שנאמר ולקחתם אגודת
אזוב וטבלתם בדם (שמות יב:כב).

─────────────

1) ורבנן אמרין] ל ח׳

4) והיו — בדמו] כך פ ; ב והיו בני המדינה מפרקסין דמו ; ל והיו בני המדינה
שלו מפרכסין לפניו

5) וטרדן] ל ואבדן

6) כך ב פ א ל ה ; ובו הוסיף אמרו אין המלך נזכר לנו אותו הדם שהיינו
מפרקסין בדם שונאיו

7) לא זכר] פ ל לא זכר לנו הקב״ה

ER 2:1 C — Sepharad

א״ר ב:א (ג) — ספרד

1) ולא זכר הדום רגליו...

2) אמר ר׳ יודן

3) למלך שתפש את שונאיו והרגן

4) והיו בני המדינה מפרכסין בדם שונאיו

5) פעם אחת הקניטוהו ודחפן והוציאן חוץ לפלטין

6) אמרו: אין המלך נזכר לנו אותו הדם שהיינו מפרכסין בדם שונאיו.

7) כך אמרו ישראל לפני הקב״ה: אין את נזכר לנו אותו הדם שבמצרים, שנאמר
ולקחו מן הדם ונתנו על שתי המזוזות ועל המשקוף (שמות יב:ז).

─────────────

3) למלך] ק משל למלך

ER 2:7 — Ashkenaz א״ר ב:ז — אשכנז

1) זנח ה׳ מזבחו

2) ר׳ חגי בשם ר׳ יצחק אמר

3) לבני מדינה שהיו עורכים שלחנות למלך

4) הקניטוהו וסבלם

5) הקניטוהו וסבלם

6) אמר המלך: כלום בני המדינה מקניטים אותי אלא בשביל השולחנות הללו שהיו עורכים לפני. הא מקלקלא לאפיהון !

7) כך אמר הקב״ה: כלום ישראל מכעיסים אותי אלא בשביל הקרבן שהיו מקריבין לפניי. הא מקלקלא לאפיהון

---

1) ב חסר כל המשל וראה הערת בו. אני העתקתי את המשל לפי פ || ר׳ חגי — ר׳ יצחק] ל ר׳ יודן בשם ר׳ יצחק

5) הקניטוהו וסבלם] כך פ ל; א ח׳

6) מקניטים] ל מכעיסים || הא-לאפיהון] ל הא אנא מקלקלא לאפיהון.

7) הקרבן — לפניי] א ל הקרבנות שהם מקריבין לפניי || הא — לאפיהון] ל הא אנא מקלקלא לאפיהון || לאפיהון] א ל מוסיפים הה״ד זנח ה׳ מזבחו.

ER 2:7 — Sepharad א״ר ב:ז — ספרד

1) זנח ה׳ מזבחו

2) ר׳ חגי בשם ר׳ יצחק אמר

3) לבני מדינה שערכו שלחנות למלך

4) הקניטוהו וסבלן

---

5)

6) אמר להם המלך: כלום אתם מקניטין אותי אלא בשביל שלחן שערכתם לי. הא לכון טרון באפיכון !

7) כך אמר הקב״ה לישראל. כלום אתם מכעיסין אותי אלא בשביל קרבנות שהקרבתם לי. הא לכון טרון באפיכון !

8) הה״ד זנח ה׳ מזבחו נאר מקדשו

---

5) מ משלים: הקניטוהו וסבלן.

ER 3:1 — Ashkenaz　　　　　　　　　　　　א״ר ג:א — אשכנז

(1) אני הגבר (איכא ג:א)

(2) אמר ר׳ יהושע בן לוי: אמרה כנסת ישראל לפני הקב״ה: רבון כל העולמים! אנא היא וילפת אנא כל מאן דאת מייתי לי.

(3) משל למטרונא שכעס עליה המלך וטרדה חוץ לפלטין.

(4) מה עשת? הלכה וצמצמה את פניה והלכה לה אחורי העמוד.

(5a) כשהמלך עבר

(5b) אמרה לו: אדוני המלך, כך נאה לי וכך יפה לי וכך הגון לי, שלא קיבלה אותך אשה אלא אני.

(6) אמר לה המלך: לאו, אלא אני שפסלתי כל הנשים בשבילך.

(7) אמרה לו: לאו! הן הן שלא קבלו אותך.

(8) כך אמרה כנסת ישראל לפני הקב״ה: רבון כל העולמים! כך הגון לי, שלא קיבלה אומה את תורתך אלא אני.

(9) אמר הקב״ה: לאו, אלא אני פסלתי כל האומות בשבילך.

(10) אמרה לו: לאו אלא הן הן שלא קיבלוה. מפני מה הלכת להר שעיר? לאו ליתן תורה לבני עשיו, ולא קיבלוה. וכן למדבר פארן? לא ליתן תורה לבני ישמעאל, ולא קיבלו אותה. מפני מה הלכת אצל עמונים ומואבים? לא ליתן תורה לבני לוט, ולא קיבלוה.

(11) הה״ד ויאמר ה׳ מסיני בא וזרח משעיר למו הופיע מהר פארן (דברים לג:ב), בתחלה הלך לו אצל עשו להר שעיר, אמר להם: מקבלים אתם התורה? אמרו לו: מה כתיב בה? אמר להם: לא תרצח (שמות כ:יג). אמרו לו: היא הברכה שברכנו אבינו — על חרבך תחיה (בראשית כז:מ). אין אנו יכולים לחיות בלא היא. ולא קיבלו אותה.

(12) הלך לו למדבר פארן אצל בני ישמעאל, אמר להם: מקבלים אתם התורה? אמרו לו: מה כתיב בה? אמר להם: לא תגנוב (שמות כ:טו), אמרו לו: היא ירושת אבינו — ידו בכל ויד כל בו. (בראשית טז:יב). אין אנו יכולים לחיות בלא היא, ולא קיבלו אותה.

(13) הלך אצל עמונים ומואבים. אמר להם: מקבלים אתם התורה? אמרו לו: מה כתיב בה? אמר להם: לא תנאף (שמות כ:יד). אמרו לו: עיקר כל אותן האנשים אינו אלא מכלל ממזרות שנאמר ותהרין שתי בנות לוט מאביהן (בראשית יט:לו), אין אנו יכולין לחיות בלא היא, ואל קיבלוה.

(14) בא לו אצל ישראל. אמר להם: מקבלים אתם התורה? אמרו לו: הין הין, כל אשר דבר ה׳ נעשה ונשמע (שמות כד:ז).

(15) אחר כל השבח הזה אמרה: אני הגבר ראה עני.

3) משל] **פ א ל ח'|| וטרדה]** בו ונודדה

(4

והלכה — עמוד] **פ ל א ה** ועמדה לאחורי העמוד

5a) עבר] **ב** העובר; ל יושב; **בו** הוסיף כאן (כנראה ע״פ הדפוס) אמר לה אקשית אפיך.

5b) אשה] **פ ח'**

6) לאו אלא] ל ח'|| אנין] **א ל אני הוא|| את** — בשבילך] כך **פ ל א**; **ב ח'**

7) שלא קבלו אותך] ל שלא קבלך אשה אלא אני

8) כך הגון — אני] ל כך נאה לי וכך יפה לי שאתה עושה לי כך לא היה אומה רוצה לקבל תורתך אלא אני

9) אני פסלתין] **א** אני הוא שפסלתי

10) וכן למדבר פארן] **פ א ל** מפני מה הלכת למדבר פארן ליתן תורה

11) אמרו — היא] **א** אמרו לו וכי ברכה שנתברך בה עשו אבינו אתה רוצה לעקרה ממנו הה״ד ועל חרבך תחיה אין אנו חפצים בתורתך.

12—13הלך — קיבלוה] **א** הלך אצל בני לוט אמר להם קבלו תורתי אמרו לו מה כתיב בה אמר להם לא תנאף אמרו לו מניאוף אנו באים ואתה רוצה לביישנו אין אנו רוצים בתורתך עוד הלך אצל בני ישמעאל ואמר להם תקבלו תורתי אמרו לו מה כתיב בה אמר להם לא תגנוב אמרו לו וכי ברכה שנתברך בה ישמעאל אבינו אתה רוצה לעקרה ממנו ה״ה ידו בכל ויד כל בו. אין אנו חפצים בתורתך חזר על כל האומות ואמר להם תקבלו תורתי אמרו לו מה כתיב בה אמר להם יודוך ה' כל מלכי ארץ כי שמעו אמרי פיך אמרו לו אנו אין רוצים בתורתך.

14) הין הין] **א ח'||ונשמע]** **א** מוסיף כמה טובות עשיתי לפניך קדשתי את שמך על הים ואמרתי לך שירה אז ישיר משה ובני ישראל וקבלתי תורתך בשמחה מה שלא קבלו האומות.

ER 3:1 — Sepharad   א״ר ג:א — ספרד

1) אני הגבר...

2) ר׳ יהושע דסיכנין בשם ר׳ לוי אמר: אני הגבר — אנא הוא דיליפנא ייסורין אהני עלי מה דאהני לך.

3) משל למלך שכעס על מטרונה ודחפה והוציאה חוץ לפלטין.

4) הלכה וצמצמה פניה אחר העמוד.

5a) נמצא המלך עובר ורואה אותה. אמר לה: אקשית אפיך.

5b) אמרה לו: אדוני המלך! כך יפה לי וכך נאה וכך ראוי לי שלא קבלה אותך אשה אחרת אלא אני.

6) אמר לה: אני הוא שפסלתי כל הנשים בעבורך.

7) אמרה לו: אם כן, למה נכנסת למבוי פלוני ולחצר פלוני ולמקום פלוני? לא בשביל אשה פלונית? ולא קבלה אותך.

8a) כך אמר הקב״ה לישראל: אקישתון אפיכון!

8b) אמרו לפניו: רבונו של עולם! כך יפה לנו וכך נאה וכך הגון לנו שלא קבלה אומה אחרת תורתך אלא אנו.

9) אמר להם: אני הוא שפסלתי כל האומות בשבילכם.

10) אמרו לו: אם כן למה החזרת תורתך על האומות ולא קבלוה?

11) דתניא: בתחלה נגלה על בני עשיו, הה״ד ויאמר ה׳ מסיני בא וזרח משעיר למו (דברים לג:ב), ולא קבלוה.

12) החזירה על בני ישמעאל ולא קבלוה. הה״ד הופיע מהר פארן (שם)

14) ולבסוף החזירה על ישראל וקבלוה. הה״ד ואתא מרבבות קדש מימינו אש דת למו (שם), וכתיב כל אשר דבר ה׳ נעשה ונשמע (שמות כד:ז).

_____

5b) אחרת] ק ח׳

ER 3:8 A — Ashkenaz   איכה ג:ח (א) — אשכנז

1) גם כי אזעק ואשוע שתם תפלתי (איכה ג:ח)

1a) ר׳ אחא ורבנן.

A   2) ר׳ אחא אמר: כל מי שמתפלל עם הצבור תפלתו נשמעת

3) משל לעשרה בני אדם שעשו עטרה למלך

4) ובא עני אחד ונתן ידו עמהם

5) מה המלך אומר? בפני העני הזה איני לובש העטרה מה דהיא היא ונלבשנה !

6) כך עשרה בני אדם צדיקים עומדים בבית כנסת ומתפללים

7) ורשע אחד עומד ביניהם

8) מה הקב״ה אומר? בפני הרשע הזה איני מקבל התפלה? נקבלה מה דהיא היא !

---

3) משל] כך ב; פ א ה ל ח׳

4) ונתן — עמהם] כך ב; א ל ונתן חלקו עמהם; ה ונטל חלק עמהן

5) בפני] פ מפני‖ מה — ונלבשנה] פ נלבשנה מה דההיא היא; א נלבישנה וקבלינה מה דהיא היא; ה נלבשנה ונקבליה מה דהיא היא; ל אלביישנה מה דהיא היא

6) צדיקים] ל ח׳

8) בפני] כך ב; א ל מפני‖ נקבלה] ל אלא אקבלה

ER 3:8 A — Sepharad   א״ר ג:ח (א) — ספרד

1) גם כי אזעק ואשוע שתם תפלתי

2) ר׳ אחא אמר: כל המתפלל עם הציבור

A) 2a) למה הוא דומה?

3) לבני אדם שעשו עטרה למלך

4) בא עני אחד ונתן חלקו בתוכה

5) מה המלך אומר? בשביל זה עני איני מקבלה? מיד מקבל המלך ונותנה בראשו

6) כך אם היו עשרה צדיקים עומדים בתפלה

7) ורשע עומד ביניהם

8) מה הקב״ה אומר? בשביל זה רשע איני מקבל תפלתם?

_____

8) תפלתם] ק מוסיף על ישראל יצא הרשע מיד מקבל הוא תפלתן של ישראל

ER 3:8 B — Ashkenaz   א״ר ג:ח (ב) — אשכנז

1) ורבנן אמרו: כל מי שמתפלל אחר הצבור מעשיו נפרטין

_____ (7-2

8) הה״ד שתם תפלתי, שתם כתיב.

_____

7-2) ב א ה ל פ המשל ח׳, ובו הוסיף על פי הדפוס.

ER 3:8 B — Sepharad

א"ר ג:ח (ב) — ספרד

B‏ 1) ורבנן אמרין: בא אחר הציבור מעשיו נפרטין

2) למה הוא דומה?

3) למלך שנכנסו אריסיו ובני־ביתו לכבדו

4) בא אחד באחרונה

5) אמר: תיסתם חביתו!

6) ומי גרם לו? הרי שבא באחרונה.

7) כך כל המתפלל לאחר הציבור מעשיו נפרטין

8) לכך נאמר: גם כי אזעק ואשוע סתם תפלתי. שתם כתיב לפי שתמו הציבור תפלתהון.

_____

5) אמר] כך ד; ק מ אמר המלך

ER 3:20 — Ashkenaz

א"ר ג:כ — אשכנז

1) זכור תזכור ותשוח עלי נפשי (איכה ג:כ)

2) תני ר' חייא

3) משל למלך שהלך לחמת גדר ונטל בניו עמו

4) פעם אחת הקניטוהו ונשבע שאין נוטלן עמו

5) והיה נזכר עליהם ובוכה ואומר: הלוואי הוו בני עמי אף על פי שמקניטין אותי.

6) כך: מי יתנני במדבר מלון אורחים (ירמיה ט:א). אמר הקב"ה: הלוואי הוו בני עמי כמה שהיו במדבר אף על פי שמליניין עלי. ודכוותיה: בן אדם בית ישראל ישבים על אדמתם ויטמאו אותה (יחזקאל לו:יז). אמר הקב"ה: הלוואי היו בני עמי בארץ ישראל אף על פי שמטמאין אותה.

_____

3) משל] פ א ל ח' ‖ ונטל בניו] ל ונטל שני בניו

5) עליהם פ א ל להם

6) כך] ב פ; בו הה"ד ‖ אמר — אותה] ל ח'

ER 3:20 — Sepharad　　　　　　　　　　　　א״ר ג:כ — ספרד

1) זכור תזכור

2) תני ר׳ חייה

3) משל למלך שיוצא למלחמה והיו בניו עמו

4) והיו מקניטין אותו

4a) למחר יצא המלך לבדו ולא היו בניו עמו.

5) אמר המלך: הלואי היו בני עמי, ואפילו היו מקניטים אותי.

6) כך המלך זה הקב״ה. בניו אלו ישראל. בשעה שהיו ישראל יוצאין למלחמה היה הקב״ה יוצא עמהם. כיון שהכעיסוהו לא יצא עמהם. וכיון שלא היה ישראל בארץ אמר: מי יתנני במדבר מלון אורחים (ירמיה ט:א) — מי יתן עמי כמראש כשהיה במדבר. וכתיב — בן אדם בית ישראל יושבים על אדמתם וגו׳ (יחזקאל לו:יז). והדין — זכור תזכור ותשוח עלי נפשי.

---

3) למלך — למלחמה] ק למלך למיומס

6) כך — אמר]ק ח׳ ומשלים: כך אמר הקב״ה הלואי היו בני בארץ ישראל ואפילו הם מקניטין אותי ואית ג׳ פסוקים מי יתנני וכו׳; מר מוסיף אחרי אמר: הלואי היו ישראל עמי ואפילו היו מכעיסים אותי, ואית ג׳ פסוקים וכו׳

ER 3:21 — Ashkenaz

א"ר ג:כא — אשכנז

1) זאת אשיב אל לבי על כל אוחיל (איכא ג:כא)

2) ר' אבא בר כהנא אמר

3) משל למלך שנשא אשה וכתב לה כתובה מרובה

4) וכתב לה : כך וכך חופות אני עושה ליך, וכך תכשיטין אני עושה ליך, וכך
וכך כסף וזהב אני נותן ליך.

5) והניחה שנים רבות והלך לו למדינת הים.

6) והיו שכנותיה מקנטרות אותה ואומרות לה: לא בעליך שבק יתיך ! זילי נסבי
לך גבר אוחרן !

7) והיתה בוכה ומתאנחת, ואח"כ היתה נכנסת לתוך חופתה וקראת כתובתה
ומתאנחת.

8) לאחר ימים ושנים בא המלך ואמר לה: תמיה אני ממך ! איך המתנת לי כל
השנים הללו?

9) אמרה לו: אדוני המלך ! אילולי כתובתך מרובה שכתבת לי כבר הטעו אותי
שכנותי.

10) כך אומות העולם מונין את ישראל ואומרות להם: אלהכון לא בעי יתכון !
שביק יתכון ! סליק שכינתיה מעליכון ! בואו אצלנו ואנו ממנים אתכם
דוכוסין ואפרכסין ואיסטרטליטין.

11) וישראל נכנסים בבתי כנסיות ובבתי מדרשות שלהם וקורין בתורה... ופניתי
אליכם והפריתי אתכם... ולא תגעל נפשי אתכם (ויקרא כו: ט, יא)
ומתנחמים.

12) למחר כשהגאולה באה, אמר הקב"ה לישראל: בני, תמיה אני מכם היאך
המתנתם לי כל השנים הללו?

13) והן אומרים לפניו: רבון כל העולמים, אילולי תורתך שנתת לנו, והיינו
נכנסים בבתי כנסיות ובבתי מדרשות, והיינו קורין ופניתי אליכם ולא תגעל
נפשי אתכם, כבר הטעונו אומות העולם ממך.

14) הה"ד לולי תורתך שעשועי אז אבדתי בעניי (תהלים קיט:צג)

2) ר׳ אבא בר כהנא **פ א ל** מוסיפים בשם ר׳ יוחנן

3) משל] **פ א ל ח׳** || מרובה] **פ א ל** ; **ב ח׳**

4) כך — ליך] ל אעשה לך כך וכך כסף וזהב כך וכך תכשיטין אתן ליך כך וכך תסבריות כך וכך אבנים טובות ומרגליות כך וכך עיירות כך וכך מדינות.

5) והניחה — הים] ל ואחר כך הלך למדינת הים והניחה שנים רבות || רבות] **א** הרבה.

6) מקנטרות] ל מקניטות || לא — אוחרן] ל ריקא לא בעליך שבקתיך זילי סבי ליך גבר אוחרן עד דאת טלייתה

7) והיתה מתאנחת] ל ח׳ || ואח״כ — נכנסת] ל מה עשתה הולכת מהן ונכנסת

8) שנים] **א ל ח׳** || בא — איך] ל חזר המלך אמר לה בתי תמיה אני האיך || איך — לי] **א** איך היית ממתנת

9) כבר — שכנותי] ל כבר היו שכנותי מטעות אותי

12) היאך המתנתם] **א** היאך הייתם ממתינים

13) שנתת] **פ** שכתבת

14) בעניין] ל ובו מוסיפים לכך נאמר זאת אשיב אל לבי על כן אוחיל

א"ר ג:כא — ספרד

ER 3:21 — Sepharad

1) זאת אשיב אל לבי על כן אוחיל

2) כי אבא בר כהנא בשם ר' יוחנן אמר

2a) משל למה הדבר דומה?

3) למלך שנשא מטרונה וכתב לה כתובה מרובה

4) ואמר לה: כך וכך חופות אני עושה ליך. כך וכך ארגוונות טובות אני נותן ליך.

5) הניחה המלך והלך לו למדינת הים ואיחר לשם

6) נכנסו שכנותיה אצלה והיו מקניטות אותה ואומרות לה: הניחך המלך והלך לו למדינת הים ושוב אינו חוזר עליך !

7) והיתה בוכה ומתאנחת. וכיון שנכנסה לתוך ביתה פותחת ומוציאה כתובתה וקוראת ורואה שבכתובתה כך וכך חופות אני עושה וכך וכך ארגוונות טובות אני נותן ליך, מיד היתה מתנחמת.

8) לימים בא המלך. אמר לה: בתי ! אני תמה איך המתנת לי כל אותן השנים.

9) אמרה לו: אדוני המלך ! אלמלא כתובה מרובה שכתבת ונתת לי כבר אבדוני שכנותי.

10) כך אומות העולם מונין את ישראל ואומרין להם: אלקיכם הסתיר פניו מכם וסילק שכינתו מכם, עוד אינו חוזר עליכם.

11) והן בוכין ומתאנחין, וכיון שנכנסין לבתי כנסיות ולבתי מדרשות וקורין בתורה ומוציאין שכתוב ופניתי אליכם והפריתי אתכם ונתתי משכני בתוככם והתהלכתי בתוככם והן מתנחמין.

12) למחר כשיבוא קץ הגאולה אומר להם הקב"ה לישראל: בני ! אני תמה מכם היאך המתנתם לי כל אותן השנים ?

13) והן אומרין לפניו: רבונו של עולם ! אילולי תורתך שנתת לנו כבר אבדונו האומות.

14) לכך נאמר זאת אשיב אל לבי (איכא ג:כא), ואין זאת אלא תורה, שנאמר וזאת התורה (דברים ד: מד). וכן דוד אמר לולי תורתך שעשועי אז אבדתי בעניי (תהלים קיט:צב), על כן אוחיל לו ומיחדים שמו שתי פעמים ביום ואומרים שמע ישראל ה' אלקינו ה' אחד (דברים ו:ד).

2a) משל — דומה] מ ח'

ER 3:24 — Ashkenaz　　　　　　　　　　　א״ר ג:כד — אשכנז

1) חלקי ה׳ אמרה נפשי (איכה ג:כד)

2) ר׳ אבהו בשם ר׳ יוחנן אמר

3) משל למלך שנכנס למדינה ועמו דוכוסין ואפרכסין ואיסטרטילוטין

4) הוה הדין אמר: דוכוס פלן אנא נסיב לגבה

5) ואחרינא אמר: אנא נסיב איסטרטילוטין לגביה

6) היה שם פיקח אחד ואמר: איני נוטל אלא המלך לבדו, דכולהו מתחלפי והוא
אינו מתחלף

7) כך אומות העולם: אלו עובדין לחמה ואלו ללבנה ואלו לעץ ואלו לאבן, אבל
הקב״ה בגורלן של ישראל הוא

8) הה״ד, חלקי ה׳ אמרה נפשי (איכה ג:כד)

9) היך מה דאת אמר, ה׳ מנת חלקי וכוסי (תהלים טז:ה)

10) ...על כן אוחיל לו: מייחדת שמו שתי פעמים ביום ואומרת שמע ישראל ה׳
אלקינו ה׳ אחד. (דברים ו:ד).

---

3) משל] כך ב; פ א ה ל ח׳

4) לגבה] ב; פ לגבי‖לגביה] פ לגבי‖היה — לגביה פ ‖ לבדו] פ פיקח אחד היה אומר
אני איני נוטל אלא המלך עצמו; א אמר אני איני לוקח אלא המלך עצמו

7) ואלו ללבנה — אבן] כך ב; פ א ה ל ו ואלו עובדין ללבנה ואלו עובדין לעץ
ואלו עובדין לאבן

8) חלקי — נפשי] ל ח׳

ER 3:24 — Sepharad　　　　　　　　　א״ר ג:כד — ספרד

1) חלקי ה׳ אמרה נפשי (איכה ג:כד)

2) רבי אבהו בשם ר׳ יוחנן אמר

3) למלך שנכנס למדינה והיו עמו דוכסין ואיפרכין ואיסטרטילוטין

3a) והיו גדולי מדינה יושבים באמצע המדינה

4) חד אמר: אנא נסיב דוכסין לגבי

5) וחד אמר: אנא נסיב איפרכין לגבי

5a) וחד אמר: אנא נסיב איסטרטילוטין לגבי

6) היה פקח אחד לשם אמר: אנא נסיב למלכא, דכולא מתחלפין ומלכא אינו מתחלף

7) כך אומות העולם: מהן עובדין לחמה ומהן עובדין ללבנה ומהן עובדים לעץ ואבן, אבל ישראל אינן עובדין אלא לקב״ה

8) הה״ד, חלקי ה׳ אמרה נפשי

10) שאני מיחד אותו שתי פעמים בכל יום ואומר שמע ישראל ה׳ אלקינו ה׳ אחד (דברים ו:ד)

_____

7) אומות העולם] כך מ ק ד; מר עובדי כוכבים

ER 4:11 — Ashkenaz　　　　　　　　א״ר ד:איא — אשכנז

1) ויצת אש בציון

2) כתיב מזמור לאסף אלקים באו גויים בנחלתך (תהלים עט:א) מזמור ! בכיה
מבעי ליה.

3) אמר ר׳ אלעזר

4) משל למלך שעשה חופה לבנו. גיידה וסיידה וצ׳יירה.

5) פעם אחת הכעיסוהו

6) וסתרה

7) התחיל פדגוג יושב ומזמר

8) אמרו לו: המלך סתר חופת בנו ואתה יושב ומזמר !

9) אמר להם: לכך אני מזמר שאמרתי מוטב ששפך חמתו על חופת בנו ולא על
בנו.

10) כך אמרו לאסף: הקב״ה החריב את בית מקדשו ואתה יושב ומזמר !

11) אמר להם: לכך אני מזמר שאמרתי מוטב ששפך הקב״ה חמתו על עצים ועל
אבנים ועל העפר ולא על ישראל.

12) הדא הוא דכתיב: ויצת אש בציון ותאכל יסודותיה.

---

4) משל] ב, פ,; א ל, ה ה ח׳ || לבנין] ב לבנו תיקן ביתו || גיידה וסיידה וצ׳יירה] א
גיירה וכיירה וצ׳יירה; ל סיידה וכיירה

6) סתר חופת בנו] ב חרב ביתו

9) שאמרתי מוטב] ב ח׳

11) שאמרתי מוטב] ב ח׳ || ועל העפר] ב ח׳

ER 4:11 — Sepharad

א״ר ד:יא — ספרד

1) ויצת אש בציון

2) כתיב מזמור לאסף אלוקים באו גויים בנחלתך (תהלים עט:א) לא הוה קרא
צריך למימר אלא בכי לאסף נהי לאסף קינה לאסף. ואת אומר מזמור לאסף!

3) אלא

4) משל למלך שעשה בית חופה לבנו וסיידה וכיירה וציירה

5) ויצא בנו לתרבות רעה

6) מיד עלה המלך לחופה וקרע את הוילאות ושיבר את הקנים.

7) ונטל פדגוג שלו איבוב של קנים והיה מזמר.

8) אמרו לו: המלך הפך חופתו של בנו ואת יושב ומזמר!

9) אמר להם: מזמר אני שהפך חופתו של בנו ולא שפך חמתו על בנו

10) כך אמרו לאסף: הקב״ה החריב היכל ומקדש ואתה יושב ומזמר!

11) אמר להם: מזמר אני ששפך הקב״ה חמתו על העצים ועל האבנים ולא שפך
חמתו על ישראל.

12) הדא הוא דכתיב ויצת אש בציון ותאכל יסודותיה

─────────────

6) מיד עלה המלך לחופה] ק מה עשה המלך? נכנס לחופה

Notes

1. Composition and Exegesis

1. For parallels, see Margulies's notes *ad locum,* esp. Koh. R. 1.3.1; B. Nedarim 3b tells the banquet story without mentioning Bar Kappara's meshalim.
2. I owe this felicitous formulation to my friend Richard Ingber; the neologism "phytomorphic" was suggested to me by Martin Ostwald. On fables in general, see B. E. Perry, "Fable," *Studium Generale* 12 (1959), 17–37. On Rabbinic fables: A. Singer's Hebrew article in *Jerusalem Studies in Jewish Folklore* 4 (1983), 79–91, with bibliography; add David Daube, *Ancient Hebrew Fables* (Oxford, 1973) and *Civil Disobedience in Late Antiquity* (Edinburgh, 1972). For the connection between fox-fables and so-called fuller's-fables *(mishlei kovesim),* see S. Jacobs, "Aesop's Fables among the Jews," *Jewish Encyclopaedia* (New York, 1901), vol. 1, 221–222.
3. Roger D. Abrahams, "Open and Closed Forms in Moral Tales," in *Studies in Aggadah and Jewish Folklore,* ed. I. Ben-Ami and J. Dan (Jerusalem, 1983), 19–33.
4. W. J. Verdenius, "AINOS," *Mnemosyne* 15 (1962), 389; cf. G. Nagy, *The Best of the Achaeans* (Baltimore, 1979), 234–241, 281–286.
5. On the account's historicity, see Emil Schürer, *The History of the Jewish People in the Age of Jesus Christ,* rev. and ed. G. Vermes, F. Millar, and M. Black (Edinburgh, 1973), vol. 1, 535–536.
6. See Minhat Yehudah ad Ber. R. 64.10, 712. The Aesopic fable most often cited is the Wolf and the Heron (#156). Cf. H. Schwartbaum, "Talmudic-Midrashic Affinities of Some Aesopic Fables," *IV International Congress for Folk-Narrative Research* (Athens, 1965), 466–483.
7. For the etymology of the root *m-sh-l,* see L. Koehler and W. Baumgartner, *Lexicon in Veteris Testamenti Libros* (Leiden, 1953), 575–576; O. Eissfeldt, *Der Maschal im Alten Testament* (Giessen, 1913); A. R. Johnson, "Mashal," in M. Noth and D. W. Thomas, eds., *Wisdom in Israel and in the Ancient Near East, SVT,* vol. 3 (Leiden, 1955), 162–169.
8. See Eliezer ben Yehuda, *Dictionary and Thesaurus of the Hebrew Language* (1910; repr. New York, 1960), vol. 4, 3386–3387; s.v. mashal,

1 and 3 in particular; cf. James Kugel, *The Idea of Biblical Poetry* (New Haven, 1981), 69n15, who suggests that the word may designate "many things written in the closural style of biblical parallelism," like proverbs, allegories, and so on. Compare, however, Ezek. 17:2, the so-called allegory of the eagle, called a *mashal*—perhaps a fable?

9. On Rabbinic use of *mashal*, its Aramaic cognate *matla*, and verb forms of the root *m-sh-l*, cf. W. Z. Bacher, *Erkhei Midrash*, trans. A. Z. Rabinowitz (Tel Aviv, 1923), vol. 1, 84; vol. 2, 231–232. For the use of the term as an exegetical category: R. Loewe, "The 'Plain' Meaning of Scripture in Early Jewish Exegesis," *Papers of the Institute for Jewish Studies, London* 1 (1964), 141–185. In B. Baba Bathra 15a, Yotham's mashal (2 Sam. 12:1ff.) and Job (the character? the story?) are both called *meshalim*, presumably meaning "fictional but exemplary."

10. For the Septuagint's translation of *mashal* as *parabolē*, see 1 Kings 5:12; Ezek. 17:2; Ps. 78:2. Note, however, that the Septuagint also translates *mashal* with other words: *paroimia*, "proverb" or "maxim," Prov. 1:1; *thrulēma*, "byword," Job 17:6; *ainigma*, "riddle," Deut. 28:37; *ainigmatistēs*, "a riddler," Num. 21:27; *apsanismon*, "byword," 1 Kings 9:7; and *threnos*, "lament," Isa. 14:4, Mic. 2:4. For the gospels: Mark 4:11,33; Matt. 13:3,24; Luke 8:4.

11. Aristotle, *The Art of Rhetoric* 2.20.1393; cf. Plato, *Timaeus* (40c4) and *Philebus* (33b2); see M. H. McCall, Jr., *Ancient Rhetorical Theories of Simile and Comparison* (Cambridge, Mass., 1969), 25–29.

12. The term "illustrative parallel" is from W. R. Roberts, quoted in McCall, 27; but for a precise and very early account of *parabolē*'s transference from figure to narrative, see Diodore of Tarsus, "Preface to the Commentary on Psalm 118," trans. in *Biblical Interpretation in the Early Church*, ed. K. Froehlich (Philadelphia, 1984), 89–90.

13. A. Jülicher, *Die Gleichnisreden Jesus* (1886; Darmstadt, 1963), vol. 1, 146 and passim. The following discussion draws on my essay, "Jesus' Parables from the Perspective of Rabbinic Literature: The Example of the Wicked Husbandmen," in *Parable and Story in Judaism and Christianity*, ed. C. Thoma and M. Wyschogrod (New York, 1989), 42–80.

14. The major proponent of this view is Paul Ricoeur, especially "Biblical Hermeneutics," *Semeia* 4 (1975); cf. *Semiology and Parables*, ed. Daniel Patte (Pittsburgh, 1976); Norman Perrin, *Jesus and the Language of the Kingdom* (Philadelphia, 1976), 89–205.

15. Sally TeSelle, *Speaking in Parables* (Philadelphia, 1975), 78–79.

16. Jülicher, 58–69; cf. R. M. Johnston, "Parabolic Interpretations Attributed to Tannaim" (Ph.D. diss., Hartford Seminary Foundation, 1977), 101.

17. Cf. T. Guttmann, *Hamashal Bitkufat Hatannaim* (Jerusalem, 1949), 75–77; D. Flusser, *Yahadut Umekorot Hanatsrut* (Tel Aviv, 1979), 207–209.

18. Jon Whitman, *Allegory* (Cambridge, Mass., 1987), 1–13, 262–268.

19. See Roman Jakobson's classic study, "Two Aspects of Language and Two Types of Aphasic Disturbances," orig. pub. as Part 2 of R. Jakobson and M. Halle, *Fundamentals of Language* (The Hague, 1956); repr. in *Language in Literature,* ed. K. Pomorska and S. Rudy (Cambridge, Mass., 1987), esp. 109–114.

20. Unlike *parabolē,* the term *dugma,* cognate to the Greek *paradeigma,* does appear in Rabbinic literature, where it is sometimes used as a synonym for the word mashal: see Shir R. 1.1.8; cf. S. Krauss, *Griechische und Lateinische Lehnworter im Talmud, Midrasch, und Targum* (Berlin, 1898), vol. 2, 187–188.

21. *Rhetoric,* 2.20.8.

22. Susan Rubin Suleiman, *Authoritarian Fictions: The Ideological Novel as a Literary Genre* (New York, 1983), 37.

23. Suleiman, 55, where she also quotes Barthes's expression from *S/Z* (Paris, 1970), 85.

24. See Abrahams, "Open and Closed Forms in Moral Tales."

25. This is the position that has been consistently taken in New Testament scholarship since Jülicher in regard to the explanations attached to the parables in the synoptic gospels. In the case of the Rabbinic mashal, no one has actually questioned the nimshal's authenticity, but see the remarks of Guttmann, *Hamashal Bitkufat Hatannaim,* 70–75. Johnston, "Parabolic Interpretations," 636–639, correctly concludes from his study of Tannaitic meshalim that nearly all of them include nimshalim, but he gives no explanation for this. In contrast, Flusser, *Yahadut Umekorot Hanatsrut,* 150–152 and 195 ff., argues for the originality of the nimshal to the mashal's form precisely because he believes the mashal to be allegorical.

26. Compare Nagy, *The Best of the Achaeans,* 281–283, on the epimythia attached to the fables of Aesop; cf. Lloyd Daly, *Aesop without Morals* (New York, 1961), 11–18. For a different view, see B. E. Perry, "The Origin of the Epimythium," *TAPA* 71 (1940), 391–419.

27. Barbara Kirshenblatt-Gimblett, "A Parable in Context: A Social Interactional Analysis of Storytelling Performance," in *Folklore: Performance and Communication,* ed. D. Ben-Amos and K. Goldstein (The Hague, 1975), 130.

28. For biblical examples: Exod. 15:18, Isa. 24:23, Ps. 93:1, and 1 Chron. 16:31; cf. Marc Z. Brettler, *God Is King: Understanding an Israelite Metaphor* (Sheffield, 1989, JSOT Sup.).

29. Thus the *'aleinu,* the *malkhuyyot* section of the Rosh Hashana *musaf,*

and the opening *berakhah* formula; for the compulsory mention of kingship in the berakhah, see J. Berakhot 9.1,12d; cf. Joseph Heinemann, *Prayer in the Talmud,* trans. R. Sarason (Berlin, 1977), 32–33, 93–97, esp. 94n26.

30. I. Ziegler, *Die Königsgleichnisse des Midrasch* (Breslau, 1903), xxii–xxiii, xxviff; S. Krauss, *Paras Veromi Batalmud Umidrashim* (Jerusalem, 1948), 34–36, 40 and n30 where, against Ziegler, he claims that any high officer in the emperor's court or service might have been called a *melekh* by the Rabbis.

31. See Ziegler, very end of book.

32. For example: S. T. Lachs, "The Pandora-Eve Motif in Rabbinic Literature," *HTR* 67 (1974), 341–345.

33. For example: Moses Hadas, "Rabbinic Parallels to *Scriptores Historiae Augustae,*" *Classical Philology* 24 (1929), 258–262 (most of which are to king-meshalim); Saul Lieberman, *Hellenism in Jewish Palestine* (New York, 1950), 4–5, discussing the mashal in Sh. R. 15.12 in connection with an incident recorded by Lactantius involving Diocletian; cf. M. Avi-Yonah, *The Jews of Palestine: A Political History from the Bar Kokhba War to the Arab Conquest* (1962; New York, 1976), 91–93; Ziegler, passim.

34. See Morton Smith, "The Image of God," *Bulletin of the John Rylands Library* 40 (1958), 481–488.

35. Since there is no complete collection of Amoraic meshalim, it is impossible to say exactly what percentage of them are king-meshalim. In Eikh. R.—which is probably as representative an Amoraic midrash as any other—there are 21 king-meshalim and 2 meshalim with protagonists who are not kings, a ratio of more than ten to one. In Johnston's anthology of Tannaitic meshalim, he lists approximately 130 king-meshalim out of a total of 324 examples; in comparison, Ziegler has roughly 800 post-Tannaitic king-meshalim. These figures, however, must remain approximate because of unanswered questions of attribution and noncritical texts.

36. See below on Sanhedrin 108a and Ber. R. 28.6 (II.1 and II.2). Cf. Guttmann, *Hamashal,* 36; and Flusser, *Yahadut,* 152f.; for the New Testament, Flusser, 143.

37. For examples: Mekhilta Beshalah 2 (anonymous) and PRK 11.3 (R. Ishmael); Mekhilta Beshalah 4 (R. Abshalom the Elder) and Sh. R. 21.8 (R. Abtulis the Elder); Mekhilta Bahodesh 6 (R. Gamliel II) and Avodah Zarah 54b (R. Gamliel II); Sifre Deut. 356 (anonymous) and Sifre Deut. 19 (anonymous); Sukkah 29a (the Rabbis) and T. Sukka 2.6 (the Rabbis); ARN A 1 (R. Simeon b. Yohai) and ARN B 1 (Rabbi). In a number of these meshalim, the changes go far beyond the revising of *adam* to *melekh*.

38. For an exhaustive listing of all variants to this formula, see Guttmann, *Hamashal,* 7–12, where he lists 75 examples though only the first 23 are actually relevant to the mashal. The most common abbreviations are *mashal le* or simple *le,* followed usually by *melekh.* In Eikh. R., the two recensions interchangeably use *mashal le* and *le* in about an equal number of cases, with no discernible pattern; see Appendix B.

39. For the kind of error that results from not understanding that this formulaic beginning is conventional, see Norman Perrin's interpretation (actually borrowed from Joachim Jeremias's famous study) of the parable of the children in the marketplace, in *Rediscovering the Teaching of Jesus* (New York, 1976), 85–87. A term, "transference of the point-of-comparison," was even invented by scholars to explain in semantic terms what is essentially a stylistic phenomenon.

40. Cf. E. E. Urbach, "The Laws of Idolatry and the Archaeological and Historical Reality in the Second and Third Centuries" [Hebrew], *Eretz Yisrael* 5 (1958), 199ff.; idem, *The Sages,* trans. I. Abrahams (Jerusalem, 1975), 87–90; in both works, Urbach cites numerous relevant meshalim.

41. For a revealing parallel to this mashal's sardonic critique of the flattery that characterized the imperial cult, see Judah Goldin's citation from Plinius Secundus's *Panegyricus* in *The Song at the Sea* (New Haven, 1971), 80–81, notes ad locum.

42. For other examples of meshalim with the *gibor* (hero) or *basar vadam* (mortal) as protagonist, see Mekhilta Shirta 4, 8.

43. In addition, note the following differences: (1) In their statements to the pedagogue, the people use different verbs in Hebrew to describe the king's destruction of the bridal-chamber: S uses *hafakh* while A uses *satar.* Note, however, that Lam. 4:11 reads *shafakh hamato,* "He poured out His anger," diction that is borrowed by A in the pedagogue's response to the people; *hafakh,* though, might have been used because of its phonetic similarity to *shafakh.* (2) In the pedagogue's concluding response, S reads "I sing because he destroyed the bridal-chamber," while A has "For this reason *(lekakh)* I sing because I said, Better *(mutav)* that he poured out his anger . . ."

44. Cf. *Lekah Tov* 35, where R. Pinhas's mashal is recorded with the additional prooftext of Ps. 39:5.

45. On this phrase and its variants, see Buber's note ad locum, and Theodor's comments in his ed. of Ber. R., 69–70.

46. *The Old Testament Pseudepigrapha,* ed. J. H. Charlesworth (Garden City, N.Y., 1983), vol. 1, 546.

47. Midrash Vayosha', in BH, vol. 1, 37; and in Yalkut Shime'oni Gen. 101.

48. Vladimir Propp, *The Morphology of the Folktale,* trans. L. Scott (1928; Austin, 1968), 20ff.
49. On the figure of the pedagogue, see H. I. Marrou, *A History of Education in Antiquity* (New York, 1956), 220–222; D. Lull, "'The Law Was Our Pedagogue': A Study in Galatians 3:19–25," *JBL* 105 (1986), 481–498.
50. Cf. Plutarch, *Moralia* 439E, cited in Lull, 491.
51. On oral literature, see J. M. Foley, *The Theory of Oral Composition* (Bloomington, Ind., 1988); Alan Dundes, in his introduction to Foley's book (pp. ix–x) connects Parry's work with Propp's.
52. *The Making of Homeric Verse: The Collected Papers of Milman Parry,* ed. Adam Parry (Oxford, 1971), 317.
53. See Jonathan Culler, *Structuralist Poetics* (Ithaca, N.Y., 1975), 113–114.
54. On orality in aggadic literature, see Joseph Heinemann, *Aggadot Vetoldoteihen* (Jerusalem, 1974), 17–47, an English translation of which is available in *Midrash and Literature,* ed. G. H. Hartman and S. Budick (New Haven, 1986), 41–55. The classic discussion of the oral "publication" of the Mishnah remains Saul Lieberman, *Hellenism in Jewish Palestine,* 83–89; cf. Jacob Neusner, "Oral Torah and Oral Tradition: Defining the Problematic," in *Method and Meaning in Ancient Judaism* (Chico, Calif., 1979), 59–75; idem, *The Rabbinic Traditions about the Pharisees before 70,* vol. 3, 143–163. On the mashal's traditional features, my own work is anticipated in David Flusser's important recent studies: in *Yahadut,* 150–209, and *Die rabbinischen Gleichnisse und der Gleichniserzähler Jesu,* part 1 (Bern, 1981), and in "Aesop's Miser and the Parable of the Talents," in *Parable and Story in Judaism and Christianity;* as their titles suggest, Flusser's focus in these works is upon the relationship between the Rabbinic meshalim and Jesus' parables. The main methodological difference between our approaches is that where Flusser adopts a more Proppian stance on the "deep structures" of the narratives, my approach is more attuned to their formulaic language and stereotyped motifs; in addition, Flusser studies the "development" of one parable from another, a tendency I avoid in analyzing Rabbinic meshalim as a group, concentrating instead on their synchronic relationships.
55. Eric A. Havelock, *The Muse Learns to Write* (New Haven, 1986), 79–116, esp. 90–92; Alain Renoir, "Oral-Formulaic Rhetoric and the Interpretation of Literary Texts," in *Oral Tradition in Literature,* ed. J. M. Foley (Columbia, Mo., 1986), 103–135; Albert B. Lord, "The Gospels as Oral Traditional Literature" in *The Relationships among the Gospels,* ed. W. O. Walker, Jr. (San Antonio, 1978), esp. 33–39; Werner Kelber, *The Oral and the Written Gospel* (Philadelphia, 1983).

None of these studies, however, considers the possibility of intentional imitation of oral forms in literary compositions.

56. On the Hebrew of the Tannaitic mashal, see Guttmann, *Hamashal,* 71–75; on Hebrew and Aramaic, E. Margoliot, "Hebrew and Aramaic in the Talmud and Midrash" (Hebrew), *Leshoneinu* 26 (1963), 20–33. For a rare example of a mashal in Aramaic attributed to a Tanna (here R. Akiba), see J. Ta'anit 3.4.

57. On the *oheiv/philos*, cf. Krauss, *Paras Veromi*, 135, 141ff.

58. M. Dahood, *Psalms* (Garden City, N.Y., 1979), vol. 2, 188; Vay. R. 17.1; L. Ginzberg, *The Legends of the Jews* (Philadelphia, 1938), vol. 6, 205. Exactly why paradoxical behavior is attributed to Asaph is unclear, but it appears to be a topos: cf. the mashal in TDE, ch. 28, 150f., in reference to Ps. 79:1, quoted and discussed in Chapter 6.

59. Cf. Targum to Psalms ad locum, and on the background of the psalm, Dahood, vol. 2, 250. This question is generic as well as lexical: if the psalm is a *kinah*, a lament, then what is it doing in a book of songs?

60. Note that the structure of the passage in its entirety resembles a petihta or classical proem, though at best this would be a pseudo-petihta: see my discussion in Chapter 5.

61. See Shir R. 3.17; Bam. R. 12.4.

62. Cf. PR 2, p. 7a, in which God explains that if He allows David to build the Temple He will never be able to destroy it and thereby take out His anger, which otherwise would be directed upon the people of Israel. For a related theme: Mekhilta Pisha 1 in connection with Exod. 32:32; cf. Baruch Bokser, "The Wall Separating God and Israel," *JQR* 73 (1983), 349–374; and idem, "Rabbinic Responses to Catastrophe," *PAAJR* 50 (1983), 37–61.

63. Such a reading of the verse makes particularly good sense because 4:11 is, in fact, the conclusion of the preceding movement in the chapter (4:1–10), which describes God's wrath against Zion; cf. Rashi on Ps. 79:1.

64. Bam. R. 12.4, which also cites the *apiryon* of Song 3:9. I wish to thank Raymond Scheindlin for suggesting this pun to me.

65. Tertullian, "An Answer to the Jews," in A. Roberts and J. Donaldson, eds., *Ante-Nicene Christian Library* (Edinburgh, 1870), vol. 18, 252–253. Cf. Justin Martyr, *The Dialogue with Trypho*, trans. A. L. Williams (London, 1930), 32–34; Aphrahat's famous comparison of the Temple's destruction to the ravaging of the vineyard, quoted in J. Neusner, *Aphrahat and Judaism* (Leiden, 1971), 119; and for background, Rowan A. Greer's discussion in Rowan A. Greer and James L. Kugel, *Early Biblical Interpretation* (Philadelphia, 1986), 120–125.

66. Cf. V. Tcherikover, "Jewish Apologetic Literature Reconsidered," *Eos* 48 (1956), 169–191.

67. For the Akiba story, see Eikh. R., 159–160, on Lam. 5:18. For the conventionality of this motif in sage-stories, see Henry A. Fischel, "Story and History: Observations on Greco-Roman Rhetoric and Pharisaism," *American Oriental Society Middle West Branch Semi-Centennial Volume,* ed. D. Sinor (Bloomington, Ind., 1969), 59–88, esp. 69–73. The obvious parallel to Akiba is Diogenes the Cynic. Cf. J. Yoma 3.9, 41a (= J. Shekalim 5.2, 49a; B. Yoma 38a), though there a child, not Akiba, does the laughing and singing.

68. For the most available description: Hermann L. Strack, *Introduction to the Talmud and Midrash* (1920; English trans. 1931; repr. New York, 1978), 93–98.

69. M. Zucker, "Towards the Solution of the Problem of the 32 Middot and 'The Mishnat R. Eliezer,'" *PAAJR* 21–23 (1952–54), 1–39; R. Loewe, "The Plain Meaning of Scripture"; I. Twersky, *Rabad of Posquieres: A Twelfth-Century Talmudist* (Cambridge, Mass., 1962), 97–106.

70. See especially the MaHaRZU's introduction to his commentary, printed at the beginning of the Vilna edition of MR.

71. Cf. Max Kadushin, *The Rabbinic Mind* (New York, 1952).

72. In particular: Lieberman, *Hellenism,* 47–82; J. Tigay, "An Early Technique of Aggadic Exegesis," in *History, Historiography, and Interpretation: Studies in Biblical and Cuneiform Literatures,* ed. H. Tadmor and M. Weinfeld (Jerusalem, 1983), 169–189; M. Fishbane, *Biblical Interpretation in Ancient Israel* (Oxford, 1985).

73. Susan Handelman, *The Slayers of Moses: The Emergence of Rabbinic Interpretation in Modern Literary Theory* (Albany, N.Y., 1982); D. Stern, "Moses-cide: Midrash and Contemporary Literary Criticism," *Prooftexts* 4 (1984), 193–204; Daniel Boyarin, *Intertextuality and the Reading of Midrash* (Bloomington, Ind., 1990).

74. *Midrash and Literature,* xi.

75. Cf. David Stern, "Midrash and the Language of Exegesis: A Study of Vayikra Rabbah, Chapter 1," in *Midrash and Literature,* 105–124.

2. Rhetoric

1. See David Daube's comments in *Ancient Hebrew Fables* (Oxford, 1973), and H. Schwartzbaum, "The Talmudic and Midrashic Affinities of Some Aesopic Fables," in *International Congress for Folk-Narrative Research,* IV (Athens, 1965), 466ff; and Schwartzbaum's magnum opus, *The Mishle Shu'alim (Fox-Fables) of Rabbi Berechiah Ha-Nakdan* (Kiron, Israel, 1979), esp. i–xviii.

2. For examples, see the two parables with which Rabban Gamliel purportedly responded to the questions of the philosopher, in Mekhilta

Bahodesh 6 and B. Avodah Zarah 54b–55a; the mashal Onkelos the proselyte is said to have told the Roman soldiers, in B. Avodah Zarah 11a; the mashal R. Gamliel used to respond to the question of Beluriah the proselyte, in B. Rosh Hashana 17b; and finally, the mashal with which R. Ami refuted the Saduccee who denied the doctrine of corporeal resurrection, in B. Sanhedrin 91a. In addition, note the following texts which, though they do not contain formal parables, relate how sages used parabolic actions as polemical instruments: PR 21, 99a–b (about R. Joshua and Hadrian); Ber. R. 4.4, (R. Meir and the Cuthite); J. Hagiga 2.1 (Akylos the proselyte and Hadrian); B. Berakhot 32b–33a (the pious man and the Roman officer).

3. B. Baba Kamma 66b, for how R. Abahu felt it necessary to apologize to R. Hiyya b. Aba when the two of them were preaching at the same time, and a far larger audience came to hear R. Abahu preach on aggadic themes than to listen to R. Hiyya teach halakhah. See also the mashal that R. Yitzhak Nafha told his disciples when one of them asked him to lecture on halakhah and the other asked for aggadah: the mashal relates the story of an elderly man with two wives, one of whom plucked all the white hairs from his head, the other all his black hairs, until the old man was left bald, in B. Baba Kamma 60b. Cf. J. Taanit 4.5, and B. Taanit 25b, for stories about sages (R. Akiba and Samuel the younger, respectively) who recited meshalim after they successfully prayed for rain and felt it necessary to justify their success.

4. Compare the story of R. Kahana, who asked his teacher R. Yohanan a parabolic legal question in order surreptitiously to gain permission to leave Palestine and return home to Babylonia, in J. Berakhot 2.8.

5. For other examples: ARN A, 14.6, p. 30, for the mashal recited by R. Eleazar b. 'Arakh to console R. Yohanan b. Zakkai; and J. Berakhot 2.8 for the mashal of Simeon b. Lakish over R. Hiyya b. Ada, both of which I quote and analyze in Chapter 3. Cf. J. Berakhot 2.8 as well for: Bar Kappara over R. Hiyya b. Abba (= Shir R. 6.5.2; Koh. R. 5.11); in memory of R. Bun (= Koh. R. 5.11); the father of Samuel over R. Levi b. Sisi (= Koh. R. 12.5.13). For the two meshalim R. Yohanan b. Zakkai recited over himself, cited in Semahot deR. Hiyya 4.1, see my discussion in Chapter 6 of the early Tannaitic mashal.

6. The closest thing to a scene describing an academic setting as the occasion for a mashal's recitation is the context depicted for the mashal R. Akiba told the woman raped as a child, in B. Niddah 45a. Cf. the context for the mashal recited in the course of the controversy between R. Ishmael and R. Eleazar b. Azariah, in B. Berakhot 11a. Compare too the brief mashal in M. Sukkah 2.5 (the other two

298 · *Notes to Pages 48–52*

"meshalim" in the Mishnah, in Niddah 2.5 and 5.7, are not narratives but extended similes at best); and such meshalim in the Tosefta as Baba Kamma 7.2, Sanhedrin 1.2, Zevahim 12.9, Niddah 34.5, all of which might have been employed in discussions of halakhah within the academy. Note also the statement of R. Yohanan, in B. Sanhedrin 38b–39a, about R. Meir, who is said to have divided his sermons into three parts, the third part being *matlei*, which could be either parables or proverbs; and to have known three hundred fables, all but three of which were lost after his death. For reconstructions of those three, cf. Rashi and MaHaRSHa ad locum and *Teshuvot Geonim* 30; interestingly, the fables, which themselves are not preserved, are referred to by their prooftexts, suggesting that even fables were used for exegetical purposes. The number three hundred, however, is conventional, *contra* Johnston who writes (in his Ph.D. diss., "Parabolic Interpretations Attributed to Tannaim," 174) that "it is tempting to conjecture that the phrase, 'Three Hundred Fables,' that occurs so often, is a reference to a standard collection which began to circulate in rabbinic circles sometime between the time of R. Johanan b. Zakkai and that of Meir." The number of one thousand king-meshalim that I cite is based upon the texts collected by Ignaz Ziegler in *Die Königsgleichnisse des Midrasch* (Breslau, 1903).

7. For fuller discussion of this scholarship, see David Stern, "Jesus' Parables from a Rabbinic Perspective: The Case of the Wicked Husbandmen," in *Parable and Story in Judaism and Christianity*, ed. C. Thoma and M. Wyschogrod (New York, 1989), 42–80.

8. Frank Kermode, *The Genesis of Secrecy* (Cambridge, Mass., 1979); cf. J. Bowker, "Mystery and Parable: Mark 4, 1–20," *JTS* n.s. 25 (1974), 300–317.

9. Tan. B. Gen., 103.

10. For an additional example, see Dev. R. (Lieberman), 8.5, 110.

11. My diagrams are based upon those of Susan Rubin Suleiman, *Authoritarian Fictions: The Ideological Novel as a Literary Genre* (New York, 1983), 33.

12. For a similar, somewhat more theologically oriented understanding of the mashal's communicative structure, see Clemens Thoma, "Literary and Theological Aspects of the Rabbinic Parables," in *Parable and Story in Judaism and Christianity*, 26–41; and Clemens Thoma and Simon Lauer, *Die Gleichnisse der Rabbinen, Erster Teil: Pesikta deRav Kahana* (Bern, 1986).

13. On praise and blame in Rabbinic society, see Urbach, *The Sages*, trans. I. Abrahams (Jerusalem, 1975), 620–630. On the language of praise and blame: Saul Lieberman, "Kaleis Kilusin" (Hebrew) in *'Alei 'Ayin* (Jerusalem, 1947), 75–81; Samuel Leiter, "Worthiness, Acclamation,

and Appointment: Some Rabbinic Terms," *PAAJR* 41–42 (1973–74), 137–168.

14. Roman Jakobson, "Concluding Statement: Linguistics and Poetics," in *Style in Language,* ed. T. Sebeok (Cambridge, Mass., 1960), 350–378.

15. Thus Saul Lieberman in his notes to Vay. R., 870; cf. S. Klein, "Zur jüdischen Altertumskunde," *MGWJ* 77 (1933), 364n9. For a different view: Margulies ad locum defines the *ma'aforet* as a special kind of turban or headdress.

16. Cf. Vay. R. 2.5; for discussion: Urbach, *The Sages,* 529–535.

17. Ed. Buber, 139.

18. My translation is based on A; S differs slightly in its language. For other parallels, see Buber's notes, 132, and add to them Midrash Shir Hashirim, ed. E. H. Grunhut (1897; 2nd ed. Jerusalem, 1981), 52–53.

19. In addition to these symbols, the mashal's narrative motifs are nearly all traditional. The narrative can be divided into the following motifs: (1) The king marries the woman; (2) the king journeys to a foreign province; (3) the wicked neighbors taunt the abandoned wife; (4) the wife reads the ketubah and is consoled; (5) the king returns. The first three motifs and the last one have many parallels: for the first motif, see Sh. R. 15.31 and Bam. R. 1.5; for the second and third, see Semahot deR. Hiyya 3.3; Tan. B. Exod., 127–128, and Num., 71. The last motif has parallels in several of these meshalim as well.

20. I owe this insight to Kathryn Hellerstein.

21. Mordechai Akiva Friedman, *Jewish Marriage in Palestine: A Cairo Geniza Study* (Tel Aviv and New York, 1981), 77, 239–262.

22. I am here reading the Hebrew *aleph-m-r* as the participle *omeir;* for the participle as future, see M. H. Segal, *A Grammar of Mishnaic Hebrew* (Oxford, 1927), 157.

23. On the interpretation of *zot,* see especially I. Heinemann, *Darkhei Haaggadah* (Jerusalem, 1970), 118. Cf. H. Fox, "As If by Finger— The History of an Anti-Anthropomorphic Figure" (Hebrew), *Tarbiz* 49 (1980), 278–291; and Betty Rojtman, *Feu Noir sur Feu Blanc* (La Grasse, France, 1986).

24. See Alan Mintz, *Hurban,* 34ff.; for his elegant analysis of this mashal (from which my own reading derives), see 82–83.

25. For the same displacement, see ARN A, ch. 17, 66 ("'for the sake of heaven' means 'for the sake of Torah'"); Judah Goldin, "The Two Versions of *Abot de Rabbi Nathan,*" *HUCA* 19 (1946), 99.

26. I wish to thank Michael Sokoloff for pointing this pun out to me.

27. Ulpian, *Digest* 50.17.30; 24.1.32.13; cited and discussed in Susan Treggiari, "Roman Marriage," in *Civilization of the Ancient Mediter-*

ranean, ed. Michael Grant and Rachel Kitzinger (New York, 1988), vol. 3, 1345.

3. Poetics

1. Hebrew *dugma:* the precise meaning of the word is unclear. A loanword from the Greek *deigma,* an "example" or "pattern," *dugma* can mean either "a figure" or "a tale with a figurative meaning"; cf. Sarah Kamin, "*Dugma* in Rashi's Commentary on the Song of Songs" (Hebrew), *Tarbiz* 52 (1982), esp. 41–45. In the latter sense, the word is a virtual synonym for mashal as parable, which seems to be the sense imputed to mashal in Eccles. 12:9 as interpreted in the midrash (in contrast to its contextual sense, which is "proverbs"); the same sense of dugma as equivalent to mashal is borne out by the continuation of the passage.
2. See Daniel Boyarin, "Two Introductions to the Midrash on the Song of Songs" (Hebrew), *Tarbiz* 56 (1986), esp. 479–491; idem, *Intertextuality and the Reading of Midrash* (Bloomington, Ind., 1990), 107.
3. Gerald Bruns, *Inventions: Writing, Textuality, and Understanding in Literary History* (New Haven, 1982), 31.
4. Susan Rubin Suleiman, *Authoritarian Fictions: The Ideological Novel as a Literary Genre* (New York, 1983), 7, 27, and in general 25–61.
5. Meir Sternberg, *The Poetics of Biblical Narrative: Ideological Literature and the Drama of Reading* (Bloomington, Ind., 1985), esp. 23–55.
6. Peter Brooks, "Fictions of the Wolfman," *Diacritics* 9 (1979), 75–81. Cf. Jonathan Culler, "Story and Discourse in the Analysis of Narrative," in *The Pursuit of Signs* (Ithaca, N.Y., 1981), 169–187.
7. Brooks, 75–76.
8. Daniel Boyarin, "Rhetoric and Interpretation: The Case of the Nimshal," *Prooftexts* 5 (1985), 272.
9. The nimshal's conclusion alludes to the alphabetic acrostics marking three of the five chapters in Lamentations.
10. Gen. 3:7 here is being interpreted in light of Gen. 3:21, which describes God as clothing Adam and Eve in garments of animal skin, believed by the Rabbis, on the basis of an independent exegesis, to be identical to the priestly garments described in Lev. 16:4. The anonymous author of this mashal assumed, against the verse's plain sense, that the true meaning of Gen. 3:21 must be retrospective: The garments referred to there must have been the clothes God made for Adam and Eve *before* they sinned, while the fig leaves in Gen. 3:7 were the clothes the first couple wore *after* their sin.
11. S reads *epikaltorin* or *plicata,* but both A and S should probably be corrected to *pilaktin,* on the basis of PRK 11.8. Mandelbaum, in his

edition, 184, connects the Hebrew to the Greek, *poikilton;* Buber, in his edition of PRK (Lyck, 1868), 150, cites the Latin *plicatus.*

12. S reads *bigdei badad,* which is closer to the scriptural text. In general, S's diction is slightly more classical and symmetrical than A's.

13. See Dev. R. 7.9 (where the special clothes that the king gives his son symbolize the mitzvot); BH vol. 3, 69 as well.

14. For R. Simlai's gloss: PRK, 184; and, in somewhat different language, Tan. B., Exod. 50a. On the *purpira,* see S. Krauss, *Paras Veromi Batalmud Umidrashim* (Jerusalem, 1948), 43–44. The bestowal of the *purpira* upon the king's son is significant since, as Krauss reminds us, the emperorship and its prerequisites, among them the privilege to wear the *purpira,* were not hereditary rights.

15. Compare Lam. 5:13 and the comment on it in Eikh. R., 157, describing the Jewish youths in captivity who were forced to carry millstones.

16. Cf. MaHaRZU and Y.A. ad locum.

17. For a dissenting view on this conventional article of belief, see the remarkable opinion of R. Akiba in B. Baba Bathra 10a.

18. See Shlomith Rimmon-Kenan, *Narrative Fiction* (London, 1983), 127–129. Note that the term gap is used in very different ways by, for example, Wolfgang Iser in *The Implied Reader* (Baltimore, 1974), esp. 274–294, and Meir Sternberg in *The Poetics of Biblical Narrative,* esp. 186–263; cf. Sternberg's earlier book, *Expositional Modes and Temporal Ordering in Fiction* (Baltimore, 1978), esp. 311n29. My own approach is much closer to Sternberg's view of gaps than to Iser's.

19. Sternberg, *Poetics of Biblical Narrative,* 191–192.

20. Buber, 90–91; MR lacks the opinion.

21. Alan Mintz, *Hurban* (New York, 1984), 26.

22. In offering his exegesis, R. Joshua may also be exploiting the unusual use of the instrumental *be* preceding *yadeiha* (rather than the more expected *et*) as an intensive indication of the son's submission to his father.

23. Note, however, that this interpretation requires excluding the second half of Lam. 1:17: "the Lord has summoned against Jacob his enemies all about him; Jerusualem has become among them a thing unclean." Something gained, another thing lost. The exegetical role this mashal plays, however, complements its function as an apologetic, for by having the son confess to his sins and willingly submit himself to his father's punishment, the mashal also recasts the entire tone of Zion's description of her persecution by God; no longer does her travail seem gratuitously and unfairly inflicted; it now has a rationale and a clear purpose.

24. Sternberg, *The Poetics of Biblical Narrative,* 235–258.

25. Quoted in François Truffaut, *Hitchcock* (rev. ed. New York, 1984), 138.

26. S reports the mashal anonymously.

27. S omits this sentence.

28. Cf. the same Talmudic passage for the tradition attributed to R. Kahana, and M. Ketubot 7.4.

29. Compare the famous passage in Eikh. R. (73–74) in which Israel complains against their treatment by God, their complaint repeatedly punctuated by the refrain, *asher lo ketoratekha,* "which is against Your Torah/Law," a phrase borrowed from Ps. 119:85.

30. Seymour Chatman, *Story and Discourse* (Ithaca, N.Y., 1978), 146ff.

31. Gerard Genette, *Narrative Discourse,* trans. Jane E. Lewin (Ithaca, N.Y., 1980), esp. 189–194.

32. See Kermode, *The Genesis of Secrecy.*

33. Gerald Prince, "Introduction to the Study of the Narratee," in *Reader-Response Criticism,* ed. Jane P. Tompkins (Baltimore, 1980), 7–25; Wolfgang Iser, *The Implied Reader;* Naomi Schor, "Fiction as Interpretation/Interpretation as Fiction," in *The Reader in the Text,* ed. S. R. Suleiman and I. Crosman (Princeton, 1980), 165–182. Cf. Wallace Martin, *Recent Theories of Narrative* (Ithaca, N.Y., 1986), 154, 156–162.

34. Schor, 170.

35. See Jonathan Culler's essay, "Literary Competence," in *Structuralist Poetics* (Ithaca, 1975), 113–130.

36. See Margulies's critical apparatus ad locum.

37. Hebrew *haviv*—on the meaning of which, see my article "Midrash and the Language of Exegesis," in *Midrash and Literature,* eds. G. H. Hartman and S. Budick (New Haven, 1986), 115ff.

38. For parallels, see Ber. R. 604n4.

39. My translation is based on the text compiled by Steven D. Fraade in his "Sifre Deuteronomy 26 (ad Deut. 3:23): How Conscious the Composition?" *HUCA* 54 (1983), 260–268; see as well Fraade's comments on this mashal: 264n45 and 274n74. For another reconstruction and discussion: Louis Finkelstein, "The Transmission of the Early Rabbinic Traditions," *HUCA* 16 (1941), 115–135.

40. Saul Lieberman, *Greek in Jewish Palestine* (New York, 1942), 163; compare as well the related mashal in Sifre Num. 137, discussed by both Lieberman and Fraade, that uses the same imagery of unripe figs.

41. Admittedly, my reading of the mashal's pun does not explain the woman's other fear, that people will say she has committed witchcraft; but that motif is, I suspect, related to the mashal's scriptural occasion, Moses' striking the rock at Zin in order to produce water. This action was susceptible to being interpreted as an act of magic or witchcraft (just as the bronze serpent was)—hence the woman's fear and her (i.e. Moses') insistence that the precise crime be stated

explicitly or put in writing. On Moses as magician, see John G. Gager, *Moses in Greco-Roman Paganism* (Nashville, 1972), 134–161.

42. Marc Z. Brettler, *God Is King: Understanding an Israelite Metaphor* (Sheffield, 1989).

43. E. E. Urbach, "The Laws of Idolatry and the Archaeological and Historical Reality in the Second and Third Centuries" (Hebrew), *Eretz Yisrael* 5 (1958), 189–205.

44. Cf. Morton Smith, "The Image of God," *John Rylands Library* 40 (1957–58), 473–512, esp. 475–481.

45. Ernst Kitzinger, *Byzantine Art in the Making* (Cambridge, Mass., 1977; 1980), 19.

46. Erwin R. Goodenough, *Jewish Symbols in the Greco-Roman Period*, 13 vols. (New York–Princeton, 1953–1968); cf. M. Smith, "Goodenough's *Jewish Symbols* in Retrospect," *JBL* 86 (1967), 53–68; and most recently, Jacob Neusner's introduction to his abridged one-volume version of *Jewish Symbols* (Princeton, 1988). For an objective survey of the artistic material: Rachel Hachlili, *Ancient Jewish Art and Archaeology in the Land of Israel* (Leiden, 1988).

47. Elias J. Bickerman, "Symbolism in the Dura Synagogue," *HTR* 58 (1965), 127–151. Cf. also the comments of J. H. Liebeschuetz on Roman worship of the sun as "an intellectual concept" or "an image of the supreme deity rather than a God of Worship" in its own right, in *Continuity and Change in Roman Religion* (Oxford, 1979), 282–284.

48. Kitzinger, 20.

49. Kitzinger, 11.

50. On the *adventus*, see Sabine G. MacCormack, *Art and Ceremony in Late Antiquity* (Berkeley, 1981); cf. A. Grabar, *Christian Iconography, A Study of Its Origins* (Princeton, 1968).

51. A. Marmorstein, *The Old Rabbinic Doctrine of God, II. Essays in Anthropomorphism* (1937; repr. New York, 1968). Cf. Urbach, *The Sages*, 37–38; Michael J. Klein, *Anthropomorphisms and Anthropopathisms in the Targumim of the Pentateuch* (Jerusalem, 1982).

52. Saadiah Gaon, *Book of Doctrines and Beliefs* II:8; cf. Julius Guttmann, *Philosophies of Judaism*, trans. D. W. Silverman (New York, 1964), 31–32 and passim; and esp. Marc Saperstein, *Decoding the Rabbis* (Cambridge, Mass., 1980), 12–20.

53. See Josef Stern, "Language," in *Contemporary Jewish Religious Thought*, ed. Arthur A. Cohen and Paul Mendes-Flohr (New York, 1986), 543–551; idem, "Logical Syntax as a Key to the Secret of the Guide of the Perplexed," *Iyyun* 38 (1989), 136–166.

54. For a comparable treatment of the rhetorical and cultural construction of the imperial cult, see S. F. R. Price, *Rituals and Power* (Cambridge, Mass., 1984). Cf. Paul de Man, "Anthropomorphism and

Trope in the Lyric," in *The Rhetoric of Romanticism* (New York, 1984), 239–262. For God's character(s) in the Bible: Yohanan Muffs, "Between Justice and Mercy: The Prayers of the Prophets" (Hebrew), in *Torah Nidreshet,* ed. A. Shapira (Tel Aviv, 1984), 39–87.

55. See M. Elon, *The Principles of Jewish Law* (Jerusalem, 1975), 419–422. The *get* in this mashal, like the *ketubah* in Eikh. R. 3.21, is a slightly incongruous presence from the perspective of the Roman court, although the king's arbitrary treatment of the consort seems more in line with Roman than with Rabbinic practice: see Jerome Carcopino, *Daily Life in Ancient Rome* (New Haven, 1940), 95–100. According to Roman law, divorce mainly required only evidence of intention. No document like a *get* existed, though Augustus's reforms required a declaration before seven witnesses; only in the case of unilateral divorce was a communication through an intermediary necessary. Cf. *Oxford Classical Dictionary,* ed. N. G. H. Hammond and H. H. Scullard, 2nd ed. (Oxford, 1970), 650.

56. Compare the anonymous interpretation for *kealmanah* (Buber, p. 45) likening Israel to the *agunah,* the woman whose husband has disappeared without divorcing her; cf. MR's version, and Rashi's famous description of the *agunah* as "living widowhood" (B. Pesahim 49a).

57. See my article, "*Imitatio Hominis:* Anthropomorphism and the Character of God," *Prooftexts* 11 (Fall 1991), which includes a lengthy analysis of two narratives about God that contain in almost pristine form these two representations of the divine personality. The narratives are found in Eikh. R. Petihta 24; cf. my translations of the two narratives in *Rabbinic Fantasies: Imaginative Narratives from Classical Hebrew Literature,* ed. D. Stern and M. J. Mirsky (Philadelphia, 1990), 47–57.

4. Thematics

1. Edgar Allan Poe, "The Short Story" (from a review of Hawthorne's *Twice-Told Tales*), in *The Portable Poe,* ed. Philip Van Doren Stern (New York, 1945), 566. Cf. Wallace Martin, *Recent Theories of Narrative* (Ithaca, N.Y., 1986), 126–129. On ideological narrative and its meanings, see: Susan Rubin Suleiman, *Authoritarian Fictions: The Ideological Novel as a Literary Genre* (New York, 1983), 25–61; Meir Sternberg, *The Poetics of Biblical Narrative: Ideological Literature and the Drama of Reading* (Bloomington, Ind., 1985), 35–41.

2. Cf. V. Tcherikover, "Jewish Apologetic Literature Reconsidered," *Eos* 48 (1956), 169–191.

3. Sifre Num. 119; Sifre Zuta, Korah 21; cf. Gedaliah Allon, *The Jews in Their Land in the Talmudic Age* (Jerusalem, 1980), 254–260, but see 257n11.

4. For another example of a mashal whose apologetic message is easily extended from its explicit exegetical occasion to later historical incidents of persecution, see Sh. R. 21.15, on Exod. 14:15, describing the lovelorn king who repeatedly sets bandits against the princess he loves so that she will have to call to him for help, and so that he will be able to hear her voice.

5. In S, the mashal is attributed to "R. Huna *and* R. Aha in the name of . . ." See Buber's note ad locum.

6. For other examples of this exegesis, see Ber. R. 98.3 (*shema' yisrael* as "Hear, O Jacob"); B. Pesahim 56a; Tan., Vayehi 8; Vay. R. 36.4; for some discussion, John Bowker, *The Targums and Rabbinic Literature* (Cambridge, 1969), 288–289.

7. For another mashal using Ephraim as the favorite son, see Dev. R. 7.12; for the general identification, see Vay. R. 2.1–3, and Margulies's notes ad locum. The words *tiferet* and *efrayim* may also be associated on account of their roots, which contain the same three letters, *aleph, peh*, and *reish*.

8. On the order of these two verses as cited, see MaHaRZU ad locum.

9. Cf. the Mekhilta mashal citation of the same verse, Hos. 11:3, but note its reading, *zero'otai*, not the MT *zero'otav;* see Lauterbach's note ad locum (vol. 1, 225) and the note to the verse in the Jewish Publication Society's *TaNaKH* (Philadelphia, 1985), 999.

10. The meaning of *arkiv* in this verse is difficult since it says that both Judah and Jacob are set to the task of plowing; JPS TaNaKH translates the word as "do advance plowing." The medieval commentators understood the verse as describing either a metaphorical yoke of the Torah, which God placed upon the neck of Ephraim, or the yoke of the kingdom of the wicked Jeroboam.

11. On its form, and on the even more truncated version in Mekhilta BaHodesh 2.31ff. (with Deut. 1:31 as its prooftext), see my exchange with Daniel Boyarin in *Prooftexts* 5 (1985), 270–280.

12. The same is true of such other father-son meshalim as in Sifra 96a and Sifre Deut. 43.

13. See Israel Cohen, *Dictionary of Parallel Proverbs* (Tel Aviv, 1961), 126.

14. Galit Hasan-Rokem, *Proverbs in Israeli Folk Narratives: A Structural Semantic Analysis* (Helsinki, 1982).

15. S attributes the mashal to R. Joshua b. Nahman, a fourth-generation Amora; R. Joshua of Sikhnin belongs to the third generation.

16. The identity of the agent who makes the object and the nature of the object made can vary of course from mashal to mashal. Note, however, that the motif seems to appear only in Amoraic meshalim, not (to my knowledge) in any Tannaitic sources.

17. On the *aurum coronarium*, see Fergus Millar, *The Emperor in the Roman*

World (London, 1977), 140–144; cf. I. Ziegler, *Die Königsgleichnisse des Midrasch* (Breslau, 1903), 7–9; S. Krauss, *Paras Veromi Batalmud Umidrashim* (Jerusalem, 1948), 46–47. Contrary, however, to the statement of Avi-Yonah, *The Jews of Palestine: A Political History from the Bar Kokhba War to the Arab Conquest* (1962; New York, 1976), 97, the *aurum coronarium* should not be confused with the crown-tax *(mas kelilah);* see Millar, 142.

18. For communal prayer, see Eikh. R. 3.8A; for the Song at the Sea, Sh. R. 23.3 and Tan. B. Exod., 60; for a specific psalm, Mid. Teh. 45.1; and for the trishagios, Vay. R. 24.8.

19. For an example, Vay. R. 2.5.

20. James Kugel, *In Potiphar's House* (San Francisco, 1990), 112–119, based on his reading of the pseudepigraphic Ladder of Jacob 1:4 (*The Old Testament Pseudepigrapha*, ed. J. H. Charlesworth [Garden City, N.Y., 1985], vol. 2, 407). For the Rabbinic sources, see Ber. R. 68.12, the locus classicus in midrash (and note in that passage the citation of Isa. 49:3, which also contains a word with the root *p-a-r*); Targum Ps. Jon. and Targum Yer. on Gen. 28:12; 78:3, 82:2; Bam. R. 4.1; Tan. Bamidbar 19; B. Hullin 81b. As MK in Eikh. R. ad locum notes, the image takes on special meanings in later Kabbalah. Cf. Targum to Ezek. 1:5,10; and Rashi ad locum, and note the textual emendations of S. H. Levey, "The Targum to Ezekiel," *HUCA* 46 (1975), 155n59; and M. McNamara, *Targum and Testament* (Shannon, 1972), 146–147.

21. On the consular diptychs, see Richard Delbrueck, *Die Consulardiptychen und Verwandte Denkmäler* (Berlin, 1929), esp. plate 39, discussed on pp. 166–167 (in which the medallion is on an elevated arch on the back of the chair); and plate 41, p. 173 (where it is carved on the actual back).

22. See the Cathedra of Maximianus (d. 556), in the Archiepiscopal Palace in Ravenna, which has both saints and biblical stories, including the story of Joseph, in ornate carvings. In the famous illustrations in the Rossano Gospels (5th c.), fol. 8r, picturing Jesus being judged before Pilate, in which the latter is seated upon an imperial throne, the twin imperial portraits are not actually on the throne but on a linen cloth spread over a table in front of the throne. See K. Weitzmann, *Late Antique and Early Christian Book Illumination* (London, 1977), 90–91. On the significance of the portraits, see, however, William C. Loerke, "The Miniatures of the Trial in the Rossano Gospels," *Art Bulletin* 43 (1961), esp. 179–182. Cf. John Beckwith, *Early Christian and Byzantine Art* (Baltimore, 1970), 35–36. I wish to thank Professor Bezalel Narkiss of Hebrew University for directing me to the pictorial sources.

23. L. Ginzberg, *The Legends of the Jews*, (Philadelphia, 1938), vol. 1, 351; vol. 5, 290–291n134. Ginzberg also pointed to the identification of Jacob with the man in the moon, and the belief that Jacob became an angel after his death: cf. Jubilees 19:25 (on which, however, see the article cited in the next note).

24. Alexander Altmann, "The Gnostic Background of the Rabbinic Adam Legends," *JQR* 35 (1944–45), 371–391. Surprisingly, Altmann does not cite our mashal in Eikh. R. though it almost perfectly fits his argument, according to which the picture of God casting down the icon of Jacob could be an allusion to or a parody of the Fall of Satan motif familiar from the Adam Books; see his highly suggestive discussion, 372–375.

25. For Jacob's immortality, see Taanit 5b; for his semi-divinity, Ber. R. 98.3 and Theodor ad locum; for Jacob's special care for Israel, Mid. Teh. 14.7 and PR 174b; for different aspects of his *zekhuyot*, Vay. R. 29.6, 36.4, and PR 191a.

26. A. Marmorstein, *The Doctrine of Merits in Old Rabbinical Literature* (1920; repr. New York, 1968), 101. For a passage in Eikh. R. that implicitly polemicizes against the doctrine of merits and suggests the futility of invoking them, see Buber, 115, on Lam. 2:10.

27. The locus classicus for the debate (originally between R. Eleazar of Modiin and R. Joshua) is found in Mekhilta Beshallah 4, (Lauterbach, p. 220); Vayasa' 3 (p. 102). On its history, see Marmorstein passim and E. E. Urbach, *The Sages* trans. I. Abrahams (Jerusalem, 1975), 496–511. For other passages, see Eikh. R. 2.10 and the aggadic, non-parabolic version of our mashal's narrative in PR 27 (p. 134a), where the angels, attempting to dissuade God from destroying the Temple, invoke "the icons of the patriarchs" that are engraved upon the divine throne; in response, God throws the icons down (for which Lam. 2:1 is cited as prooftext), after which He destroys the Temple.

28. For a brilliant example of Ammon and Moab's expertise in Scripture, which they predictably use to destroy the Temple, see B. Sanhedrin 96b. For the aggadic commonplace that the most wicked gentiles know Torah well enough to quote it, see I. Heinemann, *Darkhei Haaggadah* (Jerusalem, 1970), 40 and sources quoted there.

29. The traditional motif of the rivalry between the mistress and her maidservant goes back at least to Sarah and Hagar (cf. Gen. 21); cf. Paul's famous use of the motif in Gal. 4:21–31. For the night-and-day imagery used in the mashal, cf. Shir R. 1.6.3.

30. See, for example, the mashal in Ber. R. 74.7 (= Vay. R. 1.13); and the discussion in E. E. Urbach, "Homilies of the Rabbis on the Prophets of the Nations and the Balaam Stories" (Hebrew), *Tarbiz* 25 (1956), 272–289, esp. 279–280.

31. For Rabbinic *meshalim* that use the comparative motif, see Koh. R. 9.5.8, B. Shabbat 152b, and Sh. R. 30.20. For the figure of the *pikeiah:* Mid. Teh. 16.3, and 19.6; and PR 59a (= Tan. Num. Hukat).

32. Mid. Teh. 16.5 on Ps. 16:4.

33. R. Akiba's statement is in B. Avodah Zarah 55a. For the modern scholarly view that the Rabbis believed traditional paganism to have disappeared, see E. E. Urbach, "The Laws of Idolatry and the Archaeological and Historical Reality in the Second and Third Centuries" (Hebrew), *Eretz Yisrael* 5 (1958), 189–205. Compare, however, S. Lieberman, *Hellenism in Jewish Palestine* (New York, 1950), 120–121, 130 for types of pagan worship contemporary with the Rabbis that include worship of astral bodies, trees, stones, etc.; cf. M. Avodah Zarah 4.7, 3.7. Cf. Eikh. R. 1.2 (p. 43) for a lengthy Rabbinic polemic staged as a debate between God and the idols; though mainly an exercise in rhetorical and exegetical virtuosity, the debate would have had little purpose if the Rabbis truly had considered idolatry entirely dead. For recent studies on Late Antique paganism, see Ramsey MacMullen, *Paganism in the Roman Empire* (New Haven, 1981) and R. L. Fox, *Pagans and Christians* (New York, 1987). It should be noted that this recent scholarship only strengthens Urbach's basic thesis: that the Rabbis were willing to legislate halakhah so as to fit contemporary economic and social realities; what needs to be reformulated is the nature of those realities and their relationship to specific halakhot.

34. See W. Bacher, *Aggadot Amoraei Eretz Yisrael* (1892–1899; trans. into Hebrew, Tel Aviv, 1923) vol. 3, 46n1. Note as well that in Buber, an interpretation attributed to R. Isaac on the word *helki* immediately follows the mashal although, as Buber notes ad locum, the meaning of the interpretation is unclear. On R. Abbahu, see L. Levine, "R. Abbahu of Caesarea," in *Christianity, Judaism, and Other Greco-Roman Cults,* ed. J. Neusner (Leiden, 1975), part 4, 56–76.

35. See, for example, PR 104b (whose nimshal deals as well with God's revelation at Mt. Sinai along with Michael and Gabriel, and the difficulty the king's son has in recognizing his father among his generals); Vay. R. 1.8 (God's revelation to Moses in Lev. 1:1). For an exception to this rule, however, see Koh. R. 12.5.

36. Sabine G. MacCormack, *Art and Ceremony in Late Antiquity* (Berkeley, 1981), 17; for a general description of the imperial tours, see Millar, *The Emperor in the Roman World*, 28–57.

37. Millar, *The Emperor in the Roman World*, 37, for using imperial visits for personal requests. Our mashal's narrative does not, however, appear to describe a case of billeting, where the provincials were forced to put up Roman dignitaries and soldiers. On billeting, see

Avi-Yonah, *The Jews of Palestine*, 94; compare the anecdote about Polemo the Sophist cited in Ziegler, *Die Königsgleichnisse*, 303–304.

38. Athanasius, *De incarnatione*, 9, trans. R. W. Thomson (Louvain, 1965). Athanasius's writings, incidentally, are full of king-parables, and raise a comparative question of great interest that unhappily I cannot even broach in this book.

39. On the word *pamiliyah*, see Arukh, vol. 6, 361; on the *pamiliyah* of angels, Urbach, *The Sages*, 146–150, 764n68. For a striking portrait of the heavenly court as a divine bureaucracy in which God Himself can be overruled by His servants, see Eikh. R. (pp. 75–76), which I have translated and discussed in Appendix A under the homiletical-exegetical narrative).

40. Alan F. Segal, *Two Powers in Heaven* (Leiden, 1977), 135–146; cf. Urbach, *The Sages*, 182–183; A. Altmann, "The Gnostic Background of the Rabbinic Adam Legends," 371–395.

41. See Ber. R. 1.7, 3.8; B. Sanhedrin 38b.

42. Urbach, *The Sages*, 181–183.

43. Note that, while the two recensions of the mashal in Eikh. R. switch back and forth between Hebrew and Aramaic, the Dev. R. mashal and the "folk" expression in it are entirely in Hebrew, with no Aramaic.

44. Jastrow, 471b–482a. Israel Abrahams translates the word as "be replaced" in Urbach, *The Sages*, 182.

45. For texts, see Robert M. Grant, *Gods and the One God* (Philadelphia, 1986), 84–89.

46. Compare the famous statement likening political appointees to the "pebbles employed in calculations" by tyrants, first attributed to Solon by Diogenes Laertius, *The Lives of Eminent Philosophers* 1, 59; the translation is by R. D. Hicks, (Cambridge, Mass., 1942), vol. 1, 59. For later citations of the sentiment in Polybius, Hippolytus, and others see Millar, *The Emperor in the Roman World*, 112; on the mercurial careers of imperial *amici* and on their insecurity, Millar, 110–122. Cf. Vay. R. 23.12, for a mashal that uses as its basis the deposing of the king himself (and with the same verb, *nithaleif*).

47. Note, however, that the exact same statement appears elsewhere in Eikh. R. as a comment on Lam. 3:23, ". . . they are new every morning," where R. Helbo in the name of R. Samuel b. Nahman interprets "they" as referring to bands of angels whom God creates anew every morning to sing His praises—except for the archangels Michael and Gabriel: "For all [the angels] pass away *(mithalfin)*, but [the two archangels] do not pass away *(lo mithalfin)*." This statement directly contradicts the view of Michael's and Gabriel's lifespan stated in the Dev. R. mashal, but we will leave this contradiction for students of

Rabbinic angelology to contemplate. For mention of the difference between angels who pass away and those who don't, see Urbach, *The Sages*, 182–183, and esp. his quote from Justin Martyr, *Dialogue with Trypho*, 128.3–4, where he describes a similar belief.

48. See the famous story of Akiba's martyrdom in B. Berakhot 61b; cf. Urbach, *The Sages*, 416–417, and esp. 443–445.

49. On God as mourner, see Peter Kuhn, *Gottes Trauer und Klage in der rabbinischen Überlieferung* (Leiden, 1978); cf. Meir Eyali, "God's Sharing in the Suffering of the Jewish People," in *Studies in Jewish Thought*, ed. S. Heller Willensky and M. Idel (Jerusalem, 1989), 29–50.

50. See Sh. R. 20.7, on Exod. 13:17, in which Pharaoh laments the loss of the Israelites as his slaves(!), though this mashal may contain an element of parody. An outright literary parody of the traditional Aramaic lament, dating from the beginning of piyyut, has recently been identified by Yosef Yahalom and Michael Sokoloff, and it is possible that the genre of lament may have produced some of the earliest parodies in Hebrew literature. For another parable in which God is the mourner, but in which He laments the Jews who died in the Exodus, see Sh. R. 20.13 on Exod. 13:17.

51. Margaret Alexiou, *The Ritual Lament in Greek Tradition* (Cambridge, 1974); W. C. Gwaltney, Jr., "The Biblical Book of Lamentations in the Context of Near Eastern Lament Literature," in *Scripture in Context II*, ed. W. W. Hallo et al. (Winona Lake, Ind., 1983), 191–211; cf. F. F. Hvidberg, *Weeping and Laughter in the Old Testament* (Leiden, 1962).

52. For parallels and varying attributions, see Buber's note ad locum.

53. See the insightful reflections of Emil Fackenheim in *God's Presence in History: Jewish Affirmations and Philosophical Reflections* (New York, 1970), 8–30.

54. The form of the passage is an exegetical enumeration, on which see my discussion in the next chapter. For parallels: PRK 13.11; ARN A, ch. 34; B. Rosh Hashana 31a; note that only PRK's enumeration includes our mashal, and in briefer form.

55. Sources: Mekhilta Pisha, 14; Shirta, 3. Cf. Norman J. Cohen, "Shekhinta Ba-Galuta: A Midrashic Response to Destruction and Persecution," *JSJ* 13 (1982), 146–159; Urbach, *The Sages*, 61–65.

56. See the view of R. Yonathan in Buber's edition of Eikh. R., p. 30. Compare as well God's statement in Petihta 24 (p. 25).

57. Cf. the preceding mishnayot in M. Kelim 1 for lists of the degrees of impurity.

58. MK ad locum.

59. See Urbach, *The Sages*, 37–43.

60. For a comparable personification, also using the image of the palace,

see the mashal in Ber. R. 9.4 in which God tells the world, which He has just created, how much He loves it, and how He hopes to love it forever (knowing of course that He will be disappointed in this).

61. On "the quarrel with God" in biblical literature, see most recently Yohanan Muffs, "Between Justice and Mercy: The Prayers of the Prophets," (Hebrew) in *Torah Nidreshet* (Tel Aviv, 1984), 39–88. See as well J. Bright, "Jeremiah's Complaints—Liturgy or Expressions of Personal Distress?" in *Proclamation and Presence, Old Testament Essays in Honour of G. H. Davies* (London, 1970), 189–213; Michael Stone, "Reactions to the Destruction of the Second Temple," *JSJ* 12 (1981), esp. 200–202.

62. Cf. Alan Mintz, *Hurban* (New York, 1984), 79–83.

63. For meshalim with the reconciliation motif, see Sifra 47a; Dev. R. (Lieberman) 1.2; Yalkut 1.554. The identity of the character banished does not, of course, affect the function. For banishing the son: Mekhilta Beshalah 4 (Lauterbach vol. 1, 218–219); and in a more regularized form, Sh. R. 21.8; Sifre Num. 86 (p. 236). For banishing the king's subjects: Eikh. R. 2.1C; Tan. B., Gen., 182, in reference to Isa. 55:8. For another mashal about banishing the wife (*ishto*, however, not *matrona*), see Sifra 47a, on Lev. 9:5.

64. See, for example, the anonymous mashal in Yalkut 1.815 on Deut. 3:23; for discussion: D. Sperber, *A Dictionary of Greek and Latin Legal Terms in Rabbinic Literature* (Ramat Gan, 1984), 92–93; S. Lieberman, "Roman Legal Institutions in Early Rabbinics and in the Acta Martyrum," *JQR* 35 (1944), 17ff. Cf. Bam. R. 21.15.

65. Mintz, *Hurban*, 78.

66. See, in particular, the lengthy interpretation for Lam. 1:9 (Buber, pp. 73–74).

67. Michael Grant, *Gladiators* (London, 1967), 28–31, 55–56.

68. S attributes the mashal to R. Joshua of Sikhnin in the name of R. Levi; however, R. Joshua b. Levi and R. Levi were contemporaries, and R. Joshua of Sikhnin is known to have been a tradent for both men.

69. On this statement, see Urbach's comments in *The Sages,* 534, and especially 928n33, where he states his preference for the text in Yalkut Shimeoni (2.935 ad Lam. 3:1) that is nearly identical with S's version: "I am the one that is inured to affliction; all that You wish comes upon me."

70. Hebrew: *tzimtzemah et paneiha.* The same phrase is used in Eikh. R. 1.21; Shir R. 6.5; and Ber. R. 45.13, where, according to Theodor, the phrase connotes an act of modesty. Cf. Even-Shoshan, vol. 5, 2240. Compare also PRK 22.4 and Shir R. 4.10, where Israel at Sinai is described with the same idiom as "covering their faces in modesty

like a bride." If so, the consort in our mashal is clearly trying to conciliate the king—an attempt on her part that he clearly fails to recognize.

71. For S's different presentation of the aggadah, see Appendix B.

72. I am speaking here of the actual narrative structure. Both Eikh. R. 1.21 and Eikh. R. 2.1C actually begin with what we might call anticipatory glosses—that is, expositional material that presents background information (e.g., how the king issued the original prohibitions to his wife; how the provincials painted themselves with the blood of the king's enemies). Even though this material is presented in narrative form, it is not actually part of the mashal's basic narrative structure.

73. For Jeremiah: Eikh. R., p. 122 (R. Haninah b. Pappa); for Job, Eikh. R., pp. 123–124 (R. Joshua of Sikhnin in the name of R. Levi).

74. For the source of this aggadah, see Vay. R. 1.1 on Ps. 103:20; and Margulies's note ad locum for parallels. Note that the precise wording of the statement differs in A and S, and it is also textually problematic: see Buber's notes ad locum, as well as the classical commentators.

75. Joseph Heinemann, *Aggadot Vetoldoteihen*, (Jerusalem, 1974), 156–162.

76. The locus classicus for the apologetic version of the aggadah is in Mekhilta Bahodesh 5; Heinemann (*Aggadot*, 157–158) was the first to point out the similarities between that version and the passage in Pseudo-Philo, *Biblical Antiquities* 11.1–2; the background to the apologetic may very well have been Hellenistic Jewish; cf. Urbach, *The Sages*, 532–533.

77. Eikh. R. 3.1's use of the aggadah is not the only revisionist one in Rabbinic literature. In the Mekhilta passage itself (Bahodesh 5), R. Simon b. Eleazar gives it a polemical twist by commenting rather brutally that the gentiles couldn't observe seven laws, let alone 613 commandments! In Sh. R. 27.9, the aggadah is used to prove why the Jews, unlike the gentiles, are to be held responsible for transgressing the law and are therefore to be punished and made to suffer.

78. See Urbach, *The Sages*, 527–541; cf. the mashal about the wicked tenants in Sifre Deut. 312 (pp. 353–354), and Urbach's comments on the mashal, 925–926.

79. See Mintz, *Hurban*, 33–40.

80. The text translated is S's version, which here is clearly preferable to A's more fragmentary text.

81. Hebrew *meparkesin*. My translation follows Jastrow, 1229b; Even-Shoshan, vol. 5, 2158. Cf. Sifre Deut. 343, where Finkelstein (p. 397) connects the word to the Greek *perkazō*); B. Ketubot 54a. For alterna-

tives, see the Soncino Midrash Rabbah, which translates the word as "wallowed," and Ziegler, 125, who has "stampften."

82. This should be "province." See A.

83. Which is, indeed, the interpretation for the figure offered by the Rabbis in Eikh. R. (p. 97), as based on Ps. 99:5. See as well Ps. 132:7 and 1 Chron. 28:2.

84. Note that, in Buber, the interpretation conveyed in the nimshal of R. Yudan's mashal is also presented as an independent opinion, attributed to the Rabbis, immediately preceding R. Yudan's mashal. This independent opinion is lacking in MR.

85. A. Marmorstein, *The Doctrine of Merits in Old Rabbinic Literature;* Urbach, *The Sages,* 496–508; and most recently, Ruth N. Sandberg, "The Merit of Israel and the Redemption from Egypt: A Study of a Rabbinic Debate" (Ph.D. diss., University of Pennsylvania, 1988).

86. See Targum Pseudo-Jon. to Exod. 12:13; Sekhel Tov (ed. Buber) vol. 2, 80; Ruth R. 6.1; Sh. R. 17.3, 19.5; Tan. Vayera 4 (p. 64); Mid. Teh. 114.5; Yalkut Ezek. 354. Note as well that Eikh. R. itself preserves an interpretation of *hadom* as *hadam* qua blood of circumcision that is attributed to R. Hanina b. Isaac, and that appears as a complaint in a form exactly parallel to that of the nimshal of our mashal; the opinion immediately precedes the mashal in Buber's text. The two interpretations of Lam. 2:1 as blood of circumcision and of Passover should be viewed as complementary rather than as disagreeing; indeed, their collocation in Eikh. R. testifies to the common pedigree they share going back to their source in the Mekhilta passage discussed in the text.

87. See, however, Sh. R. 15.13, where both in an independent opinion and in a mashal the bloods of circumcision and of Passover are said to arouse God's mercy so as to make Him pardon *(lekhapeir)* Israel's sins (and thereby redeem Israel from Egypt). Saul Lieberman, in "Roman Legal Institutions in Early Rabbinics and in the Acta Martyrum," 31–32, has analyzed this parable and traced it to an anecdote related by Lactantius.

88. For general knowledge of this fact in the ancient world, see Herodotus, *The Persian Wars,* 2.43; Juvenal, Satires 15.11–12. For Rabbinic awareness, see Sh. R. 11.3, 16.3.

89. Sh. R. 16.3; Mekhilta Pisha 5.

90. Mekhilta Pisha 6 (ad Exod. 12:7), 11 (ad Exod. 12:22) (vol. 1, 44, 84), both of which have the identical opinion attributed to R. Isaac: "so that the Egyptians would see the blood and they would be cut to the quick." Cf. Sh. R. 16.3, and Ginzberg, *Legends,* vol. 5, 433n206, where he cites a tradition that the Egyptians were so provoked that they actually attacked the Jews on the 10th of Nisan; for other sources, see Ginzberg's notes.

91. On ancient atrocities, see Mars M. Westington, "Atrocities in Roman Warfare to 133 B.C." (Ph.D. diss., University of Chicago; private printing, Chicago, 1938), 46–66; see also Ziegler's comments on this mashal in *Die Königsgleichnisse*, 124.

92. The translation is taken from *Dio's Roman History*, trans. E. C. Cary (1925; repr. Cambridge, Mass., 1968), vol. 8, 421–423.

93. On the passage, see Shimon Applebaum, *Greeks and Jews in Ancient Cyrene* (Hebrew) (Jerusalem, 1969), 278–279 and notes on page with bibliography; as remarked there, Eusebius's account of the rebellion (*Historia Ecclesiastica* IV.2.4) does not mention any of these atrocities. On Xiphilinus, see briefly *Dio's Roman History*, vol. 1, xxiv–xxv.

94. Applebaum, 285–289.

95. For another example of a warning-mashal with multiple levels of meaning, see Ber. R. 99.2: overtly, the mashal admonishes the children of Jacob (the Israelites) to honor God; less obviously, the mashal warns against needlessly attempting to discover the eschatological secrets of the end-time.

96. For the text of the mashal as it appears in Eikh. R. 1.16, see Appendix B. In Eikh. R., the mashal appears as part of what looks like a circular petihta or proem on Lam. 1:16, but the exegetical connection of the mashal is obscure, as is its relevance to the Destruction: presumably, an analogy is being drawn between God's reactions to the Flood and to the Destruction (on which see Eikhah Zuta, p. 67). The mashal in Eikh. R. is borrowed almost verbatim from Ber. R., with only minor glossing. Note that the mashal appears in Eikh. R. with another mashal—about a shepherd who, after losing all his sheep to a wolf, similarly expresses regret over having bought the sheep; again, the precise sense of the mashal is slightly unclear.

97. On this word, see Theodor's note on Ber. R. 5.1, p. 32n4; Krauss, *Paras Veromi*, 81n141; and the comments of Michael Sokoloff, *Geniza Fragments of Bereishit Rabba* (Hebrew) (Jerusalem, 1982), 88n22.

98. Despite lengthy searching, I have been unable to find any historical account fully pertinent to the situation described in the narrative. However, many ancient sources depict the elaborate palaces and architectural wonders built by emperors: Nero's Domus Aurea comes first to mind; for description and discussion, see Suetonius, *The Lives of the Caesars*, Nero, 31; Axel Boethius, *The Golden House of Nero* (Ann Arbor, 1960), 121, and in general, 94–128. The detail about the mutes saluting the king by waving handkerchiefs may allude to the report about Aurelian (270–275) that he was the first to give "to the Roman people white tunics with long sleeves, brought from the various provinces, and pure linen ones from Africa and Egypt, and he was the first to give handkerchiefs to the Roman people, to be

waved on showing approval." Divus Aurelianus (The Deified Aurelian) 48.5, in *The Scriptores Historiae Augustae*, trans. D. Magie (London, 1932), vol. 3, 289. For attempts by earlier scholars to explain the mashal, none of them very convincing, see Ziegler, *Die Königsgleichnisse*, 44; Krauss, *Paras Veromi*, 81–82, and particularly n142, with its suggestion that the word *ileimim*, "mutes," may be a pun on the Latin *alimentarii*.

99. Cf. Ber. R. 27.4; John Bowker, *The Targums and Rabbinic Literature* (Cambridge, 1969), 151, 158–159.

100. S's reading here is almost certainly better. Hammat-Gader—a town near Tiberias on the shores of the Kinneret, famous then as today for its hot-baths—is probably a scribal error (though all mss. in A's recension attest it), possibly the result of a misreading of the last three letters in the word *le-milhamah*, "to war," S's text. The motif of the king going off to war is very common: see Sifre Num. 102 (and its numerous parallels); Sh. R. 30.9; and Yalkut 1.835. Cf. as well the statement about the honor of a king in Petihta 16 in Eikh. R. (p. 13); and the description of God appearing "as a mighty hero doing battle" in Mekhilta Shirta 4.

101. See the comment of David Kimhi (RaDak) in his commentary on Ezek. 36:17.

102. Cf. the interpretation of R. Yudan immediately following the mashal (Eikh. R., p. 131) and the interpretation of Lam. 3:20. Cf. the comments of MaHaRZU and the YA, who may also have understood the verse this way, and perhaps even the mashal.

103. The list form is even more explicit in S's version of the nimshal; on the form, see W. S. Towner, *The Rabbinic "Enumeration of Scriptural Examples"* (Leiden, 1973).

104. This is, of course, something of a reversed motif: it is really God who no longer accompanies Israel.

5. The Mashal in Context

1. Thus especially Jacob Neusner in a series of works; for summary, see *Midrash as Literature: The Primacy of Documentary Discourse* (Lanham, Md., 1987). For a critique that begins to point out the methodological and substantive problems in Neusner's project, see Steven Fraade's review of Neusner's *Judaism and Scripture: The Evidence of Leviticus Rabbah* (Chicago, 1986) in *Prooftexts* 7 (1987), 179–194. For an invaluable comparative perspective on redactional technique in midrashic literature, see Marc Hirshman, "The Greek Fathers and the Aggada on Ecclesiastes: Formats of Exegesis in Late Antiquity," *HUCA* 59 (1988), 137–165.

2. Judah Goldin, *The Song at the Sea* (New Haven, 1971), 3–8; J. Heinemann, "The Art of Composition in Midrash Vayikra Rabba" (Hebrew), *Hasifrut* 2 (1970/71), 809–834; Arnold Goldberg, "Form-Analysis of Midrashic Literature as a Method of Description," *JJS* 36 (1985), 159–174.

3. For the story collections, see Eikh. R., pp. 46–56 (on the wisdom of Jerusalemites and dream-interpretation); 82–87 (martyrologies); 100–107 (on Betar and the Bar Kokhba Rebellion). On the first cycle of stories, see Eli Yassif, "Traces of Folk Traditions of the Second Temple Period in Rabbinic Literature," *JJS* 39 (1988), 227–229; Galit Hasan-Rokem, "'*Echah?* . . . *Ayekah?*'—On Riddles in the Stories of *Midrash Echah Rabbah*" (Hebrew), *Jerusalem Studies in Hebrew Literature* 10–11 (1987–88), 540–544.

4. On these questions, see Paul Mandel, "Hasippur Bamidrash Eikha: Nusah Vesignon" [The Story in Midrash Ekha: A Textual and Literary Analysis] (M.A. diss., Hebrew University, Jerusalem, 1983).

5. For the best overview of Eikh. R.'s responses to the Destruction, see Alan Mintz's sensitive treatment in *Hurban* (New York, 1984), 49–83; cf. Shaye J. D. Cohen, "The Destruction: From Scripture to Midrash," *Prooftexts* 2 (1982), 18–39. For treatments of the Rabbinic and other ancient Jewish responses in general, see Jacob Neusner, "Emergent Rabbinic Judaism in a Time of Crisis: Four Responses to the Destruction of the Second Temple," *Judaism* 21 (1972), 313–327; Anthony J. Saldarini, "Varieties of Rabbinic Response to the Destruction of the Temple," *SBL Seminar Papers* (Missoula, Mont., 1982), 437–458; Michael Stone, "Reactions to Destructions of the Second Temple," *JSJ* 12 (1981), 195–204; E. E. Urbach, *The Sages,* trans. I. Abrahams (Jerusalem, 1975), 541–554, 672–676; Robert Goldenberg, "Early Rabbinic Explanations of the Destruction of Jerusalem," *JJS* 33 (1982), 517–525; idem, "The Broken Axis: Rabbinic Judaism and the Fall of Jerusalem," *JAAR* 45 (1977), 869–882; Baruch M. Bokser, "Rabbinic Responses to Catastrophe: From Continuity to Discontinuity," *PAAJR* 50 (1983), 37–61.

6. The text translated here is S's version. A preserves only the first mashal attributed to R. Aha, not the second mashal of the Rabbis, though it does preserve verbatim the Rabbis' opinion. (For his edition, Buber copied the Rabbis' mashal from the 1878 Vilna edition of MR; see his notes ad locum, and Shibolei Haleket, ed. S. K. Mirsky (New York, 1966), s. Tefilah, 9, p. 158, which has a text identical with A.) See Appendix B for further discussion of the possible history of their transmission. A's version of R. Aha's mashal differs in many points of diction but not in anything substantial.

7. Hebrew: *tisateim havito*. My translation of *tisateim* follows the Arukh,

vol. 5, 184; and I. Ziegler, *Die Königsgleichnisse des Midrasch* (Breslau, 1903), 35. For other translations, see MK ad locum, who suggests that it be read as *samekh-t-r*, "to destroy," though there is no mss. evidence for that reading; Shibolei Haleket, 158, which states that *sin-t-m* means "separation, division," and cites Gen. 30:40 as witness. Note, however, that the root *shin-t-m* means "to open"; cf. Num. 24:3 *(shatum ha'ayin)* and the classical commentators—Rashi, Nahmanides, Ibn Ezra—on the meaning of the phrase; and M. Avodah Zarah 5:3–4. If the word in this mashal is read as *tishateim*, it would mean "let his bottle be opened"—presumably to be examined and tested.

8. For the first tradition (re R. Aha's mashal), see my discussion of 2.1B in Chapter 4 and compare the mashal from Vay. R. 2.5, discussed in Chapter 2. For the tradition of the Rabbis' mashal, see the analysis of Eikh. R. 1.16.

9. Cf. YA ad locum.

10. Thus the Lehem Dim'ah in the Mikraot Gedolot edition of Lamentations, ad locum.

11. J. Heinemann, *Hatefilah Bitekufat Hatannaim Vehaamoraim* (4th ed., Jerusalem, 1984), 21.

12. Baruch M. Bokser, "The Wall Separating God and Israel," *JQR* 73 (1983), 355–357.

13. Ibid., 355nn19–20; cf. Origen, "On Prayer" 31.6–7, in *Origen*, trans. R. Greer (New York, 1979), 167–168. I have not been able to locate any Christian exegeses of Lam. 3:8 itself.

14. See R. Samuel b. Nahmani's interpretation of Lam. 3:44 (Eikh. R., pp. 137–138), on the gates of prayer (which are open only at specified times) and on the gates of repentance (which are always open); and the subsequent anecdote about R. Akiba and Turnus Rufus.

15. See Joseph Heinemann, "The Proem in the Aggadic Midrashim: A Form-Critical Study," *SH* 22 (1971), 100–122.

16. Cf. Richard Sarason, "The Petihtaot in Leviticus Rabbah: 'Oral Homilies' or Redactional Constructions?" *JSJ* 33 (1982), 557–567. For other bibliography, see my "Midrash and the Language of Exegesis," in *Midrash and Literature*, ed. G. H. Hartman and S. Budick (New Haven, 1986), 123n7.

17. The numbering of the petihta is Buber's; see his notes on p. 33. In MR, the petihta appears as a continuation of the preceding petihta, but the MaHaRZU ad locum already recognizes that it was an independent composition. In PRK 15.4, the petihta appears as an independent unit as well. The reason it was mistakenly believed not to be a separate petihta may have to do with the fact that most petihtaot, unlike this one, usually begin with the formula "R. X recited a proem" *(R. X*

patah), and are attributed to a single rabbi, presumably the one who originally recited it. S's text of the petihta is identical to A's.

18. Hebrew: *pirpeir*, literally "to flutter." See Job 16:12 and Buber's note in his edition of PRK, 120b.

19. For other examples of the motif in Eikh. R. alone, see 2.1 and S's text of 1.17.

20. The radical departure from convention that this conclusion makes is underlined by the petihta's use of the stereotyped formula *hithil mekonein 'aleihem*, whose subject is typically the prophet Jeremiah (and here God): see, for example, Petihtaot 2(1), 5, 6, 8, and so on. Some petihtaot use an even more extensive formula: "And once they sinned, they were exiled; and once they were exiled, Jeremiah began to lament over them . . ." For another variant, see Petihta 4.

21. See YA ad locum.

22. Aramaic: *ana havva detarbuti bisha.* My translation follows the consensus of the classical commentators: see MK, RaSHaSH, and Buber's note ad locum. See also the Soncino translation's note for a speculation, not entirely convincing, on the rationale behind this statement as an exegesis of Jer. 10:19.

23. Cf. David J. Lull, "'The Law Was Our Pedagogue': A Study in Galatians 3:19–25," *JBL* 105 (1986), 481–498; S. D. Benin, "Sacrifice as Education in Augustine and Chrysostom," *Church History* 52 (1983), 7–20.

24. In Petihta 24, the Patriarchs, Moses, and the angels all sing dirges before God at His request. One should, however, beware of drawing conclusions from one petihta to another; the prooftext for that petihta is a different verse, Isa. 22:12.

25. W. Bacher, *'Erkhei Midrash*, sv. *kiveyakhol*, and his reference to Rashi, B. Yoma 3b. See also Urbach, *The Sages*, 709n1; and A. Marmorstein, *The Old Rabbinic Doctrine of God, II. Essays in Anthropomorphism* (1937; repr. New York, 1968), 126–132; and now Michael Fishbane, *The Garments of Torah* (Bloomington, Ind., 1989), 19–32. Compare Rashi's comment in B. Megillah 21a and Buber's note in his edition of PRK 102a.

26. See RaSHaSH ad locum. There exist, however, traditions that the Ten Tribes were exiled in three separate exiles: Bam. R. 23.14; and in two exiles: Petihta 5 in Eikh. R.

27. "Seduction" in Hebrew is *tofteh*, which here is punned with Tofet. In actuality, Tofet is the name of a precinct in Carthage (where, incidentally, vast remains of human sacrifices have actually been discovered), and may refer to the "sacred fosses which contained the brazier" in which the bodies were burned; see A. R. W. Green, *The Role of Human Sacrifice in the Ancient Near East* (Missoula, Mont., 1975), 356n205.

28. See Targum Ps. Jon. to Deut. 34:6; Targum Jer. 7:31, and compare Rashi ad locum where he quotes our passage; Targum 2 Kings 23:10, Rashi and RaDaK ad locum; for the source of the latter's explanation and the slightly different account of the idolatrous cult in Gehennom, see Tan. B. Deut., supplement to Vaethanan, pp. 14–15.

29. "Shriekings" in Hebrew is *nehamot,* here punned on *hinnom.* MR's text lacks this opinion altogether.

30. Aramaic: *bar nash,* the equivalent to Hebrew *ben adam,* "a man." His anonymity may suggest that the story could once have been about a gentile; the only indication that the man is a Jew comes at the story's conclusion when God condemns him, but that condemnation could easily have been added.

31. Aramaic: *beveit rabeih.*

32. Hebrew: *mekudash leshamayim.*

33. Hebrew: *ohavah,* in both A and S; however, the spelling should probably be corrected to *ahuvo,* as in Yalkut Ezek. 356. The term *oheiv* refers to the king's or queen's admirer or friend in the sense of the *philos* or *amicus* or even *shushabin.* See S. Krauss, *Paras Veromi Batalmud Umidrashim* (Jerusalem, 1948), 141. I know of no meshalim in which the consort commits adultery with the *oheiv.*

34. Hebrew: *lavranatin.* S: *luratiya.* Both words are famously problematic, and may be transliterated differently, though it's quite clear that the original is a Greek or Latin loan. My translation as "laurel-[wreath]," from the Latin *laurea,* follows the suggestion of the anonymous commentary printed in Yalkut Ezek. 356; the word *laurea* can refer directly to the *laurea triumphalis,* the laurel-wreath worn at triumphs and to crown Roman emperors; for citations, see *Oxford Latin Dictionary,* ed. P. G. W. Glare (Oxford, 1982), 1010a–b; and S. W. Stevenson et al., *A Dictionary of Roman Coins* (1889; rev. London, 1964), 505b–506b. For assistance in researching this difficult word, I wish to acknowledge Dr. Yaakov Meshorer, Curator of Coins at the Israel Museum, and Professor Daniel Sperber of Bar-Ilan University. For other conjectures about its derivation and meaning, see: Arukh, vol. 2, 196b, ad *barnat* and Jacob Levy, *Neuhebräisches und chaldäisches Wörterbuch über die Talmudim und Midraschim* (Leipzig, 1876–1889), vol. 2, 471, both of whom read the word as *lavtariyon* (= *lautarion*), "a washbasin"; Samuel Krauss, *Griechische und Lateinische Lehnwörter im Talmud, Midrasch und Targum* (Berlin, 1898), part 2, 304: *libarneti,* from the Latin *liburnata,* a "litter" or "sedan-chair" *(liburnische Sanfte);* Jastrow, 691a, *labreton,* a special form of the Greek *laureaton,* "the imperial portrait as wreathed in laurels." On the latter, cf. John Beckwith, *Early Christian and Byzantine Art* (Baltimore, 1970), 35–36, where he notes that "an insult to the laureaton was an insult to the

emperor." For S's *luratiya,* see the Musafi, quoted in Buber's note, p. 72, who suggested the Greek *loutēr,* "a bath." MK proposes a lance *(romah)*.

35. Hebrew *kli,* which can refer to an object that is worn as dress: see Jastrow, 641a, ad *kli,* though note that Jastrow cites the word only in the plural form for this meaning. S reads *etsim,* "wood" or "trees," or by extension, "something from a tree," like leaves or a branch. The laurel-wreath would accordingly fit both descriptions in the two recensions.

36. This last clause—"in which I warm myself," *sheani mithameim bo* in Hebrew—makes no sense, and is entirely lacking in S. The only explanation I can see for it is a small emendation of the word *mithameim,* "I warm myself," to *mithamei,* "in which I appear"—in public ceremonies, for example. Clever as this may be, though, it has all the difficulties of any emendation that has no manuscript evidence behind it.

37. For a version of the pericope without the mashal but which nonetheless concludes with Ezek. 16:10, see the fragmentary text in PR 137b, and Ish-Shalom's notes ad locum.

38. Compare, however, the narrative about the promiscuous daughters of Zion, in Eikh. R., pp. 150–151, ad Lam. 4:15.

39. G. F. Moore's "Biblical Notes, 3: The Image of Moloch," *JBL* 14 (1895), 161–165. For the classical parallels, see especially Diodorus Siculus 20.14; and Plutarch, *De Superstitione,* 13. According to Moore, it is "probable that the authors of the Midrash borrowed their notions of Moloch and his worship from Greek sources" (164).

40. See Louis Ginzberg's *The Legends of the Jews* (Philadelphia, 1938), vol. 5, 20, where he suggests that the seven chambers mentioned in the pericope are the mundane parallel to the seven regions of Heaven's other-worldly counterpart in hell, Gehenna.

41. See M. Weinfeld, "The Worship of Moloch and the Queen of Heaven and Its Background," *Ugarit Forschungen* 4 (1972), 133–154; Green, *The Role of Human Sacrifice in the Ancient Near East;* P. G. Mosca, "Child Sacrifice in Canaanite and Israelite Religion" (Ph.D. diss., Harvard University, 1975); and most recently, G. C. Heider, *The Cult of Molek: A Reassessment* (Sheffield, 1985). Cf. Tertullian, *Apology,* 9.2–4, who writes that child-sacrifice continues to be practiced surreptitiously in North Africa "to this day" (i.e. in the 2nd c. c.e.).

42. Although our pericope does not specify a historical period, see Tan. B. Deut., suppl. to Vaethanan, 2, which explicitly dates the cult to the reign of Manasseh. Geza Vermes's contention, in *Post-biblical Jewish Studies* (Leiden, 1975), 74, that "the very idea that [a prohibition against Molokh-worship] was ever necessary must have filled the

[Rabbinic] interpreters with revulsion," need not be accepted: the fact that nonliteral interpretations are offered for verses like Lev. 18:21 or 20:2 says nothing about the Rabbis' beliefs about the past.

43. For other exegeses of the phrase, see Targum ad locum, which translates it as "from whom are destined to come forth a holy offspring" *(de'atidin lemipak minehon tuldat kudsha);* cf. also RaDaK, who translates it as "those who entered into My covenant and were Mine"; and Rashi, who interprets the phrase as referring to the firstborn "who are God's own." Rashi also quotes our aggadah, citing as his source Tanhuma though the aggadah is not preserved in our editions of Tanhuma (Buber, intro. to Tan. B., p. 91). These later medieval interpretations all seem to deny the graphic sexuality and anthropomorphization of the verse. R. Levi, in offering his exegesis, may also have been exploiting the particle *li,* "to me," in an emphatic sense; cf. Sifre Num. 92 and parallels; Vay. R. 2.2; but see also Tan. B. Exod., 101.

44. Delbert R. Hillers, *Lamentations* (Garden City, N.Y., 1972), 19, 24–26; on the background to the personification: Gerson D. Cohen, "The Song of Songs and the Jewish Religious Mentality," in *Samuel Friedland Lectures 1960–1966* (New York, 1966), 1–21.

45. For examples of meshalim using the motif of the consort's infidelity, see Bam. R. 2.15 and Yalkut 1.941 (in both of which the "other man" is a eunuch!). Cf. Ophra Meir, "Wedding Themes in King Meshalim in Rabbinic Aggadah" (Hebrew), in *Mehkerei Hamerkaz Leheiker Hafolklor* 4 (1974), 9–51.

46. Ziegler, *Die Königsgleichnisse,* 375–376.

47. Pliny, *Natural History,* trans. H. Rackham (1945; rev. Cambridge, 1968), vol. 4, 15.39, 375–383.

48. W. S. Towner, *The Rabbinic "Enumeration of Scriptural Examples"* (Leiden, 1973); for a table of the many types of lists in Rabbinic literature, 255.

49. MaHaRZU ad locum.

50. Hebrew: *shoshbin,* on which see M. A. Friedman, *Jewish Marriage in Palestine* (Tel Aviv, 1981), vol. 2, 28–30; cf. N. H. Tur-Sinai, "Shoshabin," in *Sefer Assaf,* ed. M. D. Cassuto (Jerusalem, 1953), 316–322, who notes that the character's function in the mashal has little to do with the figure's traditional function as guardian-protector in Rabbinic society.

51. For a similar idea, see Daniel Boyarin, *Intertextuality and the Reading of Midrash* (Bloomington, Ind., 1990), 80–92, who seems to believe, however, that providing a rationale for exegesis is the mashal's primary function!

52. For the text upon which my translation here is based, see Margulies's note in his edition of Vay. R., vol. 1, 43 ad locum.

53. For a comparable approach to midrash as discourse, see A. Goldberg, "Form-Analysis of Midrashic Literature as a Method of Description," *JJS* 36 (1985), 159–174; unhappily, I have been unable to get ahold of Goldberg's study of the mashal, "Das Schriftauslegende Gleichnis im Midrasch," *Frankfurter Jüdaistische Beitrage* (1981).

54. For the most available summary of the *middot*, see Hermann L. Strack, *Introduction to the Talmud and Midrash* (trans. from the 5th German ed., 1920; Philadelphia, 1931; repr. 1978), 93–98. For other "rival" systems of hermeneutical principles, see I. Heinemann, *Darkhei Haaggadah* (Jerusalem, 1970); Michael Fishbane, "Torah and Tradition," in *Tradition and Theology in the Old Testament,* ed. Douglas A. Knight (Philadelphia, 1977), 275–300.

6. The Mashal in Hebrew Literature

1. Shir R. 1.1: "Before Solomon (literally: until Solomon arose) there was no similitude *(dugma)*."

2. R. B. Y. Scott, "Solomon and the Beginnings of Wisdom in Israel" and Norman W. Porteous, "Royal Wisdom," both in *Wisdom in Israel and in the Ancient Near East,* ed. M. Noth and D. W. Thomas, *Supplements to VT* (Leiden, 1955), vol. 3, 262–279 and 247–261. Cf. 1 Kings 5:12–13.

3. On the *Streitfabel* and its influence upon the biblical parable and fable, see G. von Rad, *Wisdom in Israel,* trans. J. D. Martin (Nashville, 1972), 41–46; R. J. Williams, "The Fable in the Ancient Near East," in E. C. Hobbs, ed., *A Stubborn Faith* (Dallas, 1956), 3–26, and sources cited therein. For the texts, see W. G. Lambert, *Babylonian Wisdom Literature* (Oxford, 1960), esp. 150–212. On the biblical fable, see in particular Uriel Simon, "The Mashal of Yotham—the Fable, Its Application, and Its Narrative Framework" (Hebrew), *Tarbiz* 34 (1964), 1–34; cf. Yair Zakovitch, "On the Connections between Aesop's Fables and Biblical Literature" (Hebrew), *Yeda'-'Am* 20 (1980), 3–7. For a very early text drawing parallels between human and divine behavior, with a form very much like the *basar vadam* analogy form, see the Hittite soliloquy quoted in Moshe Greenberg, "Some Postulates of Biblical Criminal Law," *Yehezkel Kaufmann Jubilee Volume* (Jerusalem, 1960), 26.

4. Thus Uriel Simon, "The Poor Man's Ewe-Lamb: An Example of a Juridical Parable," *Biblica* 48 (1967), 207–242.

5. See H. J. Blackham, *The Fable as Literature* (London and Dover, N.H., 1985); Theodor Schulze (Etzel), *Fabeln und Parabeln der Weltliteratur* (Leipzig, 1907); Pack Carnes, *Fable Scholarship: An Annotated Bibliography* (New York, 1985).

6. The single candidate, oft-mentioned in scholarship, is the parable of

the Lame Man and the Blind Man, which is preserved in the (probably) first-century Apocryphon of Ezekiel—*The Old Testament Pseudepigrapha*, ed. J. H. Charlesworth (Garden City, N.Y., 1983), vol. 1, 487–495—which was first brought to notice by M. R. James, "The Apocryphal Ezekiel," *JTS* 15 (1913–14), 236–243. In an important article to be published shortly in *JTS*, however, Marc Bregman cogently argues for a much later date for this parable (and by extension, the Apocryphon of Ezekiel), which he tries to show is a conflation of two meshalim preserved in Tanhuma literature.

7. David Flusser, *Yahadut Umekorot Hanatsrut* (Tel Aviv, 1979), 202ff.

8. For examples of this view, see Adolph Jülicher, *Die Gleichnisreden Jesu* (Freiburg, 1886), 182; J. Jeremias, *Die Gleichnisse Jesu* (1965), 40, quoted in James C. Little, "Parable Research in the Twentieth Century," *Expository Times* 88 (1977), 40.

9. *The Old Testament Pseudepigrapha*, ed. Charlesworth, vol. 2, 480–485.

10. Note, for example, that none of the meshalim are preserved that are recited by Bar Kappara, as pure entertainment, in the story cited at the beginning of Chapter 1; as it seems, a midrashic or some other kind of "respectable" function must have been a virtual requirement for the mashal to enter the written annals of Rabbinic literature.

11. The discussion in this section draws upon my essay, "Jesus' Parables from the Perspective of Rabbinic Literature: The Example of the Wicked Husbandmen," in *Parable and Story in Judaism and Christianity*, ed. C. Thoma and M. Wyschogrod (New York, 1989), 42–80, in which I treat in detail the methodological challenges I raise here. For bibliography on parable-scholarship, see Little, "Parable Research in the Twentieth Century," *Expository Times* 87 (1976), 356–360; 88 (1977), 40–44, 71–75; Robert Johnston, "Parabolic Interpretations Attributed to Tannaim" (Ph.D. diss., University of Michigan, 1978), 1–123; W. S. Kissinger, *The Parables of Jesus: A History of Interpretation and Bibliography* (Metuchen, N.J., 1979); Bradford H. Young, *Jesus and His Jewish Parables* (New York, 1989).

12. David Flusser, *Yahadut*, 150–209. See as well Flusser's *Die rabbinischen Gleichnisse und der Gleichniserzähler Jesus*, (Bern, 1981); Clemens Thoma and Simon Lauer, *Die Gleichnisse der Rabbinen*, part 1, Pesiqta deRav Kahana (PesK) (Bern, 1986).

13. On the original language of the New Testament parables, see Young, *Jesus and His Jewish Parables*, 40–42.

14. On these dangers, see Morton Smith, "A Comparison of Early Christian and Early Rabbinic Tradition," *JBL* 82 (1963), 169–176.

15. In this paragraph, I draw upon Norman Perrin, *Rediscovering the Teaching of Jesus* (New York, 1976), 15–53, esp. 20–23.

16. By the term "narrative parable," I mean to distinguish the type of

compositions I will discuss in this essay from extended similes or illustrations, on the one hand, and from exempla or anecdotes, on the other. Similes and illustrations, like the Mustard Seed (Mark 4:30–32 and parallels) or the Tree and its Fruit (Matt. 7:16–20), tend to take the form of extended figures, rhetorical questions, and so on, rather than of past-tense narratives; both similes and illustrations tend to describe a way of acting rather than narrate an event. As for anecdotes, exempla, and pronouncement stories, such as the Prodigal Son (Luke 15:11–32), the Good Samaritan (Luke 10:29–37), or the Dishonest Steward (Luke 16:1–10), these narratives depend, like the *ma'aseh,* upon a rhetorical claim to historicity, unlike the mashal, which is self-admittedly fictional.

17. On the synoptic question in relation to the different versions of the Wicked Husbandmen in the three gospels, see J. A. T. Robinson, "The Parable of the Wicked Husbandmen: A Test of Synoptic Relationships," *NTS* 21 (1974–75), 443–461.

18. For a description of all differences, see Robinson. The major differences between Mark's version of the parable and the versions in Matthew, Luke, and in the Gospel of Thomas are as follows: (1) While Mark's and Matthew's opening descriptions of the vineyard virtually quote Isa. 5:1ff., Luke only alludes to the prophet's passage. (2) Mark and Luke describe the son as *agapetos,* "beloved" or "sole"; Matthew and Thomas do not. (3) Matthew has a plural number of servants; Mark and Luke have only a single servant. (4) Mark has the owner initially send three individual messengers, then "many others," who are in turn beaten, wounded, treated shamefully, and killed, and finally the son, who is killed; Matthew has two groups of servants, who are beaten, and then the son, who is killed; Luke has three individual servants, who are beaten, then the son, who is killed; Thomas has two servants, who are beaten, and then the son, who is killed.

19. Flusser, *Yahadut,* 181–183, who cites Sifre Deut. 312 and Sh. R. 30.6; in addition, see J. Berakhot 2.8 (the eulogy delivered by R. Simeon b. Lakish over R. Hiyya bar Ada). The separate motifs in the parable appear in many meshalim. For example, for the motif of a king (or father) who plants a field (vineyard, orchard, etc.) and gives it to his son, see: Dev. R. 5.7, Tan. B. Lev., 78, Mid. Teh. 5.1, and Yalkut 1.225; for the motif of the owner/king leasing the field to tenants: Ber. R. 61.6, Sh. R. 43.9, and ARN A 16; for the king who goes off to a foreign province, see Eikh. R. 3.21 and PR, 104b; for the king requesting his subjects to send him produce, see the rough counterpart in Vay. R. 11.7; for equivalent motifs describing the rebellion of the king's subjects (with no exact counterparts to this parable, however), see Ber. R. 5.1 (= 28.2) and Sh. R. 45.3; for an example of the

king punishing the rebellious subjects, see Mekhilta Shirta 10, ad Exod. 15:8.

20. Luke cites Ps. 118:22 alone, and then quotes the stone logion as in Matthew.

21. Irenaeus, *Against Heresies*, 36:2, in *The Ante-Nicene Fathers*, ed. A. Roberts and J. Donaldson (Grand Rapids, Mich., 1956), vol. 1, 515. For other medieval interpretations, see Kissinger, *The Parables of Jesus.*

22. Adolph Jülicher, *Die Gleichnisreden Jesu*, 405ff.

23. Joachim Jeremias, *The Parables of Jesus* (trans. S. H. Hooke from 6th German ed., 1962; rev. ed. New York, 1963), 70.

24. Jeremias, 73; cf. Jack Dean Kingsbury, "The Parable of the Wicked Husbandmen and the Secret of Jesus' Divine Sonship in Matthew: Some Literary-Critical Observations," *JBL* 105 (1986), 643–655.

25. Jeremias, 76; C. H. Dodd, *The Parables of the Kingdom*, 3rd. ed. (London, 1952), 124–132.

26. Frank Kermode, *The Genesis of Secrecy* (Cambridge, Mass., 1979), 44.

27. See K. Snodgrass, *The Parable of the Wicked Tenants* (Tübingen, 1983), esp. 80–87, and 113–118 on the possible pun between *even,* "stone," in the Psalms verse and the word *ben,* "son," which is often cited to prove that the interpretation of the verse is christological; the pun on son may refer as well to the son in the parable's narrative.

28. See, for example, Dodd, *The Parables of the Kingdom*, 131. An exception is Malcolm Lowe, "From the Parable of the Vineyard to a Pre-Synoptic Source," *NTS* 28 (1982), 257–263, who reads the parable as being about John, on the basis of the context; however, Lowe supposes that the parable was originally part of a "Baptist-sequence" that is most fully preserved in Matthew. For criticism of Lowe, see Snodgrass, 81–82 and n37.

29. See Lowe, passim.

30. On the Jewish leaders: Flusser, *Yahadut*, 426–427; D. Schwartz, "Scribes and Hypocritical Pharisees—Who Are the Scribes in the New Testament?" (Hebrew), *Zion* 50 (1985), 121–132.

31. Donald Juell, *Messiah and Temple* (Missoula, Mont., 1977), 55.

32. It is also possible to read the parable as a kind of allegory detailing Jesus' confrontation with the Jewish leaders. This confrontation begins when the Jewish leaders first challenge Jesus' authority by questioning his right to preach and teach disciples. When they initially ask him for the source of his authority, Jesus responds (in good Jewish fashion) with his own questions: What do the Jews believe about John's baptism? Was it authorized from heaven or from men? And he tells his questioners that he will answer their question if they answer his. To be sure, he also assumes rather confidently that they

won't answer him, and when they don't he refuses to reply to their question; instead, he tells them parables.

If the initial confrontation between Jesus and the Jewish leaders is over the question of authority—at first, Jesus', then John's—the parable effectively extends the challenge to the Jewish leaders' own authority. In terms of the parable's symbolism, ownership of the vineyard can be viewed as the narrative equivalent to the possession of rightful authority. The wicked husbandmen, as it were, mistake their usurpation of the vineyard for ownership. The parable not only shows the illegitimacy of the wicked husbandmen's (= Jews') claim to authority; it also exposes their attempt to usurp ownership, first by denying the authority of the rightful owner (by refusing to send back the fruits he requests) and later by murdering his son. The husbandmen's boast that they have become the owners of the vineyard by killing the son has no legal basis, as some have claimed: cf. Jeremias, p. 75, and F. W. Beare, *The Earliest Records of Jesus* (New York, 1962), 208; but see R. H. Grundy, *Matthew* (Grand Rapids, Mich., 1982), 425 and his reference to M. I. Rostovtzeff. Rather, the boast shows only that in addition to being criminals, the husbandmen are presumptuously stupid. The upshot of the parable's blame of the Jewish leaders intentionally adds insult to condemnation. For a comparable mashal that adds insult to injury, see my discussion of Eikh. R. 1.10.

33. See J. A. Fitzmeyer, *The Gospel According to Luke (X–XXIV)* (Garden City, N.Y., 1985), 1282; and Grundy, 429.

34. For summary and criticism of this view, see V. Taylor, *The Gospel According to St. Mark,* (1966, repr. Grand Rapids, Mich., 1981), 472.

35. This paradox may be related as well to the connection that Mark, for example, makes between the arrest of John and the beginning of Jesus' ministry: see Mark 1:14, particularly the awkward phrase *meta de tō paradothēnai,* literally "after the delivering up." Taylor (165) notes that the use of the articular infinitive with no qualifying clause (e.g. "to prison") suggests the fulfillment of God's will, which Jesus understood as a sign to begin preaching.

36. In early Jewish interpretation, the verse is most commonly applied to David: see Mid. Teh. 118.20; Mid. Tann. 1.17 (p. 10); B. Pesahim 118a; Mid. Hagadol on Deut. 1:17 (p. 32). A pseudo-Davidic psalm reflecting this exegesis has also been published by D. Flusser and S. Safrai in *Sefer Zikaron Liyehoshua Grintz* (Tel Aviv, 1982). For another interpretation, see Mid. Teh., 118.20, where the verse is applied to Jacob and interpreted along the same lines as those in the mashal in Sifre Deut. 312 discussed earlier. For discussion, see Young, *Jesus and His Jewish Parables,* 293–295. For early Christian interpretations, see

Acts 4:11 and 1 Peter 2:1–10, and for discussion, James L. Kugel and Rowen A. Greer, *Early Biblical Interpretation* (Philadelphia, 1986), 132–133.

37. For another example of an analogous pun on *bun-bnh,* see B. Berakhot 64a for the famous midrash attributed to R. Eleazar in the name of R. Hanina on Isa. 54:17. It is worth noting that this midrash, which is recited in the daily liturgy as a kind of peroration to the hymn *Ein Keloheinu,* is mistranslated and misinterpreted in virtually every English prayerbook. See Hanoch Yallon, *Pirkei Lashon* (Jerusalem, 1971), 123–125. For a midrashic interpretation that plays on the pun between *even* (stone) and *boneiha* (her understanders), see B. Ta'anit 4a.

38. Note that in Matthew and Luke, the question is rather more specific, and different. In Matthew (13:10), the disciples ask Jesus, "Why do you speak to them [the masses] in parables?" In Luke (8:9), they ask him "what this parable meant."

39. For a good summary of the scholarly controversy, see Kermode, *The Genesis of Secrecy,* 23–47, 149–152.

40. See Jeremias, *The Parables of Jesus,* 15; and more extensively, J. W. Bowker, "Mystery and Parable," *JTS* N.S. 25 (1974), 311–312.

41. Kermode, *The Genesis of Secrecy,* 32.

42. Ibid.

43. Albert Schweitzer, *The Quest for the Historical Jesus,* trans. W. Montgomery (New York, 1968), 263; Jeremias, 17–18.

44. A parallel version of the story, with some differences, is recorded in B. Shabbat 31a.

45. Translation based upon Judah Goldin's *The Fathers According to Rabbi Nathan* (New Haven, 1955), 80–81.

46. Bowker, "Mystery and Parable," 305.

47. Ibid., 307.

48. On the makeup of Palestinian Judaisms in Late Antiquity see Morton Smith's classic article, "Palestinian Judaism in the First Century," in *Israel: Its Role in Civilization,* ed. Moshe Davis (New York, 1956), 67–81.

49. For bibliography and summary of scholarship on these questions, see A. J. Saldarini, "Reconstructions of Rabbinic Judaism," in *Early Judaism and its Modern Interpreters,* ed. R. A. Kraft and G. W. E. Nickelsburg (Atlanta, 1986), 437–477. In dating meshalim in this book, I have generally accepted attributions to known sages as given. For anonymous passages, I have followed the collections in which they are preserved: those recorded in the Tannaitic anthologies I have treated as Tannaitic, those in Amoraic ones as Amoraic. Needless to say, many meshalim attributed to early sages were doubtless changed in transmission; problems are unavoidable.

50. For examples of "contamination," see David Weiss-Halivni, *Midrash, Mishnah, Gemara* (Cambridge, Mass., 1986); for problems in the course of transmission, see Louis Finkelstein, "The Transmission of the Early Rabbinic Traditions," in *Exploring the Talmud,* ed. H. Dimitrovsky (New York, 1976), 241–261.

51. On Semahot deR. Hiyya, see Higger's introduction, 66–72.

52. For my translation of *egemon* as procurator, see Josephus, *Antiquities* 18, 55, in reference to Pontius Pilate; cf. W. F. Arndt and F. W. Gingrich, *A Greek-English Lexicon of the New Testament and Other Early Christian Literature* (Chicago and Cambridge, 1957), 344 s.v. *hēgemon.*

53. Note, however, that the phrase concluding the second mashal, "to life in the world-to-come or to shame and everlasting contempt," is a quote from Dan. 12:3.

54. See as well the two anecdotes about Hillel recorded in Vay. R. 34.3, which also use the *kal vehomer;* note also that Hillel is attributed by early Rabbinic tradition with having invented the logical form of the *kal vehomer.*

55. Jacob Neusner, *Development of a Legend: Studies on the Traditions Concerning Yohanan Ben Zakkai* (Leiden, 1970), 224. Neusner does not seem to be aware of the text in Semahot deR. Hiyya, but treats the deathbed accounts in ARN A ch. 25, B. Berakhot 28b, J. Avodah Zarah 3.1, and J. Sotah 9.16. Only the first two accounts are relevant parallels to our passage; both collapse the two parables in Semahot into mere figurative statements that Yohanan uses in a deathbed speech. I find it more difficult than Neusner does to decide which of these versions is the "original," but I do not think the parables in Semahot could have been derived from the passages in ARN A and Berakhot.

56. Daniel Boyarin, "Rhetoric and Interpretation: The Case of the Nimshal," *Prooftexts* 5 (1985), 269–276; cf. my response in the same issue, 276–280.

57. See, for example, the various kinds of compositions listed by R. M. Johnston in "Parables among the Pharisees and Early Rabbis," in J. Neusner, *History of the Mishnaic Law of Purities,* pt. 13 (Leiden, 1976), 224–226.

58. Moshe Hadarshan borrowed most of his meshalim from the Tanhuma literature that was available to him. Yet even a figure as late as Rashi (10th c.) maintains the same stability in transmission when he quotes Moshe Hadarshan, as in his commentary on Num. 19:22; the mashal quoted there first appears in PRK 4.8. Cf. H. Albeck's introduction to Bereishit Rabbati (Jerusalem, 1940), 4.

59. For a useful summary of scholarly views about the dating and authorship of TDE, see William G. Braude and Israel J. Kapstein, *Tanna DeBe Eliyyahu* (Philadelphia, 1981), 3–12.

60. J. Elbaum, "Between a Midrash and an Ethical Treatise" (Hebrew), *Jerusalem Studies in Hebrew Literature* 1 (1981), 144–154.

61. E. E. Urbach, "On the Question of the Language and the Sources of the Book 'Seder Eliyyahu,'" (Hebrew) *Leshoneinu* 21 (1957), 183–197; esp. 184; cf. 196.

62. The best example of the mashal used as a bridge between different ideas in a passage is to be found in the very first chapter of TDE (p. 6), where one mashal is first told to illustrate the meaning of the statement that "God is fire," and a second one to illustrate the statement in Deut. 4:24 that "God is a devouring fire."

63. See, for an example of a mashal in TDE with a virtually classic form and function, the very beginning of ch. 1 (p. 4), about the king who rejoices over the refuse he sees before his palace; the parable is in praise of Israel's repentance on Yom Kippur.

64. As with nearly everything connected to Jewish mysticism, whatever we know about *Sefer Habahir* we owe almost exclusively to Gershom Scholem. This debt is especially deep in the case of *Sefer Habahir*, which was the subject of Scholem's own dissertation, a translation into German of the book, with a commentary, that was published as *Das Buch Bahir* (Leipzig, 1923). Unfortunately, Scholem never published a critical Hebrew text of the work, though an extensive treatment of the book—of the mystery of its sources; its influence upon subsequent Kabbalah; its convoluted textual history; and above all, the unresolved problems associated with *Sefer Habahir*'s own doctrines and their meaning—form the core of Scholem's monumental *Origins of the Kabbalah*, trans. Allan Arkush, ed. R. J. Z. Werblowsky (Philadelphia and Princeton, 1987), 49–198. In *Origins*, Scholem also discusses in detail the use *Sefer Habahir* makes of parabolic discourse, and specifically how it employs the Rabbinic mashal to express the gnostic doctrines that form the basis of its mystical theology. My own comments are mere elaborations upon Scholem's grand insights, a modest attempt to paint a slightly fuller picture of the parable as it was used in *Sefer Habahir* and the place of *Sefer Habahir*'s meshalim in the history of the mashal. My translations are based on *Sefer Habahir*'s most easily available edition, that of Reuben Margaliot (Jerusalem, 1951), though, as Scholem notes, the edition is far from satisfactory; I have also consulted Arkush's English translations of Scholem's German translations in *Origins*, as well as the small selection translated into English by R. C. Kiener in *The Early Kabbalah*, ed. J. Dan (New York, 1986), 57–69.

65. For an additional view of the relationship between midrash and early Kabbalah, but one whose major theses are quite opposed to those I argue in these pages, see Joseph Dan, "Midrash and the Dawn of

Kabbalah," in *Midrash and Literature,* ed. G. H. Hartman and S. Budick (New Haven, 1986), 127–139. According to Dan, *Sefer Habahir* more or less faithfully adapts the literary conventions of midrash, including those of the mashal, a claim difficult to sustain.

66. Margaliot's text reads here "a righteous man." My text follows Scholem's, in *Origins,* 189, where the parable is also discussed.

67. For other meshalim that use this motif, see Sh. R. 43.9; and B. Pesahim 128b (= Koh. R. 6.5.10). See also Sifre Deut. 312 for a mashal in which the owner of the vineyard successively throws out the tenants who prove themselves unworthy of the vineyard.

68. In its original context, the passage means the following: Ps. 105:8 appears to suggest to the Rabbis that God intended to give the Torah *(davar)* only after a thousand generations of human history had passed; once He realized, however, that the world could not sustain itself for that long without the Torah, He gave it to Israel after 26 generations. What, then, happened to the 974 generations that were supposed to exist before the giving of the Torah? According to the Hagigah passage, God took the members of those generations—wicked persons, it seems, if only because they did not deserve to live to receive the Torah—and He dispersed them through every generation, where they now constitute the evil people in each age.

69. Scholem, 188.

70. For the use of the throne, see as examples, Eikh. R. 2.1B; Bam. R. 4.1. On taking an object in his arms as a sign of affection, see Eikh. R. 2.1A, discussed in Chapter 4. For the aggadah that God wears tefillin, see B. Berakhot 6a. Professor Elliot Wolfson has informed me that the association between the throne, phylacteries, and the Shekhinah is also a traditional theme in Jewish esoteric texts.

71. Scholem, 60–61.

72. Scholem, 60. See *Sefer Habahir,* sec. 84.

73. For this reading, see Scholem, 172, and the Hagahot HaGRA of Elijah of Vilna ad locum. My reading of the parable is also based on Scholem's comments on the same page and the following ones.

74. Scholem, 170–172; cf. Elliot Wolfson, "Female Imaging of the Torah: From Literary Metaphor to Religious Symbol," in *From Ancient Israel to Modern Judaism: Intellect in Quest of Understanding,* ed. J. Neusner, E. S. Frerichs, N. M. Sarna (Atlanta, 1990), esp. 285–291.

75. For full discussion, see Scholem, 94–97.

76. Walter Benjamin, "Some Reflections on Kafka," in *Illuminations,* trans. H. Zohn (New York, 1968), 143–144; cf. Shimon Sandbank, "Parable and Theme: Kafka and American Fiction," *Comparative Literature* 37 (1985), 252–268.

77. For a sketch of these developments, see my introductory essay to

Rabbinic Fantasies: Imaginative Narratives from Classical and Medieval Hebrew Literature, ed. David Stern and Mark J. Mirsky (Philadelphia, 1990); cf. Joseph Dan, *Hasippur Ha'ivri Biyemei-Habeinayim* (Jerusalem, 1974).

78. For the text, see BH, vol. 4, 145–152. The dating of this work is disputed. M. Steinschneider, in *Manna* (Berlin, 1847), 101, no. ix, dated it to an "early period," and other scholars have placed it in the early Geonic period; however, Eli Yassif, in an unpublished article, has dated it as late as the sixteenth century, though several of the stories in it are known from much earlier sources.

79. On the exempla in *Sefer Hasidim,* see Ivan Marcus's introduction to his translations in *Rabbinic Fantasies,* 215–217. Cf. Dan, *Hasippur Ha'ivri,* 162–187; Eli Yassif, "The Exemplary Story in *Sefer Hasidim,*" *Tarbiz* 57 (1988), 217–255. For examples of the few meshalim in *Sefer Hasidim,* see the edition of J. Wistinetzki (Frankfurt a.M., 1924), 2 (a very strange parable whose protagonist is the Talmudic tractate Mo'ed Katan!), 5, 12. I wish to thank Professor Marcus for sharing these references with me.

80. On fables in medieval Hebrew literature, see H. Schwarzbaum, *The Mishle Shu'alim (Fox Fables) of Rabbi Berechiah Ha-Nakdan, A Study in Comparative Folklore and Fable Lore* (Kiron, Israel, 1979).

81. On allegory in medieval Judaism, see Frank Talmage, "Apples of Gold: The Inner Meaning of Sacred Texts in Medieval Judaism," in *Jewish Spirituality: From the Bible through the Middle Ages,* ed. Arthur Green (New York, 1986), 313–355; on the mashal, see Dan, *Hasippur Ha'ivri,* 142–147.

82. On the history of the term in medieval texts, see Elliot Wolfson, "By Way of Truth: Aspects of Nahmanides' Kabbalistic Hermeneutic," *AJS Review* 14 (1989), 124–129, and notes. Cf. E. Ben-Yehuda, *Dictionary and Thesaurus of the Hebrew Language* (repr. New York, 1959), vol. 4, 3387–3388; I. Efros, *Philosophical Terms in the Moreh Nebukim* (New York, 1924), 82; S. Lieberman, *Hellenism in Jewish Palestine* (New York, 1950), 68.

83. I wish to thank Dr. Sarah Stroumsa for sharing with me the information in this paragraph. Dr. Stroumsa, who is preparing an edition of al-Muqammis's Arabic writings, informs me that he uses at least two parables in which kings and slaves figure.

84. Dan, *Hasippur Ha'ivri,* 8–9, 144–145.

85. Moses Maimonides, *Guide of the Perplexed,* trans. S. Pines (Chicago, 1963), 12.

86. *Guide,* 619.

87. Cf. Chana Kasher, "The Parable of the Royal Palace in the *Guide of the Perplexed* as Instruction for a Student," *AJS Review* 14 (1989) (Hebrew Section), 1–19.

88. Americo Castro, *The Structure of Spanish History* (Princeton, 1954), 445–446; quoted in Talmage, "Apples of Gold," 317.

89. See, for example, Maimonides' parable of the Indian King in part I, ch. 46. On the relation of that parable to Judah Halevi's parable in Kuzari, 1.19–22, see Pines's introduction to the *Guide*, cxxxiii.

90. On the compositional makeup of the Zohar and its authorship, see Gershom Scholem, *Kabbalah* (New York, 1974), 213–222; cf. Yehuda Liebes, "How the Zohar Was Composed" (Hebrew), *Jerusalem Studies in Jewish Thought* 8 (1989), 1–71. An interesting question, worth investigating, is whether the meshalim differ in the Zohar's various sections and strata. Aside from its imitation of the classical mashal, note its equally impressive use of the classical petihta-form.

91. See Gershom Scholem, *Major Trends in Jewish Mysticism*, 3rd ed. (New York, 1961), 163–168; *Kabbalah*, 226–229.

92. Scholem, *Major Trends*, 173. Cf. I. Tishbi, *Mishnat Hazohar* (Jerusalem, 1971), vol. 2, 363–365 and 364n10 on the Zohar's relation to Bahya; Talmage, "Apples of Gold," 316 and passim.

93. Zohar, vol. 3, 152a; cf. Talmage, 324–325.

94. Zohar, vol. 2, 22b; cf. Daniel Matt, *Zohar: The Book of Enlightenment* (New York, 1983), 240–242; cf. Y. Liebes, *Perakim Bemillon Sefer Hazohar* (Jerusalem, 1976), 182–184.

95. Zohar, vol. 3, 114a; cf. Matt, 272.

96. Zohar, vol. 2, 99a–b; trans. Talmage, "Apples of Gold," 316, and discussion; cf. Elliot Wolfson, "The Hermeneutics of Visionary Experience: Revelation and Interpretation in the Zohar," *Religion* 18 (1988), 321–324; Moshe Idel, *Kabbalah: New Perspectives* (New Haven, 1988), 227–228.

97. Talmage, 316.

98. Origen, *Selecta in Psalmos* Ps. 1, in *Patrologiae cursus completus. Series graeca*, ed. J. P. Migne (Paris, 1857–1866) 12, col. 1080; cited in R. P. C. Hanson, *Allegory and Event* (London, 1959), 180. Cf. Gershom Scholem, *On the Kabbalah and Its Symbolism* (New York, 1969), 12–13.

99. For an English translation of this parable, see Aryeh Wineman, *Beyond Appearances: Stories from the Kabbalistic Ethical Writings* (Philadelphia, 1988), 18–23.

100. For other meshalim from this literature, see the parables collected and translated by Wineman from Elijah de Vidas's *Reshit Hokhmah* (1579), Moses Hagiz's *Mishnat Hakhamim* (1733), and Sasson ben Mordecai Shindookh's *Kol Sasson* (1859), in Wineman, 157–158, 164, 165–169.

101. *Sefer Shivhei Habesht*, ed. S. A. Horodezky (Tel Aviv, 1946, 1960), esp. 88–89 (the Parable of the Dog) and 93 (the King's Crown);

both anecdotes are extremely interesting because they preserve the parables, one blame, the other praise, as well as the social context in which they were first delivered. For English translation, see *In Praise of the Baal Shem Tov*, ed. and trans. Dan Ben-Amos and Jerome R. Mintz (Bloomington, Ind., 1970), 142, 236. For Yaakov Yosef of Polnoy, see Samuel H. Dresner, *The Zaddik* (New York, 1974), esp. 173–221, on the parable of the king's son.

102. Cited in Benno Heinemann, *The Maggid of Dubnow and His Parables* (New York, 1967), 190–191.

103. See, for example, Audri Durchslag, "Rabbi Nahman and His Readers," *Prooftexts* 2 (1982), 221–226; cf. Arnold J. Band, "Folklore and Literature," in *Studies in Jewish Folklore*, ed. F. Talmage (Cambridge, Mass., 1980), 33–43.

104. For some examples, see H. N. Bialik's essay "Kissui Vegilui," in *Kol Kitvei H. N. Bialik*, 2nd ed. (Tel Aviv, 1939), 191–193; and Y. H. Brenner's essay "Hevlei Bittui," in *Kol Kitvei Y. H. Brenner* (Tel Aviv, 1967), vol. 3, 456–461.

105. Thus Abraham Holtz, "The Open Parable as a Key to S. Y. Agnon's 'Sefer Hama'asim'" (Hebrew), *Hasifrut* 4 (1973), 298–333.

106. For the mashal in "Agunot," see *Kol Sippurav shel Shmuel Yosef Agnon* (Jerusalem, 1971), vol. 2, 409; on the story, see Gershon Shaked, "Midrash and Narrative: Agnon's Agunot" in *Midrash and Literature*, 285–303.

107. "Agadat Hasofer," in *Kol Sippurav*, vol. 2, 131–145.

108. *Kol Sippurav*, vol. 2, 133. Other meshalim in the story appear on 131, 139, and 141.

109. See Vay. R. 2.5 and *Shivhei Habesht* (ed. Horodezky) 93. The mashal on 139 hearkens back to the famous mashal delivered as a eulogy over R. Hiyya b. Ada (J. Berakhot 2.8) as well as to several meshalim in *Sefer Habahir*.

110. The most impressive of all the meshalim Agnon composed is the "Petihah Lekaddish," in *Kol Sippurav*, vol. 6, 288–289; trans. Judah Goldin, in *The Jewish Expression*, ed. Judah Goldin (New York, 1970), 484–485. This parable was written when Agnon was asked to compose an introduction to the Kaddish, the traditional doxology, to be recited in memory of the Jewish soldiers who died while defending the State of Israel; in response, Agnon composed a parable, using the precise language and structures of the classical king-mashal to capture the subtle, wavering quandaries of religious faith within the brutal realities of modern existence.

Appendix A. Nonparabolic Narratives in Rabbinic Literature

1. For another attempt at generic classification of aggadic narrative, see Dan Ben-Amos, "Generic Distinctions in the Aggadah," in *Studies in Jewish Folklore*, ed. F. Talmage (Cambridge, Mass., 1980), 45–71. On aggadah in general: J. Heinemann, *Aggadot Vetoldoteihen* (Jerusalem, 1974), esp. 7–15, translated into English as "The Nature of Aggadah," in *Midrash and Literature*, ed. G. H. Hartman and S. Budick (New Haven, 1986), 41–55.

2. The classic essay on the extra-biblical legend remains Shalom Spiegel's introduction to Louis Ginzberg's *Legends of the Bible* (New York, 1956); on the homiletical-exegetical narrative, see Ophra Meir, *Hasippur Hadarshani Bivreshit Rabbah* (Tel Aviv, 1987).

3. For an example: Eikh. R. 3.1's use of the legend of God offering the Torah to the gentile nations; cf. James Kugel, "Two Introductions to Midrash," in *Midrash and Literature*, 77–103.

4. For an example: the legend of Zechariah's blood (Buber, pp. 21–22; 148–149); for discussion, Heinemann, *Aggadot*, 31–39.

5. Meir, *Hasippur Hadarshani*, 63–70.

6. The first view is that of Jacob Neusner, in "Story and Tradition in Judaism," in *Judaism: The Evidence of the Mishnah* (Chicago, 1981), 307–328. The second view is that of Jonah Fraenkel: see "Hermeneutical Questions in the Study of the Aggadic Story" (Hebrew), *Tarbiz* 47 (1977–78), 139–172; *Studies in the Spiritual World of the Aggadic Story* (Hebrew) (Tel Aviv, 1981). Cf. Henry A. Fischel, "Story and History," in *American Oriental Society, Middle West Branch, Semi-Centennial Volume*, ed. D. Sinor (Bloomington, Ind., 1969), 59–88.

7. For an example: M. Baba Kamma 7.6; for discussion, Arnold Goldberg, "Form und Funktion des Ma'aseh in der Mischna," *Frankfurter Judaistische Beitrage* 1 (1974), 1–38.

8. For examples: M. Taanith 3.8; B. Yoma 53b.

9. For examples and some discussion: Gary Porton, "The Pronouncement Story in Tannaitic Literature: A Review of Bultmann's Theory," *Semeia* 20 (1981), 81–99.

10. See G. Cohen, "The Story of Hannah and Her Seven Sons in Hebrew Literature," in *Mordecai M. Kaplan Jubilee Volume* (New York, 1953), Hebrew section, 109–122; my introductions to "Midrash Eleh Ezkerah," in *Rabbinic Fantasies*, ed. David Stern and Mark J. Mirsky (Philadelphia, 1990), 19–20, 143–146.

11. Cf. Jonah Fraenkel, *'Iyyunim Be'olamo Haruhani shel Sippur Haaggadah* (Tel Aviv, 1981), 65–98; Z. Kagan, "Divergent Tendencies and Their Literary Molding in the Aggadah," *SH* 22 (1971), 151–170; S. Safrai,

"Tales of the Sages in the Palestinian Tradition and the Babylonian Talmud," *SH* 22 (1971), 209–232.

12. For the story and its versions, see G. Alon, "The Flight of R. Yohanan b. Zakkai to Yavneh," in *Jews, Judaism, and the Classical World: Studies in Jewish History in the Times of the Second Temple* (Jerusalem, 1977), 296ff. Cf. Neusner, "Story and Tradition in Judaism"; Fraenkel, "Hermeneutical Questions in the Study of the Aggadic Story"; idem, "Bible Verses Quoted in Tales of the Sages," *SH* 22 (1971), 80–99.

13. Martin Braun, *History and Romance in Greco-Oriental Literature* (Oxford, 1938).

14. Cf. my comments on Qumranic pesher in "Midrash and Indeterminacy," *Critical Inquiry* 15 (1988), 132–161.

15. Cf. Matt. 1:22, 2:17, 2:23. Cf. E. Slomovic, "Patterns of Midrashic Impact on the Rabbinic Midrashic Tale," *JSJ* 19 (1988), 66n20.

Appendix B. Hebrew Texts of the Meshalim from Eikhah Rabbah

1. For Eikh. R.'s name and dating, see M. D. Herr's article in *EJ* 10, 1377–1378; cf. H. Albeck's notes in L. Zunz, *Haderashot Biyisrael* (1892; trans. into Hebrew, Jerusalem, 1974), 78ff.

2. See Saul Lieberman, *Midrash Debarim Rabbah* (Jerusalem, 1974), intro., esp. xiii.

3. Alexander Marx, review of S. Buber's edition of Eikh. R. in *Orientalistische Litteraturzeitung* 5, no. 7 (July 1902), 293–296. Cf. Marx's "Note," *JQR* o.s. 18 (1906), 768–771; idem, "A New Collection of Manuscripts," *PAAJR* 4 (1933), 135ff. (= *Bibliographical Studies and Notes,* ed. M. H. Schmelzer, New York, 1977, 411ff.); Chaim Raphael, *The Walls of Jerusalem* (New York, 1968), 220–224.

4. *Pro tem* Paul Mandel, *Hasippur Bamidrash Eikhah: Nusah Vesignon* (The Story in Midrash Ekha: A Textual and Literary Analysis) (M.A. diss., Hebrew University, Jerusalem, 1983).

5. J. Heinemann, *Aggadot Vetoldoteihen* (Jerusalem, 1974), 156–162.

Index of Rabbinic Sources

Index

Mimesis, 221
Mintz, Alan, 58
Miracle-stories, 242
Miriam bat Nakdimon, 246
Mohar (bride-price), 57
Moloch, cult of, 169–170, 172, 173
Moses de Leon, 228, 229
Moses Hadarshan, 211
Motifs and motemes, 21, 24, 30–33, 35, 207
Motivation, unexplained, 77–78
Mustērion, 205

Nahman (rabbi), 47, 64, 65, 126
Nahman of Bratslav, 232
Narratee. *See* Interpreter, implied
Narrative: and exegesis, 1, 37–42, 67–74, 238; in mashal, 2, 12, 66; as context for mashal, 17; conventions for, 71–74; in *Sefer Habahir,* 217; homiletical-exegetical, 237–240
Narrator: absence of, 82–83; presence of, 85–86
Nimshal: definition of, 8, 13; regularized form of, 8, 249; origins of, 16–19, 69, 217; and rhetorical narrative, 51, 68, 69–70; function of, 69; gaps between mashal and, 77; omitted from *Sefer Habahir,* 217, 220; differences between Eikh. R. recensions, 249
Norms: theological, 79; violations of, 79–82, 132–134

Odyssey (Homer), 6
Oheiv, 33, 37
Oral tradition: and mashal, 6, 34; in Rabbinic literature, 7, 35; and formulaic narrative motifs and diction, 34–36; of fables, 187
Origen, 231

Palace, parable of the, 226–227, 231–232
Parable, definition of, 5. *See also* Mashal
Paradeigma, 13
Paradox. *See* Ambiguity
Paradoxical behavior, of characters in meshalim, 41–42, 78
Parry, Milman, 34

Pedagogue, as character in meshalim, 30, 33–34, 37, 41–42, 87, 212
Peshat, 183
Petihta (proem): and meshalim, 119, 153, 159–166; definition of, 159; structure of, 159–160
Philos, 33, 37
Pinhas (rabbi), 26, 31, 78
Pleroma, 221, 223
Pliny, 171
Plot: gaps in, 78–79; enigmatic, 220; differences between Eikh. R. recensions, 248
Poe, Edgar Allan, 102
Poetics of mashal, challenge of constructing, 63
Point of view, 82–86
Polemics: as theme of meshalim, 52, 53–56, 114–117; definition of, 114–115; in specific meshalim, 115–116, 117–124
Praise. *See* Apologetics; Polemics
Prince, Gerald, 86
Princess of the Palace, parable of the, 230–232
Proem. *See* Petihta
Pronouncement-stories, 243
Propp, Vladimir, 33, 34
Pseudo-*petihtaot,* 160

Quotations, 249

Rabba bar Bar Hana, 241–242, 244
Rahmai (rabbi), 217–218, 219
Reader: as implied interpreter, 86–87; of Jesus' parables, 194, 204–206. *See also* Audience
Realism. *See* Historicity
Redundancy, as a strategy in poetics, 14–15
Regret: as theme of meshalim, 145, 146–148; in specific meshalim, 148–151
Regularization, process of, 18, 19–24, 36, 45, 206–211
Rhetorical function of mashal, 41, 51–53
Rhetorical questions in mashal, 83–84
Rhetorical structures of mashal, 10, 12, 40